Our Heavenly Father

Teacher's Manual

Our Heavenly Father

Teacher's Manual

Faith and Life Series

Third Edition

BOOK ONE

Ignatius Press, San Francisco
Catholics United for the Faith, Steubenville, Ohio

Nihil Obstat: Reverend James M. Dunfee
                Censor Librorum

Imprimatur: Reverend Monsignor Kurt H. Kemo
                Diocesan Administrator of Steubenville

Director of First Edition: The late Rev. Msgr. Eugene Kevane, Ph.D.
Assistant Director and General Editor of First Edition: Patricia I. Puccetti, M.A.
First Edition Writer: Sister Theresa Wynne, I.H.M.

Director of Revision: James Halsell
Assistant Director and General Editor of Revision: Veronica A. Gutiérrez
Revision Writers: Colette Ellis, M.A.; Anne Forsythe

Catholics United for the Faith, Inc. and Ignatius Press gratefully acknowledge the guidance and assistance of the late Reverend Monsignor Eugene Kevane, former Director of the Pontifical Catechetical Institute, Diocese of Arlington, Virginia, in the production of the First Edition of this series. The First Edition intended to implement the authentic approach in Catholic catechesis given to the Church through documents of the Holy See and in particular the conference of Joseph Cardinal Ratzinger on "Sources and Transmission of Faith." The Revised Edition and Third Edition continue this commitment by drawing upon the *Catechism of the Catholic Church* (Libreria Editrice Vaticana, © 1994, 1997.)

The Subcommittee on the Catechism, United States Conference of Catholic Bishops has found this catechetical text to be in conformity with the *Catechism of the Catholic Church*.

Contents

Foreword

After a long process of updating, reformatting, editing, proofreading, and seeking ecclesiastical guidance and approval, the editorial staff of Ignatius Press gladly presents to you this Third Edition of the *Faith and Life* series. Our staff works from locations all across the country: from Florida and Michigan in the East, to Texas in the South, to California in the West. Wherever our location, we brought to the service of this project of creating a Third Edition our various talents and backgrounds, and hope to offer to you here a catechetical series that will earn the same kind of accolades we received for the Revised Edition:

"For the past two decades, *Faith and Life* has proven to be an excellent series for religious instruction in schools and family catechesis in the home. I know families who use this faith series and bear witness to the excellent fruit it has brought forth. To all who wish to transmit the faith to children in schools or in the home, I recommend the *Faith and Life* series as a textbook of refreshing and high quality" (Cardinal Christoph Schönborn).

"The *Faith and Life* series from Catholics United for the Faith provides a clear and informative presentation of what we as Catholics believe, live, and teach. With a firm grounding in the *Catechism of the Catholic Church*, *Faith and Life* reaffirms that the faith is indeed alive, a gift to be cherished, and as relevant today as when Our Lord Jesus Christ called Peter and Andrew to 'Come after me'" (Most Rev. John J. Myers, Archbishop of Newark).

"At a time when our young people so desperately need sound teaching, the *Faith and Life* catechism series is the answer to prayers. I will strongly recommend this series for use in our schools and parish-based religious education programs" (Most Reverend Michael J. Sheridan, Bishop of Colorado Springs).

"I believe that the *Faith and Life* series is a very good catechetical tool. Students who finish this series will have an excellent grasp of the deposit of faith. The material is sound and is faithful to the Magisterium of our holy Church" (Most Reverend Thomas J. Olmsted, Bishop of Phoenix, AZ).

"When CUF came out with its *Faith and Life* series, printed by Ignatius Press, and I began using it in my parish, within one year I could tell the difference for the better in the knowledge of true faith among the children of my parish" (Fr. Robert J. Fox, Fatima Family Apostolate).

"It's hard to think of anything more important than forming children in the faith. *Faith and Life* does it, and does it well" (Russell Shaw, Editor, *Encyclopedia of Catholic Doctrine*).

"Marvelous—this series will help you follow the Holy Father's desire that you teach your children" (Mother Angelica, Founder of EWTN).

"I give the *Faith and Life* series my highest recommendation. We teach our children with these texts and encourage others to do the same... [It] presents the faith with clarity, depth, and great beauty" (Scott Hahn, Steubenville, OH).

We joyfully offer this series in the spirit of our patron, Saint Ignatius of Loyola, for the greater honor and glory of God. We offer it to Catholic families, schools, and parishes in the hope of faithfully fulfilling the command of our Lord to "let the children come to me, and do not hinder them" (Mt 19:14).

The *Faith and Life* Series Editorial Staff
Ignatius Press

Introduction to the *Faith and Life* Third Edition

The *Faith and Life* series, which now includes a student text, teacher's manual, and activity book for grades one through eight, has been used in schools, parishes, and homes across the country since its original publication in 1984. This edition of the original series continues our commitment to the faithful transmission of the teachings of the Roman Catholic Church, placing special emphasis on the importance of Scripture and the *Catechism of the Catholic Church*. This edition of the series has been updated to incorporate the new translations of the Roman Missal introduced into the Mass in Advent 2011. It is our hope that additional recent changes, such as updating photographs and reformatting the teacher's manuals, will continue to make *Faith and Life* a valuable tool in catechesis.

Text and Grade Level

The first grade text, *Our Heavenly Father*, is a simple introduction to Bible stories and teachings of the Faith. The first grader has an active imagination and is easily convinced by his emotions as well as his reason. The teacher should, therefore, make use of creative presentations reinforced through repetition, such as those included in this manual, in addition to the catechist's personal good example.

The Student Textbook

The *Faith and Life* student texts are intentionally written at an advanced reading level. Doctrine is presented in a way that both challenges the student's intellect and avoids the boredom that is often fatal in catechetical efforts. The text of these books is elucidated by the material in the *Teacher's Manual*.

Each chapter opens with a passage from Sacred Scripture. Additional quotations are interspersed throughout the books to help demonstrate the Biblical backing for the Faith. The chapters close with memorization questions dealing with Church doctrines as they are presented in the *Catechism of the Catholic Church*. As students regularly review these questions they will come to recognize the significance of the *Catechism of the Catholic Church*, a fruit of the Second Vatican Council.

Each book also offers vocabulary words indicated in bold type and defined in a glossary, and a section of common Catholic prayers.

One of the first things you will notice about the *Faith and Life* student texts is the beautiful and inspiring religious artwork. Faith has inspired art for centuries, and religious art has, in turn, inspired our faith. Art is a valuable educational tool, especially in the teaching of religious truths to children, for, in addition to the oral and written word, it offers a visual image of the subject manner. Art can also be a source of meditation for students and teachers alike as they investigate the paintings, discuss the religious imagery, and come to understand the beautiful symbols and the artistic expressions of the realities they communicate.

The Activity Book

The *Faith and Life* activity books contain supplemental activities for each chapter in each grade. They offer the teacher a variety of reinforcement tools, in a text separate from the student textbook. Their purpose is to reinforce and interest the students in a new way in the material found in the student textbook.

In the primary grades, the activities focus upon drawing, coloring, and simple puzzles and exercises. In the middle grades, the activities focus on reading comprehension and integration; memorization is also emphasized. In the final grades the activities focus on comprehension and synthesis of the ideas expressed, as students are encouraged to make their own, both intellectually and actively, what they have been taught.

The Teacher's Manual

This book will be imperative for you as you guide your students through the *Faith and Life* series.

Each chapter of the teacher's manuals begins with a list of important references to the *Catechism of the Catholic Church* and Sacred Scripture that support the chapter's lessons. There are also references to Fr. Kenneth Baker's

Fundamentals of Catholicism provided for additional background reading. These are available for your own preparation, research, and reflection. You are encouraged to incorporate them into the lessons as you see fit.

This is followed by a clear and succinct summary of the doctrine discussed in the chapter's four lessons. Each chapter provides a full week of detailed color-coded lesson plans, with four days for presenting new material and one day for review and assessment.

The lesson plans are designed to be guides in teaching even the most complex truths of the Faith with age-appropriate examples. The lessons begin in the Aims section with a clear statement of the main doctrines to be discussed that day. This is accompanied by a Materials section, which allows you to know beforehand how to prepare for the various exercises and activities in the day's lesson. The Begin section provides introductory material that will help you to broach the day's topic with your students. The Develop section begins by listing the paragraphs that your students should read together in class. The student textbook pages that are used that day appear on the facing page of the *Teacher's Manual*. The specific paragraphs to be read are highlighted in accord with the color code for your easy reference.

The content of the lesson is explained in the Develop section, which also provides useful review and questions for discussion. This is supplemented with "Catholic Culture and Tradition" boxes, which include materials for the teacher, lives of the saints, explanation of terms, descriptions of Church traditions and rituals, relevant citations, suggestions for activities, additional resources, and prayers.

The Reinforce and Conclude sections help you to draw together the material covered, apply it to life, and end the classroom discussion in prayer.

Comprehensive chapter quizzes and optional unit tests are also part of each lesson and chapter. Black line masters, from which you may make copies for your students, are found in Appendix A. In addition to the review and assessment provided in the *Teacher's Manual*, each chapter's content may be reviewed and reinforced by using the *Activity Book*. The answer keys for the activities are found at the end of each chapter in this manual.

Appendix B contains additional activities such as stories, games, crafts, and skits that are often suggested in the various sections of the lesson plans.

The "Words to Know" glossary and Prayer sections from the student textbook are also available for you to view at the end of the *Teacher's Manual*, just prior to Appendix A.

Using the *Teacher's Manual* in the parish setting:
To assist Parish and CCD Programs, "once-a-week lesson plans" have been formulated and are available online at www.faithandlifeseries.com. These lesson plans cover the essential material and doctrines of each chapter in a one hour format.

In addition to following the online lesson plans, you may wish to spend time reinforcing the material learned by having students memorize questions, vocabulary words, and prayers. The quizzes can then be sent home for family reinforcement and review. The unit quizzes can still be administered in class once a month to assist the teacher in assessing the students' understanding.

Additional resources to be used with the *Faith and Life* series can be found online at www.faithandlifeseries.com.

The *Faith and Life* series Third Edition aspires to aid teachers and parents (the primary educators) in transmitting the truths, doctrines, wealth of traditions, and richness of culture found in the Roman Catholic Church.

A Note for Teachers and Catechists

Catechesis: Nature and Purpose

In recent decades the Catholic Church has given its members numerous documents and resources defining and explaining the role of catechesis in the life of Catholics. Among these are the documents of the Second Vatican Council, the *General Directory for Catechesis*, the *National Directory for Catechesis*, and *Catechesi Trandendae*. The authors and editors of the *Faith and Life* series have taken these teachings to heart in preparing a catechism for students in the first through eighth grades.

Catechesis is the systematic instruction of children, young people, and adults in the Catholic Faith and the teachings of the Church with the goal of making them into Christ's disciples (cf. CCC 5). It is the handing-on of Christ's message to His people. The *General Catechetical Directory* describes catechesis as a form of ministry of God's Word, "which is intended to make men's faith living, conscious, and active, through the light of instruction" (GCD 17; 1971).

The Role of Parents: The First Catechists

The family provides the first and most important introduction to Christian faith and practice for any child, since parents are the primary educators of their children. Instruction in the Faith, which begins at an early age, should include not only the parents' good Christian example, but also a formation in prayer and an explanation and review of what students have learned from religious instruction and from attending liturgical events, such as Mass.

Parental cooperation is very important to a teacher's success as a catechist. You should try to involve parents in their children's instruction. Discuss with them the program and methods you are using, consult them about better ways to teach their children, and ask for assistance if problems arise. Let parents know that you are there to help them fulfill their duties in forming and educating their children in Christ (cf. GCD 78, 79).

The Role of the Catechist

Put simply, "catechesis is an education in the faith" (CCC 5). To be a catechist is to be God's instrument. Every catechist has a responsibility to teach the fullness of the truth faithfully, while witnessing to those entrusted to his care. A fervent sacramental life and regular prayer life are the catechist's best personal preparation. Any instructor can use textbooks and teaching tools, learn various methods for effective classroom participation, and develop lesson plans to facilitate an academic environment. But nothing is as important as witnessing through your words and deeds and petitioning God for the on-going formation and spiritual growth of the students. No matter how much knowledge you impart to your students, you should recognize that you merely plant the seeds of faith that God Himself must cultivate in their souls.

Catechesis in today's ministry is often coupled with evangelization—a first hearing of the Good News of Salvation. Through catechesis, you should guide your students to seek, accept, and profoundly investigate the Gospel so that they in turn may become witnesses to Christ. The *Catechism of the Catholic Church*, together with Sacred Scripture, provide catechists with the tools necessary to achieve this.

John Paul II states in *Catechesi Tradendae*: "at the heart of catechesis we find . . . the Person of Jesus of Nazareth . . . in catechesis it is Christ . . . who is taught . . . and it is Christ alone who teaches . . ." (CT 5, 6). Religious education must always be centered on the Triune God and on Christ Himself. God chose to reveal Himself throughout salvation history, through His creation, the prophets, the Scriptures, and most perfectly in the Person of Jesus Christ. This revelation, preserved faithfully through Sacred Scripture and Tradition, has been entrusted to the Church that every catechist is called to serve.

As you teach, you will find that your students, like all men, have a deep desire for God and are searching for the truth. As you bring them into an environment of docility to the Holy Spirit, you will be echoing the fullness of God's revelation in Christ and helping to immerse your students into the mystery of Christ and the salvation He offers. This mirrors the divine pedagogy which ends in our salvation. Likewise, you will be creating an environment of study and prayer in which your students will be able to respond with a deepening conversion and a cultivation of the life of virtue.

Pedagogical Tools

The *General Catechetical Directory* provides an overview of various successful methodologies you may find useful. Knowledge can be transmitted through prayer and liturgy, through words and deeds, or through texts and activities, but the students learn it primarily from you, the catechist.

Induction and Deduction:	Inductive methods serve well in the presentation of facts and in considering and examining those facts in order to recognize their Christian meaning. Induction is the process of reasoning from a part to a whole, from particular to general principles. It is not independent of deductive methods, which reason from the general to the particular and include interpretation and determining cause and effect. These two methods, taken together, aid in the students' understanding of the unity of the Faith, the inter-relation of topics, and, most importantly, their practical applications.
Formulas:	Expressing thoughts or ideas succinctly and accurately in a memorable form allows for ease of memorization and better understanding of a topic. In the early stages of education, memorization should be utilized more frequently since children first need language to communicate meaning. In theology, semantics are very important, for Christians have died for their faith and schisms have occurred because of word use (e.g., the *Filioque* in the Nicene Creed still distinguishes Roman Catholics from the Eastern Orthodox). Such formulas also provide a uniform method of speaking among the faithful.
Experience:	Personal experience is reflective and practical, and it transforms abstract theories into applicable and memorable concepts. Catechists should use concrete examples in class and encourage their students to judge personal experience with Christian values.
Creativity:	Creative activities enable students to meditate upon and express, in their own words, the messages they have learned.
Groups:	In catechesis the importance of group instruction is becoming more apparent. Groups aid the social and ecclesial formation of students, and they foster a sense of Christian co-responsibility and solidarity.

The *Catechism of the Catholic Church*: An Important Tool

Today's classrooms are filled with children who have various needs and backgrounds. Complicated by an atmosphere of religious indifference, religious hostility, and an apparent absence of Catholic culture, knowledge, and meaningful practice, your catechetical work becomes especially valuable. One important tool that belongs to all the faithful is the *Catechism of the Catholic Church*, which is divided into four sections: the Profession of Faith (the Creed), The Celebration of the Christian Mystery (the Sacraments), Life in Christ (the moral life), and Christian Prayer.

The Creed:	The Creed is a summary of the Faith and the Church's baptismal promises. As a public profession of faith, Catholics find in it their identity as members of Christ's Mystical Body. This is the Faith handed down from Christ to the Apostles and to the entire Church.
Sacraments:	The seven Sacraments are outward signs instituted by Christ to confer grace. Active participation in the sacramental life of the Church, such as attending Mass prayerfully and faithfully, should be encouraged from a young age.
The Moral Life:	The moral life does not limit; instead it provides the boundaries that define the Catholic identity and allow for proper love of God and neighbor. A right moral life is man's gift to God, a response to His unconditional love, and a pathway to true freedom. Every Catholic should be an example to others.

Prayer: Prayer unites a person with God (through words, actions, silence, and presence), and should be encouraged and put into practice from early childhood. There are many forms of prayer, but each brings the soul closer to God.

The *Faith and Life Teacher's Manual* provides much of what you will need to be an effective catechist, but it will only be fruitful depending on how you utilize it and how you teach and minister the Word of God to your students. Take your responsibilities as a catechist very seriously. Call upon Christ frequently, as His witness and disciple, to help you hand on His message. Persevere and draw near to God, bringing your students with you.

Contents

A Note to Parents

Dear Parents,

The *Faith and Life* series was originally published in 1984. The book you hold in your hands is one of over 4.6 million books sold since then. From the beginning, the series was intended to provide schools, parishes, and families with the catechetical tools and essential elements of Catholic doctrine pivotal in the formation of young Catholics.

While the doctrines and Tradition of the Church remain essentially unchanged, as time has passed the editors have provided additional teaching tools that enrich the series and make it even more accessible to all types of students. Since its introduction, the series has seen the addition of activity books, teacher's manuals, numerous online resources, scriptural quotations, and correlations with the *Catechism of the Catholic Church*. Additionally, this edition has been updated to incorporate the new translations of the Roman Missal introduced into the Mass during Advent 2011.

In this first grade student text, *Our Heavenly Father*, you will find that emphasis has been given to the scriptural basis of our Faith in accord with Sacred Tradition. Every chapter opens with a Scripture passage, and important verses supplement the text where relevant. Each chapter closes with questions and answers based on Church teaching as found in the *Catechism of the Catholic Church*. Vocabulary words are indicated in bold type and in the Words to Know sections. Their definitions are found in the glossary. Common Catholic prayers are also taught in the lessons, and presented at the end of the book.

It is important to realize that, as parents, you are the primary educators of your child. Your active participation in your child's religious education is highly encouraged by the Church. As a family, you are the first witnesses of God's love to your child. If you provide a model of Catholic living at home, if as a family you participate in the sacramental life of the Church, and if you pray and attend Mass together, your child is more likely to take to heart the lessons he will learn in religion class. Family discussions of current events with a healthy religious perspective will allow your child to grow up with a better understanding of the world around him, and more importantly, help him to be a true Catholic and follower of Christ in the midst of it. As stated in the *General Directory for Catechesis*, "family catechesis precedes . . . accompanies and enriches all forms of catechesis" (GDC, 226; Congregation for the Clergy, 1998). Providing your child with a strong Catholic identity at an early age, while not ensuring a lifetime of devotion, will certainly prepare him for the challenge of becoming a faithful Catholic adult.

We encourage you to use the *Our Heavenly Father* student text, along with its resources, to assist you in the task of sharing the Good News with which you have been entrusted. More information and resources can be found at www.faithandlifeseries.com.

We sincerely hope that this series will provide parents, catechists, and teachers with the assistance they need in the task of evangelizing young people.

CHAPTER ONE
GOD IS OUR FATHER

Catechism of the Catholic Church References

Catechesis on Creation: 282–89
Dignity of Creatures: 307–8
Divine Providence: 302–14, 321–24
God as Creator of Heaven and Earth: 279–81, 325–27
God as Father: 238–42
God Created an Ordered and Good World: 299
God Created Man: 355, 369–70
God Created Man Out of Love in Order to Love: 1604

God Created Out of Nothing: 296
God is Love: 218–21, 231
God Made Everything According to His Wisdom: 295, 315
God, Sustainer of the World: 301
Human Fatherhood: 2214–20
Man's Sharing in God's Providence: 307
"Our Father Who Art in Heaven": 2777–2802
Prayer: 2559–65, 2590, 2644

Scripture References

"Behold, I have graven you on the palms of my hands":
Is 49:16a
Creation: Gen 1:1—2:25
Everything God Made Is for Man: Gen 1:29–30

Everything God Made Is Good: Gen 1:31a
Fatherhood of God and Men: Lk 11:5–13
God's Providence: Mt 6:25–33; Lk 12:22–31
The Our Father: Mt 6:9–13; Lk 11:2–4

Background Reading: *The Fundamentals of Catholicism* by Fr. Kenneth Baker, S.J.

Volume 1:
"God Our Father," pp. 30–32

Volume 2:
"The Fatherhood of God," pp. 83–86

Summary of Lesson Content

Lesson 1

God is our Father in Heaven.

God created Heaven and earth.

God made us because He loves us.

Like a good father on earth, God cares for His children by giving them every good thing.

We pray the Our Father.

Lesson 2

The natural world is the Father's gift to His children.

Our families, our faith, our education, etc., are also gifts from God.

Lesson 3

Everyone should thank our Father for His gifts, His love, and His care.

Everyone must be alert to recognize God's gifts.

Sometimes God's gifts come through other people.

Lesson 4

Just as we talk to our fathers on earth, we should talk to our Father in Heaven; prayer is talking to God.

Jesus taught that God is our Father when He gave us the Our Father.

Since God is the Father of everyone, we are all brothers and sisters, and we should love everyone in the family of God.

CHAPTER ONE: GOD IS OUR FATHER
LESSON ONE: WE HAVE A FATHER IN GOD

Aims

Students will be able to identify a good father as the source of life and provider of good things.

They will be able to explain that God is our perfect Father in Heaven Who made each of us out of love.

They will begin to learn the Lord's Prayer.

Materials

- Picture of a man with his child
- Flash card with "God" written on it
- A marble, piece of chalk, or crayon
- *Activity Book*, p. 1
- Flash cards of the Lord's Prayer

Optional:
- "God Father, praise and glory," *Adoremus Hymnal*, #464

Begin

Display the picture of the man with his child and ask the students whether:
- they know who these people are
- they think that the man and the child know each other
- they think the man and child are friends or related to each other
- they think the man is the child's father

Point out the love the father shows toward the child and how trusting the child is toward the father.

Develop

1. Read paragraph 1 of the textbook with the students. Explain that God is the Father of everyone. It is God Who is the "giver of life." Write the word "Father" on the chalkboard and point out to the children that when anyone refers to God as Father, he uses a capital letter. This signifies that He is the perfect Father of all, even all earthly fathers; this makes everyone His child.

2. Explain that fathers care very much for their children. They give their children life and then care for them as they grow up. They give their children only those things that are good for them. Have the students give examples of things that their fathers have given to them for their good. Make a list of their examples on the chalkboard. Save the list of good things on the board to use with the next lesson.

3. Ask the children to look at the painting on p. 6 of the textbook. Ask them if they know who this is supposed to represent. Explain that there is Someone Who is Father of everyone in the world; everyone in the world has the same Father. Ask whether or not they know Who this Someone is. Hold up the "God" flash card and have them look at the painting representing God the Father in their textbook again. Read the flash card with the children. Tell them that God lives in Heaven.

4. Tell the students that God made them because He loves them. He did not need to make them; He created them out of love, and He continuously loves and cares for His creatures. He made everything in the world just for man because He wants His children to be happy. He gives His children things for their good everyday. Explain that all of the good things in their lives are God's gifts to them.

Reinforce

1. God's love is greater than anyone else's love. Read the quote (Is 49:16a) on p. 7 of the student text. God assures His people that He will never forget them. He says, "Behold, I have graven you on the palms of my hands." Demonstrate (or have the children demonstrate) how safe something is when placed in the palm of the hand—use a small object such as a marble, a crayon, or a piece of chalk. Let them imagine how much safer they are in God's care since they are not only in His palm but carved on it, for this is the meaning of the word graven. Compare this to the way in which parents hold a newborn baby—cradled and therefore protected in their arms.

2. Have the children draw themselves in the palm of God's hand on p. 1 of the *Activity Book* (see *Teacher's Manual*, p. 11). Be sure to emphasize that this is an image from the Bible. Teach the children to sing "God Father, praise and glory," *Adoremus Hymnal*, #464.

Conclude

1. Ask the children to turn to p. 9 in their textbook (see *Teacher's Manual*, p. 5). Practice the answers to Questions 1 and 2 with the entire class. You should read both the question and the answer while the children listen. Then ask the question and have one child give the proper answer. Separate the students into pairs and give them a little time to practice the answers to Questions 1 and 2.

2. Read Matthew 6:9–13 from your children's Bible, then begin teaching the Our Father to the students (found on p. 9 in the text, *Teacher's Manual*, p. 5). Practice each day in the classroom. Send a flash card of the Our Father home today and ask parents to practice with their children all week.

1   God Is Our Father

"Behold, I have graven you
on the palms of my hands."
Isaiah 49:16

Did you know that you have a Father who is in Heaven? He is your Father. He is your parents' Father. He is your grandparents' Father. He is the Father of all of us. He is God.

God is the One Who made us. God made the world we live in, too. He made flowers, vegetables, trees, and animals. God made the sun and the stars and the big, blue sky. He also made rivers and lakes and oceans, and everything there is.

Why did God make you? God made you because He loves you very much. Because God loves you, He watches over you day and night. He does this by giving you all the things you need. So the food we eat, and the things we need to make clothes and houses, all come from God.

God gives you your family, the people who take

7

care of you, and all the people you love. God makes many things you like, things like warm sunshine, icy snow, and lots of water in which to swim. He also did not forget to make all the animals that make us happy.

How good our Father is! We should give thanks to God for all these gifts, like this:

Thank You, God, for everything!

When you talk to God, He always hears what you say. That is what **prayer** is—talking with God. God wants us to pray to Him. He loves us and wants us to talk to Him about everything.

God wants you to call Him "Father." So we can remember, He even gave us a prayer called the **Our Father**. It begins this way:

"Our Father, Who art in Heaven..."

8

"FOR THE KINGDOM, THE POWER AND THE GLORY ARE YOURS NOW AND FOR EVER"

After the recitation of the Our Father during the Communion Rite of Mass, the priest prays: "Deliver us, Lord, we pray, from every evil, graciously grant peace in our days, that, by the help of your mercy, we may be always free from sin and safe from all distress, as we await the blessed hope and the coming of our Savior, Jesus Christ." Following this the faithful make the above response. Protestants differ from Catholics in their recitation of the Lord's Prayer, for they add at the end without the interlude, "For Thine is the kingdom, and the power, and the glory, forever and ever. *Amen.*"

Preview

We will observe and explore the natural world that God made and gave to us, as well as some of His other gifts to us.

CHAPTER ONE: GOD IS OUR FATHER
LESSON TWO: GOD OUR FATHER GIVES US GOOD GIFTS

Aims

Students will become more aware of the natural world as a gift from God.

They will be able to explain that these gifts are a sign of His love and care.

They will become aware of some of the intangible gifts from their Heavenly Father (faith, education, etc.).

Materials

- *Activity Book*, p. 2

- Magazine pages with appropriate pictures of created things

- Children's scissors

- Bags (paper or plastic)

Optional:
- Poster board (one for each group of 4–6 children) and paste

- "God Father, praise and glory," *Adoremus Hymnal*, #464

Begin

Review Lesson 1. Tell the children that today they will step outside into the world God made in order to observe the many gifts that He has given His children. Tell them that these gifts are always there, but it is easy to forget Who created them. Encourage them to observe well today. (Note: If it is more convenient, stay in the classroom and use pictures and photographs.)

Develop

1. Read paragraph 2 of the textbook with the students.

2. Take a walk outside and encourage the children to use their senses to observe the good things that God has given to His children. Help them to listen, see, smell, and touch the elements of creation. You may pass out bags so that the students may collect some of God's gifts, such as leaves, pebbles, etc. Or, remain in the classroom and pass around pictures of nature scenes, asking the students to tell you what they observe in each picture.

3. When you return to the classroom, ask the students to name one thing they observed as a gift from God. Start a list next to the one from the last lesson (which listed the good things their earthly fathers give them) and either leave it on the board for another day or write it down and make copies for the children for tomorrow's lesson.

4. Read paragraph 3 from the text. Have the children add other things to their list of good gifts from God, e.g., faith, family, education, etc. Emphasize for them that God made them out of love, and that all of the good gifts He gives them are signs of that love. They are God's way of taking care of His children at each and every moment of every day.

5. Make a collage. As an alternative to the individual collages, you can have the children work in groups of 4–6 to make group collages using large poster board.

Reinforce

1. Using p. 2 of the *Activity Book* (see *Teacher's Manual*, p. 11), have the children work individually to make a collage of God's gifts. Distribute magazine pages and scissors and let them choose and cut out the pictures to be pasted onto the page (e.g., sun, moon, stars, rivers, oceans, birds, flowers, animals, families, food, priest, church).

2. Practice the answers to Questions 1, 2, and 3, found on p. 9, with the entire class. Then divide the students into pairs and allow a few minutes for memory work.

Conclude

1. When the drawings and the collages are complete, have the children show their work to their classmates. Then display the artwork in the classroom and hallway under the heading, Our Heavenly Father's Gifts to Us.

2. Sing with the children "God Father, praise and glory," *Adoremus Hymnal*, #464.

3. Pray the Our Father together, reminding the children that this is the prayer Jesus taught.

1   God Is Our Father

"Behold, I have graven you
on the palms of my hands."
Isaiah 49:16

Did you know that you have a Father who is in Heaven? He is your Father. He is your parents' Father. He is your grandparents' Father. He is the Father of all of us. He is God.

God is the One Who made us. God made the world we live in, too. He made flowers, vegetables, trees, and animals. God made the sun and the stars and the big, blue sky. He also made rivers and lakes and oceans, and everything there is.

Why did God make you? God made you because He loves you very much. Because God loves you, He watches over you day and night. He does this by giving you all the things you need. So the food we eat, and the things we need to make clothes and houses, all come from God.

God gives you your family, the people who take

7

care of you, and all the people you love. God makes many things you like, things like warm sunshine, icy snow, and lots of water in which to swim. He also did not forget to make all the animals that make us happy.

How good our Father is! We should give thanks to God for all these gifts, like this:

Thank You, God, for everything!

When you talk to God, He always hears what you say. That is what **prayer** is—talking with God. God wants us to pray to Him. He loves us and wants us to talk to Him about everything.

God wants you to call Him "Father." So we can remember, He even gave us a prayer called the **Our Father**. It begins this way:

"Our Father, Who art in Heaven…"

8

Words to Know:

prayer   Our Father

> **Q. 1** *Who made you?*
> God made me (CCC 355).
>
> **Q. 2** *Why is God called Father?*
> God is called Father because He is the Creator of the world (CCC 238).
>
> **Q. 3** *How does God our Father show His love?*
> God our Father shows His love by caring for His children (CCC 239).

We Pray:

OUR FATHER

Our Father, Who art in Heaven, hallowed be Thy Name; Thy Kingdom come; Thy will be done on earth as it is in Heaven. Give us this day our daily bread, and forgive us our trespasses, as we forgive those who trespass against us; and lead us not into temptation, but deliver us from evil. *Amen.*

9

PRAYER BEFORE MEALS

God gives every good gift, including the food people eat each day (Christians even pray for this in the Our Father: give us this day our daily bread). Saying a blessing before meals, often called grace, is a good way to thank God for His goodness. Many Catholics even make the Sign of the Cross and pray over their food in restaurants as an outward and public sign of their faith, such as the prayer below:

Bless us O Lord, and these Thy gifts, which we are about to receive from Thy bounty through Christ our Lord. *Amen.*

Preview

We will learn about how we should respond to God for His many gifts to us.

CHAPTER ONE: GOD IS OUR FATHER
LESSON THREE: THANKING GOD OUR FATHER

Aims

Students will learn that they should thank God their Father in Heaven for His good gifts.

They will practice thanking God for His gifts.

They will observe that some of God's gifts come to them through other people.

Materials

- A gift box containing a token gift for each member of the class (e.g., stickers, holy cards)

- Enough sentence strips for each child, with the pre-printed phrase: "God gave us _____."

- *Activity Book*, p. 3

Optional:
- "God Father, praise and glory," *Adoremus Hymnal*, #464

Begin

Pray the Our Father together. Note who is making progress in memorization and assist those who need it. Then show the children the gift box, wrapped with a beautiful bow. Tell them that in this lesson you are going to teach them something about receiving gifts.

Develop

1. Read paragraphs 4 and 5 with the students.

2. Tell the children to think back to their last birthdays. Ask them if they received anything from their family, and friends. Ask them why these people gave them presents. Did they have to do that? Or did they give the gifts out of love? Did the children say anything when they received their gifts? Of course they did; it's only good manners to say thank you when you receive a gift!

3. Pass the gift box around to a number of students and have each of them practice saying thank you. Explain that just as they thank their families and friends for the good things they give them, they must also use good manners with God, their Heavenly Father. For the many good gifts He has given out of love, they must say thank You.

4. Ask the children if God's gifts come in pretty packages like the one in the classroom. Obviously they do not.

However, tell the children that for this reason they must be ever alert for God's gifts – they can come when least expected. And they should not take them for granted just because they do not have a big, beautiful bow on them, or shiny wrapping paper.

5. Ask a student to give the gift box to another child whom you specify. Point out to the class that the gift went to the child by way of another child. Tell them that some of God's gifts are given in that way, not directly, but through other people. For example, God gave them parents who in turn give them food, clothes, a home, love, education, etc.

6. Remind the children that in the last lesson they made a list of many of the good things God has given to His creatures. Point to or pass out a copy of this list and read it with the children. Tell them that they should thank God for all of these gifts.

Reinforce

1. Pass out prepared sentence strips to every child. Demonstrate how to complete the sentence: "God gave us _____." Have them fill their own out.
   When they are finished, have each child read his own, while everyone responds: "We thank You, God our Father!" Let them take their strips home to share what they have learned.

2. Play a memory game based on what was observed during the last lesson. Give an example, such as: "God made trees; thank You, God." Explain that the first child you call on will repeat what you have said and add another gift. For instance: "God made trees and squirrels; thank You, God." The next child will repeat the first two gifts, and add a third, and so on.

3. Assign p. 3 of the *Activity Book* (see *Teacher's Manual*, p. 11). The children can use p. 9 of the student text as a guide, or ask their parents for help at home tonight.

Conclude

1. Pass out a gift to each child from the gift box, perhaps a holy card or a sticker.

2. Have pairs of students continue memorizing the answers to Questions 1, 2, and 3.

3. Explain that in addition to thanking God for all He has given us, they can also tell Him how wonderful He is in song. Then sing "God Father, praise and glory," *Adoremus Hymnal*, #464.

1   God Is Our Father

"Behold, I have graven you
on the palms of my hands."
Isaiah 49:16

Did you know that you have a Father who is in Heaven? He is your Father. He is your parents' Father. He is your grandparents' Father. He is the Father of all of us. He is God.

God is the One Who made us. God made the world we live in, too. He made flowers, vegetables, trees, and animals. God made the sun and the stars and the big, blue sky. He also made rivers and lakes and oceans, and everything there is.

Why did God make you? God made you because He loves you very much. Because God loves you, He watches over you day and night. He does this by giving you all the things you need. So the food we eat, and the things we need to make clothes and houses, all come from God.

God gives you your family, the people who take

7

care of you, and all the people you love. God makes many things you like, things like warm sunshine, icy snow, and lots of water in which to swim. He also did not forget to make all the animals that make us happy.

How good our Father is! We should give thanks to God for all these gifts, like this:

Thank You, God, for everything!

When you talk to God, He always hears what you say. That is what **prayer** is—talking with God. God wants us to pray to Him. He loves us and wants us to talk to Him about everything.

God wants you to call Him "Father." So we can remember, He even gave us a prayer called the **Our Father**. It begins this way:

"Our Father, Who art in Heaven…"

8

Words to Know:

prayer   Our Father

Q. 1   *Who made you?*
God made me (CCC 355).

Q. 2   *Why is God called Father?*
God is called Father because He is the Creator of the world (CCC 238).

Q. 3   *How does God our Father show His love?*
God our Father shows His love by caring for His children (CCC 239).

We Pray:

OUR FATHER

Our Father, Who art in Heaven, hallowed be Thy Name; Thy Kingdom come; Thy will be done on earth as it is in Heaven. Give us this day our daily bread, and forgive us our trespasses, as we forgive those who trespass against us; and lead us not into temptation, but deliver us from evil. *Amen.*

9

LITANY OF GRATITUDE

God gave us parents,
       Thank You, God our Father!

God gave us friends,
       Thank You, God our Father!

God gave us trees and plants,
       Thank You, God our Father!

God gave us animals,
       Thank you, God our Father!

God gave us His love,
       Thank you, God our Father!

Preview

We will learn to talk to God our Father in our own words.

CHAPTER ONE: GOD IS OUR FATHER
LESSON FOUR: WE PRAY TO GOD OUR FATHER

Aims

Students will be able to explain that just as they communicate with their earthly fathers, they can, and should, communicate with God, their Heavenly Father.

They will be able to define prayer as talking to God.

They will know that the Our Father is the prayer that our Lord taught in the Bible.

They will begin to understand that they are brothers and sisters in God's family and that they must behave well toward each other for this reason.

Materials

- Picture of the man and his child from Lesson 1

- *Activity Book*, p. 4

Optional:
- "God Father, praise and Glory," *Adoremus hymnal*, #464

Begin

Show the children the picture of the man and his child from Lesson 1. Ask them if they think they talk to each other, and if so, what they might say.

Develop

1. Finish reading the chapter (paragraphs 6 and 7).

2. Have the children look again at the painting representing God the Father on p. 6 of the textbook (see *Teacher's Manual*, p. 3). Point out that in the last lesson they talked to God when they thanked Him for a variety of things He has given them. In doing so, they were talking to Him in much the same way that the child in the other picture talks to his father. Tell them that there is a special word for talking to our Heavenly Father: prayer. Prayer is talking to God.

3. Emphasize that it was Jesus Himself who taught us to call God "Father." Point out that He did not say "your Father," but "our Father." This means that God the Father is the Father of Jesus and of everyone. Ask the students to think about this for a moment.

4. Ask them: If God is everyone's Father, how are they related to each other? (They are all brothers and sisters, and Jesus is their brother as well.) How, then, should they treat each other? They should be good to everyone, as Jesus would have them be. Give examples: If your friend forgets his lunch on the way to the bus, what should you do? If you see a person in the schoolyard drop something, what should you do? If your classmate is feeling sad, what should you do?

5. Explain that just as their father on earth likes to hear about what his children are interested in or worried about (like what they like and want, and how much they love him), so does God the Father in Heaven. He always hears the prayers of His children. Encourage them to talk to God often, and thank Him for the many good things He has given them. God the Father in Heaven is pleased when they talk to Him in prayer.

Reinforce

1. Have the children complete p. 4 of the *Activity Book* (see *Teacher's Manual*, p. 11), comparing the way they talk to their earthly father with the way they talk to their Heavenly Father.

2. While the children are drawing their pictures, check each student's memory work with Questions 1, 2, and 3.

Conclude

1. Allow some time for the children to review Questions 1–3.

2. Pray the Our Father together.

3. You may want to sing to reinforce this lesson with the song "God Father, praise and glory," *Adoremus Hymnal*, #464.

1   God Is Our Father

*"Behold, I have graven you
on the palms of my hands."*
Isaiah 49:16

Did you know that you have a Father who is in Heaven? He is your Father. He is your parents' Father. He is your grandparents' Father. He is the Father of all of us. He is God.

God is the One Who made us. God made the world we live in, too. He made flowers, vegetables, trees, and animals. God made the sun and the stars and the big, blue sky. He also made rivers and lakes and oceans, and everything there is.

Why did God make you? God made you because He loves you very much. Because God loves you, He watches over you day and night. He does this by giving you all the things you need. So the food we eat, and the things we need to make clothes and houses, all come from God.

God gives you your family, the people who take

7

care of you, and all the people you love. God makes many things you like, things like warm sunshine, icy snow, and lots of water in which to swim. He also did not forget to make all the animals that make us happy.

How good our Father is! We should give thanks to God for all these gifts, like this:

Thank You, God, for everything!

When you talk to God, He always hears what you say. That is what **prayer** is—talking with God. God wants us to pray to Him. He loves us and wants us to talk to Him about everything.

God wants you to call Him "Father." So we can remember, He even gave us a prayer called the **Our Father**. It begins this way:

"Our Father, Who art in Heaven..."

8

Words to Know:

        prayer   Our Father

> **Q. 1**   *Who made you?*
> God made me (CCC 355).
>
> **Q. 2**   *Why is God called Father?*
> God is called Father because He is the Creator of the world (CCC 238).
>
> **Q. 3**   *How does God our Father show His love?*
> God our Father shows His love by caring for His children (CCC 239).

We Pray:

OUR FATHER

Our Father, Who art in Heaven, hallowed be Thy Name; Thy Kingdom come; Thy will be done on earth as it is in Heaven. Give us this day our daily bread, and forgive us our trespasses, as we forgive those who trespass against us; and lead us not into temptation, but deliver us from evil. *Amen.*

9

WHAT IS PRAYER?

"For me, prayer is a surge of the heart; it is a simple look turned toward heaven, it is a cry of recognition and of love, embracing both trial and joy."

—Saint Thérèse of Lisieux

SOME FORMS OF PRAYER

Adoration/Blessing: Giving to God all our love

Petition: A prayer of supplication for oneself

Intercession: A prayer of petition on behalf of others

Thanksgiving: A prayer of gratitude to God for His goodness and mercy

Praise: A prayer that recognizes God as Himself and lauds and gives Him glory for His own sake

Preview

We will review what we have learned, play a game, and take a quiz.

CHAPTER ONE: GOD IS OUR FATHER
REVIEW AND ASSESSMENT

Aims

To review and to assess the students' knowledge of the lessons from the week.

Materials

- Appendix, p. B-1
- Quiz 1 (Appendix, p. A-1)
- "God Father, praise and glory," *Adoremus Hymnal*, #464

Review and Enrichment

1. Begin the review by praying the Our Father together (see *Teacher's Manual*, p. 9). Assess each child and assist him as needed.

2. Review the lessons of the week focusing particularly on the Words to Know, Questions 1–3 (see *Teacher's Manual*, p. 9), and the loving relationship that God has with all He has made, in particular, each of them.

3. Remind the students that each of them is a child of God. Tell them that they are all members of God's family. Remind them how special everyone is: God loves each person, He cares for each person, and He helps each person and gives him all that he needs.

4. Play Telephone (see Appendix, p. B-1 for instructions) in order to help them finalize their memorization of the Words to Know and Questions 1–3. Some suggested telephone messages you may use are: "The Our Father is a prayer that Jesus gave us"; "Prayer is talking to God"; "We are all brothers and sisters in our Heavenly Father's family."

Name:

God Is Our Father   **Quiz 1**

Fill in the blanks. *Trace the gray letters and fill in the rest.*

Word Bank

1. __G o d__ is my Father.

2. God __m a d e__ me.

3. God gives me what I __n e e d__ .

4. God loves __m e__ .

5. __T h a n k__ You, God.

Assess

1. Pass out Quiz 1 and remind the children that they should keep their eyes on their own papers. Read through the quiz with them and answer any questions they may have. Ask the children to complete the quiz and, if there is time, correct the quizzes, hand them back, and review them with the children.

2. Orally quiz the students on Questions 1–3 and the Our Father (see *Teacher's Manual*, p. 9).

Conclude

Close the lesson by singing "God Father, Praise and Glory," *Adoremus Hymnal*, #464.

CHAPTER ONE: GOD IS OUR FATHER
ACTIVITY BOOK ANSWER KEYS

Name:_____

"Behold, I have graven you on the palms of my hands."

Isaiah 49:16a

You are safe in His love and care.

Draw yourself on the palm of God's hand.

Faith and Life Series • Grade 1 • Chapter 1 • Lesson 1   1

Name:_____

Draw or cut and paste onto this page pictures of different things God gives us. Can you fill this page?

2   *Faith and Life Series • Grade 1 • Chapter 1 • Lesson 2*

Name:_____

Our Father

Use the following words and page 9 in your textbook to help you fill in the blanks.

Father	Name	evil	lead
day	bread	will	Amen
Kingdom	done	forgive	Heaven
	forgive	Heaven	

Our <u>Father</u>, Who art in <u>Heaven</u>,

Hallowed be Thy <u>Name</u>; Thy

<u>Kingdom</u> come; Thy <u>will</u>

be <u>done</u> on earth as it is in

<u>Heaven</u>. Give us this <u>day</u> our

daily <u>bread</u>, and <u>forgive</u> us

our trespasses, as we <u>forgive</u>

those who trespass against us;

and <u>lead</u> us not into

temptation, but deliver us from <u>evil</u>.

<u>Amen</u>.

Faith and Life Series • Grade 1 • Chapter 1 • Lesson 3   3

Name:_____

Draw a picture of yourself talking with your father.	Draw a picture of yourself talking to God the Father in prayer.

4   *Faith and Life Series • Grade 1 • Chapter 1 • Lesson 4*

TEACHER'S NOTES

CHAPTER TWO
HEAVEN IS OUR HOME

Catechism of the Catholic Church References

The Beatific Vision: 1023, 1028
Death and Eternal Life: 1020
Faith and Eternal Life: 163–65

Heaven: 325–27, 1023–24
"Our Father Who Art in Heaven": 2777–2802
The Sign of the Cross: 232–35, 2157

Scripture References

"Rejoice in that day, and leap for joy, for behold, your reward is great in heaven...": Lk 6:23a
"Let the children come to me...for to such belongs the kingdom of heaven": Mt 19:14

Parables of the Kingdom:
The Father's House Has Many Rooms: Jn 14:2–3

A Fine Pearl: Mt 13:45–46
A Fishing Net: Mt 13:47–50
Hidden Treasure: Mt 13:44
Kingdom Like a Sower on a Path: Mk 4:10–20
Leaven: Mt 13:33
A Mustard Seed: Mk 4:30–32
Sower of Good Seed: Mt 13:24–30

Background Reading: *The Fundamentals of Catholicism* by Fr. Kenneth Baker, S.J.

Volume 1:
"The Resurrection of the Dead," pp. 113–15
"The Life of the World to Come," pp. 116–18
Volume 2:
"The Ascension of Jesus," pp. 308–10

Volume 3:
"The Communion of Saints," pp. 149–51
"Perfect Happiness," pp. 367–70

Summary of Lesson Content

Lesson 1

Heaven is God's home.

It is a place of perfect happiness.

If a person is good and has faith he will go to Heaven after his death.

Lesson 2

Earth is only man's temporary home.

Heaven is a home that will last forever.

Forever is longer than any time we can imagine.

Lesson 3

When Jesus died on the Cross, He opened the gates of Heaven for man.

The Sign of the Cross expresses two truths of the Catholic Faith:
- There are three Divine Persons in one God.
- The death of Jesus on the Cross made it possible for man to go to Heaven.

We will learn how to make the Sign of the Cross.

Lesson 4

At Mass, Jesus Christ, true God and true man, is truly present on the altar.

Angels and saints come to the altar from Heaven to pray and worship during Mass.

The Mass is, therefore, a foretaste of Heaven—God, the angels, and saints are present.

CHAPTER TWO: HEAVEN IS OUR HOME
LESSON ONE: HEAVEN IS GOD'S HOME

Aims

Students will be able to identify Heaven as God's home and a place of perfect happiness.

They will recognize Heaven as the place where good people go after death.

Materials

- Photographs and pictures showing various nature scenes

- *Activity Book*, p. 5

Optional:
- "Our Father," *Adoremus Hymnal*, p. 85

Begin

Have the children turn to p. 10 in their textbooks. Give them a moment to look at the detail of *The Last Judgment* by Fra Angelico. Then ask them where they think this scene is located, and why they think so. Ask the following questions:
- Who are the people in this picture?
- Why do some have wings and some do not?

- Are the people happy? Are they lonely?
- What is the building in the background? Are there signs of life (like trees, or water, or light)?
- Why do people have a light near their heads?
- What are the people doing?
Tell the children that this painting clearly represents Heaven.

Develop

1. Read paragraphs 1, 2, and 3 with the class. As paragraph 3 is read, ask the students to contribute to lists (on the chalkboard) headed with:
- The Most Beautiful Place
- The Best Time
- What I Love to Do Most
- The Best Taste

2. Remind the students that in the last chapter they learned that they have a perfect Father who cares for everyone. Help them recall the first line of the Our Father so that they may identify Heaven as the place where God is.

3. When the children have finished volunteering, show them the pictures/photographs of various nature scenes—mountains, forests, meadows, beaches, etc. Tell them that although these are all beautiful places, Heaven is even more

beautiful. And it is better than any of the things listed. In a way, Heaven is all of these wonderful things wrapped up together, and so much more! It is perfect in every way because God lives there. Heaven is God's home.

4. Though it may be a sensitive topic, ask the children if they know anyone who might live with God in Heaven (some will surely know a loved one who has died). Explain that when a person dies, and if he is good during his life, he goes to Heaven where he is perfectly happy with God, our Father. Not only will a good person be with God after death, but he will also be united with family and friends who have gone before him to God. In Heaven, everyone is a saint. That is what God wants everyone to be: a saint.

5. Explain (if asked) that pets have a different kind of soul than human beings have.

Reinforce

1. Assign p. 5 in the *Activity Book* (see *Teacher's Manual*, p. 23), "Heaven!" Assist those children who need help to complete this page. You may want to do this activity together as a class.

2. Practice Question 4 with the entire class (see *Teacher's Manual*, p. 17). Then divide the students into pairs and allow a few minutes for memorization. Circulate and assist as needed.

3. Send a note home to parents asking them to help their children find a photograph of a beautiful place they have visited to bring to the classroom. (Have them write their names on the back.) As the photos are brought in, they can be posted on a bulletin board entitled: "Heaven Is More Beautiful Than . . .", or you can post various other pictures under the heading, "God Created A Beautiful World . . . Heaven is Better!" (see example on the facing page).

Conclude

Close by praying, or singing, the Our Father (see *Teacher's Manual*, p. 367), *Adoremus Hymnal*, p. 85, making special note of the phrase "Who art in Heaven."

2   Heaven Is Our Home

"…no eye has seen, nor ear heard, nor the heart of man conceived, what God has prepared for those who love him."

1 Corinthians 2:9

In the last chapter, we learned that God is our Father. In the prayer that Jesus taught us, we say "Our Father who *art* in Heaven." The word art is an old-fashioned word. It means *are*. So we see that God our Father is in **Heaven**.

Do you know what Heaven is? Heaven is God's home and a place of perfect happiness. It will never end.

Now close your eyes and think of the most beautiful place you have ever seen. Think of the best time you ever had. Think of the things you love to do and the things that taste best. Well, Heaven is better than all of that!

Now comes the best part: God wants you to come

11

SAMPLE BULLETIN BOARD

GOD CREATED A BEAUTIFUL WORLD

The Most Beautiful Place   The Best Time

What I Love to Do Most   The Best Taste

HEAVEN IS BETTER!

HEAVEN

Heaven is not a place in the sense of space; it cannot be located in one specific space as opposed to another. This is a mystery, but it can be cleared up a little by realizing that only things with bodies can be in a place in the way we normally use the term. God, however, does not have a body, and so He is not in a spatial place. The *Catechism of the Catholic Church*, in fact, defines Heaven as ". . . the state of supreme, definitive happiness" (CCC 1024), where the souls of the just are with God.

"O LORD of hosts, God of Israel, who are enthroned above the cherubim, you are the God, you alone, of all the kingdoms of the earth; you have made heaven and earth."
—Isaiah 37:16

Preview

Heaven is not only God's home, but it is also our home too.

CHAPTER TWO: HEAVEN IS OUR HOME
LESSON TWO: HEAVEN IS OUR HOME

Aims

Students will be able to identify earth as their temporary home and Heaven as their final home.

They will expand their notion of "forever."

Materials

- Photos from home of beautiful places that the children have visited
- Picture of Saint Thérèse of Lisieux
- *Activity Book*, p. 6
- Crayons

Optional:
- "Our Father," *Adoremus Hymnal*, p. 85

Begin

Ask the children, one by one, to share the photographs of beautiful places they have brought from home. As each one finishes, pin it on the bulletin board. When all have had a turn, direct the students' attention to the board and ask them to look carefully at all of these beautiful places displayed. Then ask them to close their eyes and imagine a place even more beautiful. Remind them that Heaven is even more beautiful.

Develop

1. Read paragraph 4 and the prayer with the students.

2. Remind the children that God is their Father and that they are His children. That is why He wants them to live with Him. Normally, children live with their fathers so they can be safe, sheltered, fed, and loved. Fathers and children want to live together because they love each other. It is the same with their Heavenly Father. He wants them to live with Him, too, in His home—Heaven. He made them to be happy with Him forever in Heaven. Earth is only a temporary home; their lives here will end someday, but their lives with God in Heaven will never end—they will last forever. Their lives with God in Heaven will be perfectly happy, last forever, and there will be no sadness, pain, or tears: "Rejoice in that day, and leap for joy, for behold, your reward is great in heaven . . ." (Lk 6:23a).

3. Tell the children that when they get to Heaven, they will be called saints. Ask the children if they know of any saints, and make a list on the chalk board of their responses. Tell them that angels live in Heaven, too.

4. Show the students a picture of Saint Thérèse of Lisieux and tell them that she is a great saint. She used to sit and think about what it means that Heaven lasts forever. Remind the children that they have learned that Heaven is a place of perfect happiness. Could it be perfect if it ended? Ask them to name some events or times they wish would last forever (summer vacation, a birthday party, a visit from grandparents, etc.). Explain that the joys of Heaven will never end; if they did, no one could be completely happy there.

5. To help the children better understand the concept of "forever," ask them to ponder how long a minute is (have them sit quietly and still for one minute); how long a day is; how long a week is; how long a month is; how long a year is. Then have them imagine how long one hundred years is, and one thousand years.

Reinforce

1. Have the children draw a picture of themselves in Heaven with God the Father on p. 6 of the *Activity Book* (see *Teacher's Manual*, p. 23). They can look at the detail of *The Last Judgment* on p. 10 of the text for ideas, or make up their own representation of Heaven. Remind them that Heaven is the best gift of all. They must thank God for this gift.

2. Review Questions 1–4 with the class (see *Teacher's Manual*, p. 9 and the facing page). Then have the children separate into pairs and allow a few minutes for memory work.

3. Say, "I'm getting ready for Heaven, so I am going to _____", and have the students finish the sentence. They can mention acts of charity, prayers they will say, Commandments they will keep, etc. As it goes around the circle you may want to have them add their way of getting ready for Heaven to the others as a memory exercise.

Conclude

1. Summarize what has been taught about Heaven thus far:
- Heaven is God's home, and man's final home.
- It is a place of perfect happiness.
- There is nothing sad or painful there.
- Heaven will never end.

2. Pray the Our Father together (see *Teacher's Manual*, p. 367).

3. Sing "Our Father," *Adoremus Hymnal*, p. 85.

2   Heaven Is Our Home

"…no eye has seen, nor ear heard, nor the heart of man conceived, what God has prepared for those who love him."

1 Corinthians 2:9

In the last chapter, we learned that God is our Father. In the prayer that Jesus taught us, we say "Our Father who *art* in Heaven." The word art is an old-fashioned word. It means *are*. So we see that God our Father is in **Heaven**.

Do you know what Heaven is? Heaven is God's home and a place of perfect happiness. It will never end.

Now close your eyes and think of the most beautiful place you have ever seen. Think of the best time you ever had. Think of the things you love to do and the things that taste best. Well, Heaven is better than all of that!

Now comes the best part: God wants you to come

11

to live with Him in Heaven someday. In Heaven you will be happy with God forever and ever. And in Heaven, no one is ever sad or hurt or crying. You can pray:

Thank You, God, my Father, for wanting to share Your home with me. Amen

Words to Know:

Heaven   Sign of the Cross

> **Q. 4**   *What is Heaven?*
> Heaven is God's home and a place of perfect happiness (CCC 326, 1024).

We Pray:

THE SIGN OF THE CROSS

When we talk to our Father in Heaven, we often begin and end our prayer with:

12

SAMPLE SKIT

You may want to help the students perform their arrival in Heaven as a skit, with Saint Peter at the gate asking them if they were good or not (see example). Remind them that they can only be with their Father in Heaven if they are good. Some can be already-arrived saints or angels.

Peter: Who is there?

Student 1: It is I, _____.

Peter: Have you loved God and been good?

Student 1: I have done my best to love God as I should.

Peter: Then enter and be happy forever.

Student 2: Hello, _____, welcome to Heaven.

Student 3: Yes, we are glad to see you in Heaven.

SAINT THÉRÈSE OF LISIEUX

Also known as the "Little Flower," Saint Thérèse was born in France in 1873. She became a Carmelite nun at age fifteen. She died of tuberculosis in 1897 and she was canonized in 1925. She is the patron saint of missions. Her feast day is October 1.

Preview

We will learn about Who made it possible for us to go to Heaven, and how.

Chapter Two: Heaven Is Our Home
Lesson Three: The Sign of the Cross

Aims

Students will practice making the Sign of the Cross correctly.

They will know that this prayer expresses two truths of the Catholic Faith:
• There is one God in three Divine Persons.
• Jesus opened the gates of Heaven when He died on the Cross.

Materials

• Picture of Saint Thérèse of Lisieux

• *Activity Book*, p. 7

Optional:
• "Our Father," *Adoremus Hymnal*, p. 85

Materials for optional craft:
• Large paper bags
• Children's scissors
• Construction paper
• Glue or paste
• Crayons/markers
• Glitter

Begin

Show the children the picture of Saint Thérèse of Lisieux, and tell this story from her life. As a very young girl, Saint Thérèse understood the beauty of Heaven and the joy of being with God forever. She loved her parents and God so much that she wanted her Mom and Dad to be happy with Him forever. She knew that they could only be happy with God if they died. Because of this, she was not afraid for her parents to die.

Develop

1. Read together the We Pray section in the student textbooks (see *Teacher's Manual*, pp. 367 and 368). Re-emphasize the fact that Catholics make the Sign of the Cross before and after they pray: "In the Name of the Father, and of the Son, and of the Holy Spirit." Ask them to say it with you, with their hands folded in their laps. Have the students repeat the words with you several times. You might have each student take turns saying the words. Then tell them that when Catholics say these words they are showing that they believe in the Blessed Trinity: one God in three Divine Persons, the Father, the Son, and the Holy Spirit. Each of these Persons is one and the same God.

2. Tell the children that the Sign of the Cross is the sign of a Catholic. People of other religions do not generally make this sign. Ask them if they know when Catholics make this sign (before prayers, at Mass, after prayers).

3. Ask the children if they were aware that before Jesus died on the Cross, no one could go to Heaven when he died, not even good people. The gates of Heaven were closed after Adam and Eve sinned, and remained closed until our Lord died on the Cross and opened them again. So the Cross is a great sign of hope and faith that man will one day be happy forever with God in Heaven.

4. Once all the children know the words, demonstrate for them how to make the Sign of the Cross. Read the bottom of pp. 12 and 13 of the student text with the class, then make the Sign of the Cross together. Repeat the directions slowly as you demonstrate the actions. Do this a few times until the children are comfortable with the prayer.

Reinforce

1. Assign p. 7 in the *Activity Book* (see *Teacher's Manual*, p. 23).

2. Optional craft: Have the children decorate a paper bag "suit of armor" for practicing the Sign of the Cross. For each child, provide a paper bag with holes cut out for head and arms. In the places the child will touch to make the Sign of the Cross, write Father, Son, and Holy Spirit. Have the students decorate these bags to look like armor. Tell the children that they are soldiers for Christ; their weapon is the Sign of the Cross, a very powerful prayer.

Conclude

1. Remind the class that the Sign of the Cross expresses two wonderful beliefs: that God is a Blessed Trinity and that the gates of Heaven were opened again when Jesus died on the Cross. Because He died, everyone is able to enter Heaven someday and live with God in His home forever.

2. Have the children practice the Sign of the Cross and check that they are doing it properly. Send the directions home to parents and ask them to help their children learn it correctly.

3. Spend a few minutes reviewing Questions 1–4 with the entire class (see *Teacher's Manual*, p. 9 and the facing page). Then let pairs of children practice on their own.

4. Close the lesson by singing "Our Father," *Adoremus Hymnal*, p. 85.

2   Heaven Is Our Home

"…no eye has seen, nor ear heard, nor the heart of man conceived, what God has prepared for those who love him."

1 Corinthians 2:9

In the last chapter, we learned that God is our Father. In the prayer that Jesus taught us, we say "Our Father who *art* in Heaven." The word art is an old-fashioned word. It means *are*. So we see that God our Father is in **Heaven**.

Do you know what Heaven is? Heaven is God's home and a place of perfect happiness. It will never end.

Now close your eyes and think of the most beautiful place you have ever seen. Think of the best time you ever had. Think of the things you love to do and the things that taste best. Well, Heaven is better than all of that!

Now comes the best part: God wants you to come

11

to live with Him in Heaven someday. In Heaven you will be happy with God forever and ever. And in Heaven, no one is ever sad or hurt or crying. You can pray:

Thank You, God, my Father, for wanting to share Your home with me. Amen

Words to Know:

Heaven   Sign of the Cross

> **Q. 4**   *What is Heaven?*
> Heaven is God's home and a place of perfect happiness (CCC 326, 1024).

We Pray:

THE SIGN OF THE CROSS

When we talk to our Father in Heaven, we often begin and end our prayer with:

12

In the Name of the Father, and of the Son, and of the Holy Spirit. *Amen.*

While we say the words, we make a big cross by touching with our right hand first our forehead, then our chest, our left shoulder, and finally our right shoulder.

13

PATTERN FOR OPTIONAL CRAFT

FATHER

SPIRIT   HOLY

SON

Preview

Even while we are still on earth, we can have a glimpse of Heaven.

CHAPTER TWO: HEAVEN IS OUR HOME
LESSON FOUR: THE MASS IS OUR FORETASTE OF HEAVEN

Aims

Students will be able to name those who are present at Mass.

They will know that because Jesus Christ, true God and true man, is present on the altar, Mass is like a foretaste of Heaven.

Materials

- Mural paper
- Crayons or markers
- *Activity Book*, p. 8

Optional:
- Camera for taking pictures of students
- "Our Father," *Adoremus Hymnal*, p. 85

Begin

Begin with the Sign of the Cross, then review all that has been taught about Heaven so far:
- It is God's home.
- It is perfect.
- There is nothing bad, sad, or painful there.
- It will never end.
- If a person is good in his life, he will go to Heaven when he dies.
- Jesus opened the gates of Heaven when He died on the Cross.

Develop

1. Ask the children to turn to p. 98 of their textbooks and look at the photograph of the priest offering Mass (see top left corner of facing page).

2. Remind the children that when the priest offers Mass, our Lord Himself comes down on the altar in the appearance of bread and wine. Ask whether or not they know if anyone else is present at Mass. They will easily think of the priest and the laity. Lead them to see that in addition, the angels and the saints come down to the altar from Heaven to worship our Lord in the Blessed Sacrament. They come because God is truly present in the Blessed Sacrament. It is as though Heaven comes to earth for that little while. Let the children think about this for a moment and help them to reflect on this beautiful preview of Heaven that God gives His children on earth. Athough our Lord is hidden under the appearances of bread and wine, He is truly present as both God and man.

3. Arrange with your pastor to make a brief visit to the church or see pp. 354–63 of this manual for a description of the parts of a church. Point out the tabernacle and the sanctuary lamp nearby. When the latter is lit, it indicates that the Blessed Sacrament is present in the tabernacle (see p. 356). Remind the children that it is on the altar of sacrifice that the priest offers Holy Mass, during which the bread and wine become the Body and Blood of our Lord. At that great moment, angels and saints gather around the altar to worship and adore. Make a special effort to teach the children how to genuflect (touch right knee to the floor) before the tabernacle.

4. Practice genuflecting in the classroom.

5. Take pictures of the students. Then, using poster board or a bulletin board, write the Scripture verse "Let the children come to me…for to such belongs the kingdom of heaven" (Mt 19:14). Place pictures of the students under the verse.

Reinforce

1. Divide the students into groups of 6–8 children. Provide mural paper for each group. In an open area of the classroom, secure the paper to the floor with masking tape at the corners. Instruct the children to draw a picture of those present at Mass: Jesus (in the Host and within the chalice), the priest, the people, the angels, and saints. They should first draw an altar in the middle of the paper and then fill in all those present around it.

2. When the murals are completed, hang them out in the hallway for the other children in the school to enjoy. Possible title: "Heaven Comes to Earth at Mass."

3. As the groups of children finish their mural drawings, direct them to work on p. 8 of their *Activity Book* (see *Teacher's Manual*, p. 23). They are to write to their Heavenly Father about how they would like to go to Heaven one day, and ask for help with the things they need to do to get there. For example, saying good and kind words, being honest and obedient, saying prayers, loving God and all the children in His family, etc.

Conclude

1. Provide time for pairs to finish memorizing Questions 1–4 (see *Teacher's Manual*, p. 9 and the facing page).

2. Pray the Sign of the Cross and the Our Father (see *Teacher's Manual*, p. 367). Assist those who need it.

3. Sing "Our Father," *Adoremus Hymnal*, p. 85.

to live with Him in Heaven someday. In Heaven you will be happy with God forever and ever. And in Heaven, no one is ever sad or hurt or crying. You can pray:

Thank You, God, my Father, for wanting to share Your home with me. Amen

Words to Know:

Heaven   Sign of the Cross

> **Q. 4**   *What is Heaven?*
> Heaven is God's home and a place of perfect happiness (CCC 326, 1024).

We Pray:

THE SIGN OF THE CROSS

When we talk to our Father in Heaven, we often begin and end our prayer with:

12

In the Name of the Father, and of the Son, and of the Holy Spirit. *Amen.*

While we say the words, we make a big cross by touching with our right hand first our forehead, then our chest, our left shoulder, and finally our right shoulder.

13

SAINT BENEDICT AND THE SIGN OF THE CROSS

Saint Benedict was born into a noble family in what is now Italy, around the year 490. As a young man he was sent to Rome to continue his education in the art of rhetoric. Dismayed by the licentious lives of his classmates, he left to become a hermit. He was soon discovered and asked to lead a group of monks, but his austerity led them to mix poison into his wine. When he made the Sign of the Cross over it as was his custom, the cup shattered and his life was spared. He eventually founded a monastery at Monte Cassino and wrote the Rule of Saint Benedict. He died around 547. He is often called the father of western monasticism. His feast day is July 11.

Preview

We will review what we have learned, play a new game, and take a quiz.

Aims

To review and assess the students' understanding of the material taught this week.

To hear each child's memory work.

To ensure understanding of Questions 1–4.

Materials

- Appendix, p. B-1
- "Our Father," *Adoremus Hymnal*, p. 85
- Quiz 2 (Appendix, p. A-2)

Name: _____

Heaven Is Our Home   Quiz 2

Fill in the blanks. *Trace the gray letters and fill in the rest.*

Word Bank

I	me	home	God

1. G o d lives in Heaven.

2. God wants m e to go to Heaven.

3. In Heaven I will be happy.

4. Heaven is my true h o m e .

Review and Enrichment

1. Make the Sign of the Cross with the children and pray the Our Father together (see *Teacher's Manual*, p. 367). Then sing the songs they have learned from Chapters 1 and 2. Remind them that singing is a prayer, too. Conclude with the Sign of the Cross. Be watching to see that children are correctly making the Sign of the Cross and that they are reverent during prayers.

2. Spend a few minutes reviewing Questions 1–4 with the class (see *Teacher's Manual*, pp. 9 and 21). If answers still need polishing, give pairs of children time to work together.

3. Divide the class into two groups and play Bible Baseball (see Appendix, p. B-1), asking questions about Heaven, forever, those present at Mass, and what one needs to do to get to Heaven.

Assess

1. Pass out Quiz 2 and remind the children to do their own work —no copying. Explain that you want to know if they have learned what you taught them; if not, then you want to try teaching them in a different way. It will not help them to learn if they just copy from their neighbors.

2. Have children complete Quiz 2. Observe to see whether anyone needs help.

Conclude

1. Pass out a treat for the children in recognition of their good work and reverent attitudes. Holy cards of saints are always popular.

2. Sing "Our Father," *Adoremus Hymnal*, p. 85.

Chapter Two: Heaven Is Our Home
Activity Book Answer Keys

Name:_____

HEAVEN!

Answers will vary.

Heaven is more beautiful than _____.

Heaven is more fun than _____.

Heaven is better than _____.

Heaven is prettier than _____.

Heaven lasts longer than _____.

Heaven will make me happier than _____.

The best part about _____ is that I will be with my heavenly Father!

Faith and Life Series • Grade 1 • Chapter 2 • Lesson 1   5

Name:_____

Draw a picture of yourself in Heaven with God the Father.

6   *Faith and Life Series • Grade 1 • Chapter 2 • Lesson 2*

Name:_____

Use the following words and page 13 in your textbook to help you fill in the blanks.

| Son   Spirit   Holy   Father |

In the Name of the Father
and of the Son
and of the Holy Spirit.
Amen.

Color the Picture.

Faith and Life Series • Grade 1 • Chapter 2 • Lesson 3   7

Name:_____

Write a letter to your heavenly Father.

Dear H e a v e n l y F a t h e r,

(Tell your heavenly Father how much you would like to come to Heaven.)

I would like to Answers will vary.

(Now ask your heavenly Father to help you get to Heaven.)

Please help me Answers will vary.

Love,

Student's name

8   *Faith and Life Series • Grade 1 • Chapter 2 • Lesson 4*

TEACHER'S NOTES

CHAPTER THREE
GOD WATCHES OVER EVERYTHING

Catechism of the Catholic Church References

Angels/Demons: 327–30, 350, 395, 414
Angels, Servants of Christ: 331, 351
Attributes of God Shown in and through Creation: 293–94
Fallen Angels: 391–93
God Does Not Abandon Man after the Fall: 410
God Sustains Creation: 301, 320
God's Apparent Powerlessness: 272–74

God's Goodness: 385
God's Omnipotence: 268–74
God's Providence: 302–14
Heaven, Place of Angels: 326, 1023
The Mystery of Creation: 295–301, 315, 317–18
Speaking about God: 39–43, 48

Scripture References

Creation: Gen 1
Fall of Satan and His Angels: Rev 12:7–9

Background Reading: *The Fundamentals of Catholicism* by Fr. Kenneth Baker, S.J.

Volume 2:
Creation, pp. 121–39

Summary of Lesson Content

Lesson 1

God is everywhere, all powerful, all knowing, and all good.

God's care for His children extends to every time and place.

Lesson 2

To create means "to make from nothing without effort."

Only God can create.

God created everything that exists, and gave it to us.

Lesson 3

Creating is different from making.

God creates, man makes.

Lesson 4

Angels are invisible spirits created by God. They were created to be His helpers.

Some angels turned against God and became bad; we call them devils.

Chapter Three: God Watches Over Everything
Lesson One: Qualities of God

Aims

Students will learn the meaning of four qualities of God: everywhere, all powerful, all knowing, and all good.

They will understand what these four qualities of God mean in their lives.

They will come to a deeper appreciation of God's continual care for them.

Materials

- *Activity Book*, p. 9

- Plant Clippings

- Cups

- Water

- Soil

- Appendix, p. B-2

Optional:
- "All creatures of our God and King," *Adoremus Hymnal*, #600

Begin

Help the children to recall that God is our Father who lives in Heaven. Review what they have learned thus far: God is a good Father who loves and cares for them; He gives them many gifts, such as the natural world; He wants them to be with Him in Heaven. Tell them that today they will learn four new things about God.

Develop

1. Read paragraph 1 aloud. It tells of an important way in which God differs from man: while man can only be in one place at a time, God is everywhere. Explain that if they are in one place, they simply cannot be in another place at the same time. Give examples, letting the children occupy different places in the classroom. Tell the students that though they cannot see Him, God can always see them and He is always near. He is in Heaven, on earth, and in every place, all at the same time.

2. Read paragraph 2 with the children. Remind them that God created all things. Remind them that they cannot create anything, but God can; God is all powerful. Have them compare God's work of creation with their own crafts; they work very hard when they paint or model clay, but God exerts no effort at all. Tell them that not only can God do all things, but He also does them without effort. Remember, when He created the world and all that is in it, all He did was say, "Let there be . . . ," and it began to exist. Saying words is no effort at all! There is nothing too complicated or difficult for God to do.

3. Read paragraph 3 with the children. Explain that God, having made everything that is, knows all things. Nothing is a mystery to God, and nothing is too difficult for Him to understand. He does not need to go to school, or to learn like people do. He sees all things and actions, and even knows everyone's most secret thoughts.

4. Read paragraph 4 with the children. Explain that not only did God make everything that exists, but He also cares for His creation continually. He did not just make man and the animals and the rest of the natural world, and then forget about them, as the students sometimes do with their crafts and work. Instead, God takes care of everything, and most especially He takes care of His children, keeping them always in mind.

Reinforce

1. Assign p. 9 in the *Activity Book* (see *Teacher's Manual*, p. 35).

2. Have the students work a plant project such as the example on the facing page.

3. Teach the students to sing "All creatures of our God and King," *Adoremus Hymnal*, #600.

Conclude

1. Photocopy and assign as homework p. B-2 or B-3 as appropriate from the Appendix. Give a reward to those who have a full checklist at the end of the week.

2. Practice Questions 5–7 with all of the children (see *Teacher's Manual*, p. 29). Then let them practice for a few minutes in pairs. They should also review Questions 1–4 (see *Teacher's Manual*, pp. 9 and 21).

3. End by making the Sign of the Cross, praying the Our Father, and closing with the Sign of the Cross (see *Teacher's Manual*, p. 367). Check to make sure children are doing this correctly.

God Watches Over Everything

"For you love all things that exist..."

Wisdom 11:24

God is everywhere, not just in Heaven. You cannot see God, but He looks after you all the time, wherever you are.

God is all powerful. He can do anything! No one is stronger than God.

God knows *everything*. He knows what every fish and bug and bird is doing right now. He knows what you are doing and even what you are thinking.

God created all things—every single thing! To **create** is to make something out of nothing. Once there was only God: there was no light, no outer space, no earth, no water, nothing but God. Then God said, "Let there be light! Let there be sky! Let there be land and water!" And there it was, just like that, just the way God said.

15

In order to help the students become more aware of God's constant care for them, have each child start a cutting of a plant. Then have each student care for his plant each day this week. Help them to see that in the same way they are caring for their plants' needs, God cares for their needs. However, they only keep their plants in mind for brief moments during the day. God never forgets them, not even for a moment! At the end of the week the students can take their plants home.

HOW TO PREPARE PLANT CLIPPINGS

Step 1: Choose a spider plant or a hardy vine plant that is easily trimmable.

Step 2: Cut the plant immediately above a leaf, leaving about a three inch stem.

Step 3: Soak the clippings in a cup containing at least two inches of water that is placed in direct sunlight. In a few days the roots will begin to grow.

Step 4: When the roots mature, you can transplant the clipping to a cup or flower pot of potting soil, or transplant them directly to the soil in a garden. Be sure to include all of the roots.

GOD AND THE PROBLEM OF EVIL

"Can God do bad or evil things?" If this comes up, explain to the children that God cannot do bad things. This is not because He does not have the power to do them, but because they are things that should not be done, and He is all good.

Preview

We will learn what it means to create and Who can create.

Chapter Three: God Watches Over Everything
Lesson Two: God Is the Creator of All Things

Aims

Students will understand the difference between making and creating.

They will be able to define the word *create* as "to make from nothing."

They will know that God created all things.

Materials

- Children's Bible
- *Activity Book*, p. 10
- Enlarged paper cut-outs of the six days of Creation (Appendix, pp. B-4 and B-5)
- Photocopies of Appendix, pp. B-4 and B-5 for the Creation Mobile
- Children's scissors
- Yarn

Optional:
- "All creatures of our God and King," *Adoremus Hymnal*, #600

Begin

Have the children look again at the painting on p. 14 in their textbooks. Let them name all the animals they see, even the smallest (e.g., snail, starfish). Ask them: Who is walking with the animals? Why is God shown walking with them? How is God represented in this picture? Is He old? Does God really look like this? Where is God? Is He in Heaven? Why is He with the animals? Does He like to be with people, too? Can a person see God?

Develop

1. Reread paragraph 4 in the textbook with the children. There are two important things to review in this paragraph. First, direct the children's attention to the word "create." Remind them that God has a very special way of making. In order to understand it, they must first look at how they make things. This will help the students to understand the difference.

2. Reread the line in paragraph 4 that says: "Once there was only God . . . nothing but God." Remind the children that He then created the world and everything in it. Ask the children if He used anything to make the world, as they do when they make things. Ask them to imagine what it must have been like before God made anything. Remind them that there were no stars, no sun, no moon, no world, and no outer space. Have them imagine God making the world, the sun, the moon, and the stars out of nothing. Read the last lines of paragraph 4, emphasizing that all God needed to do when He made the world was to say some words, "Let there be light." Can they do that? No. When they make something, they not only make it out of something else, but they must also work hard. This is the second important point in paragraph 4: God created everything with ease.

3. Using the enlarged paper cut-outs from pp. B-4 and B-5 play the Creation Assembly Game: first, write the names of the creatures God created on each day across the chalk board. Then tell the story of Creation (or read Gen 1 from a children's Bible). As each new creature is created by God in the story, have a student place that creature's cut-out on the chalk tray beneath the creature's name. You may want to use a bulletin board instead. Be sure to emphasize that at the end of each day God looked at what He made and saw that it was good.

Reinforce

1. On p. 10 of the *Activity Book* (see *Teacher's Manual*, p. 35), have the children draw their own picture of God's creation. Suggest that they include people, animals, plants, trees, flowers, sky, earth, etc.

2. Make a Creation Mobile. Children should color the seven pictures you have photocopied (on heavy paper if possible) from pp. B-4 and B-5 of the Appendix, cut them into squares, punch holes in the tops of each panel, and string them together with yarn. Display in the classroom, or send them home to share with families.

Conclude

1. Read Question 8 with the children. Practice the answer as a group. Then divide into pairs and give the students a few minutes to practice it and to review Questions 1–7 (see *Teacher's Manual*, pp. 9 and 21).

2. Pray the Our Father, opening and closing with the Sign of the Cross (see *Teacher's Manual*, pp. 9 and 21). Check to make sure children are doing this correctly, and encourage them to fill out their prayer checklists at home tonight.

3. Sing "All creatures of our God and King," *Adoremus Hymnal*, #600.

3   God Watches Over Everything

"For you love all things that exist..."

Wisdom 11:24

God is everywhere, not just in Heaven. You cannot see God, but He looks after you all the time, wherever you are.

God is all powerful. He can do anything! No one is stronger than God.

God knows *everything*. He knows what every fish and bug and bird is doing right now. He knows what you are doing and even what you are thinking.

God created all things—every single thing! To **create** is to make something out of nothing. Once there was only God: there was no light, no outer space, no earth, no water, nothing but God. Then God said, "Let there be light! Let there be sky! Let there be land and water!" And there it was, just like that, just the way God said.

15

God created **angels** too. Angels are like God in one way because they do not have bodies. They are invisible spirits.

All the angels were very good when God created them. Then some of the angels turned away from God. That means they chose to become bad; they became **devils**. The good angels stayed with God to be His helpers.

God is all good. Everything about God is good. He takes care of all that He has made. He takes care of the stars and the planets. He takes care of the animals and the trees. Above all, God takes care of you and loves you very much.

16

Words to Know:

create   angels   devils

Q. 5   *Where is God?*
God is in Heaven, on earth, and in every place (CCC 2794–96).

Q. 6   *Can God do all things?*
Yes, God can do all things (CCC 268–69).

Q. 7   *Does God know all things?*
Yes, God knows all things, even our thoughts (CCC 305).

Q. 8   *Why is God called "the Creator of Heaven and earth"?*
God is called the Creator of Heaven and earth because He made all things out of nothing (CCC 290–91).

Q. 9   *What are angels?*
Angels are invisible spirits. They are God's helpers (CCC 328–30).

17

ERRORS ABOUT THE WORLD'S ORIGIN

Pantheism: The world as a whole is God; the development of the world is the development of God.

Dualism, Manichaeism: Two external principles, Good and Evil, are locked in permanent conflict.

Gnosticism: The world is evil and to be rejected.

Deism: God made the world but then left it to its own devices.

Materialism: The world is merely an interplay of matter that has always existed.

Preview

We will explore how God makes things. It is very different from the way we make things.

CHAPTER THREE: GOD WATCHES OVER EVERYTHING
LESSON THREE: GOD CREATES, WE MAKE

Aims

Students will become more familiar with the difference between creating and making.

They will practice distinguishing between those things created by God and those made by men.

Materials

- Enlarged paper cut-outs from Lesson 2

- A picture or paper cut-out creature that begins with each of the letters of the word "Creator"

- A box with pictures of created things and photos of man-made things; enough for each child

- *Activity Book*, p. 11

Optional:
- Pages for the book of Creation; construction paper for covers

- "All creatures of our God and King," *Adoremus Hymnal*, #600

Begin

Play the Creation Assembly Game again as a class (from the last lesson). Pass out the paper cut-outs from Lesson 2 to each of the children (have multiple birds, fish and animals available so that each child will have a cut-out). Recount the story of Creation. Let the children participate by placing their creatures on the chalk tray or bulletin board at the appropriate time.

Develop

1. Using a chalkboard, write the word "Creator" in capital letters across the board. Remind the children that in the last lesson they learned that someone who creates is called a creator. Help them to recall that *to create* means "to make from nothing." Ask them how many Creators there are. By now they should see that there is only one, in the strictest sense of the word!

2. Under each letter on the board, draw or place a picture of a creature whose name begins with that letter, for example: C, a cat; R, a rock; E, the earth; A, an angel; T, a tree; O, an octopus; R, a rainbow. Ask the children to name other creatures that could be displayed for each letter.

3. Ask the children if they can make a rainbow, or an octopus, or a cat. Explain that only God can make these things, and, in fact, He created them from nothing. Help

them to see that they make things from things that already exist, things that God created for them to use. A carpenter makes a table from the wood of a tree, and clothing can be made from cotton that grows in the fields. Ask the students to name other things that man makes using the things God created. You may want to make a list and/or quick drawings on the chalkboard of their contributions.

4. To reinforce in the children's minds the difference between creating and making, fill a box with pictures of both created and man-made things—enough for every child in the class. Pass the box to each student and let him take out one picture. Children should hold their pictures until everyone has chosen. Then ask each student to identify the object in his picture and tell whether God created it or whether a human being made it out of things God created.

Reinforce

1. Assign p. 11 in the *Activity Book* (see *Teacher's Manual*, p. 35), a comparison of creating and making. Refer the students to your drawings or the creature cut-outs from earlier in the lesson.

2. Have the children make a storybook of the seven days of Creation. You can use the patterns from the Creation Mobile, located on Appendix, pp. B-4 and B-5. Title each section with the day, and list the creatures made by God on that day. Children should illustrate them appropriately. Or, you can use the patterns to make a display on the bulletin board (see example on facing page).

Conclude

1. Have pairs of children spend a few minutes practicing Question 8 and reviewing Questions 1-4 (see *Teacher's Manual*, pp. 9 and 21).

2. End by making the Sign of the Cross, praying the Our Father, and closing with the Sign of the Cross (see *Teacher's Manual*, p. 367). Check to make sure children are doing this correctly.

3. Together, sing "All creatures of our God and King," *Adoremus Hymnal*, #600. Verses 1–4 are appropriate and can be taught to the children over the next few weeks.

3 God Watches Over Everything

"For you love all things that exist..."
Wisdom 11:24

God is everywhere, not just in Heaven. You cannot see God, but He looks after you all the time, wherever you are.

God is all powerful. He can do anything! No one is stronger than God.

God knows *everything*. He knows what every fish and bug and bird is doing right now. He knows what you are doing and even what you are thinking.

God created all things—every single thing! To **create** is to make something out of nothing. Once there was only God: there was no light, no outer space, no earth, no water, nothing but God. Then God said, "Let there be light! Let there be sky! Let there be land and water!" And there it was, just like that, just the way God said.

15

God created **angels** too. Angels are like God in one way because they do not have bodies. They are invisible spirits.

All the angels were very good when God created them. Then some of the angels turned away from God. That means they chose to become bad; they became **devils**. The good angels stayed with God to be His helpers.

God is all good. Everything about God is good. He takes care of all that He has made. He takes care of the stars and the planets. He takes care of the animals and the trees. Above all, God takes care of you and loves you very much.

16

Words to Know:

create   angels   devils

Q. 5 *Where is God?*
God is in Heaven, on earth, and in every place (CCC 2794–96).

Q. 6 *Can God do all things?*
Yes, God can do all things (CCC 268–69).

Q. 7 *Does God know all things?*
Yes, God knows all things, even our thoughts (CCC 305).

Q. 8 *Why is God called "the Creator of Heaven and earth"?*
God is called the Creator of Heaven and earth because He made all things out of nothing (CCC 290–91).

Q. 9 *What are angels?*
Angels are invisible spirits. They are God's helpers (CCC 328–30).

17

CREATION STORY BOARD

Day 1 Light and Dark	Day 2 The Sky
Day 3 Land and Trees	Day 4 The Sun and Moon
Day 5 Fish and Birds	Day 6 Animals and Man

Day 7
God rested and blessed the seventh day.

Preview

We will learn about the invisible spirits God created.

CHAPTER THREE: GOD WATCHES OVER EVERYTHING
LESSON FOUR: ANGELS AND DEVILS

Aims

Students will learn that in addition to the visible world, God also created angels.

They will be able to define good angels as invisible spirits and God's helpers who live with Him in Heaven.

They will listen to a story of the battle between the good and bad angels.

They will be able to define devils as bad angels who turned away from God and who live in Hell.

Materials

- Enlarged paper cut-outs from Lesson 2
- Children's Bible
- *Activity Book*, p. 12

Optional:
- Popsicle puppets (see Appendix, p. B-6)
- TV show materials (Appendix, p. B-7)
- "All creatures of our God and King," *Adoremus Hymnal*, #600

Begin

Review what was learned in the last lesson by writing the word "Creator" on the chalkboard and having the children place the appropriate creatures under each letter. Remind them that only God creates because only God can make things from nothing.

Develop

1. Read paragraph 5 in the textbook with the children.

2. Point out to the students that angels are different from all other creatures of God. Ask them if they know what this important difference is. Guide them to see that angels do not have bodies and, therefore, cannot be seen; they are invisible spirits. In this way they are very much like God: He does not have a body either. Angels live with God in Heaven and act as His helpers. Artists usually portray angels with wings; they can deliver messages very quickly by flying! But remind the children that they do not really have wings; they have no bodies at all.

3. Explain to the children that though angels have no bodies, they are very powerful and great creatures. Like all of God's creatures, they were very good when God created them. Read paragraph 6 in their textbook. Tell the children you are going to read a story about the great battle that took place between the angels after God created them, and how some of the angels became bad.

4. Read the story of the fall of the bad angels from your children's Bible (Rev 12:7–9). When you are finished, check for comprehension by asking: "Who was the commander of the good angels?" (Saint Michael the Archangel) "What was the name of the leader of the bad angels?" (Lucifer) "Why did the bad angels turn against God?" (They loved themselves more than God.) "Where are the bad angels now?" (Hell) "What do we call the bad angels?" (devils) "What is Lucifer's name now?" (Satan)

5. Read paragraph 7 in the student textbook.

Reinforce

1. Have the children color the angel on p. 12 of the *Activity Book* (see *Teacher's Manual*, p. 35).

2. Dramatize the story of the fall of the bad angels by making popsicle puppets and having the children act out the parts in a shoe box theater. This is best done in groups of 6–8. Each group should make one puppet for Saint Michael, Lucifer, God, a few good angels, and a few bad angels. See Appendix, p. B-6 for directions on puppets and theater.

3. Or you may choose to make a TV show of the story of Saint Michael and the fall of the bad angels. This project is best done in small groups of 3–4 children. See Appendix, p. B-7 for directions.

Conclude

1. Spend a few minutes practicing Question 9 and reviewing Questions 5–8 with the class. Then let pairs practice them together for a few minutes.

2. Make the Sign of the Cross, then lead the students in a brief prayer thanking God for all that He has given man in creation, and conclude with the Sign of the Cross (see *Teacher's Manual*, p. 367).

3. Sing "All creatures of our God and King," *Adoremus Hymnal*, #600.

3   God Watches Over Everything

"For you love all things that exist..."
Wisdom 11:24

God is everywhere, not just in Heaven. You cannot see God, but He looks after you all the time, wherever you are.

God is all powerful. He can do anything! No one is stronger than God.

God knows *everything*. He knows what every fish and bug and bird is doing right now. He knows what you are doing and even what you are thinking.

God created all things—every single thing! To **create** is to make something out of nothing. Once there was only God: there was no light, no outer space, no earth, no water, nothing but God. Then God said, "Let there be light! Let there be sky! Let there be land and water!" And there it was, just like that, just the way God said.

15

God created **angels** too. Angels are like God in one way because they do not have bodies. They are invisible spirits.

All the angels were very good when God created them. Then some of the angels turned away from God. That means they chose to become bad; they became **devils**. The good angels stayed with God to be His helpers.

God is all good. Everything about God is good. He takes care of all that He has made. He takes care of the stars and the planets. He takes care of the animals and the trees. Above all, God takes care of you and loves you very much.

16

Words to Know:

create   angels   devils

> **Q. 5** *Where is God?*
> God is in Heaven, on earth, and in every place (CCC 2794–96).
>
> **Q. 6** *Can God do all things?*
> Yes, God can do all things (CCC 268–69).
>
> **Q. 7** *Does God know all things?*
> Yes, God knows all things, even our thoughts (CCC 305).
>
> **Q. 8** *Why is God called "the Creator of Heaven and earth"?*
> God is called the Creator of Heaven and earth because He made all things out of nothing (CCC 290–91).
>
> **Q. 9** *What are angels?*
> Angels are invisible spirits. They are God's helpers (CCC 328–30).

17

POPE LEO XIII AND THE SAINT MICHAEL PRAYER

Pope Leo XIII realized the extent of the bad angels' influence in the modern world, as well as the power of the good angels to battle against them. So he wrote a prayer to the greatest of angels, Saint Michael, who threw Lucifer and his angels into Hell:

Saint Michael the Archangel, defend us in battle, be our protection against the wickedness and snares of the devil; may God rebuke him we humbly pray; and do thou, O Prince of the heavenly host, by the power of God, cast into Hell Satan and all the evil spirits who wander about the world seeking the ruin of souls. *Amen.*

POPE LEO XIII

Leo XIII was born on March 2, 1810; elected Pope on February 20, 1878; and died in Rome on July 20, 1903.

Preview

We will practice distinguishing between things made by God and things made by man. We will play a new game to reinforce what we have learned, and we will take a quiz.

CHAPTER THREE: GOD WATCHES OVER EVERYTHING
REVIEW AND ASSESSMENT

Aims

To review and assess the children's understanding of the material taught this week.

Materials

- Pictures from Lesson 3 with safety pins

- A box or paper bag filled with things created by God and things made by man; one for each child

- Chart paper with headings: "Created by God" and "Man-Made" (to be laid on the floor)

- Quiz 3 (Appendix, p. A-3)

- "All creatures of our God and King," *Adoremus Hymnal,* #600

Review and Enrichment

1. Use the pictures of created things from Lesson 3. Lay them out on a flat surface where they can be viewed by the children.

2. Play a Creation game: using safety pins, attach to the back of each student a picture of a creature. Instruct the children not to tell each other what they have. Rather, other children should imitate or give hints about the creature until the person "wearing" it can guess what his own creature is. Once they have guessed correctly, the picture may be pinned in the front. If you have a camera in the classroom, you could take a photograph of all the children with their "creatures" pinned to them; when developed, display it and label it "God's Creatures."

3. Lay the chart you have made on the floor. Read the headings to the children. Show them the box or bag containing the items you have gathered together. Tell them that in this container there are many things, some made by people, some created by God. Each child will have a turn to pull an item out of the container and place it on the appropriate side of the chart you have prepared. Then each child should place his item on the chart under the appropriate heading: "Created by God" or "Man-Made." When the items have been sorted, ask the children to name other things that could be put on the chart, and tell which column they should go in. Don't let them forget about angels, the invisible creatures.

4. Review Questions 1–9, concentrating especially on the questions from this past week, 5–9. Review the Words to Know (see *Teacher's Manual,* pp. 9, 21, and 33).

Name:

God Watches Over Everything Quiz 3

Fill in the blanks. *Trace the gray letters and fill in the rest.*

Word Bank

made	all	God	knows	good

1. __God__ is everywhere.

2. God __knows__ everything.

3. God is __all__ powerful.

4. God is all __good__.

5. God __made__ everything.

Assess

Pass out Quiz 3. Remind the children to keep their eyes on their own papers. Read through the quiz and ask if there are any questions. Then have the children complete the quiz. Observe and provide assistance as needed. Once all the students have completed the quiz, review the correct answers with the class.

Conclude

1. Lead the children in saying a prayer of thanksgiving for all that God has given to us, beginning and ending with the Sign of the Cross (see *Teacher's Manual,* p. 367).

2. Sing "All creatures of our God and King," *Adoremus Hymnal,* #600.

CHAPTER THREE: GOD WATCHES OVER EVERYTHING
ACTIVITY BOOK ANSWER KEYS

Name:_____

Use the following words to help you fill in the blanks.

created	powerful	good
everything	everywhere	angels

God is _e v e r y w h e r e_, not just in Heaven. God looks after you all the time, wherever you are!

God is all _p o w e r f u l_, which means that He can do anything; no one is stronger than God.

God knows _e v e r y t h i n g_. He knows what we do, and even what we think!

God _c r e a t e d_ everything; this means He made everything out of nothing. When God said, "let it be," it happened.

God created _a n g e l s_. They are spirits like God, and have no bodies. They were created good, but some became devils.

God is all _g o o d_; everything about Him is good. He takes care of all that He has made, and God takes care of you!

Name:_____

Draw a picture of God's creation. Don't forget to include many of His creatures!

Name:_____

Cut and paste or draw pictures of things that are created by God and things that are man-made.

Created by God	Man-made

Name:_____

Color the angel.

TEACHER'S NOTES

TEACHER'S NOTES

CHAPTER FOUR
GOD'S SPECIAL GIFTS

Catechism of the Catholic Church References

Body and Soul: 362–68
Created in God's Image: 355–58, 380
Dignity of the Human Person: 1700–09
Equality and Differences Among Men: 1934–38, 1944–46

God Creates Out of Nothing: 296–98, 317–18
God Sustains Creation: 301, 320
Guardian Angels: 336
Spiritual and Corporeal Creation: 327

Scripture References

To Know, Love, and Serve God: Lk 10:25–28;
Jn 12:24–26; 17:3

Background Reading: *The Fundamentals of Catholicism* by Fr. Kenneth Baker, S.J.

Volume 1:
"Faith and Morality," pp. 121–23

Volume 2:
The Nature of Man, pp. 146–52
Angels and Devils, pp. 177–87, 190–93
"Each Person Has a Guardian Angel," pp. 187–90

Summary of Lesson Content

Lesson 1

Man is a composite of body and soul.

Our bodies have five senses; these are gifts from God.

Lesson 2

There is a hierarchy of "being" in creation.

Man is the only earthly creature with a soul that will live forever.

With his soul, man can think, love, and choose good.

Lesson 3

There are three things man must do to attain Heaven: know, love, and serve God.

Our senses must be used for good.

Lesson 4

God has given every person a guardian angel.

Guardian angels protect our bodies, and especially our souls.

Guardian angels help us to know, love, and serve God; devils tempt us to fail at these goals.

Everyone should pray to his guardian angel daily.

CHAPTER FOUR: GOD'S SPECIAL GIFTS
LESSON ONE: OUR BODIES

Aims

Students will be made aware that man is composed of two elements: body and soul.

They will be able to enumerate the body's five senses (touch, taste, smell, sight, and hearing).

They will develop more awareness of and appreciation for their five senses as gifts from God.

Materials

- Items for sensory observation

- Bottle of perfume

- *Activity Book*, p. 13 or large poster board divided into five sections labeled with the five senses

- Magazine pages containing appropriate pictures or ads

- Children's scissors

- Glue or paste

Optional:
- "I heard the voice of Jesus say," *Adoremus Hymnal*, #579

Begin

Ask the students to define an angel as it was studied last chapter: an invisible spirit who is God's helper. Remind them that, like God, angels do not have bodies. But when God created man, He gave him two gifts: a body and soul. Explain that the body is the part that everyone can see; no one can see the soul, but with it, everyone has life. Tell the children that today they will be learning about one marvelous gift God gave man: the body and all the things that it can do.

Develop

1. Read paragraph 1 in the textbook with the children. Have them ponder the thought that not very long ago, they did not exist. Help them to focus on the fact that they exist now because both God and their parents wanted them to live. Explain to them that life is the first and most precious gift that anyone has ever received.

2. Read the first sentence of paragraph 2 with the children. Ask the children to enumerate the many things their bodies can do: jump, run, climb, skip, turn circles, somersaults, walk on tip toes, clap hands, shout loudly, whisper quietly, etc. Then together thank God for the gift of the body and its many abilities.

3. Read the rest of paragraph 2 in the textbook with the children. As each sense is enumerated, let the children add other examples of objects of that sense.

4. In order to emphasize the importance of the senses that God has given them, present to the children various items and pictures of objects and ask them to explain which of the senses tells them the most about each particular item. For example, you may hold up a picture of a snow-covered field and ask the children what they would say if they were to stand there. (It is beautiful. It is cold.) Ask how they would know that it is beautiful or cold. (They can see the beauty and feel the cold.) Explain that God gave them bodies to see and to feel the things He made for them.

5. Hold up a perfume bottle. Explain that you will spray what is in the bottle, and when they know what is inside, they should raise their hands without saying anything to anyone else. Once all the children raise their hands, ask them what is in the bottle and how they know. Explain that God gave them the gift of smell so that they could smell beautiful things such as perfume. Tell them that the sense of smell can also warn them of danger, e.g., smoke from a fire.

Reinforce

1. Make a collage for the five senses. This can be done individually, using p. 13 of the *Activity Book* (see *Teacher's Manual*, p. 47), or as a class using a large piece of poster board. Each child should cut out five pictures from magazines—one for each of the five senses (either the part of the body that senses, or the things that are sensed). Then ask them to bring them to you and tell you to which sense each picture belongs. After that, they can paste them onto the activity page or the poster board. Display the finished product. (Note: Some pictures will fall under two categories. Let them decide which sense "likes" the item better. For example, a scoop of ice cream looks good, but if we could not see it we would still like it, because of its taste.)

2. Play "I Spy" ("I spy, with my little eye, something that is..."). Whoever guesses the object leads the next round.

Conclude

1. Practice Question 10 with the entire class (see *Teacher's Manual*, p. 41). Then divide into pairs and let the children do their memory work together for a few minutes, reviewing Questions 1–9, too (see *Teacher's Manual*, pp. 9, 21, and 33).

2. Read the prayer on p. 20 of the textbook: "Thank You, dear Father, for life and for the other wonderful gifts You have given me. *Amen.*" Teach this to the children, beginning and ending with the Sign of the Cross (see *Teacher's Manual*, p. 367).

3. Sing "I heard the voice of Jesus say," *Adoremus Hymnal*, #579.

4   God's Special Gifts

"For he will give his angels charge of you
to guard you in all your ways."
Psalms 91:11

Once upon a time, not long ago, there was *no you*! Then God decided He wanted very much to have a boy or a girl like you. So He made you. He gave you life inside your mother. You were very tiny. Then, when the right time came, you were born.

God gave you a **body** so that you can do all sorts of things. Your body can run and it can climb and jump and play. And God gave you eyes that are looking at this book right now, and ears that can listen to a story, or music, or any sound. And you can taste ice cream with your tongue, touch puppies with your fingers, and smell cookies with your nose. God gave you all these wonderful things.

God also gave you a **soul**, a very important and special thing. The soul is the part of you that makes you live. It is invisible, but real. Because you have a soul, you can think and love and choose what to do.

19

You can laugh at something funny. You can understand a story, too, and you can tell what is right and what is wrong—all because you have a soul. And your soul is the part of you that will never die.

Your body and your soul are very special to God. He gave you a **guardian angel** to help you take care of them. Your angel is always looking after you because he is your very own angel. Your guardian angel helps you to do what is right because he is your friend.

Your guardian angel helps you get to Heaven where God wants you to be with Him forever. You must be very good to go to Heaven. You must know, love, and serve God in this world. God wants you to study hard and pray often. He wants you to receive the Sacraments of Penance and Holy Communion. He also wants you to be an obedient and loving child.

Here is a prayer you can say:

Thank You, dear Father, for life and for the other wonderful gifts You have given me. *Amen.*

Words to Know:

body   soul   guardian angel

20

THE HERESY OF GNOSTICISM

Gnosticism is a doctrine of salvation by knowledge; it developed before Christianity, but many early Christians were affected by these beliefs. Gnostics felt that the body and soul were a duality, rather than a unity: the soul was of divine origin and therefore good; the body was from the earth and therefore evil. All matter was corrupt, and the ultimate end of being was to escape the prison of the body and the world, which was seen as evil from its origin. They held that a person found salvation by acquiring secret knowledge of his spiritual essence, so that the soul could then ascend to be reunited with the supreme god. Catholics must not hold this view.

Preview

In our next lesson, we will learn about the even greater gift that God gave us—the soul. It is the part of us that makes our bodies alive.

CHAPTER FOUR: GOD'S SPECIAL GIFTS
LESSON TWO: OUR SOULS

Aims

Students will become acquainted with the gradations of life present in God's creation.

They will be able to define the soul as "the source of our life, having the power to know, love, and choose."

They will know that though the body will die, the soul will live forever.

Materials

- Chalkboard or bulletin board

- Magazine pictures of a rock, a plant, an animal, and a man

- *Activity Book*, p. 14

Optional:
- Children's scissors
- Construction paper cut into 5 □ 5 inch squares

- Glue or paste

- "I heard the voice of Jesus say," *Adoremus Hymnal*, #579

Begin

Remind the children that in the last lesson they learned that they are made up of a body and a soul. They also learned a great deal about the powers that their bodies have. Ask the children to name the five senses. Tell them that today they will learn about their souls, an even greater gift from God.

Develop

1. Read paragraph 3 with the children. The first thing to point out is that the soul is what makes people alive. Some creatures of God are not alive, like rocks and water. Others are alive but do not have rational souls.

2. On a chalkboard, draw a staircase (see facing page; you may want to use a bulletin board and tacks). As each step is discussed, hold up a picture and ask the class where it belongs. First, hold up the rock. Ask the children what a rock can do. Can it grow? Can it move by itself? Can it talk, feel, or see? They should see that though a rock exists, it is not alive. It belongs on the bottom step of the staircase. Ask the children to think of other creatures that belong with the rock (e.g., mountains, lakes, stars, etc.).

3. Now show the children a plant. What can a plant do? It can grow, so it must be alive. But it cannot move like animals can. The plant should be placed on the next step of the cre-

ation staircase. Help the children to think of other creatures that should go on this step: flowers, trees, bushes, etc.

4. Next, show them an animal. Animals are alive. How is this known? Because animals grow, and eat, and move. But can animals learn or talk or laugh or pray? No they cannot. They belong on the next step. Have the students give examples.

5. Explain to the children that because they have a rational soul, they can know, love, and choose what to do. They can learn about God, love God and other people, and they can decide to do good things. Explain to the children that if they do these things well, they can go to Heaven when their bodies die, for their souls will live forever. Souls are the part of man that is like God. God will live forever, and He wants His children to live with Him in perfect happiness forever, too. Remind them that in the story of Creation God said, "Let us make man in our image, after our likeness."

Reinforce

1. Assign p. 14 of the *Activity Book* (see *Teacher's Manual*, p. 47), directing the children to draw the appropriate pictures for the hierarchy of creation. Read and discuss the four panels with them.

2. Optional craft: Have the students make a little book of the hierarchy of creation, in which case photocopies of p. 14 of the *Activity Book* might be more manageable. After the students have drawn their four pictures, have them cut out each panel and the words below it. When they have cut them out, they should glue them onto construction paper that you have cut into 5 x 5 inch squares. Check to be sure they have put the panels in the proper order; then staple on the left side to make a booklet.

Conclude

1. Review Question 10 and practice Question 11 with the class. Then divide into pairs for a few minutes of memory work.

2. Close with the prayer from p. 20 in the textbook, thanking God for the gifts of body and soul. Or help the students write a prayer thanking God in their own way and say it together.

3. Sing "I heard the voice of Jesus say," *Adoremus Hymnal*, #579.

4   God's Special Gifts

"For he will give his angels charge of you
to guard you in all your ways."

Psalms 91:11

Once upon a time, not long ago, there was *no you*! Then God decided He wanted very much to have a boy or a girl like you. So He made you. He gave you life inside your mother. You were very tiny. Then, when the right time came, you were born.

God gave you a **body** so that you can do all sorts of things. Your body can run and it can climb and jump and play. And God gave you eyes that are looking at this book right now, and ears that can listen to a story, or music, or any sound. And you can taste ice cream with your tongue, touch puppies with your fingers, and smell cookies with your nose. God gave you all these wonderful things.

God also gave you a **soul**, a very important and special thing. The soul is the part of you that makes you live. It is invisible, but real. Because you have a soul, you can think and love and choose what to do.

19

You can laugh at something funny. You can understand a story, too, and you can tell what is right and what is wrong—all because you have a soul. And your soul is the part of you that will never die.

Your body and your soul are very special to God. He gave you a **guardian angel** to help you take care of them. Your angel is always looking after you because he is your very own angel. Your guardian angel helps you to do what is right because he is your friend.

Your guardian angel helps you get to Heaven where God wants you to be with Him forever. You must be very good to go to Heaven. You must know, love, and serve God in this world. God wants you to study hard and pray often. He wants you to receive the Sacraments of Penance and Holy Communion. He also wants you to be an obedient and loving child.

Here is a prayer you can say:

Thank You, dear Father, for life and for the other wonderful gifts You have given me. *Amen.*

Words to Know:

body   soul   guardian angel

20

Q. 10   *What makes you a human person?*
I am a human person because I have a body and a soul (CCC 362–65).

Q. 11   *Will your soul ever die?*
No, my body will die, but my soul will live forever (CCC 366).

Q. 12   *What must you do to gain the happiness of Heaven?*
To gain the happiness of Heaven I must know, love, and serve God in this world (CCC 202; Mk 12:30).

Q. 13   *Does everyone have a guardian angel?*
Yes, everyone has a guardian angel who is with him all the time (CCC 336).

We Pray:

PRAYER TO MY GUARDIAN ANGEL

Angel of God, my guardian dear,
To whom God's love commits me here,
Ever this day be at my side,
To light and guard, to rule and guide. *Amen.*

21

CHALK TALK:
STAIRCASE OF CREATION

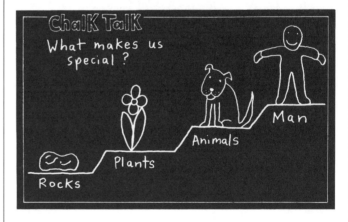

Preview

In our next lesson, we will learn more about how to use our body and soul to live good and holy lives here in this world. When we die we will then be able to go to Heaven.

CHAPTER FOUR: GOD'S SPECIAL GIFTS
LESSON THREE: OUR PATH TO HEAVEN

Aims

Students will examine the composite nature of man—the unity of body and soul.

They will know the three things they must do to attain Heaven.

They will become aware of how they can accomplish these tasks.

Materials

• *Activity Book*, p. 15

Optional:
• Pictures of children learning about, loving, and serving God

• "I heard the voice of Jesus say," *Adoremus Hymnal*, #579

Begin

Review Question 10, emphasizing the unity of body and soul. To help the students better understand, use the example of soap bubbles. (You may even want to have them make some bubbles.) Explain that a bubble needs both soap and air. Without soap, there is just air; without air, there is just soap.

In the same way, without a body, man would be more similar to an angel; without a soul, he would be an animal. But God has made man with both a body and a soul. Tell them that today they will learn about how to use these gifts well.

Develop

1. Remind the children that they have learned how God made them to live forever in His home, Heaven—a place of perfect happiness that will never end. It is because they have a soul that they can live forever with Him. But there are certain things one must do here on earth to go to Heaven.

2. Compare the journey to Heaven to a trip that the children might take here on earth. Ask them to describe what must be done before going on a family vacation: pack, put gas in the car or purchase plane/train/bus tickets, make arrangements for the family pets, etc. If these things are not done, they won't be prepared to take the trip, or at least not well prepared. What if they forget their bathing suits when they are going to the beach? They would not be able to swim. So preparations for trips here in this world are very important. How much more important are the preparations for the journey to Heaven!

3. Have the children turn to Question 12 in their textbooks. Read this aloud with them. On the chalkboard, list the three things necessary to attain the happiness of Heaven: know God, love God, and serve God. Have them think about these things for a moment. Then ask them to give examples of what they can do to meet each of these requirements.

   a. Know God: To pay attention and study hard in religion class, to read the Scriptures, to listen well to the readings and homilies at Mass

   b. Love God: To receive the Sacraments of Penance (Confession) and Holy Communion when old enough, to pray reverently at home, in the classroom, and at Mass, or during a visit to the Blessed Sacrament

   c. Serve God: To be obedient to parents and teachers, to be helpful both at home and at school, to share toys, to be kind to others

Reinforce

1. Remind the students that plants and animals cannot do any of these things. But children can because God has given them the greatest gift—a soul. With their souls they can learn and know what is right and what is wrong. They can choose to do the right thing. They have a responsibility to use the five senses for good. Tell them they should not use their eyes, for example, to look at bad pictures. Ask them to help you think of ways they can use their five senses for good.

2. Have the children complete the matching exercise on p. 15 in the *Activity Book* (see *Teacher's Manual*, p. 47). This activity is based on the lists they helped you make on the chalkboard about knowing, loving, and serving God. You may want to do it together as a class.

Conclude

1. Review Question 12 aloud with the class. Then divide the students into pairs and give them a few minutes to review Questions 1–12 (see *Teacher's Manual*, pp. 9, 21, and 33).

2. Sing "I heard the voice of Jesus say," *Adoremus Hymnal*, #579.

4   God's Special Gifts

"For he will give his angels charge of you
to guard you in all your ways."

Psalms 91:11

Once upon a time, not long ago, there was *no you*! Then God decided He wanted very much to have a boy or a girl like you. So He made you. He gave you life inside your mother. You were very tiny. Then, when the right time came, you were born.

God gave you a **body** so that you can do all sorts of things. Your body can run and it can climb and jump and play. And God gave you eyes that are looking at this book right now, and ears that can listen to a story, or music, or any sound. And you can taste ice cream with your tongue, touch puppies with your fingers, and smell cookies with your nose. God gave you all these wonderful things.

God also gave you a **soul**, a very important and special thing. The soul is the part of you that makes you live. It is invisible, but real. Because you have a soul, you can think and love and choose what to do.

19

You can laugh at something funny. You can understand a story, too, and you can tell what is right and what is wrong—all because you have a soul. And your soul is the part of you that will never die.

Your body and your soul are very special to God. He gave you a **guardian angel** to help you take care of them. Your angel is always looking after you because he is your very own angel. Your guardian angel helps you to do what is right because he is your friend.

Your guardian angel helps you get to Heaven where God wants you to be with Him forever. You must be very good to go to Heaven. You must know, love, and serve God in this world. God wants you to study hard and pray often. He wants you to receive the Sacraments of Penance and Holy Communion. He also wants you to be an obedient and loving child.

Here is a prayer you can say:

Thank You, dear Father, for life and for the other wonderful gifts You have given me. *Amen.*

Words to Know:

body   soul   guardian angel

20

Q. 10   *What makes you a human person?*
I am a human person because I have a body and a soul (CCC 362–65).

Q. 11   *Will your soul ever die?*
No, my body will die, but my soul will live forever (CCC 366).

Q. 12   *What must you do to gain the happiness of Heaven?*
To gain the happiness of Heaven I must know, love, and serve God in this world (CCC 202; Mk 12:30).

Q. 13   *Does everyone have a guardian angel?*
Yes, everyone has a guardian angel who is with him all the time (CCC 336).

We Pray:

PRAYER TO MY GUARDIAN ANGEL

Angel of God, my guardian dear,
To whom God's love commits me here,
Ever this day be at my side,
To light and guard, to rule and guide. *Amen.*

21

SAINT THÉRÈSE AND THE LITTLE WAY

Saint Thérèse of Lisieux is a good example of someone who was very aware of the difficult journey to Heaven. Her spiritual path, called the "Little Way," has become popular in modern times. Thérèse wanted to be a saint, but she felt that she could not become a great one so she comforted herself by making small daily sacrifices. This was what she called her "little way to Heaven," short and direct. By remaining childlike she asked Jesus to carry her in His arms to the Father. She felt she was too little to attain Heaven like the saints before her, so she found her own pathway. Also see p. 17 of this *Teacher's Manual* for a short biography.

Preview

In our next lesson, we will learn about some creatures that God has given to us, whose special job is to guard and protect us—our guardian angels.

CHAPTER FOUR: GOD'S SPECIAL GIFTS
LESSON FOUR: OUR GUARDIAN ANGELS

Aims

Students will become aware that God has given each of them an angel to look after him.

They will become aware that the devils tempt them to do things that are wrong.

They will learn to pray to their guardian angels for help each day.

Materials

- Bulletin board

- Pictures for staircase

- Picture of an angel

- *Activity Book*, p. 16

Optional:
- Appendix, p. B-8

- Transparencies

- Colored markers

- "I heard the voice of Jesus say," *Adoremus Hymnal*, #579

Begin

Remind the children that many of the angels help God by carrying messages from Heaven to earth. Ask if the students can think of any examples (the angel Gabriel, the angels at Christmas). Tell them that some angels help God in a different way and that they will learn about these angels today.

Develop

1. Read paragraph 4 with the children. Emphasize that it is because they are so special in God's eyes that He gives them their very own angel to help them. And because they are composed of both a body and a soul, their guardian angels are concerned about both parts of them. Let the children enumerate some of the dangers that can come their way in the course of a day (tripping in the schoolyard, a car accident, falling off a bike, etc.).

2. Read paragraphs 5–7 with the children. Explain that guardian angels are even more concerned with their souls, since souls will live forever. Their guardian angel wants them to keep their souls strong and healthy. Remind them that because they have souls, they can know God, love God and others, and choose to do the right thing. Their guardian angel's job is to help them do these things as well as they can, and help them avoid choosing to do bad or naughty things. Then their souls will be healthy and strong.

3. Using a bulletin board, review the staircase of creation. As you explain the levels of created life, have students pin the magazine pictures onto the correct step on the board. Be sure to have an additional step for the one heavenly creature: angels. Explain that of all creatures, angels are most like God, for they are purely spirits with no bodies. Pin an angel image on the top step of the staircase (you can use a photocopy of p. 12 of the *Activity Book*).

4. Direct the children's attention to the painting of *Tobit and Angel* on p. 18 of the textbook. Ask them to identify the characters: a man and an angel. Remind the children that angels do not have bodies or wings, but that people imagine them that way. This angel is talking to the man, though most angels are invisible.

5. Remind the children of the bad angels who turned away from God and were cast into Hell; they are now devils. Explain that the devils do not want them to be good because they don't want them to go to Heaven to be happy with God forever.

Reinforce

1. Teach the students the Prayer to My Guardian Angel, found on p. 21 of their textbook. You may want to write the prayer on notecards and send them home with the students as flashcards.

2. On p. 16 of the *Activity Book* (see *Teacher's Manual*, p. 47), have the children draw a picture of their guardian angels helping them in some way (kneeling up straight during Mass or prayers, sharing, helping their parents, protecting them from harm, etc.). Encourage them to make their angel beautiful, for angels are great creatures.

3. On Appendix, p. B-8 , there is a stained glass angel for the students to color. This could be copied onto transparencies for the children, colored with markers, and then hung on the windows for a beautiful effect. Alternatively, the page itself could be photocopied, colored with markers, and hung. (The effect will not be as dramatic, but it will still be pretty.)

Conclude

1. When the children have finished coloring their drawings of their guardian angels, ask them to share them, one by one, with the class. Let them share how their guardian angel is helping them in their picture.

2. Practice Question 13 with the entire class, and review Questions 1–12 (see *Teacher's Manual*, pp. 9, 21, and 33). Give pairs of children a few minutes to memorize Question 13 and to review all the others.

3. End the class by praying the prayer on p. 20 together, beginning and ending with the Sign of the Cross (see *Teacher's Manual*, p. 367).

4. Sing "I heard the voice of Jesus say," *Adoremus Hymnal*, #579.

4 God's Special Gifts

"For he will give his angels charge of you
to guard you in all your ways."

Psalms 91:11

Once upon a time, not long ago, there was *no you*! Then God decided He wanted very much to have a boy or a girl like you. So He made you. He gave you life inside your mother. You were very tiny. Then, when the right time came, you were born.

God gave you a **body** so that you can do all sorts of things. Your body can run and it can climb and jump and play. And God gave you eyes that are looking at this book right now, and ears that can listen to a story, or music, or any sound. And you can taste ice cream with your tongue, touch puppies with your fingers, and smell cookies with your nose. God gave you all these wonderful things.

God also gave you a **soul**, a very important and special thing. The soul is the part of you that makes you live. It is invisible, but real. Because you have a soul, you can think and love and choose what to do.

19

You can laugh at something funny. You can understand a story, too, and you can tell what is right and what is wrong—all because you have a soul. And your soul is the part of you that will never die.

Your body and your soul are very special to God. He gave you a **guardian angel** to help you take care of them. Your angel is always looking after you because he is your very own angel. Your guardian angel helps you to do what is right because he is your friend.

Your guardian angel helps you get to Heaven where God wants you to be with Him forever. You must be very good to go to Heaven. You must know, love, and serve God in this world. God wants you to study hard and pray often. He wants you to receive the Sacraments of Penance and Holy Communion. He also wants you to be an obedient and loving child.

Here is a prayer you can say:

Thank You, dear Father, for life and for the other wonderful gifts You have given me. *Amen.*

Words to Know:

body   soul   guardian angel

20

Q. 10 *What makes you a human person?*
I am a human person because I have a body and a soul (CCC 362–65).

Q. 11 *Will your soul ever die?*
No, my body will die, but my soul will live forever (CCC 366).

Q. 12 *What must you do to gain the happiness of Heaven?*
To gain the happiness of Heaven I must know, love, and serve God in this world (CCC 202; Mk 12:30).

Q. 13 *Does everyone have a guardian angel?*
Yes, everyone has a guardian angel who is with him all the time (CCC 336).

We Pray:

PRAYER TO MY GUARDIAN ANGEL

Angel of God, my guardian dear,
To whom God's love commits me here,
Ever this day be at my side,
To light and guard, to rule and guide. *Amen.*

21

ADDITIONAL RESOURCE

Show "My Secret Friend: A Guardian Angel Story," CCC of America, available through Ignatius Press; 30 minutes.

Preview

In our next lesson, we will review what we have learned and play some games. When we think we have learned everything we can about the great gifts God has given us, there will be a quiz and a unit test.

Chapter Four: God's Special Gifts
Review and Assessment

Aims

To review and assess the children's knowledge of the material taught this week.

Materials

- Objects and pictures from Lesson 1 for exploring with the five senses
- Appendix, p. B-1
- Quiz 4 (Appendix, p. A-4)
- "I heard the voice of Jesus say," *Adoremus Hymnal*, #579

Review and Enrichment

1. Let the children explore the objects and pictures from Lesson 1 again. They should identify the sense that each object "likes" the most.

2. Remind the children that they are very different from animals because God created children in His image, giving them a body and soul. Ask the children to contribute to a list (on the chalkboard) of all the things that a human being can do that an animal cannot do.

3. Play Telephone, Bible Baseball, or Tic-Tac-Toe (see Appendix, p. B-1 for instructions) with the students to review the material from this chapter. Make sure to include Questions 1–13 and the Words to Know (see *Teacher's Manual*, pp. 9, 21, 33, and 45).

Name:

God's Special Gifts   Quiz 4

Fill in the blanks. *Trace the gray letters and fill in the rest.*

Word Bank

| helps | me | gifts | angel |

1. God gave me life.

2. God gave me an angel to watch over me.

3. My angel helps me to know, love, and serve God.

4. Thank you, dear Father, for the gifts You have given me. Amen.

Assess

Pass out Quiz 4. Read through the quiz with the children and ask if there are any questions.

Conclude

1. When the quizzes have been completed, collect them, and if there is time, read through the quiz and ask the children to complete it orally.

2. Close the lesson by singing the songs you have learned thus far. Begin and end with the Sign of the Cross (see *Teacher's Manual*, p. 367), telling the children what Saint Augustine said about hymns sung to God: "He who sings well, prays twice."

Name:_____

Five Senses Collage

Cut photos from magazines of things having to do with each of the five senses. Paste them onto this page where they belong.

Sight   Smell

Touch

Taste   Hearing

Faith and Life Series • Grade 1 • Chapter 4 • Lesson 1   13

Name:_____

The Order of Creation

Draw and color a rock.

What can a rock do?
It cannot move by itself.
It cannot talk, or feel, or see.
It is not alive.

Draw and color a tree.

What can a tree or a plant do?
Is it alive? Yes, it grows!
It cannot move by itself, and it
cannot talk, feel, or see.

Draw and color an animal.

Do animals live?
Yes! They grow and move
around! But, they cannot think
or talk. Animals are trained.
They do not choose
as we do.

Draw and color a person.

People are special.
They have life too!
They think, understand and laugh.
They can also choose what to do.
They have a soul! They can
know, love, and serve God.

14   *Faith and Life Series • Grade 1 • Chapter 4 • Lesson 2*

Name:_____

Know, Love, and Serve the Lord!

Show how you know, love, and serve the Lord by connecting each word in the left column with the appropriate word or phrase in the right column.

Know

Love

Serve

Pray

Obey your parents

Read the Bible

Study hard

Visit the Blessed Sacrament

Share

Faith and Life Series • Grade 1 • Chapter 4 • Lesson 3   15

Name:_____

Draw a picture of your guardian angel helping you in some way.

16   *Faith and Life Series • Grade 1 • Chapter 4 • Lesson 4*

TEACHER'S NOTES

UNIT ONE TEST
CHAPTERS 1–4

> **CHAPTER ONE: GOD IS OUR FATHER**
>
> **CHAPTER TWO: HEAVEN IS OUR HOME**
>
> **CHAPTER THREE: GOD WATCHES OVER EVERYTHING**
>
> **CHAPTER FOUR: GOD'S SPECIAL GIFTS**

Aims

The students' understanding of the material covered in this unit will be reviewed and assessed.

Materials

• Unit 1 Test, Appendix, p. A-5

Assess

1. Distribute the unit tests and read through them with the students to be sure they understand the questions.

2. Administer the test.

3. After all the tests have been handed in, you may wish to review the correct answers with the class.

Name: _____

Unit 1 Test   **Chapters 1–4**

Yes or No. *Circle the correct answer.*

1. Did God make you?   (Yes)   No

2. Does God love you?   (Yes)   No

3. Can you see God?   Yes   (No)

4. Can you talk to God?   (Yes)   No

5. Do you have your own   (Yes)   No
   special angel?

Fill in the blanks.

To go to Heaven, I must know, love, and serve _God_ .

TEACHER'S NOTES

TEACHER'S NOTES

CHAPTER FIVE
ADAM AND EVE

Catechism of the Catholic Church References

Creation: 198, 280, 338, 341
Creation Entrusted to Man: 299
Grace: 1996–2005, 2021–24
Grace is Essential to Attain the End of Man: 308
The Grace of Our First Parents: 54
Heaven: 325–27, 1023–24

Man in Paradise: 374–79, 384
Man's Stewardship of Nature and Animals: 2415–18, 2456
Original Justice: 375–76
The Purpose of Man's Creation: 356–57, 381
The Reason for Creation: 293–94, 315, 319
Respect for Creation: 2415

Scripture References

"You, therefore, must be perfect, as your heavenly Father is perfect": Mt 5:48

Adam and Eve's Creation: Gen 2:7–8, 15–23

Background Reading: *The Fundamentals of Catholicism* by Fr. Kenneth Baker, S.J.

Volume 2:
"The Origin of Man," pp. 139–42
"The Idea of the Supernatural," pp. 152–55
"Adam and Eve before the Fall," pp. 155–58

Volume 3:
Grace, pp. 13–40
"Sharing in God's Life," pp. 65–68
"Children of God," pp. 68–71

Summary of Lesson Content

Lesson 1

Adam was the first man and Eve was the first woman; both were created by God.

The Garden of Eden was a happy place where Adam and Eve had everything they needed.

Among the many gifts God gave Adam and Eve was immortality.

Lesson 3

The best gift God gave Adam and Eve was grace, His own life in their souls.

Grace enables man to attain his heavenly goal: life with God in Heaven.

Lesson 2

When God created the world and all of its creatures, He made them to live in perfect harmony.

God placed Adam and Eve in dominion over the animals and the plant life He had created for them.

They were good stewards of God's creation; we must be also.

Lesson 4

Grace makes man become a child of God and His friend.

Adam and Eve are our first parents, the parents of everyone who has ever existed.

CHAPTER FIVE: ADAM AND EVE
LESSON ONE: CREATION OF ADAM AND EVE

Aims

Students will listen to the biblical story of the creation of Adam and Eve.

They will be able to identify Adam and Eve as the first man and the first woman, both of whom were created by God.

They will consider life in the Garden of Eden, particularly the gift of immortality.

Materials

- Bulletin board, cut-outs, and pictures from Chapters 1–4

- Children's Bible

- Paper cut-outs, Adam and Eve before the Fall (Appendix, p. B-9)

- *Activity Book*, p. 17

Optional:
- "All creatures of our God and King," *Adoremus Hymnal*, #600

Begin

Tell the children that today they will listen to a more detailed account of God's creation of Adam and Eve from the Bible. Before you begin to read, have them prepare the bulletin board by attaching the cut-outs used from prior lessons. Be sure they do not attach the Adam and Eve figures at this time.

Develop

1. Read paragraphs 1 and 2. Make a list of the characteristics of Eden: it was beautiful; there was plenty of food; Adam and Eve lacked nothing; they would never feel pain, become ill, or die; there was friendship between the animals and Adam and Eve.

2. Read the account of Adam and Eve's creation from your children's Bible (Gen 2:7–8; 2:21–24). As you read about God creating first Adam, and then Eve, ask the students to add these figures to the bulletin board. Be sure to retain these cut-outs for use in the lessons to come.

3. Ask the students to open their textbooks to p. 22 and to look carefully at the painting. Ask them if they see any people in the painting. If they look carefully, they will see a figure intended to represent God with Adam and Eve, who have just been created. Ask them if they know the name of this garden. (Eden)

4. Emphasize the fact that Adam and Eve were *created* by God. As Catholics, we must believe this truth. It is possible that some of the children may be aware of the scientific theory of evolution, and they may raise questions about how to reconcile these two accounts of the beginning of mankind. Without digressing into a long and detailed explanation, tell them the essential truth is that God created both a body and a soul for Adam and for Eve. Because of these two parts, humans are greater than all the other creatures on earth.

5. Tell the children that God gave Adam and Eve many gifts. The most important gift was immortality—they would live forever. They would eventually go to Heaven and be *perfectly* happy with God.

Reinforce

Have the children solve the puzzle on p. 17 of the *Activity Book* (see *Teacher's Manual*, p. 61), reinforcing the truth that God created the first man and woman, Adam and Eve, both body and soul.

Conclude

1. Ask the children to turn to Question 14 on p. 25 of the textbook (see *Teacher's Manual*, p. 57). Read both the question and answer together as a group, and then divide into pairs for further memory work.

2. Teach the students a new verse of "All creatures of our God and King," *Adoremus Hymnal*, #600.

3. Close with a prayer that they have learned such as the Our Father or Prayer to My Guardian Angel (see *Teacher's Manual*, p. 367).

5   Adam and Eve

"Then God said, 'Let us make man in
our image, after our likeness; and let them
have dominion...over all the earth...'"
Genesis 1:26

Long, long ago, God made the world. Then He made the first man and the first woman. They were called **Adam** and **Eve**.

God gave them a beautiful place in which to live. It was called the Garden of Eden. There were trees in the garden with good things on them to eat. Adam and Eve had everything they wanted. They were never sick or hurt, and they never had to die. All the animals were their friends, too.

God also gave Adam and Eve another very special gift. He gave them the gift of sharing His very own life. With God's life in their souls, Adam and Eve could know, love, and serve God. And they could live with Him forever.

23

God gives this gift to us, too. The life of God in our souls is called **grace**. Grace makes us able to go to Heaven. It makes us children of God.

Adam and Eve were our first parents because all the people of the world came from them.

24

GOD CREATED THE HUMAN SOUL

God created both a body and a soul for Adam and Eve. It is important to understand that the soul was created and infused into the body by God.

FROM *HUMANI GENERIS*

"... [T]he Teaching Authority of the Church does not forbid that, in conformity with the present state of human sciences and sacred theology, research and discussions, on the part of men experienced in both fields, take place with regard to the doctrine of evolution, in as far as it inquires into the origin of the human body as coming from pre-existent and living matter—for the Catholic faith obliges us to hold that souls are immediately created by God," *Humani Generis* [36].

See also Saint John Paul II's Address to the Pontifical Academy of Sciences; October 22, 1996.

Preview

God gave Adam and Eve many gifts when He created them in the Garden of Eden. In our next lesson, we will think about their relationship to the world of nature and the animals that God made for them.

Chapter Five: Adam and Eve
Lesson Two: Taking Care of God's Gifts

Aims

Students will consider the relationship of Adam and Eve to the animals and nature.

They will recognize that God created everything for Adam and Eve and that there was perfect harmony among all creatures.

They will learn about good stewardship and how to practice this virtue.

Materials

- *Activity Book*, p. 18
- "The Wolf of Gubbio" (Appendix, p. B-11)
- Modeling clay or play-dough
- "All creatures of our God and King," *Adoremus Hymnal*, #600

Begin

Have the children look again at the painting on p. 22. Ask them to identify the place (the Garden of Eden). Direct their attention to the animals that are pictured, noting that they all seem to be friends with each other, unlike what they might expect (e.g., dog and cat, lion and lamb, etc).

Develop

1. Reread again the last sentence in paragraph 2 with the children. Emphasize that, together with the harmony that existed among the animals, there also existed a harmony between human beings and the animals. Lions and tigers never would have attacked Adam and Eve. Snakes would not have bitten them with poisonous venom. Encourage the students to think of other examples.

2. Describe once again the perfect state in which Adam and Eve were created and lived, telling the children that God gave them all of this to care for and to use for their good. God even told Adam he could name the animals; this shows how God put Adam and Eve in charge of His creation.

3. Tell the children that there is a special word for the responsibility that God gave Adam and Eve: stewardship. They were to be good stewards of His creation. Explain that a steward is a person who is in charge of someone else's (his master's) property. Adam and Eve were stewards of God's creation; they were to take care of it and use it well.

4. To help the children realize the perfection of Adam and Eve's life, play the following game with them. Ask each student to complete this sentence: "If I lived in the Garden of Eden, I would _____" (never get sick, play with a lion, never tease the cat, etc.).

5. Tell the children that just as Adam and Eve were put in charge of creation, so too, must everyone care for the things that God has given him. Ask the children to think of ways that they may be good stewards of the world (do not waste water, do not litter, etc.). Make a list.

Reinforce

1. Have the children draw Adam and Eve in the Garden of Eden on p. 18 of the *Activity Book* (see *Teacher's Manual*, p. 61).

2. To reinforce the idea that everyone should be kind to animals, read to the children a story about Saint Francis of Assisi, such as "The Wolf of Gubbio" (see Appendix, p. B-11). Explain that Saint Francis is known for his great love for animals and the entire natural world. He called every creature brother or sister, even the sun, the moon, and all of the animals.

3. Instead of, or in addition to, the story mentioned above, you may want to show the video "Francis: Knight of Assisi," CCC of America, available through Ignatius Press; 30 minutes.

Conclude

1. Take a few minutes to review Question 14 (see *Teacher's Manual*, p. 57).

2. You may want to have the children make animals out of modeling clay or play dough (see recipe on the facing page). Tell them to take great care in their work, as God did when He created the animals. Point out that they are using something to make their animals, yet God created from nothing. When they have finished making their animals, you may want the children to demonstrate the way the animals would have behaved in the Garden of Eden.

3. Sing "All creatures of our God and King," *Adoremus Hymnal*, #600.

5   Adam and Eve

"Then God said, 'Let us make man in
our image, after our likeness; and let them
have dominion...over all the earth...'"
Genesis 1:26

Long, long ago, God made the world. Then He made the first man and the first woman. They were called **Adam** and **Eve**.

God gave them a beautiful place in which to live. It was called the Garden of Eden. There were trees in the garden with good things on them to eat. Adam and Eve had everything they wanted. They were never sick or hurt, and they never had to die. All the animals were their friends, too.

God also gave Adam and Eve another very special gift. He gave them the gift of sharing His very own life. With God's life in their souls, Adam and Eve could know, love, and serve God. And they could live with Him forever.

23

God gives this gift to us, too. The life of God in our souls is called **grace**. Grace makes us able to go to Heaven. It makes us children of God.

Adam and Eve were our first parents because all the people of the world came from them.

24

RECIPE FOR PLAY DOUGH

Combine:
3 cups of salt
6 cups of white all purpose flour
3 tablespoons of powdered alum (can be found with the spices in your local grocery)
6 cups of boiling water
1 tablespoon salad oil

Mix all the ingredients except the last, stir and cool 10 minutes, add 1 tablespoon salad oil and knead dough. You may add drops of food coloring to proportioned amounts of the dough. Wear gloves when adding the color or your hands will be stained.

Preview

In our next lesson, we will learn about the most special gift that God gave to Adam and Eve when He created them: grace.

CHAPTER FIVE: ADAM AND EVE
LESSON THREE: THE GIFT OF GRACE

Aims

Students will be able to define grace as God's life in us.

They will become aware that Adam and Eve were given this gift when they were created.

They will realize that because this was a gift for their souls, it was even better than all of the other gifts God gave them for their bodies.

They will be able to explain what grace enabled Adam and Eve to do.

Materials

• *Activity Book*, p. 19

Optional:
• "All creatures of our God and King," *Adoremus Hymnal*, #600

Begin

Review with the children what the Garden of Eden was like when God created Adam and Eve and placed them there. Make a list on the chalkboard (it was peaceful, there were no arguments, they were perfect friends, etc.). You may want to have them reassemble the bulletin board of Eden, and reread the story of Creation so that they remember the hierarchy of creatures.

Develop

1. Read paragraph 3 with the children. Emphasize that because God gave Adam and Eve His very own life, they were able to be good; they could know, love, and serve Him perfectly. Therefore, they could accomplish the mission they were given. God gave Adam and Eve grace to help them be perfect.

2. Referring again to paragraph 3 of the textbook, highlight the fact that the gift of grace was meant for Adam and Eve's souls. Explain to the children that the other gifts they have learned about had to do with the life of Adam and Eve's bodies. With God's life in their souls, they could know Him without effort, they could love Him with their whole hearts, and they could serve Him through prayer and good deeds for each other and the world He created for them. It was easy for Adam and Eve to be good with this grace.

3. Read paragraph 4 with the children. Teach the students how to use the glossary that begins on p. 117 (see *Teacher's Manual*, p. 364) at the back of their books. Ask them to look up the word "grace." They will probably need assistance with this task. Ask a student to read the definition: "The life of God in our soul."

4. Tell the students that when God created Adam and Eve, He gave them a "mission"; He had a specific reason for creating them, and they had a goal in life to accomplish. Adam and Eve were made to become saints and live with God forever in Heaven. The way to accomplish this mission was to know, love, and serve God in this world, then they could be happy with God forever in Heaven!

5. Explain that a person needs God's life in his soul to live forever with Him in Heaven. If a person does not have grace, or God's life, in his soul, then he cannot go to Heaven. Just as everyone needs food and water to remain alive here on earth, everyone also needs grace to live forever with God in Heaven.

Reinforce

1. As a class, make up an acrostic for the word "grace." Write it on the chalkboard. Example:

 G: God, the Creator
 R: Really loved
 A: Adam and Eve, and gave His human
 C: Creatures
 E: Eternal life

2. Have the children complete the word search on p. 19 of the *Activity Book* (see *Teacher's Manual*, p. 61).

Conclude

1. Read Question 15 with the entire class. Then give students time to practice Questions 14 and 15 in pairs.

2. Have the children say a prayer to God, thanking Him for His creation. Let them take turns thanking God for specific creatures, i.e., I thank God for _____ (my dog, rainbows, plants, bugs . . .).

3. Sing "All creatures of our God and King," *Adoremus Hymnal*, #600.

5   Adam and Eve

"Then God said, 'Let us make man in
our image, after our likeness; and let them
have dominion...over all the earth...'"

Genesis 1:26

Long, long ago, God made the world. Then He made the first man and the first woman. They were called **Adam** and **Eve**.

God gave them a beautiful place in which to live. It was called the Garden of Eden. There were trees in the garden with good things on them to eat. Adam and Eve had everything they wanted. They were never sick or hurt, and they never had to die. All the animals were their friends, too.

God also gave Adam and Eve another very special gift. He gave them the gift of sharing His very own life. With God's life in their souls, Adam and Eve could know, love, and serve God. And they could live with Him forever.

23

God gives this gift to us, too. The life of God in our souls is called **grace**. Grace makes us able to go to Heaven. It makes us children of God.

Adam and Eve were our first parents because all the people of the world came from them.

24

Words to Know:

Adam   Eve   grace

Q. 14 *Who were the first man and woman?*
Adam and Eve were the first man and woman (CCC 375).

Q. 15 *What was the special gift God gave Adam and Eve in the Garden of Eden?*
The special gift that God gave Adam and Eve was grace, God's life in their souls (CCC 54, 356, 375).

25

Then God said, "Let us make man in our image, after our likeness; and let them have dominion over the fish of the sea, and over the birds of the air, and over the cattle, and over all the earth, and over every creeping thing that creeps upon the earth." So God created man in his own image, in the image of God he created him; male and female he created them.

—Genesis 1:26–27

Preview

In our next lesson, we will learn more about how grace makes us God's children.

CHAPTER FIVE: ADAM AND EVE
LESSON FOUR: CHILDREN OF GOD

Aims

Students will be able to explain that with grace, Adam and Eve were both God's children and His friends.

They will learn that they can become God's children through grace.

They will be able to explain that because all people who have ever lived came from Adam and Eve, they are known as our first parents.

Materials

- *Activity Book*, p. 20

Optional:
- "All creatures of our God and King," *Adoremus Hymnal*, #600

Begin

Write on the chalkboard: "Grace is _____ _____ in our soul." Call on the children to complete this definition. Review what this means and why it so important to have grace in one's soul (to be able to live forever with God in Heaven).

Develop

1. Read paragraph 4 aloud again. Explain that when a person is born, he does not have grace in his soul, so that he is not yet God's friend and child. Remind them that it is at Baptism that God gives His life to a person's soul; at that moment he becomes God's child and friend. Ask the children to talk about a Baptism that they have attended. Tell them that they will learn more about Baptism later in the year when they study Chapter 24. What they should remember now is that at Baptism a person receives grace, God's life in their souls, and that person becomes a child of God.

2. When God created Adam and Eve, they shared His life in their souls. As their Father, God wanted to be with them. Because God is not a creature like man, He could not have walked with them in the way man walks; however, He wanted to be with the first man and woman, as a father wants to be with his children. Adam and Eve had a loving relationship with God.

3. Read paragraph 5 with the children. Tell them that no one knows what Adam and Eve looked like, or even what their personalities were like. But the Church says every human being inherits from them a composite human nature: a body and a soul. Every person can think, love, and choose, just like Adam and Eve did, so that everyone is a member of one family—Adam and Eve's family. When a person is baptized, he becomes a part of God's family.

4. Ask the students if they resemble their parents. Explain what you mean, using yourself as an example. "I have blue eyes like my mother; I have brown hair like my father." Let them volunteer, but keep to eyes and hair color in order to avoid invading anyone's privacy. Explain that these characteristics are "inherited" from our parents, and that we can inherit other types of things as well, e.g., a feisty temper, shyness, artistic or musical talent, etc.

Reinforce

Have the students draw a picture of themselves as a child of God on p. 20 of the *Activity Book* (see *Teacher's Manual*, p. 61).

Conclude

1. In pairs, have the children review Questions 1–15, concentrating on Questions 14 and 15 (see *Teacher's Manual*, pp. 9, 21, 33, 45, and 57).

2. Sing "All creatures of our God and King," *Adoremus Hymnal*, #600.

5   Adam and Eve

"Then God said, 'Let us make man in
our image, after our likeness; and let them
have dominion...over all the earth...'"

Genesis 1:26

Long, long ago, God made the world. Then He made the first man and the first woman. They were called **Adam** and **Eve**.

God gave them a beautiful place in which to live. It was called the Garden of Eden. There were trees in the garden with good things on them to eat. Adam and Eve had everything they wanted. They were never sick or hurt, and they never had to die. All the animals were their friends, too.

God also gave Adam and Eve another very special gift. He gave them the gift of sharing His very own life. With God's life in their souls, Adam and Eve could know, love, and serve God. And they could live with Him forever.

23

God gives this gift to us, too. The life of God in our souls is called **grace**. Grace makes us able to go to Heaven. It makes us children of God.

Adam and Eve were our first parents because all the people of the world came from them.

24

Words to Know:

Adam   Eve   grace

Q. 14 *Who were the first man and woman?*
Adam and Eve were the first man and woman (CCC 375).

Q. 15 *What was the special gift God gave Adam and Eve in the Garden of Eden?*
The special gift that God gave Adam and Eve was grace, God's life in their souls (CCC 54, 356, 375).

25

MADE IN THE IMAGE OF GOD

"What is it that is about to be created, that enjoys such honor? It is man—that great and wonderful living creature, more precious in the eyes of God than all other creatures! For him the heavens and the earth, the sea and all the rest of creation exist. God attached so much importance to his salvation that he did not spare his own Son for the sake of man. Nor does he ever cease to work, trying every possible means, until he has raised man up to himself and made him sit at his right hand."

Saint John Chrysostom, *In Gen. sermo* 2, 1:PG 54, 587D-588A, as quoted from the *Catechism of the Catholic Church* 358.

Preview

In our next lesson, we will review all that we have learned about how Adam and Eve were created with every good gift, the best gift being grace, and we will take a quiz.

Chapter Five: Adam and Eve
Review and Assessment

Aims

To review and assess the material taught in this chapter.

To hear each student's memory work, concentrating on Questions 14 and 15 (see *Teacher's Manual*, p. 59).

Materials

- "The Wolf of Gubbio" (Appendix, p. B-11)

- Appendix, p. B-1 for games

- Quiz 5 (Appendix, p. A-6)

- "All creatures of our God and King," *Adoremus Hymnal*, #600

Review and Enrichment

1. If you have not already, read the short story "The Wolf of Gubbio" (see Appendix, p. B-11) to the children. This is a story about Saint Francis and his gift of speaking to, being understood by, and obeyed by an animal. It will give the students a good sense of the dominion and stewardship that Adam and Eve had over the animals when they were created.

2. Play Telephone, Bible Baseball, or Tic-Tac-Toe (see Appendix, p. B-1) to help the children retain what they have learned.

Name:

Adam and Eve   Quiz 5

Fill in the blanks. *Trace the gray letters and fill in the rest.*

Word Bank

life	grace	God	Eden

1. G o d made Adam and Eve.

2. Adam and Eve lived in the Garden of E d e n .

3. God gave them the gift of g r a c e .

4. Grace is God's l i f e in us.

Assess

Pass out Quiz 5 and review it with the students. Answer any questions they may have, and remind them to do their own work.

Conclude

Collect the quizzes and review the correct answers if there is time. Conclude by singing "All creatures of our God and King," *Adoremus Hymnal*, #600.

Name:_____

Solve the Puzzle

Use the words below to help you solve the puzzle.

Adam	Eden	Garden
body	Eve	soul
	forever	

God created A d a m and E v e with a
b o d y and s o u l.

They lived in the G a r d e n of E d e n.

They could live f o r e v e r because they
had God's very own life in their souls.

Name:_____

**Draw Adam and Eve, animals, and growing things
of all kinds in the Garden of Eden. Put smiles on
Adam's and Eve's faces because they were very
happy in the garden. Then color your picture.**

Name:_____

Word Search

Can you find these words in the puzzle?

ADAM	GRACE
BODY	GOD
EVE	HEAVEN
GIFT	SOUL

H E A V E N X
X X X B O D Y
X G O D X X X
X X X X E V E
A D A M X X X
X X S O U L X
X G I F T X X
G R A C E X X

Name:_____

I am a child of God!

Draw a picture showing that you are a child of God.

TEACHER'S NOTES

CHAPTER SIX
A SAD STORY

Catechism of the Catholic Church References

Baptism and Original Sin: 405, 978, 1263
Christ Died for Our Sins: 601–23
The Consequences of Original Sin: 399–400, 402–9, 416–19
Effects of Baptism: 683, 1262, 1265–74, 1279–80
The Fall of Man: 385–90, 413
Grace: 1996–2005, 2021–24
The Hope of Salvation: 55

Loss of Eternal Life: 1472
Man Has Original Sin from Conception: 403
Necessity of Baptism: 846, 1250, 1257–61, 1277
Original Sin: 388–90, 396–401, 415
The Promise of a Redeemer: 410–12, 420–21
Sin: 1440, 1849–51, 1871–72
Teaching of Original Sin: 389

Scripture References

The Fall of Man: Gen 3:1–6, 23–24

Background Reading: *The Fundamentals of Catholicism* by Fr. Kenneth Baker, S.J.

Volume 2:
"The Sin of Our First Parents," pp. 159–62
"The Transmission of Original Sin," pp. 162–165
"What is Original Sin?" pp. 165–68

Volume 3:
"Man without Grace," pp. 34–37

Summary of Lesson Content

Lesson 1

Sin is saying no to God.

Adam and Eve committed the first sin on earth.

They had to leave the Garden of Eden because of sin.

The devil tempted Adam and Eve and he tempts us, too.

Lesson 2

When they sinned, Adam and Eve lost the special gifts God had given to them. The most important of which were the gifts of immortality and grace.

The natural world also suffered when Adam and Eve sinned.

They were very sorry for their sin, but they could not repair the damage by themselves.

Lesson 3

The most terrible loss for Adam and Eve was the loss of grace, God's life in their souls. Their minds and wills were weakened, and without grace they could not go to Heaven.

Now everyone is born with the sin of Adam and Eve on his soul.

We must be sorry for our sins and ask God for forgiveness.

Lesson 4

God still loved Adam and Eve, even though they had turned away from Him.

God felt sorry for them, and all the people who would come after them.

God promised to send a Savior. The Savior would win back God's grace and open the gates of Heaven once more.

CHAPTER SIX: A SAD STORY
LESSON ONE: THE FIRST SIN

Aims

Students will hear the story of the Fall of man.

They will learn the definition of sin.

They will be able to explain why Adam and Eve had to leave the Garden of Eden.

Materials

- Children's Bible
- A bulletin board divided into two sections, Before and After the Fall
- Paper cut-outs from Chapter 5 (Appendix, p. B-9)
- Additional paper cut-outs, Adam and Eve after the Fall (Appendix, p. B-10)
- *Activity Book*, p. 21

Optional:
- Masks (Appendix, p. B-6)
- "On this day, the first of days," *Adoremus Hymnal*, #610

Begin

Review the story of the creation of Adam and Eve and the beautiful conditions of their life in the Garden of Eden. Have the students place the appropriate paper cut-outs on the left side of the bulletin board (Before the Fall). Emphasize the fact that because Adam and Eve had grace, it was easy for them to be good and to do what God wanted them to do.

Develop

1. Remind the students that all of Adam and Eve's gifts should have passed on to their children through inheritance. Tell them that they will now learn why these gifts were not passed on. Read paragraphs 1, 2, and 3 aloud.

2. Read the story of the Fall of man from your children's Bible (Gen 3:1–6, 23–24). After reading it, help the children place the appropriate cut-out pieces on the right side of the bulletin board. This exercise will show the students how dramatic the change was after Adam and Eve sinned.

3. Highlight the most important features of this story: it was one of the fallen angels who tempted Adam and Eve; it was not as difficult for Adam and Eve to resist temptation as it is for us; they chose poorly, and said no to God's command; this was the first sin on earth. God had forbidden them to eat the fruit of one tree in the Garden of Eden and they disobeyed that command; this is called "Original Sin."

4. Read the first sentence of paragraph 4. Tell the students that Adam and Eve's sin had very serious consequences, for they were cast out of the Garden of Eden. An angel guarded the entrance so they could not return.

5. Help the students to find the definition of the word "sin" in paragraph 3 or in the glossary: "Sin is saying no to God." Explain to them that someone commits a sin whenever he says no to God, and everyone must tell God he is sorry when he does something to offend Him.

6. Recall the story of the fall of the angels from Heaven (Chapter 3) before the rest of the world was created. Remind the children that the devils try to tempt people even now, as they tempted Adam and Eve, because they do not want anyone to love God and be happy with Him in Heaven. But, by praying and staying close to his guardian angel, a person can resist these temptations.

Reinforce

1. Assign p. 21 of the *Activity Book*, "A Sad Story" (see *Teacher's Manual*, p. 73).

2. Using masks (see Appendix, p. B-6), have the students role play life in the Garden of Eden before the Fall, the snake tempting Adam and Eve, and Adam and Eve leaving the garden.

3. Teach the children an appropriate song about following God, such as "On this day, the first of days," *Adoremus Hymnal*, #610.

Conclude

1. Read and review Questions 16 and 17 with the entire class (see *Teacher's Manual*, p. 67). Then separate into groups of two and allow time for memorization.

2. Close with the Prayer to My Guardian Angel, beginning and ending with the Sign of the Cross (see *Teacher's Manual*, p. 367).

26

6   A Sad Story

"...sin came into the world through
one man and death through sin..."
Romans 5:12

One day, God gave Adam and Eve a test. He told them never to eat the fruit from one of the trees in the garden. God wanted Adam and Eve to **obey** His command, and for a while they did.

But one day, the devil pretended he was a snake and came into the garden. He told Eve to go ahead and try some of the forbidden fruit from the tree. He said it would make her just as smart as God.

Eve knew that she should obey God, but she listened to the devil instead. She ate the fruit. Then she gave some to Adam and he ate it too. This was the very first **sin**. Sin is saying no to God. That is what Adam and Eve did.

So Adam and Eve had to leave the lovely garden. Now they had to work hard for their food. And now

they had to die someday. Worst of all, Adam and Eve lost the gift of grace. Without God's life in their souls, Adam and Eve could not go to Heaven. The gates of Heaven were closed. Adam and Eve were very sad and very sorry.

Adam and Eve lost God's gift of grace for all of us too. Now everyone is born with the sin of Adam and Eve on his soul. It is called **Original Sin**.

God felt sorry for Adam and Eve because He still loved them. He felt sorry for all the people who would come after them too. So He made them a **promise**. A promise is when you say you are going to do something and really mean it. God promised to send a **Savior**. The Savior would win back God's grace for us and open the gates of Heaven again.

ASH WEDNESDAY (DIES CINERUM)

At the beginning of Mass on the first day of Lent, Catholics are exhorted to approach the altar and receive blessed ashes on their foreheads. With his thumb, the priest draws an ashen Cross on each forehead while saying, "Remember that you are dust, and to dust you shall return." The ashes used in this ceremony are made from burning the remains of the blessed palms from Palm Sunday of the previous year. The ashes are blessed with four ancient prayers, sprinkled with Holy Water, and incensed. The ashes symbolize penance, contrition, and prayer, as well as remind Catholics of their mortality. They also call to mind God's grace and mercy to the truly penitent and the promise of eternal beatitude.

Preview

In our next lesson, we will learn about the other things that happened to Adam and Eve after they sinned, in addition to leaving the Garden.

26

27

28

65

Chapter Six: A Sad Story
Lesson Two: Gifts Are Lost

Aims

Students will be able to enumerate the gifts that were lost when Adam and Eve sinned.

They will be able to make a comparison between Adam and Eve's condition before and after the Fall.

They will be able to explain that not only did Adam and Eve suffer as a result of their sin, but also the entire natural world suffered.

Materials

- Paper cut-outs, Before and After the Fall (Appendix, pp. B-9 and B-10)

- *Activity Book*, p. 22

Optional
- "On this day, the first of days," *Adoremus Hymnal*, #610

Begin

Ask student volunteers to set up the bulletin board with the Garden of Eden before the Fall on one side, and life after the Fall on the other. Retell the story of the Fall while they do this. Ask them to list some of the things that changed after Adam and Eve sinned. (The snake is wrapped around the tree, the fruit has been bitten into, Adam and Eve are sad, etc.)

Develop

1. Read paragraphs 4 and 5 with the children. On the left side of the chalkboard make a list of the consequences of Adam and Eve's sin, for example:
   - God made them leave the Garden of Eden.
   - They had to work hard for their food, clothing, and shelter.
   - They could feel pain.
   - They could get sick.
   - They would die.
   - They would not be able to go to Heaven because they had lost grace.

Let the children think about this list for a moment so that they can begin to appreciate how drastic the changes were and how much was lost through this first sin of Adam and Eve.

2. With the help of the students, on the right side of the chalkboard make a list of the gifts that Adam and Eve had when they were created, and match these to the list of lost gifts, for example:

   - Adam and Eve lived happily in the Garden of Eden.
   - They did not work or worry about food.
   - They did not feel pain.
   - They did not get sick.
   - They would never die.
   - They could go to Heaven because they had grace.

Either make a copy of this list for the next lesson, or have the children keep p. 22 of the *Activity Book* when they have completed it (see *Teacher's Manual*, p. 73).

3. Help the children to recall what they learned about the harmony that existed between the animals and Adam and Eve. All of these loving relationships changed when Adam and Eve committed Original Sin. Refer again to the cut-outs on the bulletin board which clearly show the change.

Reinforce

1. Assign p. 22 of the *Activity Book* (see *Teacher's Manual*, p. 73). Students should refer to the two lists you made on the chalkboard during this lesson presentation, and keep their lists for the next lesson.

2. Remind the children that when a person sins, he is saying no to God. Discuss ways of saying no to God and ways of saying yes to God. Help them to plan how they can say yes to God the next time they feel like doing something wrong. The children may have some good suggestions for one another.

Conclude

1. Take a few minutes to begin learning Question 18 as a group. Then let pairs of children work on Questions 16–18.

2. Make the Sign of the Cross and pray the Our Father and the Prayer to My Guardian Angel with the children (see *Teacher's Manual*, p. 367). Check to see that everyone is learning them by heart.

3. Sing "On this day, the first of days," *Adoremus Hymnal*, #610.

6   A Sad Story

*"...sin came into the world through
one man and death through sin..."*
Romans 5:12

One day, God gave Adam and Eve a test. He told them never to eat the fruit from one of the trees in the garden. God wanted Adam and Eve to **obey** His command, and for a while they did.

But one day, the devil pretended he was a snake and came into the garden. He told Eve to go ahead and try some of the forbidden fruit from the tree. He said it would make her just as smart as God.

Eve knew that she should obey God, but she listened to the devil instead. She ate the fruit. Then she gave some to Adam and he ate it too. This was the very first **sin**. Sin is saying no to God. That is what Adam and Eve did.

So Adam and Eve had to leave the lovely garden. Now they had to work hard for their food. And now

27

they had to die someday. Worst of all, Adam and Eve lost the gift of grace. Without God's life in their souls, Adam and Eve could not go to Heaven. The gates of Heaven were closed. Adam and Eve were very sad and very sorry.

Adam and Eve lost God's gift of grace for all of us too. Now everyone is born with the sin of Adam and Eve on his soul. It is called **Original Sin**.

God felt sorry for Adam and Eve because He still loved them. He felt sorry for all the people who would come after them too. So He made them a **promise**. A promise is when you say you are going to do something and really mean it. God promised to send a **Savior**. The Savior would win back God's grace for us and open the gates of Heaven again.

28

Words to Know:

obey   sin   Original Sin   promise   Savior

Q. 16   *What is sin?*
Sin is saying no to God. It is a failure to love God. It is any evil thing that we choose to do, think, or say (CCC 1849, 1850).

Q. 17   *Who committed the first sin on earth?*
Adam and Eve, our first parents, committed the first sin on earth (CCC 399, 416).

Q. 18   *What happened to Adam and Eve because of this sin?*
Because of this sin, Adam and Eve lost grace, Heaven, and life in the Garden of Eden (Gen 3:23–24; CCC 390).

Q. 19   *What has happened to us because of Adam and Eve's sin?*
Because of Adam and Eve's sin, we are born with Original Sin and without grace. We inherit their punishment (CCC 418).

29

To the woman [God] said, "I will greatly multiply your pain in childbearing; in pain you shall bring forth children, yet your desire shall be for your husband, and he shall rule over you." And to Adam he said, "Because you have listened to the voice of your wife, and have eaten of the tree of which I commanded you, 'You shall not eat of it,' cursed is the ground because of you; in toil you shall eat of it all the days of your life. . . . In the sweat of your face you shall eat bread till you return to the ground, for out of it you were taken; you are dust, and to dust you shall return."

—Genesis 3:16–18, 19

Preview

In our next lesson, we will look more closely at what it meant for Adam and Eve to lose their most precious gift from God—grace, His life in their souls.

CHAPTER SIX: A SAD STORY
LESSON THREE: GRACE IS LOST

Aims

Students will be able to identify the consequences of losing grace—minds are darkened and wills are weakened.

They will be able to explain why Adam and Eve would not be able to go to Heaven.

Now everyone is born with Original Sin, the sin of Adam and Eve, on his soul.

They will realize that sin offends God and that a person must express sorrow for his sins.

Materials

• *Activity Book*, pp. 22 and 23

• Appendix, p. B-1

Optional:
• "On this day, the first of days," *Adoremus Hymnal*, #610

Begin

Review the previous lesson, using p. 22 of the *Activity Book*. On this page, the students should have detailed the gifts that Adam and Eve had in the garden, and the gifts that were lost when they sinned. Point out the last consequence of their sin:

Adam and Eve would not be able to go to Heaven because they had lost the gift of grace. Remind the children that this was the best gift God gave them: His very life in their souls.

Develop

1. Ask the children if they remember what two special powers a person's soul has (a mind that can know, and a soul that can choose). Remind them that God made Adam and Eve with a mission: to know, to love, and to serve Him in this world. They were to use their minds to know Him, and their wills to love and serve Him. God gave them grace, His own life, so that they could accomplish this mission.

2. Reread paragraph 5 with the children. Explain that because Adam and Eve lost the gift of grace, every person is born without this grace. Everyone is born with the sin of Adam and Eve on his soul. This is called "Original Sin."

3. Explain how Adam and Eve's sin came to be passed down to all men. Everyone inherits it from Adam, like a person inherits other things from his father or his mother. For example, Johnny has blue eyes because his parents have blue eyes.

They passed them on to him. It is like that with our first parents. They have passed on to their children Original Sin.

4. Baptism is the Sacrament that washes away Original Sin and fills a soul with grace, just as God intended from the beginning. However, a person still has a darkened mind and a will that tends to want to do bad things, and sometimes, a person does commit sin; he does say no to God.

5. Explain to the class that when anyone sins, he hurts God very much. Point to the crucifix and say that Jesus died on the Cross because of man's sins. Explain that when anyone sins, it is as if he puts another thorn in Jesus' crown of thorns, and it hurts Him very much. The sinner cuts himself off from God. He loses grace, too. If someone sins very seriously, he can lose grace completely.

Reinforce

1. Read the paragraph together on p. 23 of the *Activity Book* (see *Teacher's Manual*, p. 73), then have them color the picture.

2. Reinforce all this material with a game, such as Tic-Tac-Toe (see Appendix, p. B-1).

Conclude

1. Take a few minutes to read and review Question 19 with the children as a group. Then separate into pairs and have them go over Questions 16–19.

2. As a class, make up a prayer of sorrow for sins. Write the prayer on the board and have the students say it together at the end of the lesson.

3. End the class with the Sign of the Cross, the Our Father, and Prayer to My Guardian Angel (see *Teacher's Manual*, p. 367).

4. Sing "On this day, the first of days," *Adoremus Hymnal*, #610.

6   A Sad Story

*"...sin came into the world through
one man and death through sin..."*
Romans 5:12

One day, God gave Adam and Eve a test. He told them never to eat the fruit from one of the trees in the garden. God wanted Adam and Eve to **obey** His command, and for a while they did.

But one day, the devil pretended he was a snake and came into the garden. He told Eve to go ahead and try some of the forbidden fruit from the tree. He said it would make her just as smart as God.

Eve knew that she should obey God, but she listened to the devil instead. She ate the fruit. Then she gave some to Adam and he ate it too. This was the very first **sin**. Sin is saying no to God. That is what Adam and Eve did.

So Adam and Eve had to leave the lovely garden. Now they had to work hard for their food. And now

27

they had to die someday. Worst of all, Adam and Eve lost the gift of grace. Without God's life in their souls, Adam and Eve could not go to Heaven. The gates of Heaven were closed. Adam and Eve were very sad and very sorry.

Adam and Eve lost God's gift of grace for all of us too. Now everyone is born with the sin of Adam and Eve on his soul. It is called **Original Sin**.

God felt sorry for Adam and Eve because He still loved them. He felt sorry for all the people who would come after them too. So He made them a **promise**. A promise is when you say you are going to do something and really mean it. God promised to send a **Savior**. The Savior would win back God's grace for us and open the gates of Heaven again.

28

Words to Know:

obey   sin   Original Sin   promise   Savior

Q. 16 *What is sin?*
Sin is saying no to God. It is a failure to love God. It is any evil thing that we choose to do, think, or say (CCC 1849, 1850).

Q. 17 *Who committed the first sin on earth?*
Adam and Eve, our first parents, committed the first sin on earth (CCC 399, 416).

Q. 18 *What happened to Adam and Eve because of this sin?*
Because of this sin, Adam and Eve lost grace, Heaven, and life in the Garden of Eden (Gen 3:23–24; CCC 390).

Q. 19 *What has happened to us because of Adam and Eve's sin?*
Because of Adam and Eve's sin, we are born with Original Sin and without grace. We inherit their punishment (CCC 418).

29

ORIGINAL SIN AND BAPTISM

The Sacrament of Baptism, which is the Sacrament of Christian Initiation, washes away Original Sin, and any personal sin if a person is baptized after he has reached the age of reason. The Catholic Church recognizes the validity of Protestant Baptism because this idea of one Baptism for all is found in Scripture.

"Baptism is necessary for salvation for those to whom the Gospel has been proclaimed and who have had the possibility of asking for this sacrament....God has bound salvation to the sacrament of Baptism, but he himself is not bound by his sacraments."

—*Catechism of the Catholic Church*, 1257

Preview

Though Adam and Eve sinned, and turned away from God, He still loved them. In our next lesson we will learn about the Savior that God promised Who would bring back the gift of grace.

CHAPTER SIX: A SAD STORY
LESSON FOUR: THE PROMISE OF A SAVIOR

Aims

Students will be able to explain that, because God loved Adam and Eve even after they sinned, He promised to send a Savior.

They will be able to explain that the Savior would bring grace back to the world and reopen the gates of Heaven.

They will be able to define the word "promise." They will practice making and keeping a promise.

Materials

• Prepared sentence strips for each child that say "I promise to _____"

• *Activity Book*, p. 24

Optional:
• "On this day, the first of days," *Adoremus Hymnal*, #610

Begin

Review the last few lessons with the students: when Adam and Eve committed the first sin on earth, they lost the good gifts that God had given them. The most important gift they lost was grace. They could no longer go to Heaven. Adam and Eve were terribly sorry for their sin, but they could not regain this grace on their own.

Develop

1. Read paragraph 6 with the children. Emphasize that even though Adam and Eve had deeply offended God when they sinned, God still loved them and wanted them, and all of their children, to be able to go to Heaven with Him where they would be perfectly happy. They could not, however, go there without grace. God decided to send a Savior Who would bring back grace once again so that man could be with God. The gates of Heaven would be reopened.

2. Point out the word "promise" in paragraph 6, and read its definition: to say you are going to do something and really mean it. Discuss "promises" with which the children may be familiar. For example: "I promise not to tell a secret," "I promise not to fight with my brother/sister," "I promise to do my chores," etc. Tell them that people make promises about

things that are important and difficult, and they are expected to keep these promises.

3. Explain that God made a promise to Adam and Eve and to all of their children: He would send a Savior. Ask them if God kept His promise and if they know Who the Savior is. (He did, by sending His own Son Who became a man, Jesus Christ.)

4. Explain that Jesus, our Savior, brought grace back to the world and reopened the gates of Heaven when He died on the Cross. Remind the children that they studied what Jesus did when they were learning how to make the Sign of the Cross. Tell them that they will study much more about our Savior's supreme act of love in the lessons to come. As terrible as Adam and Eve's sin was, God's love was even greater.

Reinforce

1. Show the children a sample sentence strip with "I promise to _____" written on it. Tell them that you are going to promise to do one good thing before their next religion lesson, e.g., clean off your desk, make a visit to the Blessed Sacrament, read them a story that they have been asking to hear, etc. Then fill in the blank on the sentence strip. Let them know that you are very serious about keeping your promise. Then pass out the strips to every student and let each fill in the blank himself (see examples on the facing page). Let the students take these home as a reminder of the promises they have made. Tell them that you will check back with them at the next lesson to see if they have kept their promises.

2. Have the students color p. 24 of the *Activity Book*, "God promised me a Savior!" (see *Teacher's Manual*, p. 73).

Conclude

1. Allow a few minutes for pairs to do memory work on Questions 16–19.

2. Pray the prayer that you wrote together in the last lesson, expressing sorrow for sin. Begin and end with the Sign of the Cross (see *Teacher's Manual*, p. 367).

3. Sing "On this day, the first of days," *Adoremus Hymnal*, #610.

6   A Sad Story

"...sin came into the world through
one man and death through sin..."
Romans 5:12

One day, God gave Adam and Eve a test. He told them never to eat the fruit from one of the trees in the garden. God wanted Adam and Eve to **obey** His command, and for a while they did.

But one day, the devil pretended he was a snake and came into the garden. He told Eve to go ahead and try some of the forbidden fruit from the tree. He said it would make her just as smart as God.

Eve knew that she should obey God, but she listened to the devil instead. She ate the fruit. Then she gave some to Adam and he ate it too. This was the very first **sin**. Sin is saying no to God. That is what Adam and Eve did.

So Adam and Eve had to leave the lovely garden. Now they had to work hard for their food. And now

27

they had to die someday. Worst of all, Adam and Eve lost the gift of grace. Without God's life in their souls, Adam and Eve could not go to Heaven. The gates of Heaven were closed. Adam and Eve were very sad and very sorry.

Adam and Eve lost God's gift of grace for all of us too. Now everyone is born with the sin of Adam and Eve on his soul. It is called **Original Sin**.

God felt sorry for Adam and Eve because He still loved them. He felt sorry for all the people who would come after them too. So He made them a **promise**. A promise is when you say you are going to do something and really mean it. God promised to send a **Savior**. The Savior would win back God's grace for us and open the gates of Heaven again.

28

Words to Know:

obey   sin   Original Sin   promise   Savior

Q. 16 *What is sin?*
Sin is saying no to God. It is a failure to love God. It is any evil thing that we choose to do, think, or say (CCC 1849, 1850).

Q. 17 *Who committed the first sin on earth?*
Adam and Eve, our first parents, committed the first sin on earth (CCC 399, 416).

Q. 18 *What happened to Adam and Eve because of this sin?*
Because of this sin, Adam and Eve lost grace, Heaven, and life in the Garden of Eden (Gen 3:23–24; CCC 390).

Q. 19 *What has happened to us because of Adam and Eve's sin?*
Because of Adam and Eve's sin, we are born with Original Sin and without grace. We inherit their punishment (CCC 418).

29

I PROMISE TO...

. . . clean my room without being told.

. . . sit quietly the next time I am at Mass.

. . . help my mother make dinner.

. . . do my chores without complaining.

. . . say my prayers each night before bed.

. . . take care of my little brothers and sisters.

Preview

We will see if we have kept our promises. We will also review all that we have learned, play a game, and take a quiz.

CHAPTER SIX: A SAD STORY
REVIEW AND ASSESSMENT

Aims

To review and assess the children's knowledge of the lessons of this chapter.

Materials

- Games (Appendix, p. B-1)
- Quiz 6 (Appendix, p. A-7)
- "On this day, the first of days," *Adoremus Hymnal,* #610

Review and Enrichment

1. Make the Sign of the Cross with the children and pray the Our Father and the Prayer to My Guardian Angel together (see *Teacher's Manual*, p. 367). Then sing some of the songs they have learned so far. Remind the students that singing is a prayer, too. Conclude with the Sign of the Cross. Be sure to watch that children are correctly making the Sign of the Cross and are reverent during prayers.

2. Ask the children to take out their sentence strips from the previous lesson. Ask if they have kept their promises and let them share with the class what they did. Remind them that the best promise ever made was the one God made to Adam and Eve in the Garden of Eden: He would send a Savior.

3. Spend a few minutes reviewing Questions 16–19 with the entire class (see *Teacher's Manual*, p. 71). If answers still need polishing, allow time for pairs of children to work together. Informally assess the children as they work.

4. Divide the class into two groups and play a review game such as Bible Baseball (see Appendix, p. B-1), formulating questions about sin, Original Sin, the Savior, a promise, sorrow for sin, etc.

Name:

A Sad Story   Quiz 6

Fill in the blanks. *Trace the gray letters and fill in the rest.*

Word Bank

Adam	lost	send	Sin

1. S i n is saying no to God.

2. A d a m and Eve sinned.

3. Adam and Eve l o s t the gift of grace.

4. God promised to s e n d a Savior.

Assess

Pass out and administer Quiz 6. When they are finished, orally correct the quizzes with the class.

Conclude

1. Pass out holy cards in recognition of the children's good work and reverent attitudes.

2. Sing "On this day, the first of days," *Adoremus Hymnal,* #610.

Name:_____

A Sad Story

Why are Adam and Eve sad?
Adam and Eve were sad because they lost the gift of God's grace and without it they could not go to Heaven.

Faith and Life Series • Grade 1 • Chapter 6 • Lesson 1   21

Name:_____

Fill in the blanks using this lesson's class discussion.

When Adam and Eve lived in the Garden of Eden, they:
1. lived happily in the Garden of Eden
2. did not work or worry about food
3. did not feel pain
4. did not get sick
5. would never die
6. could go to Heaven because they had grace

After Adam and Eve sinned and had to leave the Garden of Eden, they:
1. had to work for food, clothing, and shelter
2. could feel pain
3. could get sick
4. would die
5. did not have the grace necessary to go to Heaven.

22   *Faith and Life Series • Grade 1 • Chapter 6 • Lesson 2*

Name:_____

We are all born with ORIGINAL SIN, but it is washed away in Baptism and we are filled with GRACE. GRACE is GOD'S LIFE in us. This makes us children of God.

Color the picture.

Faith and Life Series • Grade 1 • Chapter 6 • Lesson 3   23

Name:_____

God promised me a Savior!

Jesus is His name.
God loves me very much.
Jesus saves me from sin through grace.

Color the picture.

24   *Faith and Life Series • Grade 1 • Chapter 6 • Lesson 4*

TEACHER'S NOTES

CHAPTER SEVEN
A TIME OF WAITING

Catechism of the Catholic Church References

Abraham and Prayer: 2569–72
The Call of Abraham: 59–61, 762
The Covenant with Noah: 56–58, 71
The Faith of Abraham: 144–46, 1080

God's Promise to Abraham: 705–6
The Promise of a Redeemer: 410–12
Salvation History: 55–59, 65–67, 71–73

Scripture References

God Tells Abraham To Go to a New Country: Gen 12:1–5
God's Promise to Abraham: Gen 13:14–17; 15:1–6;
17:15–19; 21:1–3

Noah and the Flood: Gen 6:5–22; 7:17—8:2, 15–22
The Sacrifice of Isaac: Gen 22:1–19

Background Reading: *The Fundamentals of Catholicism* by Fr. Kenneth Baker, S.J.

Volume 3:
"The Meaning of Sacrifice," pp. 256–59

"The Mass Is a True Sacrifice," pp. 259–61

Summary of Lesson Content

Lesson 1

While waiting for the Savior, most men became displeasing to God through sin.

Noah and his sons, however, were obedient to God, and they were chosen to save creation and themselves from the flood.

Obedience is doing what one is told to do.

The world had a new beginning through Noah.

Noah and his family offered a sacrifice of thanksgiving when they left the ark.

Lesson 2

Abraham obeyed God, even when it was difficult.

Abraham is a model of obedience.

We obey God by obeying those He has given to love and care for us.

Lesson 3

Faith is a gift that makes a person able to believe all that God says, even when he does not fully understand.

The Savior was one of Abraham's descendants.

Just as people before the Savior prepared for His coming by being obedient and faithful, we must prepare to see Christ in Heaven by also being obedient and faithful.

Each year, before Christmas, the Church has a special "waiting period" called Advent.

Lesson 4

God called Abraham to sacrifice Isaac.

Abraham trusted in God and did as He asked.

God rewarded Abraham for his faith.

CHAPTER SEVEN: A TIME OF WAITING
LESSON ONE: NOAH OBEYED GOD

Aims

Students will be able to explain how sin took hold of man after Adam and Eve sinned.

They will understand why God sent a flood over all the earth.

They will be able to explain what obedience is and why Noah and his family were saved—because of their obedience to God.

Materials

• Children's Bible

• *Activity Book*, p. 25

Optional:
• *Noah's Ark*, by Peter Spier

• "Noah and the Flood" skit (Appendix, p. B-12)

• "I sing the mighty power of God," *Adoremus Hymnal*, #616

Begin

Help the children to recall the main effects of Original Sin: pain, sickness, death, loss of Heaven and the friendship of God, darkened minds and weak wills, and loss of grace.

Remind them that without grace, many people turned to bad and evil ways. But God did not want them to be evil; that was no way to prepare for the coming of a Savior.

Develop

1. Read paragraphs 1, 2, and 3 of the textbook with the children. Then read the story of Noah and the flood from the children's Bible (Gen 6:5–22; 7:17—8:2, 15–22).

2. It is important to point out that Noah and his sons, Shem, Ham, and Japheth, were chosen to save creation because they were obedient to God. Have the children look up the word "obedient" in the glossary: to do what one is told to do. Noah's family loved God and did what He asked. Have the children consider what Noah's neighbors must have thought of him and of his sons as they built the ark. Tell them that Noah lived in a dry desert land far from water, so their neighbors most likely laughed at them. Where and when would they ever use this huge boat? But Noah obeyed.

3. Explain that this flood was different from any flood before or since. It covered the entire earth and washed away the sins of men; but Noah saved all the animals in the ark. He also saved his family because they were pleasing to God. When the waters began to evaporate, the world was given a fresh start in Noah, his family, and the animals he had saved.

4. Explain that the rainbow God placed in the sky was a sign of His promise that He would never again send a flood to cover the whole earth. Ask the children to explain what a promise is (see Chapter 6), and point out that often, when a person makes a promise he makes a sign, too, like shaking hands. Whenever a rainbow appears in the sky, everyone should think of God's promise and of His love.

5. Ask the children if they remember what Noah and his family did when they left the ark (offered sacrifices of thanksgiving). Point out how important it is to thank God for all that He does. Explain that Christ's death was the ultimate sacrifice and that the Mass is both a sacrifice and a prayer of thanksgiving to God.

Reinforce

1. Lead the children in completing p. 25 of the *Activity Book,* Noah's Ark (see *Teacher's Manual*, p. 85).

2. If possible, have the children look at the book *Noah's Ark* by Peter Spier. This is a wordless story; Spier's drawings give the reader a marvelous sense of what life on the ark must have been like.

3. If so desired, begin working on the short play of Noah and the flood that can be found in the Appendix, p. B-12.

Conclude

1. Give the students time to review Questions 16–19 from the last chapter, and Questions 1–15 if time allows (see *Teacher's Manual*, pp. 9, 21, 33, 45, 59, and 71). Also have them work on the definitions for "ark" and "obedient."

2. Teach an appropriate song, such as "I sing the mighty power of God," *Adoremus Hymnal*, #616.

"I will look with favor on the faithful in the land, that they may dwell with me . . ."

(Psalms 101:6)

7   A Time of Waiting

"I will look with favor on the faithful in
the land, that they may dwell with me..."
Psalms 101:6

God promised to send a Savior. But the Savior did not come right away. The people had to wait for years and years. While they waited, some of them learned to love and obey God.

Noah was one of those people. Others did not obey God and fell into sinful ways. But Noah always did what God asked of him; he was **obedient**. Since Noah and his sons were the only people on earth who loved God, He decided to begin the earth again with his family. But first He would wash the earth clean of sin with a flood.

God told Noah to build an **ark**. The ark was a big boat. Then God told Noah to fill the ark with all the different kinds of animals. After all the animals were in the boat, God told Noah and his family to climb inside and close the door very tightly. Once

they were inside, it began to rain very hard. Soon a flood covered the whole earth. Because Noah and his family obeyed God, they were safe and dry and cozy inside the ark.

Later, there was another man who loved and served God. His name was **Abraham**. He had **faith** in God, a gift that makes us able to believe all that God tells us. Abraham was always obedient to God, even when it was difficult. God promised to make of Abraham a great nation. From these people the Savior would be born. Some of Abraham's descendants are still among us today. They are the people we now call the Jewish people.

Words to Know:

Noah   obedient   ark   Abraham   faith

> **Q. 20** *What did some people do as they waited for the Savior?*
> Some people believed in God and obeyed Him so they would be ready for the Savior (CCC 58–64).

THE SACRIFICE OF THE MASS

The Mass is a true sacrifice, a mystical representation of Christ's sacrifice on Calvary. This aspect is clear in the Gospel accounts of the Last Supper, in which Christ says that His Body "will be given up," and that His Blood "will be poured out."

"It should be remembered that the Church solemnly defined at the Council of Trent in 1562 that the Mass is a sacrifice. The Council declared, 'If anyone says that in the Mass a true and proper sacrifice is not offered to God or that the sacrificial offering consists merely in the fact that Christ is given to us to eat: let him be anathema.'"

—*The Fundamentals of Catholicism,*
Fr. Kenneth Baker, Volume 3, p. 259

Preview

In our next lesson, we will learn about another good man who loved and obeyed God while he waited for the Savior—Abraham.

CHAPTER SEVEN: A TIME OF WAITING
LESSON TWO: ABRAHAM OBEYED GOD

Aims

Students will begin to learn the story of Abraham.

They will understand what obedience is and how Abraham obeyed God even when it was difficult.

Materials

• Children's Bible

• *Activity Book*, p. 26

Optional:
• "I sing the mighty power of God," *Adoremus Hymnal*, #616

Begin

Ask the children to look at the painting on p. 30 of the textbook—*Abraham with the Angels*. Tell them that the man kneeling is Abraham and the other three people are actually angels. The woman in the background is Sarah, Abraham's wife. Ask the children what they would do if angels visited them: would they kneel down, like Abraham? Explain that many years after the flood, when the world had a lot of people living in it again, there was another holy man named Abraham. God sent some of His angels to visit him and give him messages. They will learn more about him in today's lesson.

Develop

1. Read paragraph 4 of the textbook aloud. Emphasize that Abraham was always obedient to God, even when it was very difficult. Tell them that Abraham is a model of obedience for all people. God spoke to Abraham and chose him and his descendants to prepare the world for the coming of His Son, the Savior. God told Abraham things about Himself and His plans for him and his descendants. Abraham believed all that God said, and he always obeyed.

2. The story of Abraham will be divided into three parts, to be read in three lessons:
   a) God tells Abraham to move to a new country: Gen 12:1–5
   b) God promises to give him a son and descendants as numerous as the stars in Heaven and the sand on the seashore: Gen 13:14–17; 15:1–6; 17:15–19; 21:1–3
   c) God asks Abraham to sacrifice his son, Isaac: Gen 22:1–19

3. Read only the first part of Abraham's story to the students from the children's Bible. Then ask them to consider what it must have been like for Abraham to move to a new country. Abraham lived with his wife and had many animals and servants. All of these people and animals had to move with him to the new land. Help the children to compare how one moves to a new place now with how difficult it was in Abraham's time. Help them to better understand the challenge of Abraham's obedience to God.

4. Discuss with the children ways they can live the virtue of obedience in very practical ways.

5. God spoke to Abraham directly and asked him to believe what He said. Remind the children that God does not usually speak in that way, but He can speak through other people, especially the Pope, bishops, and priests. These men teach what God asks everyone to believe. Obeying them and having faith in what they say pleases God.

Reinforce

1. On p. 26 of the *Activity Book* (see *Teacher's Manual*, p. 85), have the children draw a picture of the angel giving Abraham a ram (male sheep) to sacrifice in place of Isaac.

2. Review Question 20 with the entire class, as well as the definitions of "obedient" and "faith." Then give pairs of children a few minutes to study them.

3. Teach the children a simple Act of Faith (see facing page) and pray it together.

4. "I sing the mighty power of God," *Adoremus Hymnal*, #616.

Conclude

Summarize these last two lessons by telling the children that because Adam and Eve lost the gift of grace when they committed the first sin, it was very difficult for anyone to be good. But there were some people, like Noah and Abraham, who loved, obeyed, and had faith in God. God helped them to become even better, and through them, He prepared the world for the coming of the Savior.

"I will look with favor on the faithful in the land, that they may dwell with me . . ."
(Psalms 101:6)

7   A Time of Waiting

"I will look with favor on the faithful in
the land, that they may dwell with me..."
Psalms 101:6

God promised to send a Savior. But the Savior did not come right away. The people had to wait for years and years. While they waited, some of them learned to love and obey God.

Noah was one of those people. Others did not obey God and fell into sinful ways. But Noah always did what God asked of him; he was **obedient**. Since Noah and his sons were the only people on earth who loved God, He decided to begin the earth again with his family. But first He would wash the earth clean of sin with a flood.

God told Noah to build an **ark**. The ark was a big boat. Then God told Noah to fill the ark with all the different kinds of animals. After all the animals were in the boat, God told Noah and his family to climb inside and close the door very tightly. Once

they were inside, it began to rain very hard. Soon a flood covered the whole earth. Because Noah and his family obeyed God, they were safe and dry and cozy inside the ark.

Later, there was another man who loved and served God. His name was **Abraham**. He had **faith** in God, a gift that makes us able to believe all that God tells us. Abraham was always obedient to God, even when it was difficult. God promised to make of Abraham a great nation. From these people the Savior would be born. Some of Abraham's descendants are still among us today. They are the people we now call the Jewish people.

Words to Know:

Noah   obedient   ark   Abraham   faith

> **Q. 20** *What did some people do as they waited*
> *for the Savior?*
> Some people believed in God and obeyed
> Him so they would be ready for the Savior
> (CCC 58–64).

SIMPLE ACT OF FAITH

My Lord, and My God, I trust in You, I believe in all You have revealed as taught by the Catholic Church, and in faith I give myself to You. *Amen.*

Preview

In our next lesson, we will learn more about God's promise to Abraham, and Abraham's faith.

CHAPTER SEVEN: A TIME OF WAITING
LESSON THREE: ABRAHAM HAD FAITH IN GOD

Aims

Students will learn more about the faith of Abraham.

They will be able to relate how Abraham received God's promise of many descendants.

They will be able to explain what faith is and how Abraham had great faith even when it was difficult.

Materials

- Children's Bible

- *Activity Book*, p. 27

Optional:
- Skits (Appendix, pp. B-12 and B-13)

- Manger and pieces of straw

- "I sing the mighty power of God," *Adoremus Hymnal*, #616

Begin

Remind the children that while waiting for the Savior, some people became very bad. However, there were also some people who loved God very much. Ask them to name the two great men who waited and prepared themselves for the coming Savior by loving, believing, and obeying God (Noah and Abraham). In this lesson they will learn more about Abraham and his faith in God.

Develop

1. Have the children look again at paragraph 4 in their textbooks. Point out the word "faith" and read its definition: a gift that makes us able to believe all that God tells us. Abraham had great faith in all that God told Him. That does not mean that he completely understood what God told him. For instance, did Abraham fully understand why God wanted him to move to a new and strange land? No, he did not. But Abraham believed God when He said that this new land was a good place and that God would take care of him there. Faith means to believe in things that cannot be fully understood, and that is why God gives the gift of faith so that we are able to believe everything that He tells us.

2. Read the second part of Abraham's story from the children's Bible (Gen 13:14–17; 15:1–6; 17:15–19; 21:1–3). God tells Abraham that not only will his descendants be as numerous as the stars, but also that the promised Savior would be born from his family. Point out that at the time God made this promise, Abraham did not have any children and he and his wife, Sarah, were at the age when people normally do not have children anymore (like grandparents). It must have been difficult for Abraham to believe God: How could his descendants be as numerous as the stars when he did not even have one child? But Abraham did not doubt God, he believed.

3. The gift of faith is given by God when a person is baptized (even if a person is a baby), and so is the ability to be obedient through the gift of grace. Having received these gifts, the baptized person has a responsibility to develop them as he grows up. It is important to pray and receive the Sacraments as often as possible in order for this gift of faith to grow.

Reinforce

1. Have the children complete p. 27 of the *Activity Book* (see *Teacher's Manual*, p. 85) by answering yes or no.

2. Tell the students that by being obedient and faithful, they will be preparing well for the day when they will meet Jesus, just as Noah and Abraham grew in love, obedience, and faith while they waited for the Savior to come.

3. Take some time to practice the two skits ("Noah and the Flood" and "The Sacrifice of Isaac") found in the Appendix, pp. B-12 and B-13.

Conclude

1. Give the children time to work in pairs, practicing Question 20 and the Words to Know.

2. Teach the children a simple Act of Faith (see the previous page) and pray it together.

3. "I sing the mighty power of God," *Adoremus Hymnal*, #616.

"I will look with favor on the faithful in the land, that they may dwell with me . . ."

(Psalms 101:6)

---

7   A Time of Waiting

"I will look with favor on the faithful in
the land, that they may dwell with me..."
Psalms 101:6

God promised to send a Savior. But the Savior did not come right away. The people had to wait for years and years. While they waited, some of them learned to love and obey God.

Noah was one of those people. Others did not obey God and fell into sinful ways. But Noah always did what God asked of him; he was **obedient**. Since Noah and his sons were the only people on earth who loved God, He decided to begin the earth again with his family. But first He would wash the earth clean of sin with a flood.

God told Noah to build an **ark**. The ark was a big boat. Then God told Noah to fill the ark with all the different kinds of animals. After all the animals were in the boat, God told Noah and his family to climb inside and close the door very tightly. Once

---

they were inside, it began to rain very hard. Soon a flood covered the whole earth. Because Noah and his family obeyed God, they were safe and dry and cozy inside the ark.

Later, there was another man who loved and served God. His name was **Abraham**. He had **faith** in God, a gift that makes us able to believe all that God tells us. Abraham was always obedient to God, even when it was difficult. God promised to make of Abraham a great nation. From these people the Savior would be born. Some of Abraham's descendants are still among us today. They are the people we now call the Jewish people.

Words to Know:

Noah   obedient   ark   Abraham   faith

> **Q. 20** *What did some people do as they waited for the Savior?*
> Some people believed in God and obeyed Him so they would be ready for the Savior (CCC 58–64).

ADVENT: A TIME OF WAITING

Each year the Church has a special time of waiting before Christmas called Advent (from the Latin *Advenire* meaning "to come"). As an Advent activity, prepare a classroom manger using pieces of straw. Tell the children that when Advent begins they should try very hard to perform acts of sacrifice, obedience, and love each day. Explain that an act of sacrifice means giving up something they like for love of Jesus (candy, T.V., etc.). Each time they perform an act of sacrifice, obedience, or love, they can place one piece of straw in the manger for baby Jesus. Then, when Christmas day comes, the students' good deeds will cushion the Savior's bed.

Preview

In the next lesson, we will learn about Abraham's trust in God.

CHAPTER SEVEN: A TIME OF WAITING
LESSON FOUR: ABRAHAM'S TRUST AND THANKFULNESS

Aims

Students will be able to relate the story of Abraham's call to sacrifice Isaac.

They will learn about Abraham's trust in God.

Materials

- Children's Bible

- *Activity Book*, p. 28

Optional:
- Prayer of Fatima prayer cards

- Skits (Appendix, pp. B-12 and B-13)

- "I sing the mighty power of God," *Adoremus Hymnal*, #616

Begin

Review the story of Abraham: God called him away from his homeland, then promised him many descendants (one of which would be the Savior). Tell the children that finally God sent Abraham and Sarah a son, Isaac. They loved him with all their hearts, and thanked God for keeping His promise. Then, one day God asked the most difficult thing of all from Abraham.

Develop

1. Now read the third part of the story of Abraham—the call to sacrifice Isaac (Gen 22:1–19).

2. Point out that it must have been terribly confusing for Abraham when God asked him to sacrifice Isaac. Not only was this boy his son, but Abraham must have wondered how God would keep His promise to make Abraham's descendants as numerous as the stars if he sacrificed his only child. But in trusting God and obeying God's command, Abraham proved his great love and deep faith; he believed God even when he could not understand His command. God rewarded him: Isaac went on to have two sons and these sons had many sons. These descendants were the Israelites who are now known as the Jews. Eventually, as God had promised, the Savior was born from Abraham's family.

3. Like Noah, Abraham offered a sacrifice to God, the ram caught in the bushes. Just as God called Abraham to offer his only beloved son as a sacrifice of love, God offered His only beloved Son, Jesus, as a sacrifice for the love of all. Catholics can go in faith and obedience and trust to Mass, where upon the altar, the Sacrifice of the Cross is made present during the Mass.

4. Tell the children that they will soon prepare to receive two great Sacraments: First Penance (Confession) and First Holy Communion. Until then, they can pray often to ask forgiveness when they have done something wrong, and to tell Jesus how much they love Him while at Mass and when they say their prayers each day. This way they will grow in faith, obedience, and trust, and prepare to meet their Savior (now in their hearts, soon in the Sacraments, and finally in Heaven).

Reinforce

1. Assign the matching exercise on p. 28 of the *Activity Book* (see *Teacher's Manual*, p. 85).

2. Teach the children the prayer of Fatima (see the facing page), and pray it as a group. You may want to write it on prayer cards and distribute them. This prayer is usually said during the Rosary following the Glory Be, and can be implemented when the students learn to pray the Rosary in later lessons.

3. Review Question 20 and Words to Know.

Conclude

1. Lead the children in praying for the virtues of faith, obedience, trust, and thankfulness. The students may add their own petitions, i.e., Lord, please help me to obey my mother when she asks me to do chores, etc.

2. Practice or perform the skits found in Appendix B on pp. B-12 and B-13.

3. Sing "I sing the mighty power of God," *Adoremus Hymnal*, #616.

"I will look with favor on the faithful in the land, that they may dwell with me . . ."

(Psalms 101:6)

7   A Time of Waiting

"I will look with favor on the faithful in
the land, that they may dwell with me..."
Psalms 101:6

God promised to send a Savior. But the Savior did not come right away. The people had to wait for years and years. While they waited, some of them learned to love and obey God.

Noah was one of those people. Others did not obey God and fell into sinful ways. But Noah always did what God asked of him; he was **obedient**. Since Noah and his sons were the only people on earth who loved God, He decided to begin the earth again with his family. But first He would wash the earth clean of sin with a flood.

God told Noah to build an **ark**. The ark was a big boat. Then God told Noah to fill the ark with all the different kinds of animals. After all the animals were in the boat, God told Noah and his family to climb inside and close the door very tightly. Once

they were inside, it began to rain very hard. Soon a flood covered the whole earth. Because Noah and his family obeyed God, they were safe and dry and cozy inside the ark.

Later, there was another man who loved and served God. His name was **Abraham**. He had **faith** in God, a gift that makes us able to believe all that God tells us. Abraham was always obedient to God, even when it was difficult. God promised to make of Abraham a great nation. From these people the Savior would be born. Some of Abraham's descendants are still among us today. They are the people we now call the Jewish people.

Words to Know:

Noah   obedient   ark   Abraham   faith

> **Q. 20** *What did some people do as they waited for the Savior?*
> Some people believed in God and obeyed Him so they would be ready for the Savior (CCC 58–64).

OUR LADY OF FATIMA AND SACRIFICE

In 1917 our Lady appeared to three shepherd children in Fatima, Portugal: Lucia, Francisco, and Jacinta. Among other things, she asked the children to sacrifice daily for the sins of the world and for the holy souls in Purgatory. Though their sacrifices were heroic, God does not ask such sacrifices from everyone. Tell the students that they also can make sacrifices, giving up candy or T.V. for example. To reinforce this message, you may want to show "The Day the Sun Danced," a 30 minute CCC of America video about Our Lady of Fatima, or you may want to wait until this apparition is discussed in further detail in Lesson 4 of Chapter 26 (see *Teacher's Manual*, p. 321).

PRAYER OF FATIMA

O My Jesus, forgive us our sins, and save us from the fires of Hell. Lead all souls into Heaven, especially those in most need of Thy mercy. *Amen*.

Preview

In the next lesson, we will review what we have learned, play a game, and take a quiz.

CHAPTER SEVEN: A TIME OF WAITING
REVIEW AND ASSESSMENT

Aims

To review and assess the students' knowledge of the material taught in this chapter.

Materials

- Appendix, p. B-1
- Quiz 7 (Appendix, p. A-8)
- "I sing the mighty power of God," *Adoremus Hymnal*, #616

Review and Enrichment

1. Review the stories of Noah and Abraham. Many people became sinful as they waited for the promised Savior. Noah and Abraham, among others, learned to love and obey God while they waited. Obedience is doing what one is told to do; faith is a gift that makes a person able to believe all that God tells him.

2. Remind the children that they were given the gifts of obedience and faith at Baptism and that they must practice these in order to grow in holiness. Advent is the season of waiting for the Savior when they should try particularly hard to do acts of sacrifice, love, and obedience. When they do these things, their faith will grow.

3. Play Bible Baseball or Tic-Tac-Toe (see Appendix, p. B-1) with the children to review the Words to Know as well as Question 20 (see *Teacher's Manual*, p. 83).

Name: _____

A Time of Waiting   Quiz 7

Yes or No. *Circle the correct answer.*

1. Did God send the Savior right away?   Yes   (No)

2. Did the people need to wait for the Savior?   (Yes)   No

Match the names on the left with the words on the right.

Savior ⎯⎯⎯⎯⎯⎯⎯⎯⎯ ark

Noah ⎯⎯⎯⎯⎯⎯⎯⎯⎯ faith

Abraham ⎯⎯⎯⎯⎯⎯⎯ promised by God

A-8   *Faith and Life Series • Grade 1 • Appendix A*

Assess

Distribute Quiz 7 to the children, read through it slowly with them, and answer any questions they may have.

Conclude

When the quiz has been completed, review the answers, or have the children put on their costumes, gather their props, and perform the two skits that they have practiced this week.

CHAPTER SEVEN: A TIME OF WAITING
ACTIVITY BOOK ANSWER KEYS

Noah's Ark

What was it like on the ark with all those animals?

Write a sentence and draw a picture.

Answers will vary.

Faith and Life Series • Grade 1 • Chapter 7 • Lesson 1   25

Abraham answered, "God, Himself, will provide the sheep for sacrifice."

Draw a picture of the angel giving Abraham a ram to offer in place of Isaac.

26   *Faith and Life Series • Grade 1 • Chapter 7 • Lesson 2*

Waiting

Answers will vary.

If I had to wait a long time, what would I do?

Would I be angry or impatient? _____
Would I learn about God? _____
Would I forget why I was waiting? _____
Would I read the Bible? _____
Would I waste my time? _____
Would I pray every day? _____
Would I be faithful to God? _____
What else might I do?

_____

_____

Faith and Life Series • Grade 1 • Chapter 7 • Lesson 3   27

Can you match the two lists below?

Adam and Eve — They lost grace through sin
Noah — He built an ark
Shem, Ham, Japheth — The Sons of Noah
Abraham — A faithful man, even when it was difficult
Isaac — The one who was almost sacrificed
Jesus — Our Savior and Lord
Covenant — A promise that makes us family with God

Use the list of names above to help you fill in the blanks.

1. Adam and Eve were tempted by the devil to disobey God.

2. Noah saved creation in an ark.

3. Abraham was faithful and was promised many descendants.

28   *Faith and Life Series • Grade 1 • Chapter 7 • Lesson 4*

85

TEACHER'S NOTES

CHAPTER EIGHT
GETTING READY FOR THE SAVIOR

Catechism of the Catholic Church References

The Command to Proclaim: 2
God Forms His People Israel: 62–64, 72, 218
God's Mercy: 1846–47
The Gospel and Law of the Old Covenant: 1963–64
Jesus and the Law: 574–82, 592, 2052–55
John: Forerunner, Prophet, and Baptizer: 523, 717–20

Moses and the Prayer of the Mediator: 2574–77
Obligation of the Ten Commandments: 2072–74, 2081–82
The Old Law: 1961–64, 1975, 1980–82
Preparations for Christ's Coming: 522–24
The Prophets of Israel: 64, 201
The Ten Commandments as a Way to Heaven: 1724

Scripture References

Moses and the Burning Bush: Ex 3:1–14
Moses Receives the Ten Commandments: Ex 20:1–17; 31:18
Prophecies of the Savior: Is 7:14; 9:6; 11:1–9; 53:1–12

The Story of Moses: Ex 1:22—2:10
The Story of Saint John the Baptist: Mt 3:1–17; Mk 1:1–11;
Lk 3:1–17

Background Reading: *The Fundamentals of Catholicism* by Fr. Kenneth Baker, S.J.

Volume 1:
"The Holy Spirit and Prophecy," pp. 97–99

Volume 2:
The Commandments, pp. 121–38

Summary of Lesson Content

Lesson 1

Prophets were holy men who prepared people for the coming of the Savior.

Prophets also foretold future events.

Advent is a time of preparation for Christ's coming at Christmas.

Lesson 2

Moses was the first prophet.

He was saved by God from Pharaoh's death sentence so that he could do a special job when he was a grown man.

God has a plan for each of us.

Lesson 3

God gave Moses the Ten Commandments.

The Ten Commandments are rules of life for everyone, everywhere, always.

If we obey the Ten Commandments we will come to love them.

If we disobey the Ten Commandments, we sin and must be sorry.

Lesson 4

Saint John the Baptist was the cousin of the Savior and the last prophet of the Old Covenant.

He told people to be sorry for their sins and prepared them for the Savior.

Saint John the Baptist baptized Jesus.

CHAPTER EIGHT: GETTING READY FOR THE SAVIOR
LESSON ONE: GOD SENDS PROPHETS

Aims

Students will be able to define the word "prophet."

They will be able to explain how God sent many prophets to help people be good while they waited and prepared for the Savior.

They will learn about Advent.

Materials

• Children's Bible

• *Activity Book*, p. 29

Optional:
• "O come, O come, Emmanuel," *Adoremus Hymnal*, #301

Begin

Make a simple timeline on the chalkboard and have the children assist you in putting the following in order: Noah, the promise of a Savior, the Fall of Adam and Eve, and Abraham.

Develop

1. Ask the students what they would do if you left the classroom and they had to wait for you to return. They might begin to talk or misbehave. Ask them if they think they would behave longer if you sent someone to remind them to be good because you were coming soon. Explain that God sent holy men called prophets (write this word on the board) to tell everyone to be ready for the Savior and to be good.

2. Read paragraph 1 with the children. Point out the definition of the word "prophets": holy men who prepared people for the coming of the Savior, Jesus Christ. Tell them that they did this in two ways: 1) by telling the people how God would come to earth in the future, and 2) by showing the people how to be good until He came.

3. Explain to the children that though one of the jobs of a prophet was to tell what would happen in the future, the prophets were not magical, nor did they know the future on their own. Instead, they could speak about things in the future only because God gave them that knowledge. Remind the children that one of God's qualities is that He is "all knowing" (see Chapter 3, Lesson 1; *Teacher's Manual*, pp. 26 and 27).

He gave small bits of this knowledge to the prophets in Israel and they told the people.

4. In your children's Bible, find pictures of some of the prophets. (Isaiah with the burning coal to his lips would be a good example.) Read a few of Isaiah's Christmas prophecies to the children (Is 7:14; 9:6; 11:1–9; 53:1–12), and point out that they came true—were fulfilled—in Jesus, our Savior. (For example: Jesus would be born in Bethlehem, wise men would visit Him from the East, etc.)

5. God helped the Jewish people prepare for the coming of the Savior by giving them signs to let them know when He would come. With these prophecies in mind, they would recognize the Savior when He came, and they would be ready for Him.

6. Tell the children that for the rest of this week, the class will think about the prophets' other job: to tell people how to be good while they were waiting for the Savior. The prophets' main job was to be good and to love God. Tell the children that this week they will be learning about the first prophet, Moses, and the last prophet, Saint John the Baptist.

Reinforce

1. Write the letters of the word PROPHET vertically on the chalkboard. After each letter write phrases that explain the job and purpose of a prophet such as:

P - Prepared people for the Savior
R - Reminded people of God's love for them
O - Obeyed God by telling the people what He told them
P - Proclaimed future events
H - Helped people get ready for the Savior
E - Ended with Saint John the Baptist
T - Told people about what God wanted them to do

2. Have the children complete the word search on p. 29 of the *Activity Book* (see *Teacher's Manual*, p. 97).

Conclude

1. Tell the students that the prophet Isaiah first gave the name "Emmanuel" to the Savior he foretold. The name means "God with us," which is exactly what is celebrated on Christmas. From Advent until His birth on Christmas Day the Church is waiting for Him to come.

2. Give pairs of children time to review Questions 1–20 (see *Teacher's Manual*, pp. 9, 21, 33, 45, 59, 71, and 83).

3. Teach the students an appropriate song, such as "O come, O come, Emmanuel," *Adoremus Hymnal*, #301.

8   Getting Ready
For the Savior

"The law of your mouth is better to me than
thousands of gold and silver pieces."
Psalms 119:72

Many more years passed. The descendants of
Abraham were still waiting for the Savior. God did
not forget His promise. He sent many **prophets** to the
Jewish people. Prophets were holy men who prepared
people for the coming of the Savior, Jesus Christ.

33

Moses was the first prophet. Moses was very
important because God gave him the Ten
Commandments.

The **Ten Commandments** are God's Laws for
every one of us. These Laws help us to know how God
wants us to live. When people obeyed God's Laws,
they were preparing for the coming of the Savior.

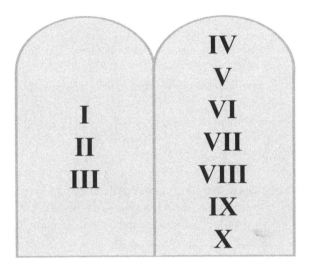

34

Then when it was almost time for the Savior
to come, God sent the last prophet of the Old
Testament. He was **Saint John the Baptist**. Saint
John was the cousin of Jesus. He lived and prayed
in the desert. He told people to be sorry for their sins.
Saint John baptized people if they were sorry for their
sins. This baptism was not the Sacrament of Baptism,
but it helped people to prepare for the Savior. Saint
John told the people that the Savior would come very
soon.

Words to Know:

prophets   Moses   Ten Commandments

Saint John the Baptist

> **Q. 21** *What are the Ten Commandments of God?*
> The Ten Commandments of God are the
> moral law that God gave to Moses on
> Mount Sinai (CCC 2056).

35

THE ADVENT WREATH

The Advent wreath originated in the folk prac-
tices of pre-Christian Germanic peoples who
gathered wreaths of evergreen and lit fires in
anticipation of the coming spring. This custom
was Christianized, so that now, during Advent,
most churches and many families display an
Advent wreath. This consists of a circle of
evergreen, three violet candles, and one rose
candle which is lit on the third Sunday, known
as "Gaudete Sunday" (Latin for "Rejoice," see
p. 91). The circular shape of the wreath represents Christ's eternal victory over death. The
evergreens are a sign of God's faithfulness to
His people, and the lighted candles are a
reminder of the light of Christ brought into the
world at Christmas.

Preview

In our next lesson, we will learn about the first prophet, a
great and holy man—Moses.

CHAPTER EIGHT: GETTING READY FOR THE SAVIOR
LESSON TWO: THE FIRST PROPHET

Aims

Students will listen to the story of Moses as a baby.

They will be able to explain that God took special care of Moses so that he could do God's work when he was a grown man.

They will be able to explain that God has special plans for each one of us.

Materials

- Map showing the Holy Land and Egypt

- Children's Bible

- *Activity Book*, p. 30

Optional:
- *Baby Moses*, by Linda Hayward

- "O come, O come, Emmanuel," *Adoremus Hymnal*, #301

Begin

Write the word "prophet" on the chalkboard and help the children to remember the definition. Then write the letters vertically (as in the last lesson) and have them help you fill in each phrase. Tell them that they will now hear a story about the first great prophet.

Develop

1. Tell the children that Abraham did in fact have many, many descendants, as many as the stars in Heaven, just as God had promised him. Over the years they had come to live far from the land that God had given to Abraham. They now lived as slaves in Egypt under the Egyptian Pharaoh, that is, the king. Locate Egypt for them on the map.

2. Now read aloud the story of baby Moses from your children's Bible (Ex 1:22—2:10), or read the story *Baby Moses* by Linda Hayward, showing pictures as appropriate.

3. Help the children to summarize and retell the story according to the following outline: first, Pharaoh sends out his soldiers; second, Moses' mother hides him in a basket and sets him on the River Nile; third, Pharaoh's daughter finds Moses and adopts him as her own son.

4. Point out that Moses grew up to be the first prophet, and that in this story of his rescue from the evil Pharaoh, God's special care for Moses is evident. God had a certain job for Moses to do, and He gave him special protection from the time he was a small baby. Through Moses, the Jewish people would become more prepared for the Savior's arrival.

5. God's plans for Moses were dramatic, and Moses grew up to be a very important man. Tell the children that they may not grow up to be prophets like Moses. Nevertheless, God loves each one of them and has a special plan for them. God takes care of everyone by giving him parents, grandparents, an angel, etc., and He wants all His children to grow up to do the job He has in mind for them. Encourage the students to pray to God often to know what it is He wants them to do or to be when they grow up. Perhaps He will even call some of them to the priesthood or religious life.

Reinforce

1. Have the children draw a picture of themselves preparing for Christ on p. 30 of the *Activity Book* (see *Teacher's Manual*, p. 97).

2. Help the students to compose a class prayer in which they tell God that they are preparing their hearts for the coming of His Son on Christmas. Post the prayer and say it throughout the Advent season.

Conclude

1. Give a few minutes for pairs of children to review Questions 1–20 in their textbooks (see *Teacher's Manual*, pp. 9, 21, 33, 45, 59, 71, and 83).

2. Sing "O come, O come, Emmanuel," *Adoremus Hymnal*, #301.

8   Getting Ready For the Savior

"The law of your mouth is better to me than thousands of gold and silver pieces."

Psalms 119:72

Many more years passed. The descendants of Abraham were still waiting for the Savior. God did not forget His promise. He sent many **prophets** to the Jewish people. Prophets were holy men who prepared people for the coming of the Savior, Jesus Christ.

33

Moses was the first prophet. Moses was very important because God gave him the Ten Commandments.

The **Ten Commandments** are God's Laws for every one of us. These Laws help us to know how God wants us to live. When people obeyed God's Laws, they were preparing for the coming of the Savior.

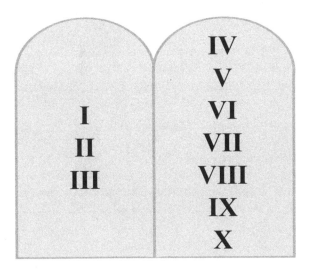

34

Then when it was almost time for the Savior to come, God sent the last prophet of the Old Testament. He was **Saint John the Baptist**. Saint John was the cousin of Jesus. He lived and prayed in the desert. He told people to be sorry for their sins. Saint John baptized people if they were sorry for their sins. This baptism was not the Sacrament of Baptism, but it helped people to prepare for the Savior. Saint John told the people that the Savior would come very soon.

Words to Know:

prophets   Moses   Ten Commandments

Saint John the Baptist

> **Q. 21** *What are the Ten Commandments of God?*
> The Ten Commandments of God are the moral law that God gave to Moses on Mount Sinai (CCC 2056).

35

GAUDETE SUNDAY IN ADVENT

The third Sunday in Advent is called Gaudete Sunday, from the first words of the Entrance Antiphon at Mass ("Gaudete in Domino semper"). About midway through a season which is otherwise of a penitential nature, it signifies the nearness of Christ's coming. Rose-colored vestments are allowed instead of the purple used throughout Advent (see *Teacher's Manual*, p. 362). Continual reference is made to Christ's Second Coming, emphasized by the signs of gladness permitted on this day. The Church asks the faithful to worship with joy: "Rejoice in the Lord always; again I say, rejoice. Indeed, the Lord is near." The joy of expectation is heightened by repeated Alleluias, which occur both during the Mass and in the Divine Office.

Preview

In our next lesson, we will learn about the rules for life that God gave to Moses for the Jewish people and for us.

CHAPTER EIGHT: GETTING READY FOR THE SAVIOR
LESSON THREE: RULES FOR LIFE

Aims

Students will listen to the story of Moses and the burning bush.

They will also hear the story of God giving Moses the Ten Commandments on Mount Sinai.

They will be able to explain that the Ten Commandments are rules of life for everyone.

Materials

- Children's Bible
- *Activity Book*, p. 31

Begin

Have the children look at the painting on p. 33 of the textbook, and tell them that this is a picture of Moses listening to God Who spoke to Him from a burning bush. Ask them to look closely at the painting to see what is so unusual about it. (The bush is not burning up, though fire rages through it.) Tell them that today they will hear a story about God and Moses.

Develop

1. From your children's Bible, read the story of Moses and the burning bush (Ex 3:1–14). Comment on how close Moses was to God—he spoke with Him. It was at this meeting that God made Moses a prophet, a messenger to the Jewish people whom He was preparing for the Savior's coming.

2. Now read the story of Moses on Mount Sinai and how God gave him the Ten Commandments (Ex 20:1–17; 31:18). These were written on tablets of stone; they could not be changed or erased. The Commandments would help the people to be good while they waited for the Savior.

3. Read paragraphs 2 and 3 with the children. Point out the definition of the Ten Commandments: God's Laws for every one of us. Explain that a law is a rule or a command. Ask if they can think of any rules everyone must follow, e.g., stop signs and stop lights. Be sure they understand that if people abide by these rules, everyone can be happy, and safe. When anyone breaks these rules, there are often punishments. Is this because parents and teachers, for example, are mean? No, it is because everyone can be happy only if everyone lives according to the rules.

4. Explain that the Ten Commandments are rules also. But they are not rules just for the classroom, or the home, or the streets; they are rules for life. By following these Commandments of God, everyone can be happy.

5. God gave Moses the Ten Commandments so that people would know how to be good. The Commandments tell everyone to love God and to treat his neighbor well. Ask the children to think of rules that help them to love God and neighbor. Write these rules on the board under two headings:

How to love God:	How to love Neighbor:
Go to Mass.	Do not tell lies.
Say daily prayers.	Obey your parents.
Say God's name with love.	Do not take other people's belongings.

6. Read the Ten Commandments to the children and help them to see how the rules you have recorded fit into these categories. Explain that God wanted the people who were waiting for the Savior to follow these rules. But He also wants all people to obey them. If anyone breaks a Commandment, he sins. Tell them that sin displeases God and a person must be sorry for his sins and try to do better.

Reinforce

1. Have the children write a letter to Jesus on p. 31 of the *Activity Book* (see *Teacher's Manual*, p. 97).

2. Read Question 21 with the children and practice it as a group.

3. Have the children begin memorizing the Ten Commandments.

Conclude

Ask the children to look at the title for this chapter in their textbook, then read aloud with them the Scripture quote below it. You might need to explain it; tell them that sometimes it is difficult to love God's Laws and to obey them. But if a person obeys them time after time, he will grow to love them, as the passage says.

8   Getting Ready For the Savior

"The law of your mouth is better to me than
thousands of gold and silver pieces."
Psalms 119:72

Many more years passed. The descendants of
Abraham were still waiting for the Savior. God did
not forget His promise. He sent many **prophets** to the
Jewish people. Prophets were holy men who prepared
people for the coming of the Savior, Jesus Christ.

33

Moses was the first prophet. Moses was very
important because God gave him the Ten
Commandments.

The **Ten Commandments** are God's Laws for
every one of us. These Laws help us to know how God
wants us to live. When people obeyed God's Laws,
they were preparing for the coming of the Savior.

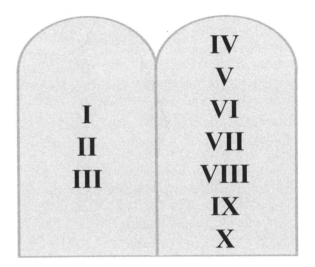

34

Then when it was almost time for the Savior
to come, God sent the last prophet of the Old
Testament. He was **Saint John the Baptist**. Saint
John was the cousin of Jesus. He lived and prayed
in the desert. He told people to be sorry for their sins.
Saint John baptized people if they were sorry for their
sins. This baptism was not the Sacrament of Baptism,
but it helped people to prepare for the Savior. Saint
John told the people that the Savior would come very
soon.

Words to Know:

prophets   Moses   Ten Commandments

Saint John the Baptist

> **Q. 21** *What are the Ten Commandments of God?*
> The Ten Commandments of God are the
> moral law that God gave to Moses on
> Mount Sinai (CCC 2056).

35

THE TEN COMMANDMENTS

1. You shall have no other gods before me.
2. You shall not take the name of the LORD
   your God in vain.
3. Remember the sabbath day, to keep
   it holy.
4. Honor your father and your mother.
5. You shall not kill.
6. You shall not commit adultery.
7. You shall not steal.
8. You shall not bear false witness against
   your neighbor.
9. You shall not covet your neighbor's wife.
10. You shall not covet you neighbor's goods.

—From Exodus 20:1–17 and
Deuteronomy 5:6–21

Preview

In our next lesson, we will learn about the last prophet—
Saint John the Baptist.

Chapter Eight: Getting Ready for the Savior
Lesson Four: The Last Prophet

Aims

Students will be able to identify Saint John the Baptist as the cousin of our Lord and the last prophet before Jesus came.

They will be able to explain that Saint John's baptism did not take away Original Sin or confer grace like the Sacrament of Baptism.

They will know that Saint John baptized Jesus, even though He did not need to be baptized.

Materials

- Children's Bible

- *Activity Book*, p. 32

Optional:
- "O come, O come, Emmanuel," *Adoremus Hymnal*, #301

Begin

Explain to the children that many, many years passed from the time of Moses until God sent the last prophet to prepare His people for the coming of the Savior. The people tried hard to obey the Ten Commandments as they waited and pre-pared for the Savior, but they often failed and fell into sin. God did not forget them. He sent many prophets to remind the people of how they should behave. Finally, He sent the last prophet; his name was Saint John the Baptist.

Develop

1. Read paragraph 4 of the textbook aloud with the children. Emphasize the fact that Saint John the Baptist was the son of Mary's cousin Elizabeth, and therefore the cousin of Jesus. He was also the last of the prophets.

2. Read the story of Saint John the Baptist from your children's Bible (Mt 3:1–17; Mk 1:1–11; or Lk 3:1–17). Highlight that both Saint John and the Savior were about the same age, for Saint John was born only a few months before our Lord. He was such a great prophet that many people thought he might be the promised Savior. But Saint John was not the Savior; he was the last prophet who directed the people to the Savior. He had to do what God asked of him; his job was to lead people to Christ and to help them to be sorry for their sins.

3. Explain that Saint John baptized people in the River Jordan. Saint John's baptism did not take away Original Sin, nor did it confer grace. Only the Sacrament of Baptism that Jesus instituted can do that. But Saint John's baptism was a sign that people were sorry for their sins; it made them ready for the Savior who was about to be revealed.

4. Explain that Jesus did not need to be baptized by Saint John because He never committed a single sin. However, He wanted to set a good example for the Jewish people and for all of his followers, including all Catholics today.

Reinforce

1. Ask the children to imagine that they are Saint John the Baptist, the cousin of Jesus, and that they are preparing people for the coming of the Savior. What would they do? They would tell the people to be sorry for what they have done that was wrong. They would tell the people to love God and try to do what pleases Him.

2. Have the children color the drawing of Saint John the Baptist and Jesus on p. 32 of the *Activity Book* (see *Teacher's Manual*, p. 97).

3. Have the students practice Question 21 and the Words to Know in pairs.

Conclude

1. Tell the children to prepare themselves for the coming of Jesus, the Savior. Encourage them to try hard to be very good and helpful before Christmas. Suggest that they choose someone in their family to do something nice for each day. They might make the person's bed or make a card saying how much they love him or her (see "Advent Angels" on the facing page).

2. Sing "O come, O come Emmanuel," *Adoremus Hymnal*, #301.

God with us

8   Getting Ready For the Savior

"The law of your mouth is better to me than thousands of gold and silver pieces."
Psalms 119:72

Many more years passed. The descendants of Abraham were still waiting for the Savior. God did not forget His promise. He sent many **prophets** to the Jewish people. Prophets were holy men who prepared people for the coming of the Savior, Jesus Christ.

33

Moses was the first prophet. Moses was very important because God gave him the Ten Commandments.

The **Ten Commandments** are God's Laws for every one of us. These Laws help us to know how God wants us to live. When people obeyed God's Laws, they were preparing for the coming of the Savior.

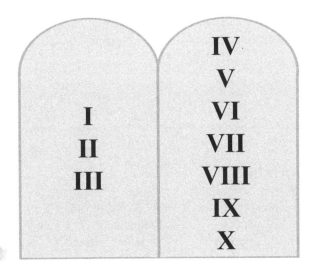

34

Then when it was almost time for the Savior to come, God sent the last prophet of the Old Testament. He was **Saint John the Baptist**. Saint John was the cousin of Jesus. He lived and prayed in the desert. He told people to be sorry for their sins. Saint John baptized people if they were sorry for their sins. This baptism was not the Sacrament of Baptism, but it helped people to prepare for the Savior. Saint John told the people that the Savior would come very soon.

Words to Know:

prophets   Moses   Ten Commandments

Saint John the Baptist

> **Q. 21**   *What are the Ten Commandments of God?*
> The Ten Commandments of God are the moral law that God gave to Moses on Mount Sinai (CCC 2056).

35

ADVENT ANGELS

Many families have a tradition of exchanging names at the beginning of Advent and secretly doing something nice for the person they choose, either weekly or daily. Sometimes this person is called by the secular name of a Secret Santa or a Kris Kringle. This exercise helps to instill the attitude of giving in the participants, especially if they are children, instead of focusing only on receiving. It also emphasizes that Advent is a season dedicated to preparing for the coming of the Savior, as Lent is a season dedicated to preparing for the Savior's Resurrection. It is important to actively observe Advent, and acting as an Advent Angel is a good way to do this.

Preview

In the next lesson, we will review what we have learned this week, play a game, and take a quiz and unit test.

CHAPTER EIGHT: GETTING READY FOR THE SAVIOR
REVIEW AND ASSESSMENT

Aims

To review and assess materials taught this week.

Materials

- Appendix, p. B-1
- Quiz 8 (Appendix, p. A-9)
- "O come, O come, Emmanuel," *Adoremus Hymnal*, #301

Review and Enrichment

1. Draw a timeline on the chalkboard like the one you made in Lesson 1. Have the children direct you as you construct it. After Abraham, add Moses and Saint John the Baptist.

2. Review prophets, Moses, the Ten Commandments, and Saint John the Baptist by playing a memory game such as Bible Baseball or Telephone (see Appendix, p. B-1).

3. Now remind the children that it is their turn to prepare for the Savior to come by trying hard to be very good and helpful before Christmas. Encourage them to choose someone in their family to do something nice for each day. Tell them that each time they do a good act they may add a piece of straw to the manger, to cushion it for baby Jesus (see *Teacher's Manual*, p. 81).

Name: _____

Getting Ready for the Savior   Quiz 8

Fill in the blanks. *Trace the gray letters and fill in the rest.*

Word Bank

John	prophets	Moses	Ten

1. God sent many p r o p h e t s .

2. God gave M o s e s the Ten Commandments.

3. The T e n Commandments teach us how to live.

4. Saint J o h n the Baptist told people that the Savior was coming very soon.

Assess

1. Pass out Quiz 8, read through it with the children, and then administer it.

Conclude

Sing "O come, O come, Emmanuel," *Adoremus Hymnal*, #301.

Name:_____

Word Search

**Can you find these words in the puzzle?
Look carefully! The words go across and down.**

ADAM	EVE	JOHN
ABRAHAM	GOD	MOSES
ANGEL	ISAAC	NOAH
DEVIL	JESUS	

```
X  J E S U S  X X  I  X X  A
X  X X X X X  X X  S  X X  N
X  A  X A  X  N O A H  X  G
X  D  X B  X X X X  A  X  E
X  A  X R  X X X X  C  X  L
X  M  X A  X X X X  X  X  X
G  X X H  X X X X  X  X  X
O  X X A  X  D E V I  L
D  X X  M O S E S  X  X
X  E V E  X X  J O H N
```

Faith and Life Series • Grade 1 • Chapter 8 • Lesson 1 29

Name:_____

Are you ready for Jesus?

God had a plan for Abraham and Moses. They were good men and helped others be good to prepare for Jesus. God has a plan for you, too!

Draw a picture of yourself doing something good to prepare for Jesus.

30 *Faith and Life Series • Grade 1 • Chapter 8 • Lesson 2*

Name:_____

The Ten Commandments:
Rules for life

Write a letter to Jesus telling Him that you will obey His Commandments because you love Him and want to be happy with Him forever.

Dear Jesus,

Answers will vary.

Love,
Student's name

Faith and Life Series • Grade 1 • Chapter 8 • Lesson 3 31

Name:_____

John the Baptist

John the Baptist was the last prophet.
He said, "Repent for the Kingdom of God is at hand."
He baptized people with the
baptism of repentance in the Jordan River.
He baptized Jesus.

Color the picture.

32 *Faith and Life Series • Grade 1 • Chapter 8 • Lesson 4*

TEACHER'S NOTES

UNIT TWO TEST
CHAPTERS 5-8

> **CHAPTER FIVE: ADAM AND EVE**
>
> **CHAPTER SIX: A SAD STORY**
>
> **CHAPTER SEVEN: A TIME OF WAITING**
>
> **CHAPTER EIGHT: GETTING READY FOR THE SAVIOR**

Aims

The students' understanding of the material covered in this unit will be reviewed and assessed.

Materials

• Unit 2 Test, Appendix, p. A-10

Assess

1. Distribute the unit tests and read through them with the students to be sure they understand the questions.

2. Administer the test.

3. After all the tests have been handed in, you may wish to review the correct answers with the class.

Name: _____

Unit 2 Test   **Chapters 5–8**

Fill in the blanks. *Trace the gray letters and fill in the rest.*

Word Bank

God	made	ark	Adam
last	Ten	send	

1. God __made__ Adam and Eve.

2. __Adam__ and Eve sinned.

3. God promised to __send__ a Savior.

4. Noah built an __ark__ .

5. Abraham had faith in __God__ .

6. God gave Moses the __Ten__ Commandments.

7. Saint John the Baptist was the __last__ prophet.

TEACHER'S NOTES

TEACHER'S NOTES

CHAPTER NINE
MARY HEARS SOME WONDERFUL NEWS

Catechism of the Catholic Church References

The Annunciation: 484–86, 494, 511, 2676
The Immaculate Conception: 490–93, 508
Mary as Virgin: 485, 496–507, 723
Mary's Divine Motherhood: 495, 509, 964

Mary in Salvation History: 488–89, 508
Obedience of Mary's Faith: 144, 148–49, 494, 511
Why the Son of God Became Flesh: 456–60

Scripture References

The Annunciation: Lk 1:26–38
The Visitation: Lk 1:39–56

Prophecy to Zechariah: Lk 1:6–16

Background Reading: *The Fundamentals of Catholicism* by Fr. Kenneth Baker, S.J.

Volume 1:
The Incarnation, pp. 55–64

Volume 2:
"Church Teaching about Mary, the Mother of God,"
pp. 315–18
"Mary, the Immaculate Mother of God," pp. 321–27

Mary, Full of Grace, pp. 327–36
"Joseph and Mary, Husband and Wife," pp. 337–40
"The Virginal Conception of Jesus," pp. 346–49
Mary's Perpetual Virginity, pp. 349–56
"Our Spiritual Mother," pp. 356–59
"Mary is Our Sure Way to Christ," pp. 378–81

Summary of Lesson Content

Lesson 1

Mary was preserved from Original Sin from the first moment of her conception.

Mary never sinned and always pleased God.

The first Joyful Mystery is the Annunciation.

Lesson 2

Mary is the perfect servant of God.

Mary's yes replaces the no of Adam and Eve.

Though Mary did not know how it could be that she would be the Mother of God, her great faith in Him prepared her to say yes.

Saint Joseph is the husband of Mary and the foster-father of Jesus.

Lesson 3

Mary's visit to Saint Elizabeth shows that her love was an active love, springing into loving service.

Saint Elizabeth's words, recorded in Scripture, form the second part of the Hail Mary.

Mary is our model for cheerful helpfulness and obedience. The Visitation is the second Joyful Mystery.

Lesson 4

Because Jesus is our brother, and Mary is His Mother, Mary is also our Mother who loves us very much.

The Rosary is her special prayer; she wants us to say it each day.

We say prayers and meditate on the lives of Jesus and Mary when we say the Rosary.

CHAPTER NINE: MARY HEARS SOME WONDERFUL NEWS
LESSON ONE: MARY, FULL OF GRACE

Aims

Students will understand how God prepared Mary for the Savior by keeping her free from Original Sin from the first moment of her life.

They will know that Mary never sinned; she was always pleasing to God.

Materials

• *Activity Book*, p. 33

Optional:
• "Immaculate Mary," *Adoremus Hymnal*, #532

Begin

Briefly review the outline of salvation history that the children have learned thus far. Tell them that from the sin of Adam and Eve until the last prophet, Saint John the Baptist, God continually prepared people for the coming of the Savior. There was one more thing that God needed to do before the Savior came. He planned to send His Son into the world as a baby. The baby needed a mother. Ask if any of the children know who the Mother of Jesus is? Tell them that today they will learn about how God prepared Mary for the birth of the Savior.

Develop

1. Read paragraph 1 aloud with the children. Then tell them that God prepared Mary for the birth of the Savior in the most careful and special way. When He promised to send a Savior, many years before, God had the Savior's Mother in mind: Mary. He wanted the Mother of His Son to be perfect in every way.

2. Remind the students that the children of Adam and Eve had Original Sin on their souls, and they did not have grace because Adam had lost the gift of grace for everyone. It would not be right for the Mother of God to be soiled in any way, so God gave Mary a wonderful gift: at the first moment of her life, God kept her from having Original Sin on her soul. He gave to her what Adam had lost for everyone—His life, the life of grace.

3. Read paragraph 2 with the children, telling them that Mary's soul was "full of grace." When Mary first began to live, hidden in the womb of her mother, Saint Anne, her soul was spotless, as though she had been baptized at that very moment. No other human person received this special gift. In fact, there is a special word to describe Mary's soul: it was *immaculate.* Ask the children if they know the meaning of this word; help them to understand that it means pure and spotless. Mary is called the Immaculate Conception.

4. Mary was the daughter of Saints Joachim and Anne. They were waiting for the Savior and preparing for His coming prayerfully and obediently. They raised her to be a loving, obedient, and faithful young woman. They lived together in a town called Nazareth.

5. Mary did not know that she was to be the Mother of the Savior. Like many other people of her day, she was waiting patiently and preparing well for the Savior. Mary did not have Original Sin on her soul; she never sinned. Because she was filled with grace, everything she did made God happy.

Reinforce

1. On p. 33 of the *Activity Book* (see *Teacher's Manual*, p. 111), have the children fill in the blanks for the Hail Mary. They can use p. 39 of their textbook as a guide (see *Teacher's Manual*, p. 107).

2. Teach the song "Immaculate Mary," *Adoremus Hymnal*, #532, reminding the children that immaculate means spotless and pure.

Conclude

Ask the children to turn to the We Pray section of their textbooks for this chapter (see *Teacher's Manual*, p. 107). Have them begin learning the Hail Mary, concentrating on the first line: "Hail Mary, full of grace!"

9   Mary Hears Some Wonderful News

"Behold, I am the handmaid of the Lord;
let it be to me according to your word."
Luke 1:38

Finally, the time came for the Savior to come into the world. There was one last thing to get ready.

There was a girl named Mary. **Mary** lived in a town called **Nazareth**. God loved her so much that He gave her the gift of grace that Adam had lost for everyone else. Mary was free from Original Sin from the very first moment of her life. She loved God so much that in her whole life she never committed even one single sin. Everything she did made God happy.

When Mary grew up, God sent the angel **Gabriel** to visit her. Gabriel told Mary some wonderful news. He said that God wanted her to be the Mother of His Son, the promised Savior.

37

Mary trusted that God knew what was best. So Mary said, "I am God's servant. Let it be done to me as you say." That is how Mary became the Mother of **Jesus**.

God's very own Son came down from Heaven to live with us. God also chose a special man named **Joseph** to be Mary's husband and to take care of Jesus. Since God is the real father of Jesus, we call Joseph the foster-father of Jesus.

Words to Know:

Mary   Nazareth   Gabriel   Jesus   Joseph

38

OUR LADY OF LOURDES AND THE IMMACULATE CONCEPTION

In 1858 our Lady appeared to fourteen-year-old Bernadette Soubiroux in Lourdes, France. As she was crossing the River Gave, Bernadette saw a beautiful lady standing above her in the hollow of a rock. The bishop doubted the heavenly nature of her visions, so on his prompting she asked the lady her name and was told, "I am the Immaculate Conception." This dogma had been declared only four years before and Bernadette was a poor girl who had no knowledge of such matters, so the bishop knew it was indeed the Queen of Heaven. A miraculous spring appeared that today still cures the sick. The feast of Our Lady of Lourdes is February 11. Also see p. 315 of this manual.

Preview

In our next lesson, we will learn how Mary came to be the Mother of the Savior.

CHAPTER NINE: MARY HEARS SOME WONDERFUL NEWS
LESSON TWO: MARY SAYS YES TO GOD

Aims

Students will be able to relate the story of the Annunciation.

They will understand how Mary is God's perfect "hand-maid."

They will be able to explain that Mary's yes to God replaces Adam and Eve's no in the Garden of Eden.

They will be able to identify Saint Joseph as the husband of Mary and the foster-father of Jesus.

Materials

- Children's Bible

- *Activity Book*, p. 34

Optional:
- Appendix, p. B-18, The Annunciation

- "Immaculate Mary," *Adoremus Hymnal*, #532

Begin

Remind the children that as Mary grew up, she was preparing for the coming of the Savior. Let them give examples of how she was obedient, prayerful, and loving.

Develop

1. Read paragraphs 3 and 4 with the children. Then read the account of the Annunciation from the children's Bible (Lk 1:26–38). Tell the students that Mary was afraid when the angel came to visit her. She did not understand how she would become the Mother of God, but she showed her faith when she agreed to do as He asked.

2. Have the children look at the painting, *Annunciation,* by Lippi on p. 36 of their text and ask the following questions:
- Who are the two main characters in the painting? (Mary and the angel Gabriel)
- Who is in the top left hand corner of the page? (the rays of light are a representation of God the Father)
- Who does the bird in the picture represent? (the Holy Spirit, sent to Mary to make her the Mother of God)
- What is happening in the picture? (the angel Gabriel has asked Mary to be the Mother of God; Mary has said yes; God the Father has sent the Holy Spirit to Mary so that Jesus will begin to live in her)

- What is Mary wearing? (a blue robe—traditionally, blue is the color of the Blessed Mother)
- Why is the angel kneeling before Mary? (because as the Mother of God and "full of grace," she is God's greatest creature, even greater than the brightest angel)
- What is the book in front of Mary? (perhaps a book of Old Testament prophecies that Mary was studying and praying when the angel Gabriel came to visit her)
- How does Mary look? (not afraid anymore as when the angel first appeared; very peaceful—how people are when they do what God asks them to do)
- What flower is the angel Gabriel holding? (a lily, which is a symbol of purity and a sign of her immaculate and pure soul)

3. Read paragraph 5 with the children. Explain that since Jesus is the Son of God, he did not have a father here on earth to take care of Him. God wanted someone who was very good to take care of Mary and Jesus. He chose Saint Joseph to be Mary's husband and the foster-father of Jesus.

Reinforce

1. On p. 34 of the *Activity Book* (see *Teacher's Manual,* p. 111) there is a short skit for pairs of children. Boys can be the angel Gabriel, girls can be our Lady.

2. You may want to pass out copies of Appendix, p. B-18, The Annunciation, for the children to color.

Note: Appendix, p. B-18 is the first of the Joyful Mysteries coloring pages. These pages may be photocopied and passed out for the children to color as each Mystery is learned and discussed. Once all five have been completed, the pages may be stapled together to form a Rosary booklet. The same can be done with the Sorrowful and Glorious Mysteries when they are taught.

Conclude

1. Practice the Hail Mary (see *Teacher's Manual,* p. 107), concentrating on the words of the angel Gabriel to Mary: "Hail Mary, full of grace! The Lord is with thee."

2. Sing "Immaculate Mary," *Adoremus Hymnal,* #532.

9   Mary Hears Some Wonderful News

"Behold, I am the handmaid of the Lord;
let it be to me according to your word."
Luke 1:38

Finally, the time came for the Savior to come into the world. There was one last thing to get ready.

There was a girl named Mary. **Mary** lived in a town called **Nazareth**. God loved her so much that He gave her the gift of grace that Adam had lost for everyone else. Mary was free from Original Sin from the very first moment of her life. She loved God so much that in her whole life she never committed even one single sin. Everything she did made God happy.

When Mary grew up, God sent the angel **Gabriel** to visit her. Gabriel told Mary some wonderful news. He said that God wanted her to be the Mother of His Son, the promised Savior.

37

Mary trusted that God knew what was best. So Mary said, "I am God's servant. Let it be done to me as you say." That is how Mary became the Mother of **Jesus**.

God's very own Son came down from Heaven to live with us. God also chose a special man named **Joseph** to be Mary's husband and to take care of Jesus. Since God is the real father of Jesus, we call Joseph the foster-father of Jesus.

Words to Know:

Mary   Nazareth   Gabriel   Jesus   Joseph

38

THE ANNUNCIATION AND MARY'S VIRGINITY

As the angel Gabriel foretold, the Holy Spirit entered the chaste womb of the Virgin Mary, forming the humanity of Christ. God not only preserved Mary's virginity before the birth of Christ, but during and after it, so that she is ever virgin. The Fathers of the Church describe Christ's passing from Mary's womb as a light passes through a window; her perpetual virginity is part of Church teaching and is found in the Creed. The Incarnation did not necessitate this exception from the laws of nature; however, it was only fitting that the Mother of God should be pure and chaste in a perfect way. Mary's virginity in no way signifies that spousal conjugal relations are unchaste; it emphasizes instead her complete dedication to God. This feast is celebrated on March 25.

THE ANNUNCIATION
Luke 1:26–38

Preview

In our next lesson, we will learn about Mary's visit to her cousin, Saint Elizabeth.

CHAPTER NINE: MARY HEARS SOME WONDERFUL NEWS
LESSON THREE: MARY, OUR MODEL

Aims

Students will listen to the story of Mary's visit to her cousin, Elizabeth.

They will learn that some of the words of the Hail Mary come from the angel Gabriel and from Saint Elizabeth.

They will see Mary's thoughtful behavior as a model for their own.

Materials

- Children's Bible

- *Activity Book*, p. 35

Optional:
- Appendix, p. B-19, The Visitation

- "Immaculate Mary," *Adoremus Hymnal*, #532

Begin

The angel Gabriel told Mary that her cousin, Elizabeth, was also expecting a baby. This was a great surprise to Mary because Elizabeth and her husband Zechariah were very old and had waited many, many years for a child (as Abraham and Sarah did). Today they will learn more about Mary's cousin and her baby.

Develop

1. Read, again, the passage where the angel Gabriel informs Mary that Saint Elizabeth is expecting a child (Lk 1:36–38). Gabriel gives Mary this news in order to help her to believe that all things are possible with God, even that she, Mary, could be the Mother of the Savior.

2. Tell the children that after the angel Gabriel leaves Mary—having secured her yes to God—the very next passage in the Bible tells us that Mary made a journey to visit her cousin, Elizabeth, who lived in the hill country a few days' journey from Nazareth. Point out to the children that this is an amazing thing, for Mary has just learned that she is soon to be the Mother of the Savior, He for whom the people have been waiting and preparing for hundreds of years. You might expect her to stay at home and begin preparations for her own wonderful child, but Mary does not do this. Encourage them to listen carefully to the story.

3. Read aloud the passage of the Visitation (Lk 1:39–56) from your children's Bible. Point out that not only did Mary visit Saint Elizabeth, but she also went "in haste" to visit and assist her. Remind the children that Saint Elizabeth was an older woman in need of help. Mary is a wonderful example of how all people should think more of others than of themselves. Mary is a good model for everyone.

4. When our Lady arrived at her cousin's home, Saint Elizabeth came out saying: "How is it that the Mother of my Lord should come to visit me?" How did Saint Elizabeth know that the Savior was hidden in Mary's womb? Somehow God gave her this knowledge.

5. Saint Elizabeth greeted the Blessed Mother with a beautiful prayer. Reread the words of Saint Elizabeth and ask if anyone recognizes them. Tell the children that some of Saint Elizabeth's words are in the Hail Mary.

Reinforce

1. Have the children give short answers to the questions on p. 35 of the *Activity Book* (see *Teacher's Manual*, p. 111), using their textbook as a guide.

2. If they have been working on their Rosary booklets, you may want to pass out copies of Appendix, p. B-19, The Visitation, for the children to color at this time.

Conclude

1. Practice the Hail Mary with the children.

2. Read Questions 22 and 23 with the class. Then give time for pairs of students to work on memorization.

3. Sing "Immaculate Mary," *Adoremus Hymnal*, #532.

Mary trusted that God knew what was best. So Mary said, "I am God's servant. Let it be done to me as you say." That is how Mary became the Mother of **Jesus**.

God's very own Son came down from Heaven to live with us. God also chose a special man named **Joseph** to be Mary's husband and to take care of Jesus. Since God is the real father of Jesus, we call Joseph the foster-father of Jesus.

Words to Know:

Mary   Nazareth   Gabriel   Jesus   Joseph

38

Q. 22 *Who is the Mother of Jesus, the Savior?* Mary is the Mother of Jesus, the Savior (CCC 488).

Q. 23 *Was Mary kept from having Original Sin?* Yes, Mary was kept from having Original Sin (CCC 491).

We Pray:

HAIL MARY

Hail Mary, full of grace! The Lord is with thee. Blessed art thou among women, and blessed is the fruit of your womb, Jesus.
Holy Mary, Mother of God, pray for us sinners, now and at the hour of our death. *Amen.*

GLORY BE

Glory be to the Father, and to the Son, and to the Holy Spirit, as it was in the beginning, is now, and ever shall be, world without end. *Amen.*

39

THE VISITATION AND SAINT ELIZABETH

When Saint Elizabeth heard Mary's greeting, her baby, filled, like his mother, with the Holy Spirit, "leaped for joy" in her womb, as if to acknowledge the presence of his Lord. At that moment, the prophecy was fulfilled that the child should "be filled with the Holy Spirit, even from his Mother's womb." Because the presence of sin is incompatible with the indwelling of the Holy Spirit in the soul, it follows that at this moment, John was cleansed from the stain of Original Sin. Thus Saint John the Baptist was conceived with, but born without, Original Sin.

PROPHECY TO ZECHARIAH

"Do not be afraid, Zechariah, for your prayer is heard, and your wife Elizabeth will bear you a son, and you shall call his name John. And you will have joy and gladness, and many will rejoice at his birth; for he will be great before the Lord, and he shall drink no wine nor strong drink, and he will be filled with the Holy Spirit, even from his mother's womb. And he will turn many of the sons of Israel to the Lord their God."

—Luke 1:13–16

"And you, child, will be called the prophet of the Most High; for you will go before the Lord to prepare his ways, to give knowledge of salvation to his people in the forgiveness of their sins."

—Luke 1:76–77

THE VISITATION
Luke 1:39–56

Preview

In the next lesson, we will learn about Mary's special devotion: the Rosary.

CHAPTER NINE: MARY HEARS SOME WONDERFUL NEWS
LESSON FOUR: THE ROSARY IS MARY'S PRAYER

Aims

Students will learn about the Rosary, our lady's prayer.

They will realize that since Jesus is their brother and Mary is His Mother, she is their Mother as well.

They will understand that the Rosary teaches about the lives of Jesus and Mary.

They will begin to pray the Rosary.

Materials

- Plastic rosaries for each child

- *Activity Book*, p. 36

Optional:
- "Immaculate Mary," *Adoremus Hymnal*, #532

Begin

Remind the children that Mary spent her entire life preparing for the Savior. Remind them also that the Church has a special time of waiting and preparation before Christmas each year. Ask them to name this season (Advent). Tell them that today they will learn about a new way to pray and prepare for the birth of Jesus.

Develop

1. Hold up a rosary so that the students can see. Point out the crucifix at the end, the short row of beads, and the longer circlet of beads. Tell them that this is a rosary, a devotion that our Lady has asked everyone to say each day.

2. Remind the children that because Jesus is their brother and Mary is His Mother, they, too, are her children. She lives in Heaven now with Jesus, and loves her children on earth very much. By staying close to her, a person will always stay close to her Son, Jesus. One way to stay close to our Lady is to pray the Rosary.

3. Pass out plastic rosaries to each of the children and let them examine them (remind them that they should treat them with reverence, i.e., do not swing or put them around their necks). Explain that the Rosary is a series of prayers that a person says with his voice while at the same time thinking about the Blessed Mother and Jesus in his heart. That sounds complicated, but it is actually not difficult. Looking at pic-

tures often helps to keep one's mind on Mary and Jesus while praying the Rosary. The class will practice doing this today.

4. Tell the class that the Rosary begins with the Joyful Mysteries. Hold your beads so they can see you move your fingers along them as you say the prayers. Announce that the first Joyful Mystery is the Annunciation, and remind them of the story. Have them turn to the first Joyful Mystery in their Rosary booklets, or place the painting of the *Annunciation* (see textbook, p. 36 on *Teacher's Manual*, p. 103) in a place where all the children can see it. Then say the Our Father and a few Hail Marys while moving your fingers along the beads. Have the children join in by saying the second half of the Hail Mary (textbook, p. 39).

5. When you are finished, have the children bless themselves with the crucifix and put the rosary beads reverently into a basket or box where they will be easily accessible.

Reinforce

1. Have the children color the rosary on p. 36 of the *Activity Book* (see *Teacher's Manual*, p. 111).

2. Give pairs of students a chance to practice their memory work with Questions 22 and 23.

Conclude

1. Encourage the students to visit a statue of our Lady on the church grounds, or have a Mary statue in the classroom at a prayer station. The children may vocalize their intentions, and all recite, "Holy Mary, pray for us."

2. Sing "Immaculate Mary," *Adoremus Hymnal*, #532. Remind the children that saying the Rosary is a wonderful devotion for Advent. It helps to put one's mind and heart on the Savior and His dear Mother.

3. Set up a Nativity Scene in the classroom, but do not add baby Jesus and the wise men until Christmas and Epiphany, respectively.

Mary trusted that God knew what was best. So Mary said, "I am God's servant. Let it be done to me as you say." That is how Mary became the Mother of **Jesus**.

God's very own Son came down from Heaven to live with us. God also chose a special man named **Joseph** to be Mary's husband and to take care of Jesus. Since God is the real father of Jesus, we call Joseph the foster-father of Jesus.

Words to Know:

Mary   Nazareth   Gabriel   Jesus   Joseph

38

Q. 22 *Who is the Mother of Jesus, the Savior?*
Mary is the Mother of Jesus, the Savior (CCC 488).

Q. 23 *Was Mary kept from having Original Sin?*
Yes, Mary was kept from having Original Sin (CCC 491).

We Pray:

HAIL MARY

Hail Mary, full of grace! The Lord is with thee. Blessed art thou among women, and blessed is the fruit of your womb, Jesus.
Holy Mary, Mother of God, pray for us sinners, now and at the hour of our death. *Amen.*

GLORY BE

Glory be to the Father, and to the Son, and to the Holy Spirit, as it was in the beginning, is now, and ever shall be, world without end. *Amen.*

39

SAINT DOMINIC AND THE ROSARY

Saint Dominic was born at Calaroga in Old Castile, Spain around the year 1170. Though tradition asserts that our Lady revealed the Rosary to him in order to combat the Albigensian heresy (see p. 121 of this manual), historical evidence shows that in the course of the twelfth century, and even before his birth, the practice of reciting 50 or 150 Hail Marys had come into general use. The date of Saint Dominic's ordination is not known, but in December 1216 the Pope granted his request to found the Order of Preachers (Dominicans) to preach against the Albigensian heresy. Dominic died on August 6, 1221; he was canonized July 13, 1234 by Gregory IX. The Feast of the Holy Rosary is October 7.

HOW TO SAY THE ROSARY

Begin with the Sign of the Cross.

On the crucifix say the Apostles' Creed.

On the first bead say the Our Father.

Say three Hail Marys.

Say a Glory Be.

Announce the Mystery.

Say the Our Father.

Say Ten Hail Marys.

Say a Glory Be.

Announce each Mystery and recite prayers until ending with the Sign of the Cross.

THE FIVE JOYFUL MYSTERIES OF THE ROSARY

1. The Annunciation
2. The Visitation
3. The Nativity
4. The Presentation
5. The Finding in the Temple

Preview

In our next lesson, we will review all that we have learned and take a quiz.

Chapter Nine: Mary Hears Some Wonderful News

Review and Assessment

Aims

To review and assess the material taught during this chapter.

Materials

- Quiz 9 (Appendix, p. A-11)
- "Immaculate Mary," *Adoremus Hymnal,* #532

Name: _____

Mary Hears Some Wonderful News   Quiz 9

Fill in the blanks. *Trace the gray letters and fill in the rest.*

Word Bank

Mary	never	angel	God	yes	Joseph

1. Mary n e v e r sinned.

2. God sent an a n g e l to Mary.

3. Mary said y e s to God.

4. M a r y is the Mother of Jesus.

5. G o d is the Father of Jesus.

6. Saint J o s e p h is the foster-father of Jesus.

Review and Enrichment

1. Review the Words to Know with the students (see *Teacher's Manual*, p. 109) and the stories of the Annunciation and the Visitation. Lastly, remind the children that God's plan for Mary was so special that He kept her from having Original Sin.

2. Play a question and answer game with the students using the following questions as models: What was Mary's soul like when she first began to live? In which town did Mary live? What was the name of the angel that God sent to Mary? What was his message? How did Mary respond? What did it mean when Mary said, "I am the handmaid of the Lord; let it be to me according to your word"? Who was Mary's husband? Was he the father of Jesus?

Assess

Pass out Quiz 9 and read through it with the children. Answer any questions they may have, then administer the quiz. Orally review the correct answers with the children once they have completed their quizzes.

Conclude

1. Reiterate the fact that because Mary is the Mother of Jesus, and He is our brother, Mary is also our Mother. We should stay close to her always; then we will never be far from her child, Jesus.

2. Sing "Immaculate Mary," *Adoremus Hymnal,* #532 and close with the Hail Mary.

Name:_____

Hail Mary

Use the following words and page 39 in your textbook to help you fill in the blanks.

death	grace	Lord
fruit	Hail	sinners
God	Holy	women
	Jesus	

<u>Hail</u> Mary, full of <u>grace</u>!

The <u>Lord</u> is with thee.

Blessed art thou

among <u>women</u>,

and blessed is the

<u>fruit</u> of thy womb, <u>Jesus</u>.

<u>Holy</u> Mary, Mother of <u>God</u>,

pray for us <u>sinners</u>,

now and at the hour of our <u>death</u>.

Amen.

Faith and Life Series • Grade 1 • Chapter 9 • Lesson 1   33

Name:_____

Here is a play for you and a friend. One of you will be Mary. The other one will be the angel Gabriel.

Mary is in her house all alone. Then the angel Gabriel comes.

Gabriel: Hail, Mary! You are full of grace. Among all women, you are most blessed. And blessed is the baby that you will have.

Mary: I don't understand. What do you mean? I'm afraid.

Gabriel: Don't be afraid, Mary. I'm an angel and God sent me from Heaven. He wants you to be the Mother of His Son.

Mary: I love God and I'll do whatever He wants.

Gabriel: Thank you, Mary. Goodbye.

Color the picture of the Annunciation.

34   *Faith and Life Series • Grade 1 • Chapter 9 • Lesson 2*

Name:_____

Answer the following questions using Chapter 9 of your textbook.

1. Where did Mary live? <u>Nazareth</u>

2. Did Mary ever sin? <u>No</u>

3. What was the name of the angel who came to visit Mary? <u>Gabriel</u>

4. What did the angel Gabriel ask Mary? <u>He asked her if she would be the Mother of God's Son.</u>

5. Did Mary accept this invitation? <u>Yes</u>

6. Who was Mary's husband? <u>Joseph</u>

Faith and Life Series • Grade 1 • Chapter 9 • Lesson 3   35

Name:_____

The Rosary

Color the Our Father beads red, and the Hail Mary beads blue.

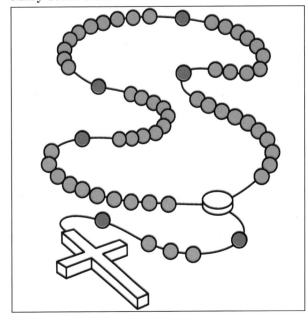

When we say the Rosary, we honor Jesus' Mother, Mary, and we stay close to both Jesus and Mary.

36   *Faith and Life Series • Grade 1 • Chapter 9 • Lesson 4*

TEACHER'S NOTES

CHAPTER TEN
THE SAVIOR IS BORN

Catechism of the Catholic Church References

The Christmas Mystery: 525–26
Humility of Our Lord's Nativity: 525
Mysteries of Christ's Infancy: 527–30, 563

Promise of a Redeemer: 410–12, 420–21
True God and True Man: 464–83
Why the Word Became Flesh: 456–60

Scripture References

The Birth of Christ: Mt 1:18–25; Lk 2:1–20
Isaiah's Prophecy regarding Christ: Is 9:2a
Savior Is Born: Lk 2:12

Joseph and Mary's Journey to Bethlehem: Lk 2:1–5
The Separation of Sheep and Goats: Mt 25:31–40

Background Reading: *The Fundamentals of Catholicism* by Fr. Kenneth Baker, S.J.

Volume 1:
The Incarnation and Nativity, pp. 55–64

Volume 2:
True God and True Man, pp. 197–225
"Why Did God Become Man?", pp. 269–72

Summary of Lesson Content

Lesson 1

Mary and Joseph obeyed the decree of Caesar Augustus and made the difficult journey to Bethlehem.

Christ was born in a stable and laid in a manger because there was no room at the inn.

By helping those in need, we express our love for Christ.

Lesson 2

The Savior did not come into the world as a worldly king, but in great humility.

His first visitors, who recognized Him as the Savior and came to worship Him, were only humble shepherds.

The third Joyful Mystery is the Nativity.

Lesson 3

Jesus is both true God and true man; this is a mystery of the Catholic Faith.

Jesus was born to save the world from sin and to open the gates of Heaven.

Jesus is the "Light of the World."

Lesson 4

Christmas trees, Christmas lights, presents, and special foods are just some of the things associated with Christmas.

The best gift to Jesus on Christmas is a loving heart offered to Him at Holy Mass.

CHAPTER TEN: THE SAVIOR IS BORN
LESSON ONE: NO ROOM AT THE INN

Aims

Students will be able to relate the events leading up to the birth of Christ.

They will understand that by helping people in need, they are expressing their love for Jesus.

Materials

- Map of the Mediterranean, including Italy, the Holy Land, and Egypt

- Children's Bible

- *Activity Book*, p. 37

Optional:
- "Away in a manger," *Adoremus Hymnal*, #336

Begin

Remind the children that Mary became the Mother of the Savior because she loved God and had faith in Him. Before Jesus was born, Mary and Joseph had difficulties, but they never doubted God. Today the class will learn about the difficult journey Joseph and Mary had to make before the Savior was born.

Develop

1. Read paragraphs 1 and 2 with the children. Tell them that the Emperor of Rome ruled the land in which Mary and Joseph lived. Show them where Rome is on the map, and then where the Holy Land is, specifically Nazareth, the home of Mary and Joseph. Just before Jesus was born, Caesar ordered that a census be taken; a census is a counting of all the people. Every family had to travel to the city of their ancestors and write their names in an official book. Even though Mary was about to give birth to the Savior of the world, she and Joseph did as Caesar commanded and went to the the town of Bethlehem. Show the children where Bethlehem is on the map.

2. Ask the children to imagine what Mary and Joseph's journey to Bethlehem must have been like.

3. Read the story of Joseph and Mary's reception in Bethlehem from your children's Bible (Lk 2:1–5). Help the students to see that people from all over the Holy Land were travelling to their home towns, so there were not enough inns to accommodate them all. Therefore, Joseph and Mary had only a stable to stay in at night.

4. Tell the children that the innkeeper is a good example for all people. Jesus asks those who love Him to help anyone who needs it, even if they are strangers, just like the innkeeper did. In this case the strangers were the Holy Family. You may read about this idea of helping others from your children's Bible (Mt 25:31–40).

5. Building upon the passage from Matthew, help the children think of examples of how they can feed the hungry and give drink to the thirsty: give a younger sibling a glass of water, share your lunch with someone at school who has forgotten his, etc. Whenever they do any of these good acts for the love of Jesus, they please Him very much. Advent is a time when everyone should try especially hard to do these kinds of good deeds and sacrifices.

Reinforce

1. Students should color the map of the Holy Land on p. 37 of the *Activity Book* (see *Teacher's Manual*, p. 123). Keep this map to use in Chapter 12.

2. Help the children to memorize Question 24 (see *Teacher's Manual*, p. 121).

3. You may want to read *The Donkey's Dream*, by Barbara Helen Berger, a lovely story told by the donkey that carried Mary to Bethlehem.

Conclude

1. Teach the children an appropriate Christmas carol, such as "Away in a manger," *Adoremus Hymnal*, #336.

2. Pray the Hail Mary (see *Teacher's Manual*, p. 367).

10   The Savior Is Born

"...you will find a baby wrapped in
swaddling cloths and lying in a manger."
Luke 2:12

One day, Mary and Joseph had to travel to **Bethlehem**. They looked and looked for a place to stay, but every inn was full and no one took them in. So they had to stay in a stable, a place where animals are kept.

This is where Jesus was born. Since Mary had no cradle for Him, she laid Him in a **manger**. A manger is a wooden box used to hold food for animals. The Son of God, our Savior, came here to earth as a poor, tiny, helpless baby.

Angels from Heaven appeared in the sky. They sang, "Glory to God in the highest. Peace on earth to men of good will."

Some **shepherds**—men who take care of sheep—saw the angels. The shepherds were afraid. "Do

41

not be afraid," said the angels. "We have good news for you and for all people. Today in Bethlehem a Savior has been born! You will find Him lying in a manger." Then the angels left.

The shepherds were amazed. They said, "Let us go to Bethlehem and see this Child about whom the angels have spoken."

The shepherds hurried away and found Jesus, Mary, and Joseph. They knelt down to **worship** their Savior. To worship means to give your best love and praise to God. The shepherds remembered to thank God the Father for sending us His Son.

Christmas is the birthday of Jesus. This is an important day because if Jesus had not come, we could not go to Heaven, ever. There would be no Christmas trees, no presents, no Christmas lights, and no Christmas songs—nothing to make you happy. But Jesus did come and we have a wonderful time every year when we celebrate His birthday.

42

AN ADVENT PREPARATION

Bring a small Christmas tree to the classroom. Each day (or as often as you wish) hand out ornaments for the students to color, cut, and hang on the tree. Before putting these on the tree, each student should write what he has done or will do to prepare for Jesus. You might write examples on the board so that the children will have something to which they can refer (help my parents, pray, clean my room, etc.) By Christmas, the tree should be full of ornaments for Jesus.

Preview

In our next lesson, we will learn about the birth of the Savior in Bethlehem.

CHAPTER TEN: THE SAVIOR IS BORN
LESSON TWO: THE NATIVITY

Aims

Students will be able to relate the story of the first Christmas.

They will be able to explain that the Savior came in humility and meekness to save the world from sin and to open the gates of Heaven.

They will learn that the third Joyful Mystery of the Rosary is the Nativity.

Materials

• Children's Bible

• *Activity Book*, p. 38

Optional:
• Appendix, p. B-15, Nativity Diorama

• Appendix, p. B-20, The Nativity

• "Away in a manger," *Adoremus Hymnal*, #336

Begin

Remind the children that in the last lesson they learned why Mary and Joseph were in Bethlehem far from their home when Jesus was born and why He was born in a stable, a place where animals are kept. In this lesson, the class will learn about what happened the night Jesus was born.

Develop

1. Read paragraphs 3, 4, 5, and 6 with the children.

2. Have the students study the painting of the Nativity on p. 40 of their textbook. Ask the following questions:
   • Where is the painting set? (the stable in Bethlehem)
   • Who is the baby in the painting? (Jesus, the Son of God)
   • In what is He lying? (a manger, a feeding box for animals)
   • Who is kneeling before Him? (Mary, His Mother)
   • How does she look? (filled with happiness at the birth of her son, the Savior)
   • Who is the man behind the Blessed Mother in the stable? (Saint Joseph, who is her husband and the foster-father of Jesus)
   • With whom is he talking at the door? (one of the shepherds)
   • To whom is Saint Joseph pointing? Why? (to the baby Jesus; the shepherds have just explained that angels told them to go and see this wonderful child)

   • What animal is looking down at the baby Jesus? (an ox)
   • Who is the baby Jesus looking at so intently? (His Mother, who has brought Him into the world because she said yes to God)

3. Read the story of the Nativity from your children's Bible (Mt 1:18–25 or Lk 2:1–20).

4. Point out that the first people to hear of the Savior's birth were not important, powerful people like kings or wealthy men, but shepherds, poor men who tended sheep. The angels visited them and told them to go to the stable where they would find the baby Jesus. Our Lord came into the world just as poor as these people were. He came in great humility, not pride or wealth or power. In doing so, He taught that everyone must be humble.

Reinforce

1. Assign p. 38 of the *Activity Book* (see *Teacher's Manual*, p. 123). See Appendix, p. B-15 for diorama patterns of the Nativity as an alternate activity.

2. If they have been working on them, have the children color the third Joyful Mystery, the Nativity, for their Rosary booklets, Appendix, p. B-20.

Conclude

1. Review Question 24 with the class (see *Teacher's Manual*, p. 121).

2. Sing together "Away in a manger," *Adoremus Hymnal*, #336.

3. You may want to say the third Joyful Mystery of the Rosary, the Nativity. The children can look at the painting of the Nativity in their textbooks to aid them in meditation.

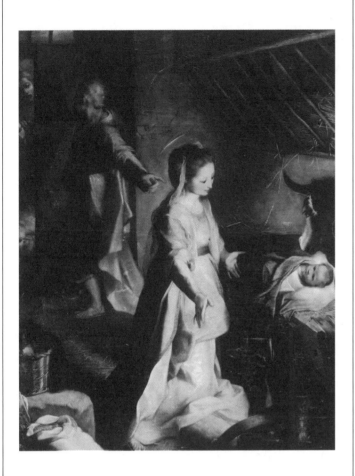

10   The Savior Is Born

"...you will find a baby wrapped in
swaddling cloths and lying in a manger."
Luke 2:12

One day, Mary and Joseph had to travel to **Bethlehem**. They looked and looked for a place to stay, but every inn was full and no one took them in. So they had to stay in a stable, a place where animals are kept.

This is where Jesus was born. Since Mary had no cradle for Him, she laid Him in a **manger**. A manger is a wooden box used to hold food for animals. The Son of God, our Savior, came here to earth as a poor, tiny, helpless baby.

Angels from Heaven appeared in the sky. They sang, "Glory to God in the highest. Peace on earth to men of good will."

Some **shepherds**—men who take care of sheep —saw the angels. The shepherds were afraid. "Do

41

not be afraid," said the angels. "We have good news for you and for all people. Today in Bethlehem a Savior has been born! You will find Him lying in a manger." Then the angels left.

The shepherds were amazed. They said, "Let us go to Bethlehem and see this Child about whom the angels have spoken."

The shepherds hurried away and found Jesus, Mary, and Joseph. They knelt down to **worship** their Savior. To worship means to give your best love and praise to God. The shepherds remembered to thank God the Father for sending us His Son.

Christmas is the birthday of Jesus. This is an important day because if Jesus had not come, we could not go to Heaven, ever. There would be no Christmas trees, no presents, no Christmas lights, and no Christmas songs—nothing to make you happy. But Jesus did come and we have a wonderful time every year when we celebrate His birthday.

42

SAINT FRANCIS AND THE NATIVITY SCENE

Saint Francis was born into a wealthy family in Assisi, Umbria (present-day Italy), around the year 1181. According to a legend that dates from the fifteenth century, he was born in a stable like our Lord. As a young man he enjoyed music, fine clothes, and showy display. He soon embraced poverty and founded the Franciscan Order in 1209 by permission of Pope Innocent III. During Christmastime of 1223 the saint reproduced in a church at Greccio a manger scene, laicizing an ecclesiastical custom. He has thus come to be regarded as the person responsible for popularizing devotion to the Crib. He died October 3, 1226; he was canonized by Gregory IX on July 16, 1228; his feast day is October 4.

THE NATIVITY
Matthew 1:18–25   Luke 2:1–20

Preview

In our next lesson, we will learn about Jesus, the Savior, and how He is both God and man.

CHAPTER TEN: THE SAVIOR IS BORN
LESSON THREE: SON OF GOD, SON OF MARY

Aims

Students will be able to explain that Jesus is both God and man.

They will know that this a mystery of faith that no one can fully understand.

They will be able to define the Savior's mission: to save man from sin and to regain Heaven for everyone.

They will understand what it means to call Jesus the "Light of the World."

Materials

- *Activity Book*, p. 39

Optional:
- A book of collected paintings of the Nativity

- "Away in a manger," *Adoremus Hymnal*, #336.

Begin

Remind the students of the sin of Adam and Eve, and review the consequences of this first sin for everyone except the Blessed Mother. Help them to see how deeply man needed a Savior to rescue him from sin and to reopen the gates of Heaven.

Develop

1. Explain to the students that because Jesus had a human Mother, Mary, He was truly human. He was born as a baby just like every other human, dependent on His Mother and foster-father for food, clothing, shelter, love, and education.

2. Ask the children to tell you who the father of Jesus is. It is not Saint Joseph—he was our Lord's foster-father. Jesus' Father is God the Father, the First Person of the Blessed Trinity.

3. Summarize what they have just learned: Jesus the Savior is both human and divine (God). Tell them that this is a mystery of the Catholic Faith that no one can completely understand. In the natural world, for instance, a tree is not also a bear, nor is a fish also a cat. But in the case of our Savior, God worked a marvelous miracle so that He was both God and man in one Divine Person: Jesus (see facing page).

4. Ask the children to look again at the painting on p. 40 of their textbooks. Ask them if they can locate a bright light in the picture. Help them to locate the light coming from the baby Jesus as a symbol of his being God.

5. Mention Isaiah's prophecy: "The people who walked in darkness have seen a great light" (Is 9:2a). Explain that everyone walked in the darkness of sin from the time of Adam and Eve until the coming of the Savior (except Mary). Then, when the Savior was born into the world, it was as though a bright light began to shine. He had come to save man from the darkness of Adam's sin; thus Jesus is called the "Light of the World."

6. Reread paragraph 6 of the textbook that tells how the shepherds arrived at the stable and knelt down to worship the Christ Child in the manger.

Reinforce

1. Study Questions 25 and 26 together as a group (see *Teacher's Manual*, p. 121). Separate the students into pairs to memorize the answers.

2. Have the children complete the word search on p. 39 of the *Activity Book* (see *Teacher's Manual*, p. 123).

3. If you have not already assigned it, you may have the children color the Nativity in their Joyful Mysteries of the Rosary booklet.

4. Obtain a book of collected Nativity paintings and have the children view these. Help them to compare and contrast them with each other and the painting they studied in their textbook. Discuss the various aspects of the first Christmas as different artists highlight them.

Conclude

1. Sing "Away in a manger," *Adoremus Hymnal*, #336.

2. Pray the third Joyful Mystery of the Rosary.

10   The Savior Is Born

"...you will find a baby wrapped in
swaddling cloths and lying in a manger."
Luke 2:12

One day, Mary and Joseph had to travel to **Bethlehem**. They looked and looked for a place to stay, but every inn was full and no one took them in. So they had to stay in a stable, a place where animals are kept.

This is where Jesus was born. Since Mary had no cradle for Him, she laid Him in a **manger**. A manger is a wooden box used to hold food for animals. The Son of God, our Savior, came here to earth as a poor, tiny, helpless baby.

Angels from Heaven appeared in the sky. They sang, "Glory to God in the highest. Peace on earth to men of good will."

Some **shepherds**—men who take care of sheep —saw the angels. The shepherds were afraid. "Do

41

not be afraid," said the angels. "We have good news for you and for all people. Today in Bethlehem a Savior has been born! You will find Him lying in a manger." Then the angels left.

The shepherds were amazed. They said, "Let us go to Bethlehem and see this Child about whom the angels have spoken."

The shepherds hurried away and found Jesus, Mary, and Joseph. They knelt down to **worship** their Savior. To worship means to give your best love and praise to God. The shepherds remembered to thank God the Father for sending us His Son.

Christmas is the birthday of Jesus. This is an important day because if Jesus had not come, we could not go to Heaven, ever. There would be no Christmas trees, no presents, no Christmas lights, and no Christmas songs—nothing to make you happy. But Jesus did come and we have a wonderful time every year when we celebrate His birthday.

42

THE LIGHT OF THE PASCHAL CANDLE

The blessing of the paschal candle takes place during the Holy Saturday Vigil. While a prayer is chanted, the candle is ornamented with five grains of incense. It is then lighted with the newly blessed fire and plunged three times into the baptismal font. The paschal candle signifies Christ, "the true light that enlightens every man" (Jn 1:9). The five grains of incense set cross-wise in it recall the wounds retained in Christ's glorified body. The wax, often produced by virgin bees, symbolizes the pure flesh which Christ derived from His Blessed Mother, the wick is emblematic of Christ's human soul, while the flame represents His divinity. The lighting of the candle serves as an image of the Resurrection.

SPEAKING OF CHRIST

Who is Christ? A Divine Person.
What is Christ? God and man.
Christ is two natures in one Person,
the Second Person of the Blessed Trinity.

Preview

In our next lesson, we will learn about some Christmas traditions that help us to celebrate the birth of Jesus.

CHAPTER TEN: THE SAVIOR IS BORN
LESSON FOUR: THE CELEBRATION OF CHRISTMAS

Aims

Students will learn about several Christmas traditions.

They will understand that the best gift they can give Jesus is a loving heart at Christmas Mass.

Materials

- Two wrapped boxes—one in birthday paper, one in Christmas paper

- *Activity Book*, p. 40

Optional:
- A statue or ornament of Santa Claus kneeling at the manger

- "Nicholas: The Boy Who Became Santa," video, CCC of America, available through Ignatius Press

- "Away in a manger," *Adoremus Hymnal*, #336

Begin

Show the children the birthday present and ask them to tell you what it is and when they would receive or give such a package (on their birthday or that of a friend). Then show them the Christmas present and ask them on whose birthday they would give or receive a present such as this one (on Christmas, the birthday of Jesus). In this lesson the class will consider the meaning of Christmas presents and other traditions that are part of Christmas.

Develop

1. Read paragraph 7 with the children. This paragraph lists a few of the things that we associate with Christmas: trees, lights, carols, presents. List these on the chalkboard and let children add other items such as special foods and crafts.

2. Ask the children if any of their families have their Christmas tree yet. The Christmas tree reminds people of the Tree of Life in the Garden of Eden. It also reminds people of the Cross upon which Jesus died to save man from sin. The trees are decorated with Christian symbols, like lights (Jesus is the Light of the World), and ornaments which remind us of Christmas stories.

3. Discuss the custom of singing Christmas carols. They remind everyone of the angels who sang praises to God on the first Christmas when they announced the birth of the baby Jesus to the shepherds.

4. Ask the students if any of them have given up certain foods during Advent as a way of preparing their hearts for the birth of the Savior (e.g., candy, cookies, etc.). Many families engage in baking and cooking in the days leading up to Christmas, so that when Christmas arrives they will be able to celebrate with the foods that they enjoy and have denied themselves during Advent.

5. Remind the children that Christmas is Jesus' birthday. It is good to have a present for the infant Jesus. During Advent everyone prepares his heart for Christ's birth by doing acts of kindness and sacrifice.

Reinforce

1. If possible, show the children a small statue, ornament, or picture of Santa Claus kneeling at the Christ Child's manger. This is an image that has been popularized in recent years as a way of putting Santa Claus and Christmas presents into the proper perspective. The video about Saint Nicholas also ends with this image. Discuss the meaning of this image with the children.

2. Have the children draw their own picture of Santa kneeling before the Christ Child on p. 40 of the *Activity Book* (see *Teacher's Manual*, p. 123).

3. You may want to show the video "Nicholas: The Boy Who Became Santa" (available through Ignatius Press; 30 minutes).

4. Discuss the Albigensian heresy (see facing page). Discuss how Christmas (God becoming man) testifies to the goodness of God and the material world He created and redeemed.

Conclude

1. Sing together "Away in a manger," *Adoremus Hymnal*, #336.

2. Pray together the prayer found on p. 43 of the student text.

not be afraid," said the angels. "We have good news for you and for all people. Today in Bethlehem a Savior has been born! You will find Him lying in a manger." Then the angels left.

The shepherds were amazed. They said, "Let us go to Bethlehem and see this Child about whom the angels have spoken."

The shepherds hurried away and found Jesus, Mary, and Joseph. They knelt down to **worship** their Savior. To worship means to give your best love and praise to God. The shepherds remembered to thank God the Father for sending us His Son.

Christmas is the birthday of Jesus. This is an important day because if Jesus had not come, we could not go to Heaven, ever. There would be no Christmas trees, no presents, no Christmas lights, and no Christmas songs—nothing to make you happy. But Jesus did come and we have a wonderful time every year when we celebrate His birthday.

42

Bethlehem   manger   shepherds   worship

Christmas

Q. 24 *Where was Jesus Christ born?*
Jesus Christ was born in a stable in Bethlehem, and was placed in a manger (CCC 525; Lk 2:7).

Q. 25 *Who is Jesus Christ?*
Jesus Christ is the Second Person of the Blessed Trinity, the Son of God made man (CCC 454, 495).

Q. 26 *Why did the Son of God become man?*
The Son of God became man to save us from sin and to regain Heaven for us (CCC 457–60).

We Pray:

Thank You, dear Jesus, for coming down from Heaven to save us. Thank You for Christmas time. Help us to get ready for Your coming this year. *Amen.*

43

SAINT NICHOLAS AND SANTA CLAUS

Though one of the most popular saints in the Church, little is known about Saint Nicholas except that he was born in Parara, a city of Lycia in Asia Minor, and that he was the bishop of Myra in the fourth century. His relics are preserved today in the church of San Nicola in Bari, Italy. He is the patron saint of mariners, merchants, bakers, travelers, and children, and his feast day is December 6. Tradition asserts that he became well-known during his life for giving generous gifts to many people, including the poor. In the United States he is identified with Santa Claus, the jolly man in a red suit who brings presents to children every Christmas Eve.

THE ALBIGENSIAN HERESY

The Albigensians were a sect that flourished in southern France in the twelfth and thirteenth centuries. They believed in the co-existence of two mutually opposed principles, one good, and the other evil. They held that the good principle was the creator of the spiritual world, while the latter was the creator of the material world. This dualism was also the basis of their moral teaching, for they taught that man is a living contradiction. Hence, suicide was commendable for it was a liberation of the soul from its captivity in the body. They taught that this liberation was the true end of man's existence, and that the resurrection of the body would not take place, since by its nature all flesh is evil. Also see p. 109 of this manual.

DECEMBER SIXTH CUSTOMS

Every year on the night of December 5, Saint Nicholas passes through towns in Germany, Switzerland, and the Netherlands and leaves coins or other small gifts for the children to discover the next day, which is his feast day.

Preview

In our next lesson, we will review what we have learned in this chapter and take a quiz.

CHAPTER TEN: THE SAVIOR IS BORN
REVIEW AND ASSESSMENT

Aims

To review and assess what has been learned in this chapter.

Materials

- Appendix, p. B-1
- Quiz 10 (Appendix, p. A-12)
- "Away in a manger," *Adoremus Hymnal*, #336

Review and Enrichment

1. In a large group, have the children retell the story of the birth of our Lord. Encourage them to include all the details they can remember.

2. Review Questions 24, 25, and 26 with the children and the Words to Know (see *Teacher's Manual*, p. 121) by playing Bible Baseball or Tic-Tac-Toe (see Appendix, p. B-1).

Name: _____

The Savior is Born   **Quiz 10**

Fill in the blanks. *Trace the gray letters and fill in the rest.*

Word Bank

Jesus	no	baby	went
sang	Mary	was	

1. __Mary__ and Joseph went to Bethlehem.

2. There was __no__ room for them at the inn.

3. Jesus __was__ born in a stable.

4. Mary laid __baby__ Jesus in a manger.

5. Angels __sang__ , "Glory to God."

6. The shepherds __went__ to see Jesus.

7. __Jesus__ is the Savior of the world.

Assess

1. Pass out Quiz 10 and read through it with the children. Answer any questions which they might have.

2. After they have finished, review the correct answers with the children.

Conclude

1. Sing an appropriate Christmas carol, such as "Away in a manger," *Adoremus Hymnal*, #336.

2. Pray the prayer on p. 43 of the student text (see *Teacher's Manual*, p. 121).

3. If a Nativity scene has been set up in your church, take the children for a visit, or encourage them to go with their parents. Remind the children that the baby Jesus will not be in the manger until Christmas.

CHAPTER TEN: THE SAVIOR IS BORN
ACTIVITY BOOK ANSWER KEYS

Name:_____

The Holy Land

On this map of the Holy Land, color the land brown and the sea blue. Then draw a star on the city where Jesus was born.

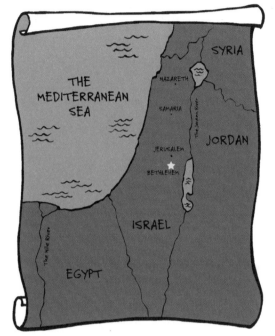

Name:_____

The Nativity

Color the picture and then answer the question.

Who came to see baby Jesus?

Shepherds

Name:_____

Word Search

Can you find these words in the puzzle?
Look carefully! The words go across and down.

BETHLEHEM	BIRTHDAY
MANGER	MARY
SHEPHERDS	JOSEPH
CHRISTMAS	SAVIOR
JESUS	

```
X C H R I S T M A S
X B I R T H D A Y A
X J X X X E X X X V
X O X X X P X X X I
X S X X X H X X X O
B E T H L E H E M R
X P X M A R Y X X X
X H X X X D X X X X
X J E S U S X X X X
X X X M A N G E R X
```

Name:_____

Draw a picture of Santa Claus kneeling before baby Jesus.

TEACHER'S NOTES

CHAPTER ELEVEN
THREE WISE MEN ARRIVE

Catechism of the Catholic Church References

The Blessed Sacrament: 1373–81, 1418
Christ's Mission of Salvation: 456–60
The Epiphany: 528, 1171

Mysteries of Christ's Infancy: 527–30, 563
Places Favorable to Prayer: 2691, 2696

Scripture References

The Wise Men: Mt 2:1–12

Background Reading: *The Fundamentals of Catholicism* by Fr. Kenneth Baker, S.J.

Volume 3:
"The Catholic Doctrine of the Real Presence," pp. 229–31
"My Flesh Is Real Food and My Blood Is Real Drink," pp. 232–35
"Water into Wine, Wine into Blood," pp. 235–38

"A Wonderful Change," pp. 238–40
"Presence of the Whole Christ," pp. 241–43
"How Long Is the Lord Present in the Eucharist?", pp. 244–47

Summary of Lesson Content

Lesson 1

Three wise men from the East came to worship the Christ Child.

These wise men represent all gentiles; their visit is a sign that Christ came into the world to save everyone, not just the Jewish people.

Christ is the "King of Kings."

Lesson 3

Mary and Joseph, poor and humble, received the wise men who worshiped their divine Son.

Every person should offer his talents and do his best for Jesus always.

The story of the Little Drummer Boy teaches that a person need not be rich, powerful, nor important to be loved by Jesus.

Lesson 2

Jesus is truly and really present in the Blessed Sacrament.

Catholics can worship Him in the Blessed Sacrament as the wise men worshiped Him at the stable in Bethlehem.

Benediction is a special service during which Catholics worship our Lord in the Blessed Sacrament.

Lesson 4

Though the wise men offered magnificent gifts, everyone can offer gifts to Jesus.

In the Morning Offering, a person offers all of his daily activities to Jesus. In doing so, they become gifts to Jesus and He blesses them.

CHAPTER ELEVEN: THREE WISE MEN ARRIVE
LESSON ONE: THREE WISE MEN VISIT JESUS

Aims

Students will listen to the story of the visit of the wise men.

They will be able to explain that Christ came into the world to save everyone.

They will understand why Christ is called the "King of Kings."

Materials

- Children's Bible

- *Activity Book*, p. 41

Optional:
- A large star, perhaps made of cardboard and covered with aluminum foil

- "We three kings of Orient are," *Adoremus Hymnal*, #350

Begin

Ask the children if they are familiar with the Christmas carol "The Twelve Days of Christmas." Tell them that the twelve days in the song refer to the twelve days between Christmas and Epiphany, the feast commemorating the visit of the three wise men. Epiphany used to be celebrated exactly twelve days after Christmas, on January 6th, and has only recently been moved to the Sunday closest to this date. In the song, gifts are given on each of these twelve days of Christmas.

Develop

1. Read paragraphs 1, 2, and 3 of the text with the class.

2. Return to the first line of paragraph 1, which says: "Jesus came to save everybody." Remind them that they have learned that God prepared the Jewish people for the coming of the Savior. Mary, Joseph, the shepherds, and some other Jews were truly prepared for His arrival, but many others were not; they were looking for a more worldly king. The three wise men were not Jews at all. They came from far away lands, and practiced other religions. However, in their arrival at the stable in Bethlehem and their worship of the baby Jesus, they reveal the truth that God sent His Son into the world not just for the Jews whom He had so carefully prepared, but for all men everywhere.

3. Read the story of the visit of the wise men from your children's Bible (Mt 2:1–12).

4. Point out to the children the contrast between the humble conditions surrounding the Christ Child and the wealth and power of the three wise men. Comment on the fact that these men had a deep faith. Though Jesus looked poor, their faith let them know He was the greatest King of all.

5. Help the children to find the definition of "king" in the text: someone who rules over a land. Tell them that Jesus rules over the Kingdom of Heaven.

6. Talk about the gifts of the three wise men. Explain that gold was given to Jesus because He is a King. Frankincense signifies the divinity of Christ. Myrrh is used for anointing the dead. Jesus' death on the Cross would be the salvation of the world; thus myrrh was an apt gift for our Lord.

Reinforce

1. Lead the children to the classroom manger, holding up a star for them to follow. When you arrive at the Nativity scene (the Christ Child should be waiting in the manger), have the children move the wise men to the stable. Say a prayer together at the manger, thanking God for His best gift—Jesus.

2. Have the children color the wise men on p. 41 of the *Activity Book* (see *Teacher's Manual*, p. 135).

3. Practice Question 27 with the children as a class, then allow pairs to practice (see *Teacher's Manual*, p. 133).

Conclude

1. Teach the children an appropriate Christmas carol, such as "We three kings of Orient are," *Adoremus Hymnal*, #350.

2. Pray and make a sacrificial gift to Jesus.

GT APERTIS THESAVRIS SVIS OBTVLERVT EI AVRVM THVS Z MIRRAM. MACH. I. C.

44

11   Three Wise Men Arrive

"Where is he who has been born king of the Jews?
For we have seen his star in the East,
and have come to worship him."

Matthew 2:2

Jesus came to save everybody. He loves the people of every part of the world and He loves them very, very much.

Three **wise men** came to Bethlehem from a far away land when Jesus was born. The wise men knew many things about God and the world He made by studying His creation. They did not get lost because they followed a star that brought them to Jesus. The wise men knew that Jesus was a great **king**. A king is someone who rules over a land. Jesus rules over all kings of the world and over the Kingdom of Heaven too. He is the King of Kings. So the wise men knelt before Jesus and gave Him gifts fit for a king. His Kingdom will never end!

Jesus was glad to see the wise men. Although He was a baby, He really was their God and King.

45

WISE MEN, NOT KINGS

Although there is a tradition of calling the wise men kings, their proper name is Magi. Magi were a priestly caste or order of ancient Media and Persia whose religion was similar to that of Zoroaster. There is no scriptural evidence to support the wise men's kingship, nor that they were three in number. Some Fathers of the Church speak of three Magi, but they were very likely influenced by the number of gifts.

LITTLE CHRISTMAS

The feast of the Epiphany is sometimes called "Little Christmas," for it was on this day that the birth of the Savior was revealed to the entire world, as He had been revealed to the Jewish people on Christmas Day.

ADDITIONAL RESOURCE

The Gifts of the Magi is a Metropolitan Museum of Art boxed book set that also contains small samples of gold, frankincense, and myrrh.

EPIPHANY

Epiphany comes from the Greek word *epiphaneia,* which means "manifestation."

Preview

In our next lesson, we will learn about how we can visit Jesus and bow down in worship, like the wise men.

Chapter Eleven: Three Wise Men Arrive
Lesson Two: We Visit Jesus and Worship

Aims

Students will be able to explain that Jesus is truly and substantially present in the Blessed Sacrament in the tabernacle.

They will be inspired to visit our Lord often in the Blessed Sacrament, and worship Him as the wise men did.

Materials

• *Activity Book*, p. 42

Optional:
• A visit to Adoration and/or Benediction

• "We three kings of Orient are," *Adoremus Hymnal*, #350

Begin

Review the last lesson about the three wise men, highlighting the fact that they bowed down in worship before the Christ Child. Ask the students if they would have liked to be present at the stable in Bethlehem to worship the baby Jesus. Tell them that today they will learn about how they can worship Jesus more than 2,000 years after His birth.

Develop

1. Read paragraphs 4 and 5 with the children. Explain that at church they can worship Jesus as the wise men did, because Jesus is truly present in the tabernacle.

2. Tell them that when the priest says the words of Consecration at Mass, "This is my Body" and "This is the chalice of my Blood," the bread and wine truly become the Body and Blood of Jesus, our Lord. It is proper to kneel down at this most sacred part of the Mass, just as the wise men knelt down before the baby Jesus at the stable in Bethlehem. Christ is truly present on the altar, just as He was in Bethlehem.

3. Ask the children if they know what the red lamp in the sanctuary of their church signifies (when lit, it means Jesus is present in the tabernacle; see p. 229 of this manual).

4. Take a few minutes to practice genuflecting (see Chapter 2, Lesson 4, see *Teacher's Manual*, pp. 20–21).

5. If possible, attend Adoration and/or Benediction as a class. Explain that the focus is on worshiping our Lord in the Blessed Sacrament. There are special hymns and prayers that are always sung and said at Benediction. Also, incense (similar to frankincense) is used to signify the divinity of Christ, truly present in the Blessed Sacrament, as well as the prayers being offered to Him. When Jesus is exposed in the monstrance, everyone genuflects on both knees. Model this for the children: a quick kneel and bow on both knees.

6. If you cannot have the children attend Adoration and/or Benediction, make a visit to the Blessed Sacrament. In either case, emphasize how important it is to visit Jesus in the tabernacle, even just for a few minutes.

Reinforce

1. Have the children answer the questions on p. 42 of the *Activity Book* (see *Teacher's Manual*, p. 135).

2. Read Question 28 with the children and review Question 27 (see *Teacher's Manual*, p. 133). Then give pairs time to practice as you circulate and assist.

Conclude

1. Close by singing "We three kings of Orient are," *Adoremus Hymnal*, #350.

2. Pray, expressing love to Jesus in the Blessed Sacrament.

11   Three Wise Men Arrive

"Where is he who has been born king of the Jews?
For we have seen his star in the East,
and have come to worship him."

Matthew 2:2

Jesus came to save everybody. He loves the people of every part of the world and He loves them very, very much.

Three **wise men** came to Bethlehem from a far away land when Jesus was born. The wise men knew many things about God and the world He made by studying His creation. They did not get lost because they followed a star that brought them to Jesus. The wise men knew that Jesus was a great **king**. A king is someone who rules over a land. Jesus rules over all kings of the world and over the Kingdom of Heaven too. He is the King of Kings. So the wise men knelt before Jesus and gave Him gifts fit for a king. His Kingdom will never end!

Jesus was glad to see the wise men. Although He was a baby, He really was their God and King.

45

Can you do what the wise men did? Can you visit Jesus and give Him gifts? Yes, you can! Jesus is always waiting for you in church. You can visit Him any time the church is open.

If you are at home you can visit Jesus, too. All you have to do is stop what you are doing and talk to Him. God is everywhere and can always hear you.

Your gift to Jesus is your love for Him. Your prayers are a gift to Him. Your good deeds are a gift to Him too. Each time you chose right over wrong, that is a gift to Jesus.

Words to Know:

wise men   king

46

ADORATION
OF THE BLESSED SACRAMENT

The practice of formal Exposition and Adoration of the Blessed Sacrament first appeared in the later Middle Ages, about the beginning of the thirteenth century. During exposition there should be group prayers and songs to direct the faithful's attention to the true presence of Christ on the altar. Readings from Scripture followed by a homily or a brief exhortation are also encouraged. However, some periods of silence should be reserved for private, personal prayer. The Liturgy of the Hours may also be said before the Blessed Sacrament.

BENEDICTION
OF THE BLESSED SACRAMENT

Benediction of the Blessed Sacrament is ordinarily an afternoon or evening devotion, and consists in singing hymns or litanies before the Blessed Sacrament which is exposed upon the altar in a monstrance and surrounded by candles. It usually opens with singing "O Salutaris Hostia" and concludes with "Tantum Ergo," though these may be replaced with other appropriate hymns. The priest says a prayer; then, his shoulders covered in a humeral veil, he takes the monstrance into his hands and with it makes the Sign of the Cross in silence over the kneeling congregation.

"Where is he who has been born king of the Jews? For we have seen his star in the East, and have come to worship him.

—Matthew 2:2

Preview

In our next lesson, we will learn more about the visit of the wise men, as well as about a poor boy and the gift he gave to baby Jesus.

CHAPTER ELEVEN: THREE WISE MEN ARRIVE
LESSON THREE: A POOR BOY'S GIFT

Aims

Students will learn more about the wise men.

They will learn about a little boy's simple gift to baby Jesus.

Materials

- *Activity Book*, p. 43

Optional:
- "Little Drummer Boy," video, Family Home Entertainment

- Collected paintings of the Epiphany

- "We three kings of Orient are," *Adoremus Hymnal*, #350

Begin

If you have made a visit to Benediction, ask the children what struck them most about it (e.g., the incense—the way it rose up to Heaven, the way it smelled; the priest's special vestment, called a "cope"; the monstrance; etc.). Or, if you took the students to visit the tabernacle, discuss this experience with them. If you did not make a class visit, encourage them to go with their parents. Remind them that Jesus is waiting in the Blessed Sacrament for His children to visit Him.

Develop

1. Have the children turn to p. 44 of their textbooks and give them a moment to study *The Adoration of the Magi* by Fra Angelico. Then ask the following questions:

- What is the setting for this painting? (outside the stable at Bethlehem)
- Who is in the doorway of the stable? (Mary and baby Jesus)
- How could you tell it was them? (they have halos)
- Who else has a halo, to the right of Mary? (Saint Joseph)
- Who is kneeling before Mary and Jesus? (one of the wise men)
- Where is his crown? (a man on the right is holding it)
- Who is the man holding the crown? (probably a servant)
- Where is this wise man's gift? (the Christ Child is holding it in his left hand)
- What is Jesus doing with His right hand? (possibly blessing the wise man)
- Can you point out the other two wise men? (one is talking to Saint Joseph, the other is to the left of the kneeling wise man)

- Who do you think the other people are? (servants or other worshipers)
- Can you see animals in the background on the left? What are they? (horses or camels the Magi travelled with)
- What is in the background of the painting? (Bethlehem)

2. Ask the children to consider how the Blessed Mother and Saint Joseph may have felt about this amazing visit. Remind the children that Mary and Joseph were humble people, and now they were receiving visitors and magnificent gifts. They must also have rejoiced to know that others shared their belief that Jesus was the Savior.

3. Ask the students to imagine what they would give the Christ Child if they had accompanied the wise men to the stable (sing a song, do a dance, etc.). Emphasize the importance of giving their BEST to Jesus.

Reinforce

1. Assign p. 43 of the *Activity Book* (see *Teacher's Manual*, p. 135). Children will draw pictures of themselves at Bethlehem, offering the Christ Child their special gifts and talents.

2. Practice Questions 27 and 28 (see *Teacher's Manual*, p. 133).

3. Optional: Show the video "The Little Drummer Boy," which combines the visit of the Magi with the legend of the drummer boy (available through Family Home Entertainment; 30 minutes).

4. If you have them, display and discuss paintings or pictures of the Epiphany.

Conclude

1. Pray, offering our best to God.

2. Sing "We three kings of Orient are," *Adoremus Hymnal*, #350.

GT APERTIS THESAVRIS SVIS OBTVLERVT EI AVRVM THVS Z MIRRAM. MACTH. 1. C.

44

11   Three Wise Men Arrive

"Where is he who has been born king of the Jews?
For we have seen his star in the East,
and have come to worship him."

Matthew 2:2

Jesus came to save everybody. He loves the people of every part of the world and He loves them very, very much.

Three **wise men** came to Bethlehem from a far away land when Jesus was born. The wise men knew many things about God and the world He made by studying His creation. They did not get lost because they followed a star that brought them to Jesus. The wise men knew that Jesus was a great **king**. A king is someone who rules over a land. Jesus rules over all kings of the world and over the Kingdom of Heaven too. He is the King of Kings. So the wise men knelt before Jesus and gave Him gifts fit for a king. His Kingdom will never end!

Jesus was glad to see the wise men. Although He was a baby, He really was their God and King.

45

Can you do what the wise men did? Can you visit Jesus and give Him gifts? Yes, you can! Jesus is always waiting for you in church. You can visit Him any time the church is open.

If you are at home you can visit Jesus, too. All you have to do is stop what you are doing and talk to Him. God is everywhere and can always hear you.

Your gift to Jesus is your love for Him. Your prayers are a gift to Him. Your good deeds are a gift to Him too. Each time you chose right over wrong, that is a gift to Jesus.

Words to Know:

        wise men   king

46

THE LITTLE DRUMMER BOY

According to legend, a little drummer boy was present in Bethlehem when Jesus was born. When he saw the magnificent gifts of the Magi, he was saddened because he was poor and had no gift to bring to the Christ Child. As the Magi left, he stood alone, then softly began to play his drum for the holy Baby: pa-rum-pum-pum-pum. Walking forward and playing more loudly, he saw Jesus smile at him. With a heart full of love, he continued to play. No longer sad, the little drummer boy's heart sang for he knew that his was the greatest gift of all, the gift of love. It is important to remember that Jesus does not want extravagant or expensive gifts, only the best a person has. Using one's God-given talents for God's glory will certainly make the Christ Child smile.

Preview

In our next lesson, we will learn about how we can give gifts to Jesus every day of our lives.

Chapter Eleven: Three Wise Men Arrive
Lesson Four: Daily Gifts for Jesus

Aims

Students will learn how to divide their day into prayers, works, joys, and sufferings.

They will understand what these divisions mean.

They will learn how to offer all of their daily activities as gifts to Jesus.

They will learn a Morning Offering prayer.

Materials

- *Activity Book*, p. 44

Optional:
- "We three kings of Orient are," *Adoremus Hymnal*, #350

Begin

Review with the children the gifts that the wise men brought to the Christ Child (gold, frankincense, and myrrh), the gift that the drummer boy gave to Jesus (playing his drum), and the gifts that everyone can give to Jesus (their talents). Then tell them that today they will learn about some gifts that they can give to Jesus every day.

Develop

1. Read paragraph 6 in the textbook with the children.

2. Discuss as a group the activities that the children engage in each day. Make four headings on the chalkboard and let them fill these in:
   - Prayers (morning and evening, at mealtime, at school, at church, for help for themselves and others)
   - Works (chores at home, schoolwork, sports, music, and other activities)
   - Joys (doing well on a test, getting a new puppy, seeing grandparents)
   - Sufferings (losing a game, getting a skinned knee)

3. Explain to the children that they should offer all of these activities to Jesus each day. Because He loves everyone, He also loves the good things that each person does each day. By offering them to Jesus, these activities become gifts to Him.

4. Focus on how the children can offer their joys to Jesus. Let them talk about those things that give them joy: e.g., surprises, treats, friends, family, etc. By offering these joys to Jesus, they will be reminded to thank Him.

5. Focus on how the children can offer sufferings to Jesus. Let them tell you about sufferings they experience; e.g., falling and getting hurt, hurt feelings, being afraid of the dark, etc. Remind them that Jesus suffered, too, most especially when He died on the Cross. Anyone can comfort Jesus by uniting his sufferings to Christ's, and He will help that person to bear sufferings well.

6. As a class, design your own Morning Offering prayer. It should specify prayers, works, joys, and sufferings, and how the students can offer these things to our Lord and unite them to His sacrifice on the Cross. Also see examples at right.

Reinforce

1. Complete p. 44 of the *Activity Book* together as a class (see *Teacher's Manual*, p. 135). This page is based on the lists you made during this lesson; answers may vary by student.

2. Practice Questions 27 and 28 as a class, allowing time for personal memorization.

Conclude

1. Pray a morning offering (see facing page).

2. Close by singing "We three kings of Orient are," *Adoremus Hymnal*, #350.

11   Three Wise Men Arrive

"Where is he who has been born king of the Jews?
For we have seen his star in the East,
and have come to worship him."

Matthew 2:2

Jesus came to save everybody. He loves the people of every part of the world and He loves them very, very much.

Three **wise men** came to Bethlehem from a far away land when Jesus was born. The wise men knew many things about God and the world He made by studying His creation. They did not get lost because they followed a star that brought them to Jesus. The wise men knew that Jesus was a great **king**. A king is someone who rules over a land. Jesus rules over all kings of the world and over the Kingdom of Heaven too. He is the King of Kings. So the wise men knelt before Jesus and gave Him gifts fit for a king. His Kingdom will never end!

Jesus was glad to see the wise men. Although He was a baby, He really was their God and King.

45

Can you do what the wise men did? visit Jesus and give Him gifts? Yes, you always waiting for you in church. You ca any time the church is open.

If you are at home you can visit Jesus, you have to do is stop what you are doing and talk to Him. God is everywhere and can always hear you.

Your gift to Jesus is your love for Him. Your prayers are a gift to Him. Your good deeds are a gift to Him too. Each time you chose right over wrong, that is a gift to Jesus.

Words to Know:

    wise men   king

46

Q. 27   *What did the wise men do when they found Jesus?*
They knelt before Jesus and gave Him gifts (CCC 528).

Q. 28   *Where can we go to kneel before Jesus?*
We can kneel before Jesus in the Blessed Sacrament (CCC 1373, 1378).

MORNING OFFERING

Dear Jesus, I give You my day and everything in it. Please keep me close to You, Your Mother Mary, and my guardian angel as I live today for Your glory. *Amen.*

47

A SIMPLE MORNING OFFERING

Dear Jesus, I give You my day and everything in it. Please keep me close to You, Your Mother Mary, and my guardian angel as I live today for Your glory. *Amen.*

A MORNING OFFERING

O Jesus, through the Immaculate Heart of Mary, I offer You all my prayers, works, joys, and sufferings of this day, for the intentions of Your Sacred Heart, in union with the Holy Sacrifice of the Mass throughout the world, in reparation for my sins, and for the conversion of all sinners. *Amen.*

Preview

In our next lesson, we will review what we have learned in this chapter and take a quiz.

Chapter Eleven: Three Wise Men Arrive
Review and Assessment

Aims

To review and assess the students' understanding of the material taught in this chapter.

Materials

- Quiz 11 (Appendix, p. A-13)
- "We three kings of Orient are," *Adoremus Hymnal*, #350

Review and Enrichment

1. Review Questions 27 and 28 and the Words to Know (see *Teacher's Manual*, p. 133).

2. Use the following questions as a guide to review the material from this chapter:
- Who came from the East to worship Jesus?
- Did Jesus come to save the Jewish people only?
- What gifts did the wise men bring?
- Why didn't the wise men tell King Herod where Jesus was after they found Him?
- How can we visit Jesus? Can you visit Jesus at church? Can you visit Jesus at home?
- The wise men brought gifts to the Christ Child. Can you bring Him gifts, too?
- Who is in the tabernacle?

Name: _____

Three Wise Men Arrive   **Quiz 11**

Fill in the blanks. *Trace the gray letters and fill in the rest.*

Word Bank

gifts	star	good	save

1. Jesus came to s a v e everybody.

2. A s t a r led the three wise men to Jesus.

3. They gave g i f t s to Jesus.

4. My g o o d deeds are my gifts for Jesus.

Assess

Pass out Quiz 11 and read through it with the children, answering any questions they may have. Administer the quiz. Review the correct answers with the children when everyone has finished.

Conclude

1. Practice the Morning Offering prayer you have written in class.

2. Sing "We three kings of Orient are," *Adoremus Hymnal*, #350.

Name:_____

Three wise men followed a star. They came to worship Jesus.

Name:_____

Let the wise men be our examples.

The wise men traveled a long way to visit Jesus and bring Him gifts.

Answer the following questions.

1. Can you visit Jesus, as the wise men did?
Yes. Jesus is waiting for you in the church.

2. Can you visit Jesus at church? You can visit Him anytime the church is open.

3. Can you visit Jesus at home? Yes. All you have to do is stop what you are doing and talk to Him.

4. The wise men brought gifts. What gifts can you take to Jesus? Your love for Jesus, your prayers, and your good deeds are all gifts to Jesus.

Name:_____

A Gift of Love

If you were at the first Christmas, what special gift or talent would you bring to Jesus? Draw yourself bringing your gift of love to Him.

Name:_____

The Morning Offering

There are many things you can offer in your morning offering.

Match the words in the left column with the correct words in the right column.

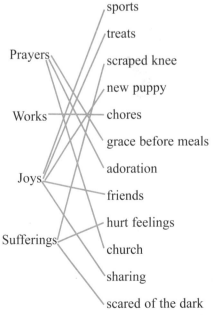

Prayers
Works
Joys
Sufferings

sports
treats
scraped knee
new puppy
chores
grace before meals
adoration
friends
hurt feelings
church
sharing
scared of the dark

TEACHER'S NOTES

CHAPTER TWELVE
JESUS GROWS UP

Catechism of the Catholic Church References

Christ's Obedience Replaces Man's Disobedience: 615
Duties of Children to Parents: 2214–20, 2247–48, 2251
The Family and the Call to Follow Christ: 2232–33
The Family as Natural Society: 1882
The Family as the Original Cell of Society: 2207

The Family as a Privileged Community: 2206
Jesus as Teacher and Model of Holiness: 516, 519–21, 561
The Model of the Domestic Chuch: 1655–58, 1666
Mysteries of Christ's Hidden Life: 531–34, 564
Relations Between Siblings: 2219

Scripture References

The Finding of the Child Jesus in the Temple: Lk 2:41–52
The Flight into Egypt: Mt 2:13–23

The Presentation in the Temple: Lk 2:22–40
Jesus Grows Up: Lk 2:52

Background Reading: *The Fundamentals of Catholicism* by Fr. Kenneth Baker, S.J.

Volume 1:
The Fourth Commandment, pp. 182–87

Volume 2:
"Jesus Possessed Both Infused and Acquired Knowledge,"
pp. 253–56
"Jesus' Suffering and Human Feelings," pp. 266–69

Summary of Lesson Content

Lesson 1

Baby Jesus was presented to God in the Temple.

Simeon and Anna recognized Him as the promised Savior.

Because King Herod wanted to kill the Christ Child, Saint Joseph and Mary fled to Egypt with Him.

The fourth Joyful Mystery is the Presentation.

Lesson 3

Jesus led a simple, humble life in Nazareth.

We will study the Holy Family's life in Nazareth.

Statues may represent the saints in Heaven.

Lesson 2

Saint Joseph, as head of the Holy Family, was its protector and provider.

Saint Joseph is protector of the Catholic Church.

Honest, hard work is pleasing to God.

Lesson 4

Everyone should follow the example of Jesus in his life.

In the Fourth Commandment God tells us we must love and obey our parents.

Jesus was lost for three days in the Temple.

Mary and Saint Joseph rejoiced greatly upon finding Him; the Finding in the Temple is the fifth Joyful Mystery.

CHAPTER TWELVE: JESUS GROWS UP
LESSON ONE: THE EARLY CHILDHOOD OF JESUS

Aims

Students will be able to relate the events of the Presentation in the Temple.

They will learn the story of the flight into Egypt and will be able to explain why it was necessary.

Materials

- Children's Bible

- *Activity Book*, p. 37 for the map of the Holy Land

- *Activity Book*, p. 45

Optional:
- Appendix, p. B-21, The Presentation

- Mural paper for small groups of 2–3 students

- "Come, thou long expected Jesus," *Adoremus Hymnal*, #310

Begin

Review the sequence of events in the Christmas story: the Annunciation, the Visitation, the journey to Bethlehem, the Nativity, the visit of the shepherds, and the visit of the wise men. List these on the chalkboard and draw a simple sketch for each episode. Tell the children that today they will find out what happened in Christ's life after the wise men left and returned safely to their own far-away lands.

Develop

1. From your children's Bible, read the story of the Presentation of baby Jesus to God in the Temple (Lk 2:22–40). Explain to the children that Jewish law instructed parents to offer their firstborn son to God, to give him over to God's service. Mary and Joseph obeyed this law, even though Jesus was God Himself. They were very humble and happily brought Jesus to the Temple, His Father's house. The holy old man, Simeon, had waited patiently and faithfully for the Savior all of his life. God rewarded his faithfulness by letting him know that Jesus was the Savior. Simeon called Him "a light" to all people.

2. Now read the story of the flight into Egypt from your children's Bible (Mt 2:13–23). Point out that once again, an angel was sent from God to help Joseph protect the Christ Child. Saint Joseph immediately obeyed the angel and "flew" to Egypt. (It may be necessary to define *flight* and *flew* as "travel done in great haste," to distinguish it from airplane flying.) Have the children refer to p. 37 of their *Activity Books* (see *Teacher's Manual*, p. 123) where they colored a simple map of the Holy Land and the nearby Mediterranean area. Point to Egypt and trace the journey that Joseph and Mary had to make. Discuss the difficulties of this journey. It was much like their travel to Bethlehem, only much longer and they were afraid for their precious child. They must have prayed fervently that the Christ Child would be preserved from the evil intent of Herod.

3. Once again, an angel visited Saint Joseph in a dream and told him that Herod had died and it would be safe to return to his homeland. So Joseph took Mary and Jesus and made the long journey back to Israel. They settled in the town of Nazareth. That is where Jesus lived as a little boy and where He grew up and became a man. In the coming chapters the early life of Christ will be explained in greater detail.

Reinforce

1. On *Activity Book* p. 45 (see *Teacher's Manual*, p. 147), have the students draw Jesus, Mary, and Joseph on the flight to Egypt. Encourage them to include some of the harsh conditions they probably encountered, such as the fierce desert sun, the sand, and riding on camels.

2. If they have been making Rosary booklets, pass out photocopies of Appendix, p. B-21, the Presen-tation, for the students to color. This will be p. 4 in their Joyful Mysteries Rosary booklet.

3. In order to review all of the events of the Christmas story and the first few years of Jesus' life, separate the children into small groups of 2–3 children. Each group will work on one panel of an 8-part mural. Refer the children to the chalkboard list you made at the beginning of the lesson, and add to it the Presentation and the Flight into Egypt. Assign one part of the story to each group and let them tell that part of the story in a picture.

Conclude

1. When all of the groups have completed each panel, have the children help you post them in the proper sequence in the classroom or in the hallway.

2. Pray the fourth Joyful Mystery of the Rosary—the Presentation in the Temple.

3. Sing "Come, thou long expected Jesus," *Adoremus Hymnal*, #310.

12   Jesus Grows Up

"And Jesus increased in wisdom and
in stature, and in favor with God and man."
Luke 2:52

The boy Jesus lived and worked and played in a little house in Nazareth. Jesus is the Son of God. Mary is His Mother. And Saint Joseph is His foster-father.

Saint Joseph did everything for Jesus just like a real father should. Saint Joseph was a **carpenter** who made chairs, tables, and many other things out of wood. Jesus liked to help him in the shop because He wanted to learn to be a carpenter, like Joseph.

Jesus loved His parents. He obeyed them and helped them with their work. He grew up and was strong and good. Jesus did all these things to show us how to **honor** our parents. When we love and obey them, we honor our parents and make our heavenly Father happy with us.

49

---

carpenter   honor

Q. 29 *Is Saint Joseph the father of Jesus?*
No, Saint Joseph is the foster-father of Jesus and the husband of Mary (CCC 484, 497).

Q. 30 *What does Jesus teach us in His family life?*
Jesus teaches us in His family life to love and obey our parents (CCC 520, 532).

50

THE PRESENTATION = THE PURIFICATION OF MARY = CANDLEMAS DAY

February 2nd, forty days after Christmas, is a feast of various names. It commemorates the day that Joseph and Mary presented Jesus to God in the Temple, along with a sacrifice of a pair of turtle doves. It reminds us that Mary underwent the Jewish purification rites following childbirth like any other woman of her faith; she redeemed her firstborn from the Temple and was purified by the prayer of Simeon in the presence of the prophetess Anna. The least known name for this feast refers to a candle procession that the early Christians instituted to counter a pagan Roman holiday. This Roman feast fell in mid-February, forty days after the Eastern rite's celebration of Christmas on January 6th.

SUGGESTED BACKGROUND READING

"Guardian of the Redeemer" by Saint Pope John Paul II. This encyclical examines the relationship between Saint Joseph and Jesus.

THE PRESENTATION
Luke 2:22–40

Preview

In our next lesson, we will learn about Saint Joseph, the foster-father of Jesus, and how he cared for Jesus and Mary.

CHAPTER TWELVE: JESUS GROWS UP
LESSON TWO: SAINT JOSEPH—PROVIDER, PROTECTOR, AND PATRON

Aims

Students will understand Saint Joseph's role as provider and protector of the Holy Family.

They will realize that just as Saint Joseph protected Jesus and Mary, he is the protector of the Catholic Church.

Materials

- *Activity Book*, p. 46

Optional:
- Pictures of fathers with their children and at work

- Materials to make cards for their fathers

- "Come, thou long expected Jesus," *Adoremus Hymnal*, #310

Begin

Read paragraph 1 of the textbook with the children. This paragraph reminds students that Jesus is both the Son of God, and the Son of Mary; He is both divine and human. God is His Father. He had no earthly father; rather, Saint Joseph is His foster-father. Explain that Saint Joseph, Mary, and Jesus are the Holy Family, a model for all families. Saint Joseph was the head of the holiest of families.

Develop

1. Help the children to recall the story of the Flight into Egypt as read from Scripture. Highlight Saint Joseph's role as the protector of the Christ Child and His Mother. Discuss how seriously Saint Joseph took his role by pointing out that as soon as the angel warned him in a dream that Herod wanted to kill baby Jesus, he immediately obeyed and took Mary and Jesus in the middle of the night. His main concern was the safety of the Christ Child and His Mother because he was their protector. When Herod died, and the Christ Child was no longer threatened, they could return to Nazareth. Once there, Saint Joseph continued to protect Jesus and Mary.

2. Direct the children's attention to the painting on p. 48 of their textbooks—*Saint Joseph the Carpenter*. Help them to analyze the painting by asking the following questions:
- Who is the man in the painting? (Saint Joseph)
- Who is the child in the painting? (Jesus)
- Where is this scene taking place?

- What time of day is it?
- How do you know?
- What is the Christ Child doing?
- What is Saint Joseph doing?
- How are they dressed?
- Who do you think made the clothes they are wearing? (Mary)
- At what or at whom is Saint Joseph looking? (Jesus)

3. Explain that just as Saint Joseph was the protector of the Holy Family, he is now the protector of the Church that Jesus founded before He returned to His Heavenly Father.

4. Read paragraph 2 with the class. Have the students find the meaning of the word "carpenter" in the text and/or glossary: "someone who makes chairs, tables, and many other things out of wood." Tell them that God likes to see people involved in honest, hard work.

Reinforce

1. Show the students pictures of fathers and their children at work. Then have them color the picture of Jesus helping Saint Joseph in the workshop in Nazareth on p. 46 of the *Activity Book* (see *Teacher's Manual*, p. 147).

2. Have the children make cards out of folded construction paper for their fathers, thanking them for all they do for their families.

Conclude

1. Practice Question 29 with the class.

2. Recite the Litany of Saint Joseph on p. 51 of the text. Have the children respond: Pray for us.

3. Teach the children this prayer: Jesus, Mary, Joseph, I love you. Save souls.

4. Sing "Come thou long expected Jesus," *Adoremus Hymnal*, #310.

12   Jesus Grows Up

"And Jesus increased in wisdom and
in stature, and in favor with God and man."
Luke 2:52

The boy Jesus lived and worked and played in a little house in Nazareth. Jesus is the Son of God. Mary is His Mother. And Saint Joseph is His foster-father.

Saint Joseph did everything for Jesus just like a real father should. Saint Joseph was a **carpenter** who made chairs, tables, and many other things out of wood. Jesus liked to help him in the shop because He wanted to learn to be a carpenter, like Joseph.

Jesus loved His parents. He obeyed them and helped them with their work. He grew up and was strong and good. Jesus did all these things to show us how to **honor** our parents. When we love and obey them, we honor our parents and make our heavenly Father happy with us.

49

---

carpenter   honor

> **Q. 29** *Is Saint Joseph the father of Jesus?*
> No, Saint Joseph is the foster-father of Jesus and the husband of Mary (CCC 484, 497).
>
> **Q. 30** *What does Jesus teach us in His family life?*
> Jesus teaches us in His family life to love and obey our parents (CCC 520, 532).

50

Litany to Saint Joseph

Let Us Pray:

Saint Joseph...
Foster-father of the Son of God...
Head of the Holy Family...
Joseph most just...
Joseph most strong...
Joseph most obedient...
Joseph most faithful...
Pillar of families...
Protector of Holy Church...

Pray for us.

51

SAINT JOSEPH'S DEATH

Devout people everywhere have long believed that Saint Joseph died in the arms of Jesus and Mary. There is no more beautiful or holy way to leave this world. For this reason, Saint Joseph is known as the patron saint of a happy death and of the dying.

SAINT JOSEPH THE WORKER

In addition to being the Protector of the Church, Saint Joseph is the patron saint of workers because he always did his work perfectly for the love of God. He is the saint that working people can pray to for help in making their own work a gift to God. The feast of Saint Joseph the Worker is May 1.

SAINT JOSEPH'S DAY

March 19 is the day the Church celebrates Saint Joseph as the Provider and Protector of the Christ Child and the Church and the patron saint of the dying.

Preview

In our next lesson, we will learn more about the life of the Holy Family in Nazareth.

CHAPTER TWELVE: JESUS GROWS UP
LESSON THREE: GROWING UP IN NAZARETH

Aims

Students will consider the circumstances of the Child Jesus' life.

They will learn about the daily life and duties of the boy Jesus.

They will understand that statues may represent saints who are in Heaven.

Materials

- *Activity Book*, p. 47

Optional:
- Pictures of families imitating the Holy Family (working, praying, singing, reading, playing, eating a meal together)

- "Come, thou long expected Jesus," *Adoremus Hymnal*, #310

Begin

Tell the children that very few details are known about the life of the Child Jesus in Nazareth, because the Bible is nearly silent about this time. This period of the Savior's life is sometimes referred to as "the hidden years." However, one can imagine what His childhood may have been like from what is known about Mary, Joseph, Jesus, and the community in which they lived.

Develop

1. Ask the children to imagine that they are living at the time of Jesus, more than 2000 years ago. They can imagine that they are neighbors of the Holy Family. They do not have TVs, stereos, or video games. In fact, there is no electricity in their homes (no lights, refrigerator, heating, washing machine, etc.). The children would probably spend their days helping their parents. At that time, mothers cared for the homes by making clothes, cooking meals, cleaning, etc. Children might carry water from the village well to the home so that dishes could be cleaned and clothes washed by hand. They probably helped their fathers in whatever trade they pursued (cobbler, carpenter, blacksmith, farmer). They would have only a few toys, but they would amuse themselves with balls, marbles, and other simple games. When it got dark at night, they would light oil lamps to see.

2. Explain to the children that it was this kind of life that Mary, Joseph, and Jesus knew. In some ways it was a difficult life, but it was also a simple and good life. Mary took care of the home, making and mending clothes, cooking meals, and cleaning. She also taught Jesus about God and the Jewish laws, prayers, and rituals. Joseph worked hard in his carpentry shop, making furniture for the people of the town of Nazareth.

3. Discuss with the children what sort of a son Jesus must have been to Mary and Joseph (helpful, cheerful, obedient, etc.). Also discuss what kind of a friend and neighbor He, Mary, and Joseph must have been (friendly, generous, kind, helpful, humble).

4. Show pictures of families imitating the Holy Family and ask individual children to explain how each family is acting like the Holy Family.

Reinforce

1. Help the children to complete p. 47 of the *Activity Book* as a class (see *Teacher's Manual*, p. 147). This is a chart that sorts out the various duties and qualities of Mary and Joseph as they have been discussed.

2. If possible, make a visit to the Blessed Sacrament in church and point out the statues of Mary and Joseph to the children. Explain that statues help people remember the holy men and women who are now saints in Heaven, like Mary and Saint Joseph. It is much like having family pictures on your wall or on display at home. No one prays to statues, but a person may ask the saints they represent to pray for them, similar to asking family or friends to pray for one's needs.

Conclude

1. Practice Question 29.

2. You may want to say together the Litany to Saint Joseph from p. 51 of the textbook.

3. Close by singing: "Come thou long expected Jesus," *Adoremus Hymnal*, #310.

12   Jesus Grows Up

"And Jesus increased in wisdom and
in stature, and in favor with God and man."
Luke 2:52

The boy Jesus lived and worked and played in a little house in Nazareth. Jesus is the Son of God. Mary is His Mother. And Saint Joseph is His foster-father.

Saint Joseph did everything for Jesus just like a real father should. Saint Joseph was a **carpenter** who made chairs, tables, and many other things out of wood. Jesus liked to help him in the shop because He wanted to learn to be a carpenter, like Joseph.

Jesus loved His parents. He obeyed them and helped them with their work. He grew up and was strong and good. Jesus did all these things to show us how to **honor** our parents. When we love and obey them, we honor our parents and make our heavenly Father happy with us.

49

carpenter   honor

Q. 29   *Is Saint Joseph the father of Jesus?*
No, Saint Joseph is the foster-father of Jesus and the husband of Mary (CCC 484, 497).

Q. 30   *What does Jesus teach us in His family life?*
Jesus teaches us in His family life to love and obey our parents (CCC 520, 532).

50

Litany to Saint Joseph

Let Us Pray:

Saint Joseph...
Foster-father of the Son of God...
Head of the Holy Family...
Joseph most just...
Joseph most strong...
Joseph most obedient...
Joseph most faithful...
Pillar of families...
Protector of Holy Church...

Pray for us.

51

No matter what [Mary's] jobs were—ordinary, commonplace, or seemingly more important ones—they revealed to her, sometimes quite clearly, sometimes obscurely, the activity of the Almighty and were an opportunity for her to praise God.

—Jean-Pierre de Caussade

Preview

In our next lesson, we will learn about how Jesus, by His own example, teaches us how to keep the Fourth Commandment: Honor thy father and mother.

CHAPTER TWELVE: JESUS GROWS UP
LESSON FOUR: THE FOURTH COMMANDMENT

Aims

Students will be inspired to follow the example of Jesus, Who was a child like them at one time.

They will memorize the Fourth Commandment.

They will be able to describe ways that they can keep the Fourth Commandment.

They will learn the story of the Finding of the Child Jesus in the Temple.

Materials

- Children's Bible

- *Activity Book*, p. 48

Optional:
- Paintings of the Holy Family by various artists

- Appendix, p. B-22, The Finding of the Our Lord in the Temple

- "Come, thou long expected Jesus," *Adoremus Hymnal*, #310

Begin

Show the children various paintings of the Holy Family and discuss them in terms of the previous lesson—how people lived at that time and how Jesus' family was the holiest family of all.

Develop

1. Read paragraph 3 and help the children to consider the boy Jesus as their model. Remind them that although He was God, He was also truly human; this means that He did many of the same things the students do, felt many of the feelings they feel (joy, sorrow, fear, etc.), and He worked hard and learned as He grew. Tell them that He understands what it is like to be six or seven years old. By following His example, they can become holy, as He was. The one thing Jesus does not share with man is sin; Jesus never committed a single sin in His life. However, He was tempted to sin, so when anyone has a temptation, he can pray to Jesus; He will understand and help the person say no to the temptation.

2. Help the students to recall the Ten Commandments that they studied in Chapter 8. Remind them that the Ten Commandments are rules to live by, for all people, at all times, everywhere (refer to Chapter 8, pp. 92–93 of this manual for explanation if necessary). Write the Fourth Commandment on the chalkboard: "Honor your father and your mother."

3. Explain to the students that Jesus kept the Fourth Commandment perfectly when He was a child. He obeyed Saint Joseph and Mary cheerfully and quickly when they asked Him to do something.

4. Ask the children in what ways they can imitate Jesus. Have them repeat and complete the following sentences: "I want to be like Jesus of Nazareth. I will . . ." (always obey my parents, be a cheerful helper, never talk back, etc.).

5. Read the story of the Finding of the Child Jesus in the Temple (Lk 2:41–52). Tell the children that this event in the life of Christ occurred when He was around the age of twelve. Discuss the fact that although Jesus was God and was fully aware of that, He nevertheless returned to Nazareth with Mary and Joseph and was obedient to them.

Reinforce

1. Help the children to complete p. 48 of the *Activity Book*—Jesus as a boy (see *Teacher's Manual*, p. 147).

2. If available, show the children paintings of the Holy Family by various artists, and have them help you to make a list of the ways that Jesus honored Mary and Joseph. Write these on the chalkboard. Then have them list the ways that they can honor their own parents. Write these on the chalkboard as well.

3. If they have been working on making a Rosary booklet, pass out photocopies of Appendix, p. B-22, The Finding of the Our Lord in the Temple. This will be the last page in their Joyful Mysteries. When completed, have the children put them in order before you check and staple them.

Conclude

1. Practice Question 30 with the students, and review Question 29.

2. Sing "Come thou long expected Jesus," *Adoremus Hymnal*, #310.

3. Pray the fifth decade of the Joyful Mysteries of the Rosary, The Finding of the Child Jesus in the Temple.

12   Jesus Grows Up

"And Jesus increased in wisdom and
in stature, and in favor with God and man."
Luke 2:52

The boy Jesus lived and worked and played in a little house in Nazareth. Jesus is the Son of God. Mary is His Mother. And Saint Joseph is His foster-father.

Saint Joseph did everything for Jesus just like a real father should. Saint Joseph was a **carpenter** who made chairs, tables, and many other things out of wood. Jesus liked to help him in the shop because He wanted to learn to be a carpenter, like Joseph.

Jesus loved His parents. He obeyed them and helped them with their work. He grew up and was strong and good. Jesus did all these things to show us how to **honor** our parents. When we love and obey them, we honor our parents and make our heavenly Father happy with us.

49

---

carpenter   honor

Q. 29 *Is Saint Joseph the father of Jesus?*
No, Saint Joseph is the foster-father of Jesus and the husband of Mary (CCC 484, 497).

Q. 30 *What does Jesus teach us in His family life?*
Jesus teaches us in His family life to love and obey our parents (CCC 520, 532).

50

Litany to Saint Joseph

Let Us Pray:

Saint Joseph...
Foster-father of the Son of God...
Head of the Holy Family...
Joseph most just...
Joseph most strong...
Joseph most obedient...
Joseph most faithful...
Pillar of families...
Protector of Holy Church...

Pray for us.

51

THE FOURTH COMMANDMENT: A CHILDREN'S EXAMINATION OF CONSCIENCE

Do you obey your parents?

Do you complete your household chores?

Do you speak respectfully to those in authority?

Do you remember to pray for your parents?

Do you ask permission to do things that are not part of your ordinary life?

Do you humbly accept correction from your parents?

THE FINDING IN THE TEMPLE
Luke 2:41–52

Preview

In our next lesson, we will review all that we have learned and take a quiz and a unit test.

CHAPTER TWELVE: JESUS GROWS UP
REVIEW AND ASSESSMENT

Aims

To review and assess children's knowledge of the material covered in this chapter.

Materials

- Appendix, p. B-1
- Quiz 12 (Appendix, p. A-14)
- "Come, thou long expected Jesus," *Adoremus Hymnal*, #310

Review and Enrichment

Play a game of Bible Baseball or Tic-Tac-Toe using the following types of questions (see Appendix, p. B-1 for instructions):

- Whom did Mary and Saint Joseph meet in the Temple at the Presentation?
- What did Simeon say about the baby Jesus?
- Why did the Holy Family have to leave Bethlehem?
- To which country did they flee?
- Does Jesus have a father on earth?
- Who is the foster-father of Jesus?
- What was his job in the Holy Family?
- What was Saint Joseph's occupation?
- Saint Joseph is the patron of whom?
- Who is the Protector of the Church?
- What types of things did the Blessed Mother do for her family?
- What is the Fourth Commandment?
- How did Jesus show Mary and Joseph that He honored them?
- Whose example should we follow/imitate if we want to be holy?
- When Mary and Saint Joseph found Jesus in the Temple, what did Jesus do?

Name: _____

Jesus Grows Up   **Quiz 12**

Yes or No. *Circle the correct answer.*

1. Did Joseph make things?   (Yes)   No

2. Did Jesus help Joseph?   (Yes)   No

3. Did Jesus disobey His parents?   Yes   (No)

4. Does Jesus teach us to love our parents?   (Yes)   No

5. Is Jesus the Son of God?   (Yes)   No

Assess

1. Pass out Quiz 12 and read through it with children, answering any questions they may have. Administer the quiz and observe the students, then review the correct answers.

Conclude

1. Review and pray the Joyful Mysteries of the Rosary. The children may look at the Joyful Mysteries of the Rosary books they have completed to help them meditate while they pray.

2. Sing "Come thou long expected Jesus," *Adoremus Hymnal*, #310.

Name:_____

Flight into Egypt

Traveling to Egypt was very difficult for Joseph, Mary, and baby Jesus. The days were very hot and the nights were very cold.

Draw a picture of Joseph taking Mary and Jesus on this difficult journey.

Faith and Life Series • Grade 1 • Chapter 12 • Lesson 1   45

Name:_____

Joseph the Carpenter
Jesus liked to help his foster-father.

Color the picture.

46   *Faith and Life Series • Grade 1 • Chapter 12 • Lesson 2*

Name:_____

Using the words below, write the words for Mary under the title "Mary" in the chart. Do the same for Joseph.

Carpenter	Husband
Beautiful	Teacher
Foster-father	Mother
Handmaid of God	Sinless

Mary	Joseph
1. Beautiful	1. Carpenter
2. Handmaid of God	2. Foster-father
3. Mother	3. Husband
4. Sinless	4. Teacher

Faith and Life Series • Grade 1 • Chapter 12 • Lesson 3   47

Name:_____

Jesus was young once, just like you!
He understands you and all you think and do!

List some things you can share with Jesus.

1. Answers will vary
2._____
3._____
4._____
5._____

48   *Faith and Life Series • Grade 1 • Chapter 12 • Lesson 4*

TEACHER'S NOTES

UNIT THREE TEST
CHAPTERS 9–12

> **CHAPTER NINE: MARY HEARS SOME WONDERFUL NEWS**
>
> **CHAPTER TEN: THE SAVIOR IS BORN**
>
> **CHAPTER ELEVEN: THREE WISE MEN ARRIVE**
>
> **CHAPTER TWELVE: JESUS GROWS UP**

Aims

The students' understanding of the material covered in this unit will be reviewed and assessed.

Materials

• Unit 3 Test, Appendix, p. A-15

Assess

1. Distribute the unit tests and read through them with the students to be sure they understand the questions.

2. Administer the test.

3. After all the tests have been handed in, you may wish to review the correct answers with the class.

Name: _____

Unit 3 Test   **Chapters 9–12**

Fill in the blanks. *Trace the gray letters and fill in the rest.*

Word Bank

Jesus	Mary	sin	God
baby	men	His	

1. **Mary** is the Mother of Jesus.

2. Christmas is the birthday of **Jesus**.

3. Jesus came to save us from **sin**.

4. The angels sang, "Glory to **God**."

5. The shepherds went to see **baby** Jesus.

6. A star led three wise **men** to Jesus.

7. Jesus obeyed **His** parents.

TEACHER'S NOTES

TEACHER'S NOTES

CHAPTER THIRTEEN
JESUS BEGINS HIS WORK

Catechism of the Catholic Church References

Christ, the Heart of Catechesis: 426–29
Christ Gathers the Apostles: 542, 787, 1506
Christ Reveals Himself to the Apostles: 645, 647
Christ Reveals the Father: 238–41, 262
The Church Is Apostolic: 857, 860

The Commission of Christ: 2, 858–60
The Holy Spirit Guides the Apostles: 243, 725
Proclaiming the Gospel: 425, 1816
Proclaiming the Paschal Mystery: 571
The Twelve Apostles: 551–53

Scripture References

The Blessing of the Children: Mk 10:13–15; Lk 9:46–48
The Call of Matthew: Mt 9:9
The Call of Peter: Mt 4:18–22
The Call of the Twelve: Mt 10:1–4; Mk 3:13–19;
Lk 6:12–16

The Last Instructions to the Apostles: Mt 28:16–20
Mary Magdalene: Lk 8:2; Mk 14:3–9
The Samaritan Woman at the Well: Jn 4:1–30
Strength of God's Love: Is 49:16a
Fishers of Men: Mk 1:17

Background Reading: *The Fundamentals of Catholicism* by Fr. Kenneth Baker, S.J.

Volume 3:
"Jesus Personally Founded the Catholic Church," pp. 92–94
"Why Did Christ Establish His Church?", pp. 95–98
"A Hierarchical Church," pp. 101–4
"Bishops Are Successors of the Apostles," pp. 104–7

"What Is a Bishop?", pp. 119–22
"Some Notes on Collegiality," pp. 122–25

Summary of Lesson Content

Lesson 1

Jesus spent His public life teaching—in word and in deed—about God's love for man.

Jesus was called "rabbi."

Lesson 3

Jesus called twelve Apostles to be His helpers.

The Apostles lived with and learned from Jesus for three years.

When Jesus returned to Heaven, the Apostles carried on His work on earth.

Lesson 2

Jesus has a special love for children.

Today, priests bless children just as Jesus did.

Lesson 4

The Pope and bishops, with assistance from priests, are the successors of the Apostles and carry on their work.

Everyone can be an apostle of Jesus by behaving as He would and by learning about Him in order to teach others.

Chapter Thirteen: Jesus Begins His Work
Lesson One: Jesus Taught by Word and Deed

Aims

Students will learn that Jesus was called "rabbi."

They will learn that Jesus went from town to town teaching people.

They will be able to explain that our Lord taught about God by His words and by His actions.

Materials

- *Activity Book,* p. 49

- Children's Bible

Optional:
- Pictures of the Holy Land

- "To Jesus Christ, our sov'reign King," *Adoremus Hymnal,* #480

Begin

Write the word "Rabbi" on the board and say it with the children. Explain that the word "rabbi" is a Hebrew word for Jewish teachers. They were men who taught people about God and they were considered to be very wise and holy. Today, the class will learn why our Lord was called "rabbi" when He lived on this earth.

Develop

1. Read paragraphs 1 and 2 with the children. Then help the children to imagine what it would have been like to walk from town to town in Jesus' day. If possible, show them pictures of the dry, arid landscape of the Holy Land. Direct their attention to the painting of our Lord by the Sea of Galilee on p. 52 of their textbooks. Have them notice that our Lord is wearing only sandals on His feet, and that the men with Him are barefoot. Help them to appreciate the difficulties involved when walking from town to town: heat, dust, blisters, insects, etc.

2. Emphasize that Jesus went from town to town teaching people about God. Remind the children that through the prophets and holy men and women, God had already told the Jewish people some things about Himself and how He wanted people to live their lives. But Jesus told them much more: He told them about God's great love for them and God's desire that they love Him in return.

3. Because Jesus was teaching people about God, some of them called Him "rabbi" and this was a good name for Him. He was, however, different from every other rabbi because Jesus is God and, therefore, the best teacher of all. Who could better teach man about God than God Himself?

4. Tell the children that Jesus did not only teach with words, but also by His actions. By His perfect example of love, Jesus taught how people should behave toward one another. Talk briefly about how Jesus, a Jew, spoke to the Samaritan woman at the well, even though the Jews and Samaritans despised each other (Jn 4:1–30). Other examples might be: Jesus' tender care for Mary Magdalene, a notorious sinner shunned by all respectable people (Lk 8:2; Mk 14:3–9), and His friendship with Matthew, a hated tax collector (Mt 9:9).

Reinforce

Have the children answer the questions found on p. 49 of the *Activity Book* (see *Teacher's Manual,* p. 161). These questions pertain to paragraphs 1 and 2 in the text. You may want to assist them with this page.

Conclude

1. Ask the children to bring in a photograph of themselves to put on a bulletin board during the next class. Remind them to write their names on the back.

2. Sing "To Jesus Christ, our Sov'reign King," *Adoremus Hymnal,* #480.

52

13   Jesus Begins His Work

"And when Jesus had finished instructing his
twelve disciples, he went on from there to
teach and preach in their cities."

Matthew 11:1

When Jesus had grown up and was thirty years old, He left Nazareth. He knew it was time to begin His work. He walked from town to town and taught. He was a **teacher**, someone who shares with others the things that he knows so that they can know them too. He wanted everyone to learn about God.

He told people things about God that they never knew before, and He taught them how to love God better. Sometimes Jesus would teach large crowds, lots and lots of people. Sometimes He spoke to people one at a time.

Jesus liked to spend time with children. He liked to tell them how much their heavenly Father loved them. He put His arms around the children and then gave them His blessing.

53

Jesus picked twelve men to help him in a special way. These men were called the Twelve Apostles. They left their homes and went everywhere with Jesus. The Twelve Apostles listened to His teachings and then they told other people about Jesus. Later, additional men were chosen to be Apostles. The Apostles were the first bishops of the Church. They helped other people to follow Jesus. These other followers of Jesus we call disciples.

We, too, can be disciples of Jesus. We must listen to what our parents and teachers say about Him. We should tell others about Him. We should remember that Jesus is always near us.

Words to Know:

teacher   Apostles

Q. 31 *Who are the Apostles?*
The Apostles were special men who helped Jesus teach and lead his followers. Their successors today are called bishops (CCC 551).

54

GEOGRAPHY: GALILEE

On a hill near the town of Capernaum in Galilee, also known as the Mount of the Beatitudes, Christ preached the Sermon on the Mount (see Mt 5—7). This location provided a natural setting conducive to Christ's teaching: the landscape was naturally shaped like an amphitheater so His holy message was heard by the multitude who followed Him. Likewise, the Sea of Galilee (also called the Lake of Tiberias) is surrounded by mountains so that when Christ preached to his followers from the boat (see Mk 4:1), His voice projected and everyone present clearly heard His holy words.

Preview

In our next lesson, we will learn about Jesus' special love for children.

CHAPTER THIRTEEN: JESUS BEGINS HIS WORK
LESSON TWO: JESUS' LOVE FOR CHILDREN

Aims

Students will become aware of Jesus' special love for children.

They will learn about a priest's special blessing for children.

Materials

- *Activity Book*, p. 50

- Photographs of the students

Optional:
- Children's Bible

- "To Jesus Christ, our sov'reign King," *Adoremus Hymnal*, #480

- Have a priest visit

Begin

Remind the students that Jesus came into the world as a baby and grew up as a child in the care of Mary and Joseph. He knew what it was like to be a child: to laugh and play, to do chores, to love His family, and obey His parents. He also knew what it was like to be sad, and how it felt to be afraid. Jesus knows that children have a special love for God, and they please Him very much. Today, the class will learn about Jesus' special love for children.

Develop

1. Read paragraph 3 in the textbook. Emphasize that Jesus liked to tell the children how their Heavenly Father loved them very much. Ask the children to tell you how a father loves his children: he cares for their needs, gives them love, corrects them when they do something wrong, forgives them, encourages them to grow, shares their joys and sadness. He listens to his children, and he spends time with them.

2. Explain that God the Father has given each of the students a father here on earth. Earthly fathers are to be examples of God the Heavenly Father. They are to care for their children and love them. Although they are not perfect, they are a gift from God, and God chose each father for each child.

3. Refer back to the last sentence in paragraph 3 where it relates how Jesus put His arms around the children and blessed them. How much He loved the children! Ask the students how they feel when they receive hugs. Do they feel happy, safe, warm, and loved? Jesus gives them such love. He also gives His blessing. A blessing is a sign of love. It is when something is set apart for God, like when you save your favorite toy or food. Jesus blessed the children because He loves them and wants them to be set apart for Him. You might read the story of Jesus blessing the children from a children's Bible (Mk 10:13–15).

4. If possible, have a priest visit the classroom and ask him to give a special blessing to the children. Ask him to explain how he is acting in the person of Christ and how, through the priest, Christ Himself is blessing the students, just as He did in the Bible passage they just heard.

5. Remind them that they learned about the strength of God's love in Chapter 1, Lesson 1: "Behold, I have graven you on the palms of my hands" (Is 49:16a).

Reinforce

1. Have the students work on p. 50 of the *Activity Book* (see *Teacher's Manual*, p. 161). The children may draw themselves into this picture.

2. Gather the photographs of the children and attach them to the bulletin board under the title "Jesus Loves the Little Children." You may ask the students to assist you.

Conclude

1. Practice Question 31 with the class (see *Teacher's Manual*, p. 157).

2. Pray the Our Father (see *Teacher's Manual*, p. 367).

3. Close by singing "To Jesus Christ, our sov'reign King," *Adoremus Hymnal*, #480.

13   Jesus Begins His Work

"And when Jesus had finished instructing his twelve disciples, he went on from there to teach and preach in their cities."

Matthew 11:1

When Jesus had grown up and was thirty years old, He left Nazareth. He knew it was time to begin His work. He walked from town to town and taught. He was a **teacher**, someone who shares with others the things that he knows so that they can know them too. He wanted everyone to learn about God.

He told people things about God that they never knew before, and He taught them how to love God better. Sometimes Jesus would teach large crowds, lots and lots of people. Sometimes He spoke to people one at a time.

Jesus liked to spend time with children. He liked to tell them how much their heavenly Father loved them. He put His arms around the children and then gave them His blessing.

SAINT DOMINIC SAVIO

Saint Dominic Savio was born in Italy on April 2, 1842. As a small child he showed signs of great holiness. At the age of twelve, he entered the school founded by Saint John Bosco (see p. 231 of this manual). Though younger than the other boys, Dominic worried about their souls being stained by sin. He constantly reminded them to be good, to pray, and to confess their sins. Upon being falsely accused of mischief, he endured the punishment in imitation of our Lord, who was silent in His sufferings. He died in 1857 at the age of fifteen and was canonized in 1954. His feastday is May 6. He is the patron saint of youth, choir boys, and the falsely accused.

SAINT MARIA GORETTI

Saint Maria Goretti was born on October 16, 1890 in Corinaldo, Italy, the daughter of humble sharecroppers. Always cheerful in her daily duties even after her father's death, she was soon propositioned by her neighbor, 20-year-old Alessandro Serenelli. On July 5, 1902, after refusing him again, he stabbed her fourteen times. Maria died the next day at the age of eleven after forgiving her killer. Pius XII canonized her on June 24, 1950. The youngest officially recognized saint, she is the patroness of modern youth. Her feastday is July 6. Serenelli converted after Maria appeared to him in prison. He was present at her canonization.

"Let the children come to me, do not hinder them; for to such belongs the kingdom of God. Truly, I say to you, whoever does not receive the kingdom of God like a child shall not enter it."

—Mark 10:14–15

Preview

In the next lesson, we will learn about the men Jesus asked to help Him to do His work on earth: the Apostles.

CHAPTER THIRTEEN: JESUS BEGINS HIS WORK
LESSON THREE: JESUS CALLS THE APOSTLES

Aims

The students will learn about the call of the twelve Apostles and, in particular, the call of Peter.

They will be able to explain the mission of the Apostles.

Materials

- Children's Bible

- *Activity Book*, p. 51

Optional:
- "To Jesus Christ, our sov'reign King," *Adoremus Hymnal*, #480

Begin

Write two words on the board: "Disciple" and "Apostle." Explain that as Jesus traveled the Holy Land teaching people about God, there were many who became devoted to Him, and some even followed Him from town to town. That is what *disciple* means—a person who follows another. But even those who did not travel with Jesus followed the teach-ings of Jesus and the way of life he taught them in their hometowns. Explain that the "Apostles" were followers, too, but they were sent forth to do special jobs for which Jesus prepared them while He was on earth. Today, the class will learn more about the Apostles.

Develop

1. Read paragraph 4 aloud with the students.

2. From your children's Bible, read the account in Mark 3:13–19 of the call of the twelve Apostles.

3. Explain that Jesus chose twelve men to be His closest followers, or Apostles. They lived with Him, traveled with Him, ate with Him, learned from Him when He spoke publicly to people and when he spoke privately to them. They were Jesus' closest friends on earth.

4. Tell the children that in addition to being Jesus' closest friends, Jesus prepared these twelve men to carry on His work after He returned to Heaven. Before Jesus ascended to the Father after His death, He spoke to the Apostles one last time. Read Matthew 28:16–20, the passage where our Lord sends the Apostles out into the world to carry on the work He had begun. That is the meaning of the word *apostle*: "one who is sent out by another to help do his work."

5. Have the students look at the painting *The Calling of the First Apostles* on p. 52 in their textbooks. Tell the children that this is an unusual painting because it depicts two different events as though they happened at the same time: the call of the twelve Apostles and the specific call of Saint Peter. Ask these questions about the painting:
- Who is in the center of the painting, in the foreground? (Jesus)
- To whom is He speaking? (two men, with halos, who kneel before Him—two of the Apostles)
- Who is in the background, to the far right? (Jesus, again)
- To whom is He speaking? (to three men in a fishing boat)
- How are the men reacting to Jesus, both the two kneeling and those in the boat? (kneeling with their hands/arms crossed in prayer)

Reinforce

1. Have the students draw a picture of the twelve Apostles on p. 51 of the *Activity Book* (see *Teacher's Manual*, p. 161).

2. Practice Question 31 with all of the children. Then have pairs of students practice.

Conclude

1. Read the Scripture passage found on p. 55 of the text (see *Teacher's Manual*, p. 159): "Follow me and I will make you become fishers of men." Explain if need be.

2. Pray the Our Father (see *Teacher's Manual*, p. 367).

3. Sing "To Jesus Christ, our sov'reign King," *Adoremus Hymnal*, #480.

52

13   Jesus Begins His Work

"And when Jesus had finished instructing his twelve disciples, he went on from there to teach and preach in their cities."

Matthew 11:1

When Jesus had grown up and was thirty years old, He left Nazareth. He knew it was time to begin His work. He walked from town to town and taught. He was a **teacher**, someone who shares with others the things that he knows so that they can know them too. He wanted everyone to learn about God.

He told people things about God that they never knew before, and He taught them how to love God better. Sometimes Jesus would teach large crowds, lots and lots of people. Sometimes He spoke to people one at a time.

Jesus liked to spend time with children. He liked to tell them how much their heavenly Father loved them. He put His arms around the children and then gave them His blessing.

53

Jesus picked twelve men to help him in a special way. These men were called the Twelve Apostles. They left their homes and went everywhere with Jesus. The Twelve Apostles listened to His teachings and then they told other people about Jesus. Later, additional men were chosen to be Apostles. The Apostles were the first bishops of the Church. They helped other people to follow Jesus. These other followers of Jesus we call disciples.

We, too, can be disciples of Jesus. We must listen to what our parents and teachers say about Him. We should tell others about Him. We should remember that Jesus is always near us.

Words to Know:

teacher   Apostles

Q. 31 *Who are the Apostles?*
The Apostles were special men who helped Jesus teach and lead his followers. Their successors today are called bishops (CCC 551).

54

THE TWELVE APOSTLES

1. Simon Peter
2. Andrew, his brother
3. James the Greater
4. John, his brother
5. Philip
6. Thomas, the Twin
7. Bartholomew
8. Matthew (Levi)
9. James (the Lesser), son of Alpheus
10. Jude Thaddeus
11. Simon the Zealot
12. Judas Iscariot

You may want to teach the children "There Were Twelve Disciples," from *Wee Sing More Bible Songs*, pp. 20–21. This song lists the names of the twelve Apostles; it is a good tool for learning their individual names. See also Matthew 10:1–4; Mark 3:13–19; or Luke 6:12–16 for a biblical listing of the twelve Apostles.

Preview

In our next lesson, we will learn about how the work of the Apostles has gone on for more than 2000 years, and how we can do our part in spreading the message of Jesus.

CHAPTER THIRTEEN: JESUS BEGINS HIS WORK
LESSON FOUR: JESUS' WORK CONTINUES

Aims

Students will be able to explain that today's bishops carry on the work of the twelve Apostles, and that priests help them in their work.

They will be able to explain that they, too, can be apostles of Jesus in their daily lives.

Materials

- A picture of the Pope

- A picture of the local bishop

- *Activity Book*, p. 52

Optional:
- "To Jesus Christ, our sov'reign King," *Adoremus Hymnal*, #480

Begin

Tell the children that before Jesus went back to Heaven, He left one of His twelve Apostles, Saint Peter, in charge of the other Apostles and all of His followers. Saint Peter was the first Pope, and the other Apostles were the first bishops. Jesus left them in charge of His new Church.

Develop

1. Show the children a picture of the Holy Father and ask them to name him. Write his name on the chalkboard. Explain that the Pope is the successor of Saint Peter, which means that He has all the authority that Christ gave to Saint Peter when He was on this earth: to teach and to rule over the whole Church (they will learn more about this in Chapter 20). The Catholic Church was tiny when Jesus returned to Heaven, but because the first Apostles followed His command to go out into the whole world and teach everyone about Jesus, the Church is now everywhere and has millions and millions of members.

2. Explain that just as Saint Peter had the other Apostles to help him, so too, our Holy Father has helpers throughout the world. These men are called bishops. Show the children a picture of your local bishop and write his name on the chalkboard. Point out that both the Pope and the bishop have "crosiers," or staffs, much like the staff that a shepherd uses to herd his sheep. The members of the Church are the sheep, and the Pope and bishops are the shepherds who teach, guide, and protect the Church because they love her, just as Christ the Good Shepherd loved His Church (see the diagrams of Apostolic Succession on p. 205 of this manual).

3. Mention the name of your parish pastor (or priest), and write it on the chalkboard. Explain that, he, along with all the other priests, helps the bishop in caring for the members of the Church. Each pastor is in charge of a parish and is responsible for offering Mass, administering the Sacraments, and teaching his parishioners.

4. Explain to the children that everyone can be a "little apostle" for Jesus. Read paragraph 5 of the text with them. Ask them to think of ways that they can carry on Jesus' work. Remind them that in Lesson 1 they learned that Jesus taught both by His words and by His deeds.

Reinforce

1. Have the children complete little stories showing how an Apostle would act in a given situation. For example, "John's mother is sick in bed. John wants to be Jesus' Apostle, so John..." (helps around the house, is quiet, reads to his younger brothers and sisters, etc.). Or, "Tony was watching his favorite show just when his father asked him to run an errand. Tony immediately..." (turned off the T.V. and went on the errand).

2. Have the children color the picture on p. 52 of the *Activity Book* (see *Teacher's Manual*, p. 161).

3. Practice Question 31 in the textbook.

Conclude

1. Pray the Our Father (see *Teacher's Manual*, p. 367).

2. Sing "To Jesus Christ, our sov'reign King," *Adoremus Hymnal*, #480.

Jesus picked twelve men to help him in a special way. These men were called the Twelve Apostles. They left their homes and went everywhere with Jesus. The Twelve Apostles listened to His teachings and then they told other people about Jesus. Later, additional men were chosen to be Apostles. The Apostles were the first bishops of the Church. They helped other people to follow Jesus. These other followers of Jesus we call disciples.

We, too, can be disciples of Jesus. We must listen to what our parents and teachers say about Him. We should tell others about Him. We should remember that Jesus is always near us.

Words to Know:

teacher   Apostles

> **Q. 31** *Who are the Apostles?*
> The Apostles were special men who helped Jesus teach and lead his followers. Their successors today are called bishops (CCC 551).

54

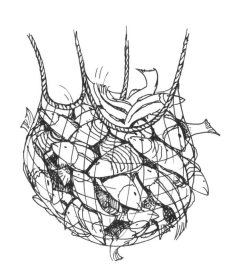

"Follow me and I will make you become fishers of men."
Mark 1:17

55

DEATHS OF THE TWELVE APOSTLES

Simon Peter: Crucified head downward.
Andrew: Crucified with ropes rather than nails.
James the Greater: Put to death by the sword.
John: Died naturally in Ephesus at an old age.
Philip: Cause of martyrdom unknown.
Thomas: Death by spearing.
Bartholomew: Either flayed alive and crucified head downward, or beheaded.
Matthew: Burned, stoned, or beheaded.
James, son of Alpheus: Put to death by the Jews.
Jude Thaddeus: Thrown from atop the Temple and beaten to death with a club; beheaded post-mortem.
Simon the Zealot: His body was sawed to pieces.
Judas: The betrayer of Christ who hanged himself; the Church has never pronounced judgment on him.

SAINT MATTHIAS

In Jerusalem in the days following the Ascension, Peter proposed that the Apostles choose someone to fill the place of the traitor Judas. Lots were drawn and Matthias was chosen. It is unclear whether the Jews crucified or stoned him in Jerusalem before beheading him.

For further reading see Acts 1:15–26.

Preview

In our next lesson, we will review what we have learned this week and take a quiz.

CHAPTER THIRTEEN: JESUS BEGINS HIS WORK
REVIEW AND ASSESSMENT

Aims

To review the material taught this week, and to assess the children's understanding of it.

Materials

- Quiz 13 (Appendix, p. A-16)

Optional:
- "To Jesus Christ, our sov'reign King," *Adoremus Hymnal*, #480

Review and Enrichment

1. Ask the following questions to help the students review the material from the week:
- How old was Jesus when He began His public life? (thirty years old)
- Whom did Jesus teach? (people of all ages)
- Whom did He particularly love? (little children)
- How many men did Jesus choose to be His helpers? (twelve)
- What were these men called? (Apostles)
- What did the Apostles do? (they lived with and learned from Jesus; when He returned to Heaven, they went out to the whole world and taught others about God)
- Whom did Jesus name as the head of the Apostles? (Saint Peter)
- Who is Saint Peter's successor? (the Pope)
- Who are the successors of the Apostles? (the bishops; their helpers are the pastors and priests)
- Can we be Apostles, too? How? (yes, by behaving as Jesus would, and by learning all we can about Him and teaching others what we learn)

2. Review Question 31 with the children as well as the Words to Know (see *Teacher's Manual*, p. 159).

Name: _____

Jesus Begins His Work   **Quiz 13**

Fill in the blanks. *Trace the gray letters and fill in the rest.*

Word Bank

God	sent	men	twelve	loves

1. Jesus told people about _God_ .

2. Jesus _loves_ little children.

3. Jesus chose _twelve_ men to be His helpers.

4. These _men_ were the Apostles.

5. Jesus _sent_ the Apostles to teach everyone about Him.

A-16   *Faith and Life Series • Grade 1 • Appendix A*

Assess

Pass out Quiz 13. Read through it with the children and answer any questions which they may have. Administer the quiz. When they have completed it, review the correct answers.

Conclude

Sing "To Jesus Christ, our Sov'reign King," *Adoremus Hymnal*, #480.

Chapter Thirteen: Jesus Begins His Work
Activity Book Answer Keys

Name:_____

Answer the following questions.

1. How old was Jesus when He began teaching?
<u>30 years old</u>

2. Where did Jesus teach?
<u>He walked from town to town.</u>

3. What did He want people to know?
<u>He wanted everyone to learn about God.</u>

4. Whom did Jesus teach?
<u>He taught large crowds.</u>

5. Whom did Jesus bless?
<u>Children</u>

6. Who were Jesus' special helpers?
<u>The Apostles</u>

7. How many helpers did He have?
<u>Twelve</u>

8. How can you be an Apostle?
<u>By listening to what our teachers and parents say about Jesus, and telling others what we have learned</u>

Name:_____

Jesus liked to spend time with children. He told them how much their heavenly Father loves them.

Color the picture.

Jesus put His arms around the children and He gave them His blessing.

Name:_____

Jesus chose twelve Apostles. They listened to His teaching. Then they taught others about Jesus.

Draw and color a picture of Jesus teaching His twelve Apostles.

Name:_____

It is important to listen to your teacher and to learn about Jesus, so you can teach others and be Apostles.

Color the picture.

In the Name of the Father and of the Son and of the Holy Spirit. Amen

TEACHER'S NOTES

CHAPTER FOURTEEN
JESUS TELLS THE GOOD NEWS

Catechism of the Catholic Church References

Christ: the One Word of Holy Scripture: 101–4, 134–35

Christ's Life Is a Mystery: 514–15, 534

The Good News of Christ: 422–29, 2763

The Inspiration and Truth of Scripture: 105–8, 136, 304, 702

The Interpretation of Scripture: 109–14, 128–33, 137

Jesus Teaches Us How To Pray: 2607–15, 2621

The Kingdom of God Is Near: 541–46, 567

The New Testament: 125–27

Proclamation of the Gospels: 2, 75, 875, 888, 1565, 2044

Scripture and Tradition: 78, 80–84, 95

The Transmission of the Gospels: 76–79

The Word Became Flesh: 456–60

Scripture References

The Beatitudes: Mt 5:1–12

The Great Commandment: Mt 22:37–40

The Last Supper: Mt 26:26–29; Mk 14:22–25; Lk 22:14–20

Background Reading: *The Fundamentals of Catholicism* by Fr. Kenneth Baker, S.J.

Volume 2:
"The Divine Teacher," pp. 279–82

Summary of Lesson Content

Lesson 1

The Good News tells of God's love for everyone.

God wants all people to be His children.

God wants everyone to live with Him forever in Heaven.

Lesson 3

The Good News is in the Bible, to be read and heard by everyone.

The Bible is God's Word.

Though God is the author of Sacred Scripture, Jesus' friends were inspired to write down in the Gospels the things He said and did.

Lesson 2

Jesus taught the Good News by word and deed.

Many people were happy to hear the Good News.

Jesus taught everyone how to love God and one another.

Lesson 4

Catholics can hear the Good News at Mass.

Everyone can learn the Good News by reading the Bible.

All people can live the Good News by loving God and neighbor as Jesus taught in Scripture.

CHAPTER FOURTEEN: JESUS TELLS THE GOOD NEWS
LESSON ONE: THE GOOD NEWS OF GOD'S LOVE

Aims

Students will understand that the Good News tells about God's love for all men.

They will know that God loves all people and wants everyone to be His child.

They will come to know that the Good News is for man now and always.

God wants everyone to be with Him forever in Heaven.

Materials

• A newspaper

• *Activity Book*, p. 53

Optional:
• "I heard the voice of Jesus say," *Adoremus Hymnal*, #579

Begin

Review with the children the teaching that the Pope, bishops, and priests are continuing Jesus' work here on earth.

Following the Apostles' example, they teach today what Jesus taught and did while He was on earth.

Develop

1. Hold up a newspaper and ask the children if they know what it is. Next, ask if they know its use (to tell the news, to let people know what is going on in the world, and other things people want to know).

2. Ask the children if they have ever received good news. For example, have they heard that a sick friend is now feeling better, or that they did well on a test? How did the good news make them feel? (happy, proud, thankful)

3. Explain that Jesus, the Son of God, brought some Good News to man. Write "Good News" on the board. Tell the children that it is capitalized because this "Good News" is important for every person on earth. Ask the children what they think this Good News is.

4. Now read paragraphs 1 and 2 from the textbook with the children. Repeat that the Good News is that God loves every-

one and wants every person to be with Him forever in Heaven. God loves man as a father loves his children. Ask the students what kind of love a father gives (protective, forgiving, unconditional). If God is their Father, they are His children. How can they be like children of God?

5. Remind the children that this Good News is important and that it is for everyone. Reread paragraph 1. Jesus told everyone the Good News. In fact it was so important that He went from town to town. How can people hear the Good News today? (at Mass, through the clergy, by reading the Bible, from parents and teachers)

6. Ask the children why Jesus wants them to hear the Good News. (So they can come to know, love, and serve God, and be happy with Him forever in Heaven!) Have the children think of ways they can give love to God, so that they can be with Him now in their hearts, and with Him forever in Heaven (pray, obey parents, do good deeds, etc.).

Reinforce

1. As a class, discuss the questions on p. 53 of the *Activity Book* (see *Teacher's Manual*, p. 173), then have the children complete the activity.

2. Have the children work with a partner and memorize Question 32 from the textbook. Also have them begin memorizing the Words to Know (see *Teacher's Manual*, p. 169).

3. Assign Good News stories and have the children write a simple report, then display the newspapers on the bulletin board (see example on the facing page).

Conclude

1. Teach the children a song to implement the lesson, such as "I heard the voice of Jesus say," *Adoremus Hymnal*, #579.

2. Lead the children in a closing prayer thanking God for His Good News. You may want to close with the Our Father (see *Teacher's Manual*, p. 367).

14   Jesus Tells the Good News

"Let the children come to me, and do not hinder them;
for to such belongs the kingdom of heaven."
Matthew 19:14

Jesus and His Apostles went from town to town. Jesus taught the people. He told everyone about the Good News of God's Kingdom everywhere He went.

The **Good News** is that God loves us all. Jesus told the people that God is their Father Who loves them very much. He told them that God wants them to be His children. He also said that God wants them to live in the Kingdom of Heaven.

Many people were happy to hear this Good News. They had waited all their lives for Jesus to come and show them the way to Heaven. Jesus taught them many other things. He taught them how to pray. He taught them how to love God and one another. Jesus came to show all of us the way to Heaven.

We can hear the Good News of Jesus too. The friends of Jesus wrote down the things He said and did while He was living here on earth. You can read about them in the **Bible**.

The Bible has other things in it, too. As you know, it tells the story of the sin of Adam and Eve. It tells of Noah, Abraham, and Moses. It also has prayers and songs. The Bible is God's book.

"THE GOOD NEWS"

Have the children make "Good News" newspapers and display them on the bulletin board under these headings:

- What is the Good News?
- How can we live the Good News?
- Who told the Good News?
- Who receives the Good News?

The Good News is that God loves everyone!

Preview

In our next lesson, we will learn about Jesus teaching the Good News and how people received it.

Chapter Fourteen: Jesus Tells the Good News
Lesson Two: Jesus Teaches the Good News

Aims

Students will be able to relate Christ's preaching of the Good News of the Kingdom.

They will be able to understand what the Good News is.

Materials

- Children's Bible

- *Activity Book*, p. 54

- Poster board and crayons

Optional:
- "I heard the voice of Jesus say," *Adoremus Hymnal*, #579

Begin

Have the children open their textbooks to p. 56 to the picture of Christ preaching. Discuss this picture with questions such as the following:
- What does this picture depict? (Jesus is preaching the Good News.)
- To whom is Jesus preaching? (He is preaching to many people—men, women, children.)

- Are the Apostles there? (Yes, they are the men on the right with halos.)
- Were people happy to hear the Good News? (Some look happy, like the women on the bottom right; all are listening carefully.)

Explain that today the children will learn more about how Jesus preached the Good News.

Develop

1. Read paragraph 3 with the children.

2. Read aloud to the class the Beatitudes from your children's Bible (Mt 5:1–12).

3. Discuss the Beatitudes with the children:
- Who is considered blessed?
- What is promised to them?
- For whom was the Good News preached? (Name specific people, such as your name and the names of the students in the class, their parents, friends, etc.)

4. Explain that the Good News tells of God's love for everybody (even those who think that God does not love them, like the poor, those who are sad, etc.). God's promises give people hope. Reinforce the promises for each Beatitude, and the hope to be united with God in Heaven.

5. Ask the children to whom Jesus taught the Good News. (everyone) To whom did He show the way to Heaven? (all people) How can the Beatitudes be lived? (see examples below)
- Poor in spirit—being humble
- Those who mourn—when a person is sad about a bad thing
- Those who hunger and thirst for what is right—loving justice
- Those who are merciful—when a person forgives another
- Those who are pure in heart—when a person is loving to God and neighbor
- Those who are peacemakers—when a person stops arguments
- Those who are persecuted for what is right—when it is difficult to do what is good, but one does it anyway

Reinforce

1. Assign the word search on p. 54 of the *Activity Book* (see *Teacher's Manual*, p. 173). You may want to assist them with this activity.

2. Have the children make posters for each Beatitude on a large piece of construction paper or poster board, and then arrange them into a long mural. It can be hung in the classroom or out in the hallway.

Conclude

1. Lead the class in prayer. Students may pray for those mentioned in each Beatitude: i.e., "God, please bless the poor in spirit."

2. Sing "I heard the voice of Jesus say," *Adoremus Hymnal*, #579.

56

14   Jesus Tells the Good News

"Let the children come to me, and do not hinder them; for to such belongs the kingdom of heaven."
Matthew 19:14

Jesus and His Apostles went from town to town. Jesus taught the people. He told everyone about the Good News of God's Kingdom everywhere He went.

The **Good News** is that God loves us all. Jesus told the people that God is their Father Who loves them very much. He told them that God wants them to be His children. He also said that God wants them to live in the Kingdom of Heaven.

Many people were happy to hear this Good News. They had waited all their lives for Jesus to come and show them the way to Heaven. Jesus taught them many other things. He taught them how to pray. He taught them how to love God and one another. Jesus came to show all of us the way to Heaven.

57

We can hear the Good News of Jesus too. The friends of Jesus wrote down the things He said and did while He was living here on earth. You can read about them in the **Bible**.

The Bible has other things in it, too. As you know, it tells the story of the sin of Adam and Eve. It tells of Noah, Abraham, and Moses. It also has prayers and songs. The Bible is God's book.

58

THE BEATITUDES

Blessed are the poor in spirit, for theirs is the kingdom of heaven.

Blessed are those who mourn, for they shall be comforted.

Blessed are the meek, for they shall inherit the earth.

Blessed are those who hunger and thirst for righteousness, for they shall be satisfied.

Blessed are the merciful, for they shall obtain mercy.

Blessed are the pure in heart, for they shall see God.

Blessed are the peacemakers, for they shall be called sons of God.

Blessed are those who are persecuted for righteousness' sake, for theirs is the kingdom of heaven.

—Matthew 5:3–10

Preview

In our next lesson, we will learn more about the Bible, God's book.

CHAPTER FOURTEEN: JESUS TELLS THE GOOD NEWS
LESSON THREE: THE BIBLE IS THE WORD OF GOD

Aims

Students will realize that the Bible is the Word of God.

They will learn that the Bible has two parts: the Old Testament and the New Testament.

They will understand that the New Testament contains the words and deeds of Jesus, including His teaching of the Good News.

They will learn that God is the author of the Bible, but that He had different people write it.

Materials

- Bible

- Children's Bible

- *Activity Book*, p. 55

Optional:
- "I heard the voice of Jesus say," *Adoremus Hymnal*, #579

Begin

Begin by showing the children a Bible, and write the word "Bible" on the chalkboard. Explain that the Bible has two parts to it, the Old Testament and the New Testament. Write these words on the board. Explain that the Old Testament tells about God preparing everyone for the coming of Jesus, and the New Testament tells about the life of Jesus, His teaching the Good News, and His works.

Develop

1. Read aloud the boxed-in description of the Bible found in the textbook on p. 58.

2. Explain that a children's Bible has the same stories as the Bible, but it is easier to understand. It is written for children, because God also wants children to understand His love for them. Hold it up for them to see.

3. Explain that God is the author of the Bible. It contains all that He wanted written and no more. Tell the children that many people wrote different parts of the Bible, and God told them what to write. They were obedient to God in what they wrote. The Bible was written over a long period of time, and many people helped God in writing it.

4. Ask the children to describe how you look. Some will tell you what you are wearing, some may focus on your features. The answers will each be different, but correct. Using this as an example, read from the different Gospels to show that they, too, are all correct but that the writers may say things differently. They were all obedient to God by writing what He wanted, just like the children obeyed you in your instructions. You may want to read a passage from each of the Gospels relating the same event.

Scriptural example: The Last Supper
- Mt 26:26–29
- Mk 14:22–25
- Lk 22:14–20

Reinforce

Help the children think of people with whom they can share the Good News. Have them write these names on p. 55 of the *Activity Book* (see *Teacher's Manual*, p. 173).

Conclude

1. End class by rereading the Beatitudes from the Bible as a prayer (see complete listing on p. 167). Together, offer thanksgiving for the Word of God. You may want to have all the children kiss the Bible, then place it in a prominent place, such as a Bible stand, or small altar.

2. Sing "I heard the voice of Jesus say," *Adoremus Hymnal*, #579.

We can hear the Good News of Jesus too. The friends of Jesus wrote down the things He said and did while He was living here on earth. You can read about them in the **Bible**.

The Bible has other things in it, too. As you know, it tells the story of the sin of Adam and Eve. It tells of Noah, Abraham, and Moses. It also has prayers and songs. The Bible is God's book.

58

Words to Know:

Good News   Bible

Q. 32 *What did Jesus tell the people?* Jesus told the people the Good News of God's love for them (CCC 543–544).

59

GROUPING THE BOOKS OF THE OLD TESTAMENT

The Pentateuch: Genesis, Exodus, Leviticus, Numbers, Deuteronomy

The Historical Books: Joshua, Judges, Ruth, 1 and 2 Samuel, 1 and 2 Kings, 1 and 2 Chronicles, Ezra, Nehemiah, Tobit, Judith, Esther, and 1 and 2 Maccabees

The Wisdom Books: (also known as the Poetic Books): Job, Psalms, Proverbs, Ecclesiastes, the Song of Solomon, the Wisdom of Solomon, and Sirach

The Major Prophets: Isaiah, Jeremiah, Ezekial, and Daniel

The Minor Prophets: Hosea, Joel, Amos, Obadiah, Jonah, Micah, Nahum, Habakkuk, Zephaniah, Haggai, Zechariah, Malachi, Baruch, and Lamentations

Scripture has a sacredness peculiar to itself.
—Saint Augustine

Preview

In our next lesson, we will learn that the Word of God is for children too.

CHAPTER FOURTEEN: JESUS TELLS THE GOOD NEWS
LESSON FOUR: THE BIBLE IS FOR ALL PEOPLE

Aims

Students will know that God's Word is for all people; God wants all people to know Him and His Good News.

The children will realize that they hear God's Word at Mass in the readings.

They can also learn God's Word by reading the Bible.

The children will understand how they can respond to God's Word by loving God and neighbor.

Materials

- Sunday missal with the readings for the week marked

- *Activity Book*, p. 56

Optional:
- "I heard the voice of Jesus say," *Adoremus Hymnal*, #579

Begin

Hold up a Sunday missal or missalette. Open to the readings of the week and explain that these readings come from the Bible. You may want to find them in the Bible for the children so they can see them there.

Develop

1. Explain to the children that at Mass, God's Word is read aloud so that all people can come to know, love, and serve God. By doing this, everyone can prepare to be with God forever in Heaven.

2. Explain that the priest, at every Mass, reads the Gospel. Remind them that the Gospel teaches what Jesus said and did. Tell the children that if they listen at Mass, Jesus can be their teacher and example. The readings from the Bible are for all people, of all ages, for people long ago, and people now, and even those yet to be born. God's Word is the same for everyone—it is what He wants man to know. If anyone wants to know God and what God wants him to know, he should read the Bible, and listen to God's Word at Mass.

3. Tell the children that the Good News is summarized in the Great Commandment that is found in Matthew 22:37–40. Read the passage to them, and then repeat the Great Commandment:
   - You shall love the Lord your God with all your heart, and with all your soul, and with all your mind.
   - You shall love your neighbor as yourself.

You may want to write these on the board and/or have the students repeat them after you.

4. Discuss ways that anyone can love God and neighbor. Have the children think of things they have done and can do, for example, pray, go to Mass, visit the Blessed Sacrament, do a kind deed, etc. List these examples on the chalkboard.

Reinforce

1. Have the children complete p. 56 of the *Activity Book* on the Great Commandment (see *Teacher's Manual*, p. 173). They can refer to the list on the chalkboard for help.

2. Review memorization of Question 32 in their textbook, and the Great Commandment. They should memorize these if possible.

Conclude

1. As a class, say a prayer asking God for help in living the Good News. The children may add their intentions, asking God's help to live the Good News in a specific way, i.e., "Please God, help me to be kind to my brother/sister."

2. Sing "I heard the voice of Jesus say," *Adoremus Hymnal*, #579.

We can hear the Good News of Jesus too. The friends of Jesus wrote down the things He said and did while He was living here on earth. You can read about them in the **Bible**.

The Bible has other things in it, too. As you know, it tells the story of the sin of Adam and Eve. It tells of Noah, Abraham, and Moses. It also has prayers and songs. The Bible is God's book.

58

Words to Know:

Good News   Bible

Q. 32 *What did Jesus tell the people?*
Jesus told the people the Good News of God's love for them (CCC 543–544).

59

GROUPING THE BOOKS OF THE NEW TESTAMENT

The Narrative Books: Matthew, Mark, Luke, John, and the Acts of the Apostles

The Letters and Epistles: Romans, 1 and 2 Corinthians, Galatians, Ephesians, Philippians, Colossians, 1 and 2 Thessalonians, 1 and 2 Timothy, Titus, Hebrews, James, 1 and 2 Peter, 1, 2, and 3 John, and Jude

Apocalyptic Literature: Revelation

Ignorance of Scripture is ignorance of Christ.
—Saint Jerome

THE SYNOPTIC GOSPELS

Matthew, Mark, and Luke are called the Synoptic Gospels because they "view together" (from the Greek *synoptikos*) the events in the life of Christ.

THE GREAT COMMANDMENT

"You shall love the Lord your God with all your heart, and with all your soul, and with all your mind."

"You shall love your neighbor as yourself."
—Matthew 22:37, 39

Preview

In our next lesson, we will review this week's materials and take a quiz.

171

CHAPTER FOURTEEN: JESUS TELLS THE GOOD NEWS

REVIEW AND ASSESSMENT

Aims

To review and reinforce the materials taught this week, and assess the children's understanding.

Materials

- Quiz 14 (Appendix, p. A-17)
- "I heard the voice of Jesus say," *Adoremus Hymnal*, #579

Review and Enrichment

1. Ask questions to review the chapter with the children, such as:
   - To whom did Jesus teach the Good News?
   - What is the Good News?
   - What is the Bible?
   - What are the Beatitudes?

2. Ask the children to explain what is happening in the picture in the textbook on p. 56 (see *Teacher's Manual*, p. 167). Correct any mistakes they make.

3. Review the following words:
   - Old Testament
   - New Testament
   - Gospels
   - Bible
   - Apostle
   - Good News

Name: _____

Jesus Tells the Good News   Quiz 14

Fill in the blanks. *Trace the gray letters and fill in the rest.*

Word Bank

Bible	News	Jesus	love
went	all	pray	

1. Jesus and His Apostles **went** from town to town.

2. They told people the Good **News**.

3. The Good News is that God loves us **all**.

4. Jesus taught us to **love** God and one another.

5. Jesus also taught us to **pray**.

6. The **Bible** is the holy book that God gave us.

Assess

1. Pass out Quiz 14 and read through it with the children; then administer the quiz. After the students have finished, review the answers with them aloud.

2. Take time to quiz the children on their memory work, including the Great Commandment.

Conclude

Conclude by singing "I heard the voice of Jesus say," *Adoremus Hymnal*, #579, or saying a prayer, such as the Our Father (see *Teacher's Manual*, p. 367).

Name:_____

The Good News!

Answer the following questions.

Who? (Who preached the Good News?)

Jesus and the Apostles

What? (What is the Good News?)

God loves us all.

Where? (Where did Jesus tell the Good News?)

Everywhere He went

When? (When did people first hear the Good News?)

When Jesus came

Name:_____

Word Search

Can you find these words in the puzzle?
Look carefully! The words go across and down.

GOOD NEWS	HEAVEN	PRAY
EVERYWHERE	BIBLE	APOSTLES
KINGDOM	JESUS	CHILDREN
TEACH	FATHER	EVERYONE

```
X  X  C  H  I  L  D  R  E  N  X  E
X  X  X  X  X  J  B  I  B  L  E  V
G  O  O  D  N  E  W  S  X  X  X  E
T  X  X  X  X  S  X  X  X  X  X  R
E  X  X  X  X  U  X  X  P  R  A  Y
A  X  X  X  X  S  X  X  X  X  X  W
C  X  X  X  X  X  X  X  X  F  X  H
H  X  H  E  A  V  E  N  X  A  X  E
X  E  V  E  R  Y  O  N  E  T  X  R
A  P  O  S  T  L  E  S  X  H  X  E
X  X  X  X  X  X  X  X  X  E  X  X
K  I  N  G  D  O  M  X  X  R  X  X
```

Name:_____

Every Sunday at Mass we hear the Gospel. It is the Good News of God's love for us. It helps us to love God. It tells us all about Jesus our Lord and Savior.

I can listen at Mass to understand the readings. My parents can help me when I do not understand.

List some people to whom you can tell the Good News.

Answers will vary

Name:_____

Memorize the Great Commandment.

"You shall love the Lord your God with all your heart, and with all your soul, and with all your mind.

You shall love your neighbor as yourself."

Matthew 22:37, 39

Can you give some examples of how to live this Commandment?

Love God

Answers will vary

Love Neighbor

Answers will vary

TEACHER'S NOTES

TEACHER'S NOTES

CHAPTER FIFTEEN
JESUS DOES WONDERFUL THINGS

Catechism of the Catholic Church References

Christ the Physician: 1503–5
Christ: True God and True Man: 464–70, 480–83
Contrition: 1451–54, 1492
Forgiveness: 2842–45, 2862
"Give Us This Day Our Daily Bread": 2828–37, 2861
God Alone Forgives Sin: 1441–42

Jesus: The Only Son of God: 441–45, 454
Mercy and Sin: 1846–48
Miracles and Signs of the Kingdom: 156, 547–50, 567
Healings as a Sign of Christ's Divinity: 515, 517, 1507
Exorcisms: 517, 1673

Scripture References

The Calming of the Storm: Mt 8:23–27; Mk 4:35–41;
Lk 8:22–25
The Healing of the Paralytic: Mt 9:2–8; Mk 2:2–12;
Lk 5:17–26
Messiah Prophesy: Is 29:18–19
Sacrament of Penance: Mt 16:19; 18:18; Jn 20:23

Anointing the Sick: Mk 16:13; Jas 5:14–15
Truly You Are the Son of God: Mt 14:33; Jn 6:1–15
The Raising of Jairus' Daughter: Mt 9:18–19, 23–26;
Mk 5:22–24, 35–43; Lk 8:41–42, 49–56
Apostles' Breakfast of Fish: Jn 21:9–14

Background Reading: *The Fundamentals of Catholicism* by Fr. Kenneth Baker, S.J.

Volume 1:
"The Power of Christ," p. 263–66

Summary of Lesson Content

Lesson 1

Jesus performed miracles to show He is the Son of God.

We will learn the miracle of the multiplication of loaves and fishes.

God continues to feed His children today in the Eucharist.

Lesson 2

Miracles are not magic.

Only God can work miracles.

We will learn the miracle of the calming of the storm.

Lesson 3

Jesus, as God, has the power to perform miracles.

Jesus will perform miracles if they are for a person's good.

We will hear the miracle of the raising of Jairus' daughter, and other healings.

Lesson 4

We will learn how Jesus miraculously healed the paralyzed man.

Only God can forgive sins.

Today, Jesus still heals people and forgives sins in the Sacraments of the Anointing of the Sick and Reconciliation.

CHAPTER FIFTEEN: JESUS DOES WONDERFUL THINGS
LESSON ONE: JESUS FEEDS THE HUNGRY

Aims

Students will learn that Jesus performed many miracles.

They will see that these miracles reveal that Jesus is the Son of God.

They will hear about the multiplication of loaves and fishes.

They will realize that Jesus feeds the hungry today in the Eucharist, which is His Body.

Materials

- Dinner roll

- Children's Bible

- *Activity Book*, p. 57

Optional:
- "Jesus, my Lord, my God, my all!" *Adoremus Hymnal*, #516

Begin

Draw a diagram of the Blessed Trinity on the chalkboard (see example on the opposite page) and add the word "Jesus" beside God the Son. Remind the children that God the Son became man in the person of Jesus; Jesus is both God and man.

Develop

1. Read paragraphs 1 and 2 aloud with the children.

2. Using a small amount of food (e.g., a dinner roll), break it into enough pieces for all the students. Explain that this is not a miracle, because you provided the bread. As the roll is broken, the pieces become smaller and there is not enough to feed everyone, especially if someone is hungry. Remind them that Jesus fed five thousand people with some bread and fish.

3. From your children's Bible, read the account of the multiplication of loaves and fishes (Jn 6:1–15). Jesus did not just share His bread and fish. He performed a miracle and made more loaves and fish so that there was plenty for everyone to eat. Ask the children if they can do this. Why can Jesus do it? (Jesus is God.) Ask the students why Jesus did the miracle (for the good of the people; because He loved them; to show that He is God).

4. Explain that a miracle is something that only God can do. It is not a magic trick, and it is not a coincidence. It is when God does what man and nature cannot do. Sometimes God uses what is available, such as fish and bread; sometimes He uses nothing at all and He does what is not possible for any man to do.

5. Explain that Jesus performed miracles to show that He is God, and because He loves all people. He performed miracles that helped people and taught them about God's love.

6. Discuss how Jesus still feeds people today in the Eucharist. Just as people become hungry and must eat to nourish their bodies, so too, the soul must be fed to be healthy and strong. Jesus gives nourishment for the soul in the Eucharist. He does this because He loves His children. Jesus comes as the Bread of Life to nourish the soul. He is true food for the spiritually hungry (the Eucharist and the Mass will be studied in Chapter 25).

Reinforce

1. Have the children draw and color a picture of Christ's miracle of the multiplication of loaves and fish on p. 57 of the *Activity Book* (see *Teacher's Manual*, p. 185).

2. Teach and sing with the children an appropriate song, such as "Jesus, my Lord, my God, my all!" *Adoremus Hymnal*, #516.

Conclude

End the class with a prayer. If possible, take the children for a visit to the Blessed Sacrament. Encourage them to pray before the Blessed Sacrament often.

15   Jesus Does Wonderful Things

"Truly you are the Son of God."
Matthew 14:33

To show us that He is really the Son of God, Jesus did many wonderful things that were beyond human power. We call these things **miracles**. Here are some of the miracles of Jesus:

One time, Jesus finished teaching five thousand people. Then it was late and everyone was hungry, but there wasn't enough food for everyone. So Jesus took five loaves of bread and two fishes and made them into enough for all of them, all five thousand people.

Another day Jesus and the Apostles were out on a boat when a big storm came. The Apostles were afraid the boat would sink so they called to Jesus, "Save us, Lord." Jesus told the wind and waves to be quiet, and everything grew calm, just like that! Only God can make the weather obey.

THE SYMBOLISM OF THE FISH

The symbol of the fish in Christian art may have been suggested by the miraculous multiplication of the loaves and fish, or by the Apostles' breakfast of fish on the shore of the Sea of Galilee after the Resurrection (Jn 21:9–14). However, the fish's popularity among Christians is likely the result of the acrostic forming the Greek word for fish (*Ichthys*), which briefly but clearly describes the character and divinity of Christ: *Iesous Christos Theou Yios Soter*, i.e., *Jesus Christ, Son of God, Saviour*. This word, as well as the representation of the fish, is a brief profession of faith. Tertullian called Christians "little fishes," who, after the image of the Ichthys, are born in the water.

CHALK TALK: THE BLESSED TRINITY

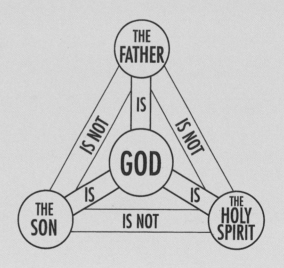

Man does not live by bread alone, but . . . man lives by everything that proceeds out of the mouth of the LORD.

—Deuteronomy 8:3

Preview

In our next lesson, we will study Jesus' miracle of the calming of the storm.

CHAPTER FIFTEEN: JESUS DOES WONDERFUL THINGS
LESSON TWO: JESUS CALMS THE STORM

Aims

Students will understand that because Jesus is God, He can perform miracles; even the weather obeys Him.

They will understand the difference between miracles and magic.

Only God can work true miracles.

Materials

- Any children's trick
- Children's Bible
- *Activity Book*, p. 58

Optional:
- "Jesus, my Lord, my God, my all!" *Adoremus Hymnal*, #516

Begin

Gather the students and perform a children's trick. Then show the students how the trick was done. Ask them if this is a miracle. Explain that a trick fools the audience. A miracle is not a trick, nor is it meant to fool anyone; it can only be performed by God. A trick is performed to entertain or to receive a reward. A miracle is done to help someone, to show God's love, and reveal that Jesus is God. Review the multiplication of loaves and fish with the children, and reinforce how this miracle showed that Jesus is God. Explain that Jesus worked many miracles, another of which will be told about in this lesson.

Develop

1. Read aloud paragraph 3 in the student text, then read the calming of the storm from a children's Bible (Mt 8:23–27; Mk 4:35–41; or Lk 8:22–25).

2. Have the students imagine that they are disciples in the boat with Jesus. Would they be scared in the storm? Would they be cold and wet? Would they wonder why Jesus would sleep during the storm? Would they have faith to ask Jesus to save them? Then have the children imagine the storm clearing away immediately at the command of Christ. How would they feel? What would they think? Would they recognize Jesus as the Son of God?

3. Ask the students to think about what might have happened if Jesus had not calmed the storm. Would it have cleared away on its own? Was this a coincidence?

4. Remind the children that the calming of the storm was not done by the power of man. No man can control the weather, not even the weatherman! Jesus is not just a man, He is God, so He was able to make the storm obey Him. He did this to save the Apostles, to calm their fear, to show His love for them, to reveal that He is God, and to give them faith.

5. Ask the children to name some of the similarities between the miracles of the multiplication of loaves and fish and the calming of the storm. For example:
- Man alone could not do these works; only God has the power.
- These miracles gave faith to the people involved and revealed that Jesus is the Son of God.
- The miracles helped people.
- Both miracles show God's love for man and His concern for man's well being.

Reinforce

1. Have the children fill in the blanks on p. 58 in their *Activity Book* (see *Teacher's Manual*, p. 185). You may want to do this activity with them.

2. Have the children separate into pairs to review Question 33 in the textbook.

Conclude

1. End the class with a prayer, thanking Jesus for His miracles.

2. Sing "Jesus, my Lord, my God, my all!" *Adoremus Hymnal*, #516.

15   Jesus Does Wonderful Things

"Truly you are the Son of God."
Matthew 14:33

To show us that He is really the Son of God, Jesus did many wonderful things that were beyond human power. We call these things **miracles**. Here are some of the miracles of Jesus:

One time, Jesus finished teaching five thousand people. Then it was late and everyone was hungry, but there wasn't enough food for everyone. So Jesus took five loaves of bread and two fishes and made them into enough for all of them, all five thousand people.

Another day Jesus and the Apostles were out on a boat when a big storm came. The Apostles were afraid the boat would sink so they called to Jesus, "Save us, Lord." Jesus told the wind and waves to be quiet, and everything grew calm, just like that! Only God can make the weather obey.

61

Another time a man came to Jesus. "Please come to my house," he said. "My little girl is sick." Jesus was sad about this so He went with him. On the way, someone from the man's house met them and he said, "It is too late. She's dead." But Jesus went right on to the house and He took the child's hand. "Get up little girl," Jesus said. The little girl opened her eyes and got up. Jesus had brought her back to life.

Jesus did many other miracles too. He made blind people see, He made deaf people hear, and He made sick people well.

Because Jesus is God, He could help anyone who asked Him for help. But He would only help them if it really was good for them, and if it was for the best. Jesus wants you to ask Him for help when you need it too. In the prayer Jesus gave us, we say, "Give us this day our daily bread," and that means asking for just about anything we need.

One day, some people carried a very sick man to Jesus. The man couldn't walk or even move his arms. But before Jesus made him better, He said, "Your sins are forgiven." Then He said, "Get up and walk." The

62

man got up and walked. He felt so much better because his sins were gone too.

Because Jesus is God, He could heal the sick. Because Jesus is God, He can **forgive** sins. If we are sorry for our sins, Jesus will forgive them too.

Words to Know:

miracle   forgive

> **Q. 33** *Why did Jesus perform miracles?*
> Jesus performed miracles to show us that He is truly the Son of God (CCC 515).

63

INSTRUCTIONS FOR A SIMPLE TRICK

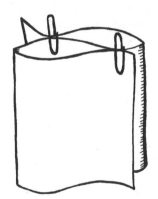

Materials: two paper clips and a sheet of paper

Fold the sheet of paper in three.

Fasten a paper clip at the two places indicated.

Pull the ends of the paper outward and the two paper clips will be interlocked.

Preview

In our next lesson, we will learn about some of Christ's miracles of healing.

CHAPTER FIFTEEN: JESUS DOES WONDERFUL THINGS
LESSON THREE: JESUS HEALS THE SICK

Aims

Students will understand that Jesus, because he is God, has the power to heal people and even raise them from the dead.

They will realize that Jesus does miracles only if it is for the good of the person.

They will see that Jesus can work miracles in their lives, too.

Materials

- Children's Bible

- *Activity Book*, p. 59

Optional:
- "Jesus, my Lord, my God, my all!" *Adoremus Hymnal*, #516

Begin

Review the different miracles you have taught to the class. Explain that the miracles discussed so far changed bread and fish and the weather, but not people. However, Jesus can work miracles for people too; Jesus can heal both their bodies and souls. Tell them to listen carefully as you read about one of these bodily miracles.

Develop

1. Read paragraph 4 with the class.

2. You may now want to read about the raising of Jairus' daughter from your children's Bible (Mt 9:18–19, 23–26; Mk 5:22–24, 35–43; or Lk 8:41–42, 49–56). Explain that because He is God, Jesus raised this girl from the dead. This is a very great miracle.

3. With the students, read paragraph 5. Ask the children to tell you what other miracles Jesus did for people:
- He gave the blind sight.
- He made the deaf hear.
- He cured the sick.

4. Explain that these miracles showed the Jewish people that Jesus is the Messiah, the Son of God. Isaiah, a great prophet, told the Jewish people that the Messiah would do these things so that they would be able to recognize Him when He came.

Read Isaiah's prophecy (Is 29:18–19), so the children will hear what the Jewish people who saw Jesus already knew about Him. Some Jews recognized Him and followed Him, but others did not.

5. Read paragraph 6. Tell the students that because Jesus is God, He can work miracles in their lives, too. If they ask Jesus for something, and it is for their own good, Jesus can work a miracle in their lives. For example, Jesus can make sick people well. Miracles also happen at church, when bread and wine become the Body and Blood of Jesus Christ; in this way, He feeds hungry souls in a more real way than when he multiplied the loaves and fish.

6. You may want to lead the children in a discussion of miracles of which they have knowledge, i.e. in the lives of the saints, other miracles of Jesus in the Bible, or maybe even a healing in their family.

Reinforce

1. Have the children match the miracles with the pictures on p. 59 of the *Activity Book* (see *Teacher's Manual*, p. 185).

2. Students may draw pictures of Jesus' miracles, then take turns showing them to the class.

Conclude

1. Sing with the children "Jesus, my Lord, my God, my all!" *Adoremus Hymnal*, #516.

2. Say a prayer thanking Jesus for His miracles and His love for all people, especially those with faith who are ill or disabled.

Another time a man came to Jesus. "Please come to my house," he said. "My little girl is sick." Jesus was sad about this so He went with him. On the way, someone from the man's house met them and he said, "It is too late. She's dead." But Jesus went right on to the house and He took the child's hand. "Get up little girl," Jesus said. The little girl opened her eyes and got up. Jesus had brought her back to life.

Jesus did many other miracles too. He made blind people see, He made deaf people hear, and He made sick people well.

Because Jesus is God, He could help anyone who asked Him for help. But He would only help them if it really was good for them, and if it was for the best. Jesus wants you to ask Him for help when you need it too. In the prayer Jesus gave us, we say, "Give us this day our daily bread," and that means asking for just about anything we need.

One day, some people carried a very sick man to Jesus. The man couldn't walk or even move his arms. But before Jesus made him better, He said, "Your sins are forgiven." Then He said, "Get up and walk." The

62

man got up and walked. He felt so much better because his sins were gone too.

Because Jesus is God, He could heal the sick. Because Jesus is God, He can **forgive** sins. If we are sorry for our sins, Jesus will forgive them too.

Words to Know:

miracle   forgive

Q. 33 *Why did Jesus perform miracles?*
Jesus performed miracles to show us that He is truly the Son of God (CCC 515).

63

SAINT ANTHONY OF PADUA

Born in Lisbon in 1195, Saint Anthony was baptized Ferdinand. At the age of fifteen he joined a group of Augustinian friars. In 1220 he joined the Franciscans to preach against heretics and perhaps suffer martyrdom for Christ's sake. At this time he took the name Anthony. He soon became a well-known preacher and miracle worker in Italy, and was given the name "Hammer of the Heretics." He died on June 13, 1231. At the time of his death, even young children considered him a saint. He was quickly canonized on Pentecost, May 30, 1232, by Gregory IX, who knew him personally. In 1263, it was discovered that his tongue is incorrupt; he is a Doctor of the Church.

MIRACLES OF SAINT ANTHONY

- A horse fasting for three days, refused oats until it had knelt down and adored the Blessed Sacrament in Saint Anthony's hand.
- The poisoned food offered him by some Italian heretics was rendered harmless by the Sign of the Cross.
- He preached a sermon to the fishes on the bank of a river near Padua.
- After telling a young man who kicked his mother in a fit of anger that the foot of one who kicks his mother deserved to be cut off, the man ran home and did so. The saint took the amputated foot and miraculously rejoined it to the leg.

MORE MIRACLES OF SAINT ANTHONY

- Preaching one Holy Thursday he remembered he had to sing a Lesson of the Divine Office. Suddenly he appeared at that moment among the friars in choir to sing his Lesson, after which he continued his sermon.
- While preaching, he miraculously preserved his audience from the rain.
- He predicted during a sermon that the devil would break down the pulpit, but that all should remain safe. The pulpit was overthrown while he was preaching but no one was hurt.

Preview

In our next lesson, we will learn about the healing of the paralytic.

CHAPTER FIFTEEN: JESUS DOES WONDERFUL THINGS
LESSON FOUR: JESUS HEALS US, BODY AND SOUL

Aims

Students will hear the miracle of the paralytic.

They will learn that Jesus has the power to forgive sins.

They will understand that through the Church, Jesus still works miracles in the Sacraments of the Anointing of the Sick and Penance.

Materials

- Children's Bible

- *Activity Book*, p. 60

Optional:
- Have a priest explain the Sacraments of the Anointing of the Sick and Penance

- "Jesus, my Lord, my God, my all!" *Adoremus Hymnal*, #516

Begin

Remind the students how they learned that Jesus is able to heal sick bodies. Tell them that Jesus can also heal souls. Write the words "Body" and "Soul" on the chalkboard, and list types of miracles under each title. For example, "the blind see" belongs under "body," and "the Eucharist" under "soul." Tell the children that today they will learn about a miracle that shows Jesus has the power to heal both body and soul.

Develop

1. Read paragraph 7 from the text. You may also want to read this story from a children's Bible (Mt 9:2–8; Mk 2:2–12; or Lk 5:17–26). Then ask the following questions:
   - Did Jesus go to the sick man, or did the sick man come to Jesus? (The sick man came to Jesus.)
   - What was wrong with the man? (He could not move his arms and legs.)
   - What did Jesus first say? (His sins were forgiven.)
   - Why would Jesus say this if his body was sick? (Jesus healed his body as a sign of healing his soul.)
   - When Jesus said, "Get up and walk," what happened? (The man got up and walked and his sins were forgiven.)

2. Read paragraph 8 with the students and emphasize that Jesus still offers His healing and forgiveness through the Church. If a priest visited during Chapter 13, Lesson 2, remind the students of his special blessing for children. If not, explain that a priest not only gives blessings through Christ, but heals and forgives sins in the Sacraments.

3. Explain the Sacrament of the Anointing of the Sick: Sometimes when a person is sick and even when he is in the hospital, Jesus wants to give him healing, just as He did while on earth. A priest will go to the sick person and anoint him with oil. If it is for the person's good, Jesus will heal his body. Sometimes, Jesus heals a person spiritually so he can be happy and ready to be with Him in Heaven. In this way, through the priest, Jesus still works healing miracles.

4. Explain the Sacrament of Penance (Confession): Just as the paralyzed man's sins were forgiven, Catholics may go to Jesus in the Sacrament of Penance. The priest acts in the person of Christ to forgive sins. This Sacrament is a great miracle for it cleanses the sinner's soul and gives back God's grace.

5. If possible, have a priest visit the classroom and discuss these Sacraments with the students.

Reinforce

1. The best reinforcement is a priest's visit.

2. Have the children complete p. 60 of the *Activity Book* on the Sacraments of Healing (see *Teacher's Manual*, p. 185).

Conclude

1. Lead the children in prayer.

2. Sing, in closing, with the children "Jesus, my Lord, my God, my all!" *Adoremus Hymnal*, #516.

Another time a man came to Jesus. "Please come to my house," he said. "My little girl is sick." Jesus was sad about this so He went with him. On the way, someone from the man's house met them and he said, "It is too late. She's dead." But Jesus went right on to the house and He took the child's hand. "Get up little girl," Jesus said. The little girl opened her eyes and got up. Jesus had brought her back to life.

Jesus did many other miracles too. He made blind people see, He made deaf people hear, and He made sick people well.

Because Jesus is God, He could help anyone who asked Him for help. But He would only help them if it really was good for them, and if it was for the best. Jesus wants you to ask Him for help when you need it too. In the prayer Jesus gave us, we say, "Give us this day our daily bread," and that means asking for just about anything we need.

One day, some people carried a very sick man to Jesus. The man couldn't walk or even move his arms. But before Jesus made him better, He said, "Your sins are forgiven." Then He said, "Get up and walk." The

62

man got up and walked. He felt so much better because his sins were gone too.

Because Jesus is God, He could heal the sick. Because Jesus is God, He can **forgive** sins. If we are sorry for our sins, Jesus will forgive them too.

Words to Know:

miracle   forgive

> **Q. 33** *Why did Jesus perform miracles?*
> Jesus performed miracles to show us that He is truly the Son of God (CCC 515).

63

THE ANOINTING OF THE SICK

Christ instituted this Sacrament (Mk 6:13 and Jas 5:14, 15) to give spiritual health, including the remission of sins, to Christians who are seriously ill; it may also restore bodily health. The Sacrament consists in the anointing of the sick person by a priest, accompanied by certain special prayers. The priest uses oil made from olives and blessed by the bishop to anoint the organs of the five senses (eyes, ears, nose, lips, hands), and the feet. It may only be administered to baptized Catholics who retain the use of reason and who are in danger of death due to illness (i.e., not a condemned criminal, nor a martyr). All sin, including mortal, is forgiven.

THE SACRAMENT OF PENANCE

Christ instituted this Sacrament after His Resurrection (see Mt 16:19, 18:18, and Jn 20:23) to forgive post-baptismal sins and to impart grace to the soul. This occurs through the priest's absolution to penitents, who, with true sorrow, confess their sins and promise to do penance. The penitent is at once the accuser, the person accused, and the witness. The priest, in the person of Christ, pronounces judgment and sentence. This Sacrament is supported in Scripture. It is not enough for a Catholic to confess his sins to himself, or to a layman. Sincere sorrow is also necessary in order to receive absolution.

SCRIPTURAL SUPPORT

"Is any among you sick? Let him call for the elders of the Church, and let them pray over him, anointing him with oil in the name of the Lord; and the prayer of faith will save the sick man, and the Lord will raise him up; and if he has committed sins, he will be forgiven."
—James 5:14–15

"If you forgive the sins of any, they are forgiven; if you retain the sins of any, they are retained."
—John 20:23

Preview

In our next lesson, we will review what we have learned about miracles, and take a quiz.

CHAPTER FIFTEEN: JESUS DOES WONDERFUL THINGS
REVIEW AND ASSESSMENT

Aims

To review the materials taught this week and assess the children's understanding of it.

Materials

- Quiz 15 (Appendix, p. A-18)
- "Jesus, my Lord, my God, my all!" *Adoremus Hymnal,* #516

Review and Enrichment

1. Review Question 33 from the textbook with the children (see *Teacher's Manual*, p. 183).

2. Ask the following questions for review:
- Why did Jesus perform miracles? (to show He is the Son of God and that He loved the people He healed)
- What was the first miracle we learned about this week? (multiplication of loaves and fish)
- How does Jesus still feed the hungry today? (in the Eucharist)
- Could Jesus also make the weather obey? (yes, He calmed the storm)
- How powerful is Jesus? Can He raise someone from the dead? (yes, Jairus' daughter is an example)
- What other miracles did Jesus do?
    - a. Made the blind see
    - b. Made the deaf hear
    - c. Made the sick well
    - d. Made the paralyzed walk
- How does Jesus heal our bodies and souls today? (in the Sacraments of the Anointing of the Sick and Penance/Confession)
- Why can Jesus work all these miracles? (He is God)

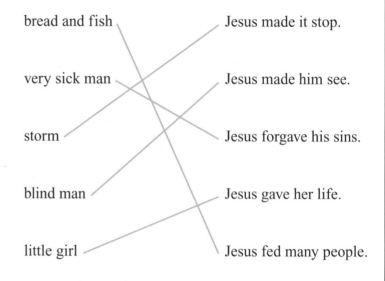

Name: _____

Jesus Does Wonderful Things   **Quiz 15**

Matching. *Draw a line from the words to their matches.*

bread and fish — Jesus made it stop.

very sick man — Jesus made him see.

storm — Jesus forgave his sins.

blind man — Jesus gave her life.

little girl — Jesus fed many people.

Assess

Distribute Quiz 15. Read through the quiz with the children and answer any questions they may have. Adminster the quiz. After all the students have handed in the quiz, and if there is time, review the correct answers with them.

Conclude

Close by singing "Jesus, my Lord, my God, my all," *Adoremus Hymnal*, #516.

CHAPTER FIFTEEN: JESUS DOES WONDERFUL THINGS
ACTIVITY BOOK ANSWER KEYS

Name:_____

Jesus multiplies loaves and fish to feed 5000 people!

Draw and color a picture of the small boy giving Jesus the loaves of bread and fish.

Name:_____

What did Jesus do to calm the storm?

<u>Jesus told the wind and the waves to be quiet, and everything grew calm, just like that! It was a miracle.</u>

Name:_____

Jesus did miracles to show us that He is the Son of God.

Label the pictures of the miracles that Jesus did.

Jesus heals the sick girl.

Jesus calms the storm.

Jesus feeds 5000.

Jesus makes the man walk.

Jesus makes the blind man see.

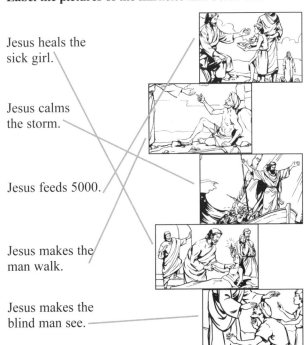

Name:_____

Jesus still does miracles today!

Color the pictures.

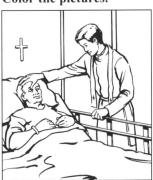

Even today, Jesus still heals people and forgives sin.

He does this through His Church.

TEACHER'S NOTES

CHAPTER SIXTEEN
WE BELIEVE IN JESUS

Catechism of the Catholic Church References

The Consequences of Faith in One God: 150, 200, 202, 222–229, 233
Cooperation of Intellect, Will, and Grace: 155
Duties of Faith: 2087–89
Faith and Understanding: 156–59
Faith Is a Grace: 153, 179

Faith Is a Human Act: 154–55, 180
Faith in Jesus: 151, 202, 463
Faith: The Beginning of Eternal Life: 163–65, 184
Freedom of Faith: 160
Necessity of and Perserverance in Faith: 161, 162, 183, 846
Unity of Faith: 172–74

Scripture References

The Healing of the Centurion's Servant: Mt 8:5–13; Lk 7:1–10

The Healing of the Blind Man: Mk 10:46–52; Lk 18:35–43
We Believe in Jesus: Mt 21:22

Background Reading: *The Fundamentals of Catholicism* by Fr. Kenneth Baker, S.J.

Volume 1:
"Faith and the Good News," pp. 21–22
"Submission to God," pp. 32–35

"The Center of Christian Faith," pp. 25–27
"Faith and Morality," pp. 121–23

Summary of Lesson Content

Lesson 1

Jesus is the Son of God and the Savior of the world.

He wants all people to believe in this truth.

He taught people to live as God's children.

He performed many miracles so that people might believe.

Lesson 3

Jesus cured the centurion's servant.

The centurion had great faith and he was humble.

Jesus cured the servant without being present at his side.

Lesson 2

Jesus healed a blind man.

He healed him because of his faith.

He cured him immediately.

Lesson 4

Jesus also wants us to believe in Him.

The faith of the people in these stories pleased Jesus.

The reward for steadfast faith is happiness with God forever in Heaven.

Chapter Sixteen: We Believe in Jesus
Lesson One: Jesus Is the Son of God

Aims

Students will know that Jesus is the Son of God and the Savior of the world.

They will know that Jesus taught and did miracles so that everyone would believe in Him.

Materials

• A wrapped box containing a toy or another small object

• *Activity Book*, p. 61

• Prepared index cards with a simple Act of Faith, to be distributed

Optional:
• "At the Name of Jesus," *Adoremus Hymnal*, #602

Begin

Write the word "Believe" on the board. Ask if any of the children know what it means to believe in something. Explain that it means that the person accepts that something is true, even if he does not fully understand it. All people today can believe in Jesus because they have seen His miracles and heard His teachings. Because Jesus is the Son of God, we know that Jesus will only speak the truth.

Develop

1. Read all but the last sentence of paragraph 1 aloud, then use the following example to help the children understand the meaning of belief. Hold up a box and tell them what you have in your hand. Ask the children if they believe that there is something (a toy perhaps) in the wrapped box. You can describe the toy's shape or color, and you may pass the box around and allow the students to hold it, shake it, etc. Ask them if they believe you about the contents of the box. Why? (because you said so, and you have not lied to them before) Unwrap the box and show them that they were right to believe you, because of what you said, because of what you did, and what they saw was true. If you are only a human teacher, how much more should they believe Jesus, Who is the divine teacher (see facing page to review personhood of Christ).

2. Explain that to trust in something or someone is to have faith. A person has faith if he believes. So a person has faith in Jesus if he believes in Him and what He said and did.

3. Ask the children how they act if they believe in something. Their actions should reflect what they believe. So if they believe in Jesus, they will do what He says to do. They will trust Him. They will love Him because of His love for all of them. They will obey His teachings too.

4. Ask the children how they will react:
  • If Jesus says to love one another?
  • If Jesus says to be kind to one another?
  • If they believe in Jesus and do all He says, what will be their reward? (Heaven)

5. At this point you may read through the rest of the chapter with the children. Discuss both miracles with the students, emphasizing that it was each man's faith that Jesus looked for when he healed him or his servant. Jesus heals only those who believe in Him. Encourage the students to pray often for the gift of faith to be strengthened in their hearts.

Reinforce

1. Have the children complete the exercise on p. 61 of the *Activity Book* (see *Teacher's Manual*, p. 197).

2. Divide the students into pairs and have them begin memorizing Question 34 in the text (see *Teacher's Manual*, p. 195).

3. Teach and sing with the children "At the Name of Jesus," *Adoremus Hymnal*, #602.

Conclude

1. Read the prayer on p. 66 of the textbook together. This is a simple Act of Faith that may be repeated at the end of each lesson.

2. Distribute index cards of the above prayer that the children can read and memorize. Or, use the simple Act of Faith found on the facing page.

64

16   We Believe in Jesus

"And whatever you ask in prayer,
you will receive, if you have faith."
Matthew 21:22

Jesus is God's Son and the Savior of the world. He wants everyone to **believe** in Him. To believe is to accept that what someone says is true, even if you have never heard it before. That is why Jesus did all those miracles, and that is why He taught people. If you believe in Jesus, He will give you a reward, like in this real story:

Once there was a blind man. When Jesus was walking by, the blind man called out, "Jesus help me." "What do you want me to do?" Jesus asked. "Please make me see," begged the blind man. "Because you believe that I can do this, you will see," Jesus said. And He cured the blind man then and there.

Another day, a man came to ask Jesus to cure his dying servant, who was at home. "Lord," the man said, "I am not worthy (that means 'not good enough')

65

for you to enter my house. But I know that if you just say one word, you can cure my servant from here." Jesus was so pleased with the man's faith that when the man came home, the servant was better. Jesus had cured him.

Jesus wants you to believe in Him too. You can pray:

Lord, I believe in You. Please help those
who do not believe in You. *Amen.*

They did this:	And this is what happened:
The blind man believed in Jesus.	Jesus made him see.
The man with the dying servant believed in Jesus.	Jesus cured the servant.

You do this:	And this is what will happen:
You believe in Jesus.	Jesus promises to bring you to Heaven to be happy with Him forever.

66

Preview

In our next lesson, we will learn how the blind man showed faith and how Jesus rewarded him.

Chapter Sixteen: We Believe in Jesus
Lesson Two: The Blind Man Sees

Aims

Students will learn how the blind man acted in faith.

They will understand that, because of his faith, Jesus healed the blind man.

Jesus cured the blind man immediately.

Materials

- Children's Bible

- *Activity Book*, p. 62

Optional:
- Appendix, p. B-16, "The Healing of the Blind Man" skit

- Simple Act of Faith

- "At the Name of Jesus," *Adoremus Hymnal*, #602

Begin

Review with the children the meaning of the words "believe" and "faith." Remind them that if they believe, they will act in faith. Tell them that they will learn about such faith in the story of the blind man.

Develop

1. Read the story of the healing of the blind man from the children's Bible (Mk 10:46–52 or Lk 18:35–43).

2. Ask the students the following questions about the story:
   - Why did the blind man call out to Jesus to help him? (He believed that Jesus would cure him.)
   - Why did the blind man have faith? (Maybe he heard about Jesus, His teachings, and His miracles.)
   - Why did Jesus ask the blind man what he wanted Him to do? If He is God, did He not already know? (Yes, but God wants people to ask Him for what they need or want.)
   - Why did Jesus cure the blind man? (He cured him because of his faith.)
   - Did it take a long time for Jesus to cure the blind man? (No, he cured him immediately.)

3. Reread paragraphs 1 and 2 from the textbook. Ask the children what rewards they can receive because of their faith (God's love, Heaven, comfort, healing). God does not always reward His children with miracles in this life, but to those who love Him and are faithful and good throughout their lives on earth, God will welcome them into Heaven.

4. Ask the children how they can respond to God in faith. List on the board ways they can do this (e.g., prayer, being kind to others, obeying parents, studying religion, going to church, etc.).

5. Discuss prayer and how to pray. People can thank God for His blessings (thanksgiving), they can ask God for what they need (petition), they can praise Him for His Goodness (praise), and they can pray for others (intercession). This may be a time to lead the children in prayer (see p. 9 of this manual for a brief overview of the various types of prayer).

Reinforce

1. Have the children color the picture of the blind man on p. 62 of the *Activity Book* (see *Teacher's Manual*, p. 197).

2. Read through the skit found on p. B-16 of the Appendix, "The Healing of the Blind Man." Choose individual students to read each part as they act out the scenes.

3. Discuss with the children the idea that they can also respond to God in faith by acting in love toward their neighbor, and by helping those in need. A class project may be undertaken, such as making sandwiches for the poor, cleaning up the playground, etc. Encourage them to be kind to their brothers and sisters, and to do their chores and help their parents at home without being told. Emphasize that it is as important to help those they know as it is to help strangers.

Conclude

1. Lead the class in a prayer if you did not do this during the lesson (see Develop #5).

2. Or pray a simple Act of Faith (see two versions on p. 189 of this manual).

3. Close by singing "At the Name of Jesus," *Adoremus Hymnal*, #602.

16   We Believe in Jesus

"And whatever you ask in prayer,
you will receive, if you have faith."
Matthew 21:22

Jesus is God's Son and the Savior of the world. He wants everyone to **believe** in Him. To believe is to accept that what someone says is true, even if you have never heard it before. That is why Jesus did all those miracles, and that is why He taught people. If you believe in Jesus, He will give you a reward, like in this real story:

Once there was a blind man. When Jesus was walking by, the blind man called out, "Jesus help me." "What do you want me to do?" Jesus asked. "Please make me see," begged the blind man. "Because you believe that I can do this, you will see," Jesus said. And He cured the blind man then and there.

Another day, a man came to ask Jesus to cure his dying servant, who was at home. "Lord," the man said, "I am not worthy (that means 'not good enough')

for you to enter my house. But I know that if you just say one word, you can cure my servant from here." Jesus was so pleased with the man's faith that when the man came home, the servant was better. Jesus had cured him.

Jesus wants you to believe in Him too. You can pray:

Lord, I believe in You. Please help those who do not believe in You. *Amen.*

They did this:	And this is what happened:
The blind man believed in Jesus.	Jesus made him see.
The man with the dying servant believed in Jesus.	Jesus cured the servant.

You do this:	And this is what will happen:
You believe in Jesus.	Jesus promises to bring you to Heaven to be happy with Him forever.

SAINT MARTIN DE PORRES: RESPONDING TO GOD IN FAITH AND DEED

Saint Martin de Porres was born in Lima, Peru in the year 1579. The unwanted son of a Spanish gentleman and a colored freed woman from Panama, he became a lay Dominican brother at the age of fifteen. Unable to travel and earn for himself the crown of martyrdom, he made a martyr out of his body with his many strict penances. As a reward, God granted him the gifts of prophecy, bilocation, and aerial flight. As a barber and farm laborer, Saint Martin showed love for all those around him, including animals and the poor. He died on November 3, 1639 and was canonized in 1962. His feast day is November 3. He is the patron saint of public education, social justice, and interracial relations.

Preview

In our next lesson, we will learn about the healing of the centurion's servant.

CHAPTER SIXTEEN: WE BELIEVE IN JESUS
LESSON THREE: JESUS HEALS THE CENTURION'S SERVANT

Aims

Students will learn of the miracle of Jesus curing the centurion's servant.

They will learn about humility.

They will learn that Jesus can work miracles from a distance.

Materials

- Children's Bible

- *Activity Book*, p. 63

Optional:
- Appendix, p. B-17, "The Healing of the Centurion's Servant" skit

- "At the Name of Jesus," *Adoremus Hymnal*, #602

Begin

Explain to the class that Jesus can work miracles for anyone who has faith. The blind man was a Jewish person, like Jesus. Tell the children that in the next miracle account, they will learn about a man who was not Jewish, but who had great faith. Jesus rewarded his faith with a miracle.

Develop

1. Reread paragraph 3 from the text. Then read from the children's Bible the account of the healing of the centurion's servant (Mt 8:5–13 or Lk 7:1–10).

2. Using the picture on p. 64 of the text to reinforce the passages you have just read, ask the following questions:
- What is the centurion wearing? (He has on a soldier's outfit.)
- Is Jesus dressed the same? (No, He has a simple cloak and tunic.)
- Why is the centurion kneeling? (He is kneeling in humility; this means that even though he is a gentile, he knows that Jesus is God.)
- Does Jesus look upset with him? (No, He is looking with concern upon him, he is listening to him.)
- How does the centurion look? (He is sad and pleading for help for his servant.)
- What happened after this meeting? (His servant was healed from afar, at the moment that Jesus told the centurion he would be cured.)

3. For the following exercise, see the chart on the facing page. Make a copy of this chart on the chalkboard, leaving the far right sections blank. Then ask the children to tell you how to fill in the empty sections of the chart. Ask the students about each situation and be sure they understand the significance of each particular miracle.

4. Based on what the students have said in the above exercise, ask them why these miracles can strengthen their faith so that they will believe in Jesus. Answers may be as follows:
- Jesus does things only God can do.
- Jesus rewards a person's faith.
- Jesus cures both bodies and souls.
- Jesus still works miracles today.

5. Explain to the students that in the Old and New Testaments, the word "gentile" referred to anyone who was not a Jew, one of the Chosen People.

Reinforce

1. Have the children read the chart on p. 66 of the textbook and repeat the contents of the boxes in their own words and/or memorize the contents. They may separate into groups to do this.

2. Assign the word search on p. 63 of the *Activity Book* (see *Teacher's Manual*, p. 197).

3. Separate the students into groups to read the skit found on p. B-17 of the Appendix, "The Healing of the Centurion's Servant."

Conclude

1. Lead the children in prayer, perhaps a thanksgiving for the gift of faith or for miracles that Jesus performs today.

2. You may lead them in singing "At the Name of Jesus," *Adoremus Hymnal*, #602.

16 We Believe in Jesus

"And whatever you ask in prayer,
you will receive, if you have faith."
Matthew 21:22

Jesus is God's Son and the Savior of the world. He wants everyone to **believe** in Him. To believe is to accept that what someone says is true, even if you have never heard it before. That is why Jesus did all those miracles, and that is why He taught people. If you believe in Jesus, He will give you a reward, like in this real story:

Once there was a blind man. When Jesus was walking by, the blind man called out, "Jesus help me." "What do you want me to do?" Jesus asked. "Please make me see," begged the blind man. "Because you believe that I can do this, you will see," Jesus said. And He cured the blind man then and there.

Another day, a man came to ask Jesus to cure his dying servant, who was at home. "Lord," the man said, "I am not worthy (that means 'not good enough')

for you to enter my house. But I know that if you just say one word, you can cure my servant from here." Jesus was so pleased with the man's faith that when the man came home, the servant was better. Jesus had cured him.

Jesus wants you to believe in Him too. You can pray:

Lord, I believe in You. Please help those who do not believe in You. *Amen.*

They did this:	And this is what happened:
The blind man believed in Jesus.	Jesus made him see.
The man with the dying servant believed in Jesus.	Jesus cured the servant.

You do this:	And this is what will happen:
You believe in Jesus.	Jesus promises to bring you to Heaven to be happy with Him forever.

CHALK TALK: MIRACLES OF JESUS

The blind man believed	Jesus made him see	Jesus gives us the sight of faith
The centurion believed	Jesus healed his servant	Jesus heals those for whom we pray
The paralyzed man believed	Jesus forgave his sins and made his body well	Jesus forgives sins in the Sacraments of Penance and the Anointing of the Sick
The 5000 were hungry	Jesus multiplied bread and fish	Jesus feeds us Himself in the Eucharist
A man's daughter died	Jesus raised her back to life	Jesus promises us eternal life if we have faith

Preview

In our next lesson, we will learn that Jesus also wants us to believe in Him.

CHAPTER SIXTEEN: WE BELIEVE IN JESUS
LESSON FOUR: JESUS DESIRES OUR FAITH

Aims

Students will learn that Jesus wants them to believe in Him, too.

They will understand that their faith pleases Jesus, just like the faith of the men in the stories.

They will realize that the reward for faith is Heaven.

Materials

• *Activity Book*, p. 64

Optional:
• "At the Name of Jesus," *Adoremus Hymnal*, #602

Begin

1. Review some of the ways God has shown His love for man:
   • Creation
   • Noah and the Ark
   • Abraham
   • Moses
   • God sends His Son, Jesus
   • Jesus' teaching and miracles

2. Ask the children to tell you how God has revealed His love for them in their own lives.

Develop

1. Take some time to ensure that the children recognize God's great love, His plan for them, and His great care in preparing their hearts to receive the gift of faith. Explain to the children that from the beginning of the world, God has prepared man for the coming of the Son. His teachings reveal God's love for all men.

2. Remind the students that God freely offers His love and that He wants everyone to believe in Jesus. Every person is called to have faith like the blind man and the centurion. God gives the gift of faith, but a person can strengthen it by learning about Jesus.

3. Encourage the children to pray to Jesus and to ask Him to strengthen their faith. A good prayer to learn and pray is an

Act of Faith. As a class, say the prayer found on p. 66 in the textbook, or say one of the two versions of the Act of Faith found on p. 189 of this manual. If the children have their prayer cards from Lesson 1, everyone may read their cards together.

4. Review the stories of the healing of the blind man and the centurion's servant. Call on the students and ask them to retell the events of each story. Have them refer to the text if necessary. Be sure to tell the children how much the faith of these two men pleased Jesus, and that He rewarded them with healing miracles. Remind the students that their faith pleases Jesus too. The reward for their faith is the promise of Heaven, where they can be united with Jesus forever (you may want to read through the skits once more).

Reinforce

1. Have the students complete the letter to Jesus found on p. 64 of their *Activity Book* (see *Teacher's Manual*, p. 197). You may want to assist them with this exercise (see example on the facing page).

2. Separate the children into small groups so that they may work on memorizing Question 34.

3. Maintaining the small groups, ask the students to read and learn the chart on p. 66 of the textbook.

Conclude

1. Have the children take turns reading their "Dear Jesus" letters.

2. Pray the Act of Faith found on p. 66 of the textbook if you have not already done so.

3. End with the song "At the Name of Jesus," *Adoremus Hymnal*, #602.

16   We Believe in Jesus

"And whatever you ask in prayer,
you will receive, if you have faith."
Matthew 21:22

Jesus is God's Son and the Savior of the world. He wants everyone to **believe** in Him. To believe is to accept that what someone says is true, even if you have never heard it before. That is why Jesus did all those miracles, and that is why He taught people. If you believe in Jesus, He will give you a reward, like in this real story:

Once there was a blind man. When Jesus was walking by, the blind man called out, "Jesus help me." "What do you want me to do?" Jesus asked. "Please make me see," begged the blind man. "Because you believe that I can do this, you will see," Jesus said. And He cured the blind man then and there.

Another day, a man came to ask Jesus to cure his dying servant, who was at home. "Lord," the man said, "I am not worthy (that means 'not good enough')

65

for you to enter my house. But I know that if you just say one word, you can cure my servant from here." Jesus was so pleased with the man's faith that when the man came home, the servant was better. Jesus had cured him.

Jesus wants you to believe in Him too. You can pray:

Lord, I believe in You. Please help those
who do not believe in You. *Amen.*

They did this:	And this is what happened:
The blind man believed in Jesus.	Jesus made him see.
The man with the dying servant believed in Jesus.	Jesus cured the servant.

You do this:	And this is what will happen:
You believe in Jesus.	Jesus promises to bring you to Heaven to be happy with Him forever.

66

Word to Know:

believe

> **Q. 34** *What is the reward for faith?*
> The reward for faith is pleasing God and attaining Heaven (CCC 161).

67

A SAMPLE LETTER TO JESUS

Dear Jesus,

I believe in You because:

You are the Son of Mary and the Son of God.

You loved me so much that You came to earth as a tiny baby so that one day I could be with You in Heaven.

You performed miracles, something only God can do. You are the Second Person of the Blessed Trinity.

You gave me Your Mother as my own.

Preview

In our next lesson, we will review what we have learned and take a quiz and a unit test.

CHAPTER SIXTEEN: WE BELIEVE IN JESUS

REVIEW AND ASSESSMENT

Aims

To review the materials taught this week and assess the children's understanding of them.

Materials

- Quiz 16 (Appendix, p. A-19)
- "At the Name of Jesus," *Adoremus Hymnal*, #602

Review and Enrichment

1. Review Question 34 with the children by reading it aloud and having them repeat the answer (see *Teacher's Manual*, p. 195).

2. Have the children describe the miracles of the healing of the blind man and the centurion's servant.

3. Ask the students to define the words "faith" and "believe."

4. Ask the children how they should respond to Jesus if they believe in Him. Some sample answers may be:
   - obey His laws
   - love God and neighbor
   - read the Bible
   - pray

5. Ask the children what reward is promised to those who have faith? (Heaven)

Name: _____

We Believe in Jesus   **Quiz 16**

Yes or No. *Circle the correct answer.*

1. Did Jesus do miracles?   (Yes)   No

2. Can a miracle happen without God's help?   Yes   (No)

3. Does everyone believe in Jesus?   Yes   (No)

4. Does Jesus want everyone to believe in Him?   (Yes)   No

5. Is faith in Jesus pleasing to God?   (Yes)   No

Faith and Life Series • Grade 1 • Appendix A   *A-19*

Assess

1. Distribute the quizzes. Read through the questions and answer any questions that the children may have. After all the quizzes have been turned in, review the answers with the children.

Conclude

End with a prayer of thanksgiving for the gift of faith and then sing "At the Name of Jesus," *Adoremus Hymnal*, #602.

Name:_____

I believe in Jesus.

Put an X in the correct boxes.

Because I believe in Jesus...

[X] I know that Jesus is the Son of God.

[ ] I know how to tie my shoes.

[X] I know that Jesus worked miracles.

[X] I know that Jesus can forgive sins.

[X] I can be happy with Him in Heaven.

[ ] I can make my bed.

Faith and Life Series • Grade 1 • Chapter 16 • Lesson 1   61

Name:_____

The blind man believed in Jesus.

Color the picture.

Jesus made him see!

62   *Faith and Life Series • Grade 1 • Chapter 16 • Lesson 2*

Name:_____

Word Search

Can you find these words in the puzzle?
Look carefully! The words go across and down.

BELIEVE	STORM	SINS
FAITH	SICK	MIRACLES
HEAL	CURE	WALK
CALM	FORGIVE	LIFE

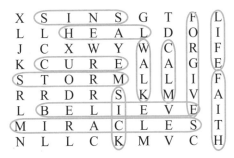

Faith and Life Series • Grade 1 • Chapter 16 • Lesson 3   63

Name:_____

Dear Jesus,

I believe in You because:

Answers will vary

_____

_____

_____

_____

_____

_____

Love,

Student's name

64   *Faith and Life Series • Grade 1 • Chapter 16 • Lesson 4*

TEACHER'S NOTES

UNIT FOUR TEST
CHAPTERS 13–16

> ### CHAPTER THIRTEEN: JESUS BEGINS HIS WORK
> ### CHAPTER FOURTEEN: JESUS TELLS THE GOOD NEWS
> ### CHAPTER FIFTEEN: JESUS DOES WONDERFUL THINGS
> ### CHAPTER SIXTEEN: WE BELIEVE IN JESUS

Aims

The students' understanding of the material covered in this unit will be reviewed and assessed.

Materials

• Unit 4 Test, Appendix, p. A-20

Assess

1. Distribute the unit tests and read through them with the students to be sure they understand the questions.

2. Administer the test.

3. After all the tests have been handed in, you may wish to review the correct answers with the class.

Name: _____

Unit 4 Test   **Chapter 13–16**

Fill in the blanks. *Trace the gray letters and fill in the rest.*

Word Bank

sins	You	loves	News
Apostles	sick	fed	

1. Jesus chose Apostles.

2. Jesus and His Apostles spread the Good News.

3. The Good News is that God loves us.

4. Jesus healed the sick.

5. Jesus fed many people.

6. Jesus forgave sins.

7. Jesus, I believe in You.

TEACHER'S NOTES

TEACHER'S NOTES

TEACHER'S NOTES

CHAPTER SEVENTEEN
THE BEST GIFT OF ALL

Catechism of the Catholic Church References

Apostolic Succession: 75–79, 96, 861–62, 880–87, 935–38

"Do this in memory of me": 1341–44, 1409

The Fruits of Holy Communion: 1391–1401, 1416

The Institution of the Eucharist: 1337–40

The Last Supper: 610–11, 621

The Mass as Memorial Celebration: 1356–57, 1362–66, 1372

The Paschal Banquet: 1355, 1382–90

The Presence of Christ in the Eucharist: 1373–81, 1410

The Signs of Bread and Wine in the Eucharist: 1333–36, 1412

The Sunday Eucharist: 1193, 2177–79

Scripture References

The Agony in the Garden: Mt 26:36–56; Mk 14:32–50; Lk 22:39–54; Jn 18:1–12

The Last Supper: Mt 26:17–19, 26–28; Mk 14:12–16, 22–25; Lk 22:7–20

The Scourging at the Pillar: Mt 27:26–28; Mk 15:15; Lk 22:63–65; Jn 19:1

The Crowning of Thorns: Mt 27:29–31; Mk 15:16–20; Jn 19:2–3

The Carrying of the Cross: Mk 15:21–22; Lk 23:26–32; Jn 19:17

John: Mt 17:1; 26:37; Mk 3:17; 5:37; Lk 22:8; Jn 13:23, 25; 19:26–27; 20:2–10; 21:7

Background Reading: *The Fundamentals of Catholicism* by Fr. Kenneth Baker, S.J.

Volume 3:

"Jesus Personally Founded the Catholic Church," pp. 92–94

"Bishops are Successors of the Apostles," pp. 104–7

"Jesus Gave Thanks," pp. 226–28

The Real Presence in the Blessed Sacrament, pp. 229–46

The Eucharist, pp. 247–56

The Mass as Sacrifice, pp. 256–70

"Each Mass Benefits All," pp. 271–73

Summary of Lesson Content

Lesson 1

Jesus promised to remain with the Church for all time.

He instituted the Eucharist at the Last Supper.

By receiving the Eucharist, a person receives Christ and His grace.

The Agony in the Garden is the first Sorrowful Mystery.

Lesson 2

The Apostles, through Jesus, received the power to change bread and wine into the Body and Blood of Jesus, our Lord.

This power has been passed on through Apostolic Succession.

The Scourging at the Pillar is the second Sorrowful Mystery.

Lesson 3

The Eucharist is the source and summit of Catholic life.

We will hear the Bread of Life discourse.

The third of the Sorrowful Mysteries is the Crowning with Thorns.

Lesson 4

The Real Presence of Jesus is in the Eucharist: Body, Blood, Soul, and Divinity.

The Eucharist is reserved in the tabernacle of every Catholic church.

The fourth Sorrowful Mystery is the Carrying of the Cross.

Chapter Seventeen: The Best Gift of All
Lesson One: The Last Supper

Aims

Students will learn that Jesus wanted to remain on earth after He died.

They will learn that at the Last Supper Jesus changed bread and wine into His Body and Blood.

They will understand that Jesus lives in those who receive Him by eating His Body and drinking His Blood.

Materials

- Children's Bible

- *Activity Book*, p. 65

- Appendix, p. B-23, The Agony in the Garden

Optional:
- "O Jesus, we adore thee," *Adoremus Hymnal*, #517

Begin

Review the many miracles Jesus worked. Explain to them that Jesus gives the best gift of all: He gives us Himself in the Eucharist. Tell the children that today they will learn about the night Jesus performed this great miracle.

Develop

1. Read paragraphs 1 and 2 aloud with the children.

2. Now read the story of the Last Supper from a children's Bible (Mt 26:17–19, 26–28; Mk 14:12–16, 22–25; or Lk 22:7–20).

3. Have the students open to p. 68 of their textbooks and discuss the painting with them:
   - Where is Jesus in the picture? (Point out our Lord celebrating the Eucharist.)
   - Who is present? (The Apostles are present.)
   - What is Jesus doing? (They may discuss this in as much detail as they wish, from commenting on His act of changing the bread and wine, to remembering and repeating the words that Jesus said.)

4. Ask the children discussion questions about this chapter:
   - When did Jesus share this special meal with the Apostles? (at the Last Supper, the night before He died)
   - What did Jesus change? (bread and wine)
   - Into what did Jesus change the bread and wine? (His Body and Blood)
   - Why did Jesus give the gift of Himself? (so He can live in us and remain with us)
   - How do we know the bread and wine really and truly become Jesus' Body and Blood? (He said so; He is God)
   - How could Jesus do this; change bread and wine into His Body and Blood? (He is God; He can do all things)
   - Does Jesus want all of us to receive Him in Holy Communion? (yes)
   - Why? (He loves us so much)

Reinforce

1. Assign p. 65 of the *Activity Book*, the coloring page of the Last Supper. (see *Teacher's Manual*, p. 211).

2. You may want to pass out copies of Appendix, p. B-23, The Agony in the Garden, for the children to color. Read aloud the relevant passages from the children's Bible as they work (Mt 26:36–56; Mk 14:32–50; Lk 22:39–54; or Jn 18:1–12), or wait until this is studied in the next chapter.

Note: Appendix, p. B-23 is the first of the Sorrowful Mysteries coloring pages, whose incidents are not mentioned until Chapter 18. These pages may be photocopied and passed out for the children to color either during this or the next chapter's lessons. Once all five have been completed, the pages may be stapled together to form a Rosary booklet, following the pattern of the Joyful Mysteries.

Conclude

1. Lead the children in a prayer, thanking Jesus for the miracle of the Eucharist.

2. Sing "O Jesus, we adore thee," *Adoremus Hymnal*, #517.

17   The Best Gift of All

"I made known to them your name, and I will make
it known, that the love with which you have
loved me may be in them, and I in them."

John 17:26

Jesus worked many miracles on earth. He taught us that He is God, and how much God loves us. But, Jesus knew that He was going to die soon. He loved us so very much that He found a way to be with us after He died.

The special supper Jesus shared with His Apostles on the night before He died is called the **Last Supper**. At the Last Supper, Jesus took bread and blessed it. He said, "Take this and eat of it. *This is My Body.*" Then Jesus took a cup of wine and said, "*This is the chalice of My Blood.*" Jesus changed bread and wine into His own Body and Blood. When the Apostles ate this Bread, Jesus lived inside them.

Then Jesus did something amazing. He gave His Apostles the power to change bread and wine into His

69

Body and Blood. The Apostles, in turn, passed on this power to all the bishops and priests who came after them, right up to today.

The **priest** at your church has received this power too. Because he has this power, when your priest offers **Mass**, he does what Jesus did at the Last Supper. When he says the words of Jesus, the bread and wine become the Body and Blood of Jesus. And when the people receive **Holy Communion**, Jesus comes to live in them. This is the best gift Jesus could have given us. It is the gift of Himself.

Words to Know:

Last Supper   Mass   priest

Holy Communion

70

HOLY THURSDAY MASS

The feast of Maundy (or Holy) Thursday commemorates the institution of the Eucharist and is the oldest observance particular to Holy Week. The priest celebrates Mass in white vestments with joyous solemnity, for the Gloria is said and the bells are rung. Often the service of the Maundy, or Washing of the Feet, occurs. After Mass, the ringing of bells ceases until the Easter Vigil, the altar is stripped, and the Eucharist is borne in solemn procession to the Altar of Repose, which is surrounded with flowers and candles. Other Hosts are reserved for the Good Friday service. These ceremonies are performed to express the sense of the Church's bereavement during the time of Christ's Passion and Burial.

THE AGONY IN THE GARDEN
Matthew 26:36–56   Mark 14:32–50   Luke 22:39–54
John 18:1–12

Preview

In our next lesson, we will learn how Jesus gave the power to the Apostles to change bread and wine into His Body and Blood.

CHAPTER SEVENTEEN: THE BEST GIFT OF ALL
LESSON TWO: THE APOSTLES RECEIVE THE POWER

Aims

Students will hear again how Jesus changed bread and wine into His Body and Blood at the Last Supper.

They will learn that Jesus gave this power to His Apostles.

They will learn that this power has been passed on to all bishops and priests from the Apostles.

Materials

• A small object, such as a ball or toy

• A missal or missalette

• *Activity Book*, p. 66

Optional:
• Appendix, p. B-24, The Scourging at the Pillar

• "O Jesus, we adore thee," *Adoremus Hymnal*, #517

Begin

Review with the children the events of the Last Supper, focusing on Jesus instituting the Sacrament of the Eucharist. Point out the words: "Do this in memory of Me." Be sure the children know that when Jesus said this to the Apostles, He gave them the power, through Him, to do the same: to change bread and wine into His Body and Blood.

Develop

1. To reinforce this idea, gather the children and pass an object from one child to the next. You may use a ball or a toy. Ask the children if the object being passed around has changed? (no) Is the object still from you? (yes, ultimately)

2. Explain that just as the object remains the same, so too does the power to change the bread and wine which was passed from Christ to the Apostles, and from them to bishops and priests today. This power is still from Christ, and changes bread and wine into His Body and Blood, when the bishop or priest uses what Jesus used (bread and wine) and says what Jesus said: "This is my Body"; "This is the chalice of my Blood." The bread and wine are then changed during Mass into the Body and Blood of Jesus through the power given by Jesus.

3. Read paragraphs 3 and 4 with the children. Ask if they know the names of their parish priests and write them on the board (review from Chapter 13, Lesson 4; p. 158 of this manual). Ask the name of the local bishop and write his name on the board, drawing a line from the bishop to each priest. Then connect the bishop with a line to the word "Apostles," and "Apostles" with a line to "Christ Jesus" (see diagrams on the facing page). This line-chart will help the students see the passing of the power to consecrate the Eucharist.

4. Emphasize that the priest at Mass says and does what Jesus did at the Last Supper and thus acts in the person of Christ. Using a missal (or church missalette), you may want to go through the Mass, emphasizing the words, gestures, matter, and form used to celebrate this Sacrament. Be sure the children know that Jesus works through the priest. It is very important that the words and actions of the priest are the same ones Jesus used because this is the very same celebration that Jesus made, not a new celebration over and over again, but the very same one (outside of time).

Reinforce

1. Have the children complete p. 66 of the *Activity Book* (see *Teacher's Manual*, p. 211), comparing Christ's actions at the Last Supper to the priest's actions at Mass.

2. You may want to pass out copies of Appendix, p. B-24, The Scourging at the Pillar, for the children to color. Read aloud the relevant passages from the children's Bible (Mt 27:26–28; Mk 15:15; Lk 22:63–65; or Jn 19:1), or wait until Chapter 18 for this activity.

Conclude

1. End with a brief class prayer, to which the children may add their intentions, i.e., "Please bless priests and bishops," etc.

2. Sing an appropriate song, such as "O Jesus, we adore thee," *Adoremus Hymnal*, #517.

17   The Best Gift of All

*"I made known to them your name, and I will make
it known, that the love with which you have
loved me may be in them, and I in them."*

John 17:26

Jesus worked many miracles on earth. He taught us that He is God, and how much God loves us. But, Jesus knew that He was going to die soon. He loved us so very much that He found a way to be with us after He died.

The special supper Jesus shared with His Apostles on the night before He died is called the **Last Supper**. At the Last Supper, Jesus took bread and blessed it. He said, "Take this and eat of it. *This is My Body*." Then Jesus took a cup of wine and said, "*This is the chalice of My Blood*." Jesus changed bread and wine into His own Body and Blood. When the Apostles ate this Bread, Jesus lived inside them.

Then Jesus did something amazing. He gave His Apostles the power to change bread and wine into His

69

Body and Blood. The Apostles, in turn, passed on this power to all the bishops and priests who came after them, right up to today.

The **priest** at your church has received this power too. Because he has this power, when your priest offers **Mass**, he does what Jesus did at the Last Supper. When he says the words of Jesus, the bread and wine become the Body and Blood of Jesus. And when the people receive **Holy Communion**, Jesus comes to live in them. This is the best gift Jesus could have given us. It is the gift of Himself.

Words to Know:

Last Supper   Mass   priest

Holy Communion

70

APOSTOLIC SUCCESSION
Example One

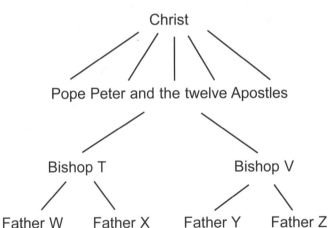

Christ

Pope Peter and the twelve Apostles

Bishop T   Bishop V

Father W   Father X   Father Y   Father Z

APOSTOLIC SUCCESSION
Example Two

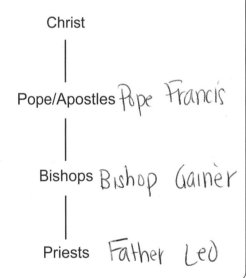

Christ

Pope/Apostles   *Pope Francis*

Bishops   *Bishop Gainer*

Priests   *Father Leo*

SAINT PAUL ON THE EUCHARIST

For I received from the Lord what I also delivered to you. . . . For as often as you eat this bread and drink the chalice, you proclaim the Lord's death until he comes.

—1 Corinthians 11:23, 26

THE SCOURGING AT THE PILLAR
Matthew 27:26–28   Mark 15:15   Luke 22:63–65
John 19:1

Preview

In our next lesson, we will hear the Bread of Life discourse from the Gospel of John and learn what Christ's words mean.

CHAPTER SEVENTEEN: THE BEST GIFT OF ALL
LESSON THREE: THE BREAD OF LIFE

Aims

Students will come to understand the tremendous gift of Jesus in the Eucharist.

They will review the Bread of Life discourse from Saint John's Gospel.

Materials

- Holy cards or medals (small gifts)

- *Activity Book*, p. 67

Optional:
- Construction paper and crayons

- Appendix, p. B-25, The Crowning with Thorns

- "O Jesus, we adore thee," *Adoremus Hymnal*, #517

Begin

Give each of the children a small present, such as a prayer card or medal. Explain that you want them to have it because you care about them and when they look at it or pray the prayer, you want them to remember you. Further explain that this gift is a little extension of yourself (you are giving a sign of your love, or your presence). A perfect gift would be the gift of yourself, rather than a mere reminder.

Develop

1. Ask the children to reread paragraph 1 of the textbook. Then ask them how Jesus can remain with us always (in the Eucharist). Explain that Jesus, Who is God, can give the perfect gift, the gift of Himself in the Eucharist. This is not merely a reminder, like a prayer card or medal, or just a sign of His love, or even a part of Him like His heart. It is all of Him, Body, Blood, Soul, and Divinity, really and truly present. It is the most perfect gift of all.

2. Have the children turn to p. 71 of the textbook. Read aloud the Bread of Life discourse from Saint John's Gospel that is found at the bottom of the page. Ask the children if they understand what it means when Jesus says: "If any one eats of this bread, he will live forever"? Explain that anyone who receives Christ in the Eucharist and has Jesus living (God's life) in him, will be able to go to Heaven. Ask them if they remember another name for God's life? (grace) So if a person has grace in his soul, he can be with God forever in Heaven. If a person receives Jesus in the Eucharist, Christ lives in him at that moment here on earth. This prepares him for the glory of Heaven. A Catholic receives Jesus and His grace when he receives Jesus in the Eucharist.

3. Reread the last three lines of the chapter: "And when the people receive Holy Communion, Jesus comes to live in them. This is the best gift Jesus could have given us. It is the gift of Himself." Explain that Jesus wants His children not only to have a picture of Him or a statue of Him as a reminder. Instead, Jesus wants everyone to have the gift of Himself, really and truly present, living in our hearts. Ask the children why this is the best gift:
- Because Jesus is God
- Because Jesus gives the gift of His life
- Because Jesus loves every person so much that He wants to be physically united to him

Reinforce

1. Have the children answer the multiple choice questions on p. 67 in their *Activity Book* (see *Teacher's Manual*, p. 211).

2. The children may use construction paper and crayons or markers to make thank you cards for Jesus, thanking Him for the gift of Himself in the Eucharist.

3. You may want to take this time to pass out copies of Appendix, p. B-25, The Crowning of Thorns, for the children to color. You may read aloud the relevant passages from the children's Bible (Mt 27:29–31; Mk 15:16–20), or wait until Christ's Passion is studied in Chapter 18.

Conclude

1. Lead the children in prayer, thanking Him for the gift of Himself, and for the promise of eternal life if they receive Him.

2. Sing "O Jesus, we adore thee," *Adoremus Hymnal*, #517.

17   The Best Gift of All

> "I made known to them your name, and I will make
> it known, that the love with which you have
> loved me may be in them, and I in them."
>
> John 17:26

Jesus worked many miracles on earth. He taught us that He is God, and how much God loves us. But, Jesus knew that He was going to die soon. He loved us so very much that He found a way to be with us after He died.

The special supper Jesus shared with His Apostles on the night before He died is called the **Last Supper**. At the Last Supper, Jesus took bread and blessed it. He said, "Take this and eat of it. *This is My Body*." Then Jesus took a cup of wine and said, "*This is the chalice of My Blood*." Jesus changed bread and wine into His own Body and Blood. When the Apostles ate this Bread, Jesus lived inside them.

Then Jesus did something amazing. He gave His Apostles the power to change bread and wine into His

69

Body and Blood. The Apostles, in turn, passed on this power to all the bishops and priests who came after them, right up to today.

The **priest** at your church has received this power too. Because he has this power, when your priest offers **Mass**, he does what Jesus did at the Last Supper. When he says the words of Jesus, the bread and wine become the Body and Blood of Jesus. And when the people receive **Holy Communion**, Jesus comes to live in them. This is the best gift Jesus could have given us. It is the gift of Himself.

Words to Know:

Last Supper   Mass   priest

Holy Communion

70

Q. 35   *At the Last Supper, what did Jesus do with the bread and wine?*
At the Last Supper, Jesus changed the bread and wine into His Body and Blood (CCC 1339).

Q. 36   *Why can priests today change bread and wine into the Body and Blood of Jesus?*
Jesus gave this power to His Apostles and they gave it to the bishops and priests who came after them (CCC 1341).

Q. 37   *Why is Holy Communion a special gift from God?*
Holy Communion is a special gift from God because, in Communion, Jesus Himself comes to live in us (CCC 1384).

Jesus said to them, "I am the bread of life;
he who comes to me shall not hunger,
and he who believes in me shall never thirst....
I am the living bread which came down from
heaven; if any one eats of this bread,
he will live for ever; and the bread which I shall
give for the life of the world is my flesh."

John 6:35, 51

71

JOHN, THE BELOVED DISCIPLE

John, the son of Zebedee and Salome, was the younger brother of James the Greater; Christ called these brothers the "sons of thunder". With their father, they fished on Lake Genesareth, became followers of John the Baptist, then Apostles of Jesus. John alone of the Apostles remained at the foot of the Cross and took Mary into his care at the request of Christ. After the Resurrection, John, with Peter, was the first disciple to hasten to the tomb, and he was the first to believe that Christ had truly risen. John wrote the fourth Gospel, three Epistles, and the Book of Revelation. Tradition relates that by order of the Emperor Diocletian he was cast into a cauldron of boiling oil. Emerging unharmed, John was then exiled to the island of Patmos for a year. He died at an advanced age in Ephesus about the year 100, the last of the Apostles. A church was built over his tomb which was afterwards converted into a mosque. His feastday is December 27. He is the patron saint of Asia Minor. (See Mt 17:1; 26:37; Mk 3:17; 5:37; Lk 22:8; Jn 13:23, 25; 19:26–27; 20:2–10; 21:7.)

THE CROWNING OF THORNS
Matthew 27:29–31   Mark 15:17–20   John 19:2–3

Preview

In our next lesson, we will learn of the Real Presence of Jesus in the Blessed Sacrament.

Chapter Seventeen: The Best Gift of All
Lesson Four: Jesus Remains with Us

Aims

Students will better understand that Jesus is really and truly present in the Blessed Sacrament.

They will learn that they can visit Jesus in the Blessed Sacrament in the tabernacle of any Roman Catholic church.

Materials

- *Activity Book*, p. 68

Optional:
- Missal

- *The Caterpillar that Came to Church* by Irene Hooker, et. al.

- Appendix, p. B-26, The Carrying of the Cross

- "O Jesus, we adore thee," *Adoremus Hymnal*, #517

Begin

Ask the students to think about the Mass, particularly the moment when the bread and wine become the Body and Blood of Jesus. Explain that this change is called "Transubstantiation." Repeat this word again slowly, saying that it is a big word that means what they have already learned—that it is no longer bread and wine even though it looks/tastes/smells/feels like it. It is really the Body and Blood of Jesus.

Develop

1. Explain to the children that "Transubstantiation" occurs during a part of the Mass called the Consecration (you might want to write this word on the board and explain that it means "set apart by God to give His grace"). You might read the words from the Roman Missal to remind the children of what the priest says and does to change the bread and wine into the Body and Blood of Jesus. Explain that after Transub-stantiation occurs, Jesus remains in the Blessed Sacrament.

2. Ask the children if they know what happens to the Blessed Sacrament after Mass? Jesus is placed in the tabernacle (the gold box usually found on or near the altar; see p. 229 and We Go To Mass, p. 356 of this manual). He is there waiting for His children to visit with Him. You can explain that Jesus is kept in the tabernacle so priests can take Him to sick people, so people can visit Him and pray to Him, and for Adoration/Benediction.

3. If possible, take the children on a visit to the Blessed Sacrament. Teach/remind them how to genuflect (kneel on the right knee and make the Sign of the Cross). Explain that this is a way of greeting Jesus and recognizing that He is present in the tabernacle. Catholics can genuflect/kneel to the Blessed Sacrament because it is truly Jesus, Who is God and the King of Kings.

4. If a visit to the tabernacle is not possible during class, encourage the students to go at another time with their parents. Tell them they can talk to Jesus in the tabernacle, pray to Him in their hearts or out loud, and even sing to Him.

5. Briefly describe the lives of two young saints who loved the Blessed Sacrament: Saint Gemma Galgani and Saint Tarsicius of Rome (see the facing page).

Reinforce

1. Have the students complete the word search found on p. 68 of the *Activity Book* (see *Teacher's Manual*, p. 211).

2. Read aloud *The Caterpillar That Came to Church: A Story of the Eucharist*, by Irene Hooker, Susan Brindle, and Miriam Lademan, or another appropriate story.

3. You may want to pass out copies of Appendix p. B-26, The Carrying of the Cross, for the children to color at this time. Read aloud the relevant passages from the children's Bible (Mk 15:21–22; Lk 23:26–32; Jn 19:17; or Mt 27:32), or wait until the next chapter.

Conclude

1. Remind the children to visit Jesus whenever they can, to genuflect whenever they pass the tabernacle, and to pray to Jesus truly present in the Blessed Sacrament.

2. Sing "O Jesus, we adore thee," *Adoremus Hymnal*, #517.

Body and Blood. The Apostles, in turn, passed on this power to all the bishops and priests who came after them, right up to today.

The **priest** at your church has received this power too. Because he has this power, when your priest offers **Mass**, he does what Jesus did at the Last Supper. When he says the words of Jesus, the bread and wine become the Body and Blood of Jesus. And when the people receive **Holy Communion**, Jesus comes to live in them. This is the best gift Jesus could have given us. It is the gift of Himself.

Words to Know:

Last Supper   Mass   priest

Holy Communion

70

Q. 35 *At the Last Supper, what did Jesus do with the bread and wine?*
At the Last Supper, Jesus changed the bread and wine into His Body and Blood (CCC 1339).

Q. 36 *Why can priests today change bread and wine into the Body and Blood of Jesus?*
Jesus gave this power to His Apostles and they gave it to the bishops and priests who came after them (CCC 1341).

Q. 37 *Why is Holy Communion a special gift from God?*
Holy Communion is a special gift from God because, in Communion, Jesus Himself comes to live in us (CCC 1384).

Jesus said to them, "I am the bread of life; he who comes to me shall not hunger, and he who believes in me shall never thirst.... I am the living bread which came down from heaven; if any one eats of this bread, he will live for ever; and the bread which I shall give for the life of the world is my flesh."

John 6:35, 51

SAINT GEMMA GALGANI

Saint Gemma was born on March 12, 1878 in a small town near Lucca, Italy. Though her mother died when she was only seven, she instilled in Gemma the love of God so that at age nine, overcome with desire to receive Jesus in the Eucharist, Gemma begged her father, her confessor, and her teachers to allow her to make her First Communion. They relented, and it was the most joyous day in her young life. Many mystical experiences followed, including the stigmata. In January of 1903 Gemma was diagnosed with tuberculosis. She died quietly on April 11 at age twenty-five. She was beatified in 1933 and canonized by Pius XII on May 2, 1940, only thirty-seven years after her death.

SAINT TARSICIUS

Saint Tarsicius was a young acolyte or deacon in Rome in the third century. Little is known about his life other than a poem written by Pope Saint Damasus I in the fourth century. It relates that Saint Tarsicius, while carrying the Blessed Sacrament to some Christians in prison, was attacked by a mob on the Appian Way. Rather than surrender the Body of Christ to be desecrated, he fought his attackers as they beat and stoned him to death. His martyrdom probably occurred during a persecution against Christians in Rome. He was buried in the catacombs of Pope Saint Callistus on the Appian Way. He is the patron saint of first communicants, altar boys, and teenagers.

Jesus has nourished me with His Blessed Sacrament alone!

—Saint Gemma

I no longer take pleasure in perishable food or in the delights of the world. I want only God's bread, which is the Flesh of Christ... and for drink I crave His Blood which is love that cannot perish.

—Saint Ignatius of Antioch

THE CARRYING OF THE CROSS
Mark 15:21–22   Luke 23:26–32   John 19:17

Preview

In our next lesson, we will review what we have learned and take a quiz.

Chapter Seventeen: The Best Gift of All
Review and Assessment

Aims

To review and assess the children's knowledge of the materials taught in this chapter.

Materials

- Quiz 17 (Appendix, p. A-21)
- "O Jesus, we adore thee," *Adoremus Hymnal*, #517

Review and Enrichment

1. Review the story of the Last Supper, highlighting the institution of the Eucharist.

2. Reinforce the passing on of the power to change bread and wine into the Body and Blood of Jesus.

3. Review the gift of Jesus Himself in the Eucharist. Know that He comes to live in those who receive Him and gives them His life (called grace).

4. Remind the children that Jesus remains and is really and truly present in the Eucharist after the Consecration. The children should know that they can visit Jesus in the tabernacle, and that they should genuflect.

5. Review the words "tabernacle," "genuflect," "priest," "Mass," "Last Supper," "Holy Communion," and "Real Presence."

Name: _____

The Best Gift of All   Quiz 17

Fill in the blanks. *Trace the gray letters and fill in the rest.*

Word Bank

Last	Holy	Body	Mass	Blood

1. At the Last Supper, Jesus was with the Apostles.

2. Jesus changed bread and wine into His Body and Blood.

3. At Mass, Jesus gives us His Body and Blood.

4. Holy Communion is the best gift of all.

Faith and Life Series • Grade 1 • Appendix A   A-21

Assess

Distribute Quiz 17 and read through it with the children. Answer any questions that they may have, then administer the quiz. Once the quiz is completed, review the correct answers with the children.

Conclude

Close by singing "O Jesus, we adore thee," *Adoremus Hymnal*, #517.

Name:_____

Jesus gave us His Body and Blood at the Last Supper.

Color the picture.

Faith and Life Series • Grade 1 • Chapter 17 • Lesson 1   65

Name:_____

At Mass, the priest does what Jesus did. He says the words of Jesus and the bread and wine become the Body and Blood of Jesus.

66   *Faith and Life Series • Grade 1 • Chapter 17 • Lesson 2*

Name:_____

Use the following words and phrases to fill in the blanks.

bread and wine	Eucharist
grace	all
Bread of Life	Body and Blood
bishops and priests	

1. Jesus can be with us always through the
Eucharist.

2. The Eucharist is not part of Jesus, but **all** of Jesus.

3. Jesus is the **Bread of Life**.

4. A Catholic receives Jesus and His **grace** when he receives Jesus in the Eucharist.

5. Jesus gave the Apostles the power to change the **bread and wine** into His **Body and Blood**. The Apostles then gave the power to the **bishops and priests**.

Faith and Life Series • Grade 1 • Chapter 17 • Lesson 3   67

Name:_____

Word Search

Can you find these words in the puzzle? Look carefully! The words go across and down.

BLOOD	MASS
BODY	PRIEST
BREAD	TABERNACLE
CUP	WINE

```
J  Q  M  A  S  S  B  P  T  J
L  G  L  F  N  H  L  Y  A  J
Z  B  N  M  N  W  O  V  B  X
P  R  I  E  S  T  O  W  E  J
Q  E  K  K  H  T  D  N  R  N
H  A  R  W  I  N  E  V  N  C
P  D  N  C  K  R  L  P  A  L
G  C  Q  U  L  P  Q  H  C  L
X  C  G  P  B  O  D  Y  L  L
B  C  F  T  X  C  Y  M  E  J
```

68   *Faith and Life Series • Grade 1 • Chapter 17 • Lesson 4*

TEACHER'S NOTES

CHAPTER EIGHTEEN
JESUS DIES FOR US

Catechism of the Catholic Church References

Christ's Redemptive Death in God's Plan of Salvation: 599–605, 619–620

Christ Offered Himself to the Father for Our Sins: 606–18, 621–23

Jesus at Prayer: 2599–2606, 2620

Jesus' Mission of Salvation: 456–60

Paschal Mystery: 571

Scripture References

The Crucifixion: Mt 26:47—27:54; Mk 14:43—15:39; Lk 22:47—23:47; Jn 18:12—19:30

A Sword Pierces Mary's Soul: Lk 2:35

Mary's Grief: Jn 19:25

Jesus Gives Mary to John: Jn 19:26–27

Jesus Dies for Us: Jn 15:13

Background Reading: *The Fundamentals of Catholicism* by Fr. Kenneth Baker, S.J.

Volume 1:
"The Death of Jesus," pp. 67–69

Volume 2:
"Jesus' Sacrifice on the Cross," pp. 289–92
"What Do We Mean by 'Redemption'?", pp. 292–95
"Jesus Died Not for Himself but for All Men," pp. 295–98

Summary of Lesson Content

Lesson 1

Jesus suffered and died for the sins of man.

We will hear an age-appropriate account of the sufferings of Christ.

The Passion of Christ should inspire thankfulness and a conversion of heart to all those who hear it.

We will learn about the fifth Sorrowful Mystery, The Crucifixion.

Lesson 2

We will hear the Passion narrative.

We will learn how to pray a simple version of the Stations of the Cross.

Lesson 3

The Blessed Virgin Mary had an important role in the Passion of Christ.

Mary suffered with Jesus.

Jesus gave Mary to man to be the Mother of all the living by order of grace.

Mary is an example of faithful discipleship.

The Sacrifice of the Cross is present at Mass.

Lesson 4

Christ is the New Adam.

Jesus' sacrifice on the Cross made up for Adam's sin and won back grace for mankind.

By virtue of His death Jesus opened the gates of Heaven.

CHAPTER EIGHTEEN: JESUS DIES FOR US
LESSON ONE: JESUS DIES ON THE CROSS

Aims

Students will be able to discuss the sufferings of Jesus.

They will know that Jesus suffered and died for them.

They will be inspired to thank Jesus for loving them enough to die on the Cross for them.

Materials

- A crucifix

- *Activity Book*, p. 69

Optional:
- Appendix p. B-27, The Crucifixion of Our Lord

- "O Cross of Christ, immortal tree," *Adoremus Hymnal*, #361

Begin

Open with a discussion of the sufferings of Christ, either by providing pictures (see Appendix pp. B-23–B-27) for this meditation, or by visiting the Stations of the Cross in church. Point out the sufferings of Jesus on the Cross: the crown of thorns, the nails, His pierced side, His wounds. Emphasize that Jesus suffered and died because He loves everyone so much and He wants all people to be able to go to Heaven and to be with Him forever.

Develop

1. Read paragraphs 1, 3, and 5 with the children as an overview of Christ's suffering and death.

2. Enumerate and write on the chalkboard the sufferings of Christ as found in the textbook:
- Jesus knew He was going to die.
- Soldiers took Him away.
- He was beaten with whips.
- He was crowned with thorns.
- He was nailed to a Cross.
- He died.

3. Lead the children in meditation, asking them how each suffering listed on the board might have made Jesus feel. Would He be sad, or angry? How much would this hurt? Would He be embarrassed to be taken away by soldiers? Would He worry what His followers might think about Him? Would He worry that people might lose faith? Hold up a crucifix. Have the children look upon it and in silence consider the wounds of Jesus.

4. Read paragraph 2 aloud to the class. Emphasize the fact that because Jesus is God, He could have stopped the men from hurting Him, but He wanted to suffer and die because He loves us so much. When you love someone, you want to do good things for that person, like giving a gift, offering help if needed, spending time together, and loving him. Because Jesus was God, He could make the perfect sacrifice and total gift of love by offering Himself on the Cross, so He did.

5. Explain that Jesus wanted to suffer and die on the Cross because His sacrifice, being perfect, would win for us God's grace and open the gates of Heaven, so we can be with Him forever.

6. Tell the children that Catholics meditate on the sufferings of Christ (e.g., in the Stations and Rosary) in order to thank Him for His gift of love, and to know Him and love Him better in return.

Reinforce

1. Have the children complete the letter to Jesus on p. 69 of the *Activity Book* (see *Teacher's Manual*, p. 223). In this letter the emphasis should be on gratitude for the Savior's death.

3. You may want to pass out copies of Appendix, p. B-27, The Crucifixion, for the children to color. Read aloud the relevant passages from the children's Bible (Mt 26:47—27:54; Mk 14:43—15:39; Lk 22:47—23:47; or Jn 18:12—19:30) to add to what they have learned from the textbook.

Conclude

1. Teach the children to sing an appropriate song, such as "O Cross of Christ, immortal tree," *Adoremus Hymnal*, #361.

2. Or have the children take their rosaries out of their basket or box (see Chapter 9, Lesson 4, Develop #5, on p. 108 of this manual) and pray together the fifth Sorrowful Mystery, the Crucifixion.

18   Jesus Dies for Us

"Greater love has no man than this,
that a man lay down his life for his friends."
John 15:13

The Last Supper happened on a Thursday. That night, after the Supper was over, Jesus went out to a garden to pray. He knew that soon He would be killed, but He wanted to give His life to save us. When soldiers came and took Jesus away the Apostles were afraid, but Jesus was brave. The next day, on Friday, they beat Him with whips. They pressed a crown of thorns onto His head and made fun of Him.

Because Jesus was God He could have stopped them from hurting Him, but He did not. That is because He wanted to suffer for us, because He loves us. His suffering and dying would bring us the gift of grace, God's life, and the ability to go to Heaven.

Later that day, bad men decided to kill Jesus. Jesus had to carry a heavy Cross through the city of Jerusalem and sometimes it made Him fall.

73

Mary met her Son on the way and she suffered very much when she saw the way people were hurting Jesus. Then a man named Simon helped Jesus to carry the Cross until they came to the top of a hill. That is when soldiers crucified Jesus (this means they nailed Him to a wooden cross to die). Mary and Saint John the Apostle stood by Jesus the whole time because they loved Him so much.

After three hours, Jesus died. His friends took Him down from the Cross and buried Him.

Jesus died to make up for Adam's sin and for our sins too. Jesus died to win back the gift of grace for us. Jesus died so that we could live in Heaven forever and ever. We call the day He died **Good Friday** because it is good that Jesus died and opened up the gates of Heaven.

74

SAINT CATHERINE OF SIENA

The 25th child of dyer Giacomo di Benincasa and his wife Lapa, Saint Catherine was born in Siena in 1347. From a young age she began to have mystical experiences, seeing guardian angels as clearly as people. At age 16 she became a Dominican Tertiary and her visions of Jesus, Mary, and other saints continued. She experienced a "mystical espousal" in 1366, and she received the stigmata in 1375, visible only after her death in Rome in 1380. She died at age 33, the age of Christ at His death, and her body was found incorrupt in 1430. Her feast day is April 29. She is one of three female Doctors of the Church. She is the patroness of Italy.

THE CRUCIFIXION
Mathew 26:47—27:54	Mark 14:43—15:39
Luke 22:47—23:47	John 18:12—19:30

Preview

In our next lesson, we will continue our meditation on the Passion of Christ.

Chapter Eighteen: Jesus Dies for Us
Lesson Two: The Passion

Aims

The students will become familiar with the Passion narrative.

They will learn how to pray a simple version of the Stations of the Cross.

Materials

- Children's Bible

- Pictures of the Stations

- *Activity Book*, p. 70

Optional:
- Sorrowful Mysteries of the Rosary booklet

- "O Cross of Christ, immortal tree," *Adoremus Hymnal*, #361

Begin

Review with the students the sufferings of Christ as enumerated in the textbook and the previous lesson: He knew He was going to die, soldiers came to take Him away, they whipped Him, crowned Him with thorns, and nailed Him to a Cross to die. Tell them that now they will hear about Christ's suffering from the Bible.

Develop

1. Read the Passion of Christ from a children's Bible (Mt 26:47—27:54; Mk 14:43—15:39; Lk 22:47—23:47; or Jn 18:12—19:30). As these are long passages you may choose to read shorter sections aloud, or simply show a video on the Passion.

2. Display pictures of the Stations in the front of the classroom, or pass around other appropriate images. Then teach the children a simple way of praying the Stations. First, read the title of each aloud, then pray together as a response: "We adore You, O Christ, and we bless You, because by Your Holy Cross, You have redeemed the world." You may want to write this prayer on the chalkboard or pass out printed copies they can read at their desks.

1st Station: Jesus is condemned to die
2nd Station: Jesus takes up His Cross
3rd Station: Jesus falls the first time
4th Station: Jesus meets His Mother, Mary
5th Station: Simon of Cyrene helps Jesus carry His Cross
6th Station: Veronica wipes the face of Jesus
7th Station: Jesus falls the second time
8th Station: Jesus speaks to the women of Jerusalem
9th Station: Jesus falls the third time
10th Station: Soldiers remove the clothes of Jesus
11th Station: Jesus is nailed to the Cross
12th Station: Jesus dies on the Cross
13th Station: Jesus is taken down from the Cross
14th Station: Jesus is laid in the tomb

3. After this exercise, ask the students if they have any questions about the Stations and discuss these with them. Also discuss how each person in the Station might have felt. For example, how would Mary feel when she met Jesus carrying His Cross? Would she be sad? Would Simon be happy to help Jesus? Did he know who Jesus was? How would Veronica feel as she wiped Christ's face of sweat and blood?

Reinforce

1. Assign p. 70 of the *Activity Book* (see *Teacher's Manual*, p. 223), which is a page of questions about the Passion of Christ.

2. Have the children read Questions 38 and 39 in the textbook and begin memorization.

3. If they have begun them, the children may work on their Sorrowful Mysteries of the Rosary booklets (see Appendix, pp. B-23–B-27).

Conclude

1. Lead the children in prayer, thanking Jesus for suffering for them, and for His love.

2. Or have the children take out their rosaries and pray the fifth Sorrowful Mystery as a class.

3. Sing "O Cross of Christ, immortal tree," *Adoremus Hymnal*, #361.

18   Jesus Dies for Us

"Greater love has no man than this,
that a man lay down his life for his friends."
John 15:13

The Last Supper happened on a Thursday. That night, after the Supper was over, Jesus went out to a garden to pray. He knew that soon He would be killed, but He wanted to give His life to save us. When soldiers came and took Jesus away the Apostles were afraid, but Jesus was brave. The next day, on Friday, they beat Him with whips. They pressed a crown of thorns onto His head and made fun of Him.

Because Jesus was God He could have stopped them from hurting Him, but He did not. That is because He wanted to suffer for us, because He loves us. His suffering and dying would bring us the gift of grace, God's life, and the ability to go to Heaven.

Later that day, bad men decided to kill Jesus. Jesus had to carry a heavy Cross through the city of Jerusalem and sometimes it made Him fall.

73

Mary met her Son on the way and she suffered very much when she saw the way people were hurting Jesus. Then a man named Simon helped Jesus to carry the Cross until they came to the top of a hill. That is when soldiers crucified Jesus (this means they nailed Him to a wooden cross to die). Mary and Saint John the Apostle stood by Jesus the whole time because they loved Him so much.

After three hours, Jesus died. His friends took Him down from the Cross and buried Him.

Jesus died to make up for Adam's sin and for our sins too. Jesus died to win back the gift of grace for us. Jesus died so that we could live in Heaven forever and ever. We call the day He died **Good Friday** because it is good that Jesus died and opened up the gates of Heaven.

74

Words to Know:

Good Friday

Q. 38 *How did Jesus suffer?*
Jesus was scourged, crowned with thorns, He carried His Cross, He was crucified, and He died (CCC 572, 596, 619).

Q. 39 *Why did Jesus suffer?*
Jesus suffered to atone for Adam's sin and our sins, and to open again the gates of Heaven (CCC 615).

We Pray:

Thank you, Jesus, for loving me so much.
I am sorry my sins made You suffer.
Thank You for giving Your life for me. *Amen.*

75

GOOD FRIDAY

Good Friday is the only day in the Church year that Mass is not celebrated anywhere in the world. During the first part of the day's service, lessons are read from Sacred Scripture, followed by a long series of prayers for various intentions. As the priest prays, the deacon directs the congregation by saying, "Let us kneel" (Flectamus genua), then, "Let us stand" (Levate). The second part of the ceremony consists of the unveiling and veneration of the Cross as the priest states "Ecce lignum Crucis," etc. (Behold the wood of the Cross, on which hung the salvation of the world), to which the choir answers, "Venite adoremus" (Come, let us adore). The third part is the Mass of the Presanctified; the priest uses Hosts that were consecrated on Holy Thursday.

Preview

In our next lesson, we will learn about Mary's role in the Passion of Christ.

CHAPTER EIGHTEEN: JESUS DIES FOR US
LESSON THREE: THIS IS YOUR MOTHER

Aims

Students will learn of the role of Mary in the Passion of Christ, and her faithfulness.

They will know that Jesus gave Mary to us to be our Mother.

They will learn from Mary's example to remain faithful to Christ.

They will learn that Mass is the Sacrifice of the Cross, and that those at Mass stand with Mary under the Cross, faithful to Christ.

Materials

- Children's Bible
- Crucifix
- *Activity Book*, p. 71

Optional:
- Sorrowful Mysteries of the Rosary booklet
- "O Cross of Christ, immortal tree," *Adoremus Hymnal*, #361

Begin

Tell the children that in the last chapter they learned that Jesus gives Himself in the Eucharist at Mass and is made present during the Consecration. Remind them that He died on the Cross, in a sacrifice of Himself, and that this, too, is made present at Mass. When Catholics receive the Eucharist they receive the gift of Jesus as He gave Himself up on the Cross for the sins of man.

Develop

1. Read paragraph 4 from the textbook. Mary and John the beloved disciple were present under the Cross when Jesus was crucified, because they loved Him so much.

2. Read from the children's Bible the passage when Jesus gives Mary to John (Jn 19:26–27). Tell the children that in this way, Jesus gave Mary to all of us to be our Mother. As our Mother, she is the best example of how to live faithfully in Christ.

3. Ask the children some ways that Mary is a good example for everyone:
   - She said yes to become the Mother of God.
   - She loved Jesus very much.
   - She was faithful to Jesus.
   - She loved others.
   - She prayed.
   - She stayed with Jesus, even when it was very difficult (under the Cross).

4. Ask the children what Mary did when Jesus suffered and died. (She was with Him; she loved Him.) Tell the children that they too can be with Jesus on the Cross, by praying at Mass. In doing so, they are like Mary and John, being faithful to Christ and loving Him as He gives Himself up, just as He did 2000 years ago on Calvary. His sacrifice on the Cross is made present on the altar at every Mass.

5. Show the children a crucifix. Explain that God does not live in time like people do. He created time and at every Mass, Jesus is really made present and gives Himself up for us; it is the *same* sacrifice as on the Cross. One day soon, when the children have prepared and are ready, they can receive Him in a special way in Holy Communion.

Reinforce

1. On p. 71 of the *Activity Book* (see *Teacher's Manual*, p. 223), have the children draw themselves under the Cross as faithful disciples.

2. Students may continue coloring their Sorrowful Mysteries Rosary booklets.

Conclude

1. Lead the children in asking Mary to intercede for their intentions in order to grow in her example:
   Child 1: Mary help me to be faithful like you.
   All: Mary, please pray for us.
   Child 2: Mary, help me to love Jesus more.
   All: Mary, please pray for us.

2. Close with the Hail Mary (see *Teacher's Manual*, p. 367).

3. Sing "O Cross of Christ, immortal tree," *Adoremus Hymnal*, #361.

18   Jesus Dies for Us

"Greater love has no man than this,
that a man lay down his life for his friends."
John 15:13

The Last Supper happened on a Thursday. That night, after the Supper was over, Jesus went out to a garden to pray. He knew that soon He would be killed, but He wanted to give His life to save us. When soldiers came and took Jesus away the Apostles were afraid, but Jesus was brave. The next day, on Friday, they beat Him with whips. They pressed a crown of thorns onto His head and made fun of Him.

Because Jesus was God He could have stopped them from hurting Him, but He did not. That is because He wanted to suffer for us, because He loves us. His suffering and dying would bring us the gift of grace, God's life, and the ability to go to Heaven.

Later that day, bad men decided to kill Jesus. Jesus had to carry a heavy Cross through the city of Jerusalem and sometimes it made Him fall.

73

Mary met her Son on the way and she suffered very much when she saw the way people were hurting Jesus. Then a man named Simon helped Jesus to carry the Cross until they came to the top of a hill. That is when soldiers crucified Jesus (this means they nailed Him to a wooden cross to die). Mary and Saint John the Apostle stood by Jesus the whole time because they loved Him so much.

After three hours, Jesus died. His friends took Him down from the Cross and buried Him.

Jesus died to make up for Adam's sin and for our sins too. Jesus died to win back the gift of grace for us. Jesus died so that we could live in Heaven forever and ever. We call the day He died **Good Friday** because it is good that Jesus died and opened up the gates of Heaven.

74

DEVOTION TO OUR LADY OF SORROWS

Our Lady, as the first and greatest disciple of Christ, participated in His redemptive suffering in a profound way. Devotion to the Sorrowful Mother can be traced back to apostolic times, beginning with John's account of Mary's grief while standing at the foot of the Cross (Jn 19:25). Luke records the prophecy of Simeon at the Presentation at the Temple: "and a sword will pierce through your own soul also" (Lk 2:35). During the Middle Ages this devotion became popular, thus the well-known medieval hymn Stabat Mater. In art, Our Lady of Sorrows is traditionally depicted in black with seven swords piercing her heart. Her feast day is September 15.

THE SEVEN SORROWS OF MARY

1. The prophecy of Simeon

2. The flight into Egypt

3. The loss of the Child Jesus for three days

4. Meeting Jesus on the way to Calvary

5. The Crucifixion and death of Jesus

6. Jesus taken down from the Cross

7. Jesus laid in the tomb

The seven sorrows of Mary are also known as the seven dolors. *Dolor* is a Latin word that means "pain" or "sorrow."

Preview

In our next lesson, we will learn about Christ as the New Adam, just as Mary is the New Eve.

CHAPTER EIGHTEEN: JESUS DIES FOR US
LESSON FOUR: THE NEW ADAM

Aims

Students will learn that Christ is the New Adam.

They will learn that Jesus' sacrifice on the Cross made up for Adam's sin and won back grace for the world.

They will learn that Jesus opened the gates of Heaven.

Materials

- *Activity Book*, p. 72

Optional:
- Paper/poster board and crayons

- "O Cross of Christ, immortal tree," *Adoremus Hymnal*, #361

Begin

Review the story of Adam and Eve with the children and the effects of Original Sin, namely suffering, death, loss of grace, and the inability to go to Heaven. Remind them that these are caused by the sin of Adam. Then tell them that today they will learn how Christ repaired the damage from Adam's sin, and therefore, He can be called the New Adam.

Develop

1. Read paragraph 6 aloud from the textbook.

2. Make a chart on the chalkboard and compare Adam (left side) and Jesus (right side). Contrast the disobedience and sin of Adam (and the effects of sin) with the obedience and sacrifice of Christ and the graces He won for mankind.

ADAM	CHRIST
Disobedience	Obedience
Selfish sin	Sacrifice on the Cross
Loss of grace	Won back grace
Loss of Heaven	Opened gates of Heaven
Death	Eternal life

3. Expand upon the importance of Christ as the New Adam, using the information below:

Obedience: Christ's obedience pleased God greatly. Because of Adam's sin, people could not please God perfectly because their hearts were torn between good and evil. Even great people who were faithful had a hard time choosing to do good. But Jesus, being perfect, was able to be obedient to God in all things. Jesus was able to undo the harm of Adam's sin.

The Cross: Jesus gave Himself as a gift to God, holding nothing back, not even His life or sufferings. Jesus was generous, not selfish in any way like Adam.

Grace/Eternal Life: Jesus won back grace for all men, so God would be pleased. Christ lives in man through the Eucharist, and man can live forever in Heaven.

Heaven: Before Jesus died, people could not go to Heaven, not even good people like Noah, Abraham, Moses, or David. Jesus wanted them to be with Him in Heaven, so by dying on the Cross, He opened Heaven's gates and brought these faithful people into Heaven to be happy with God forever.

Reinforce

1. Have the children complete the word search on p. 72 of the *Activity Book* (see *Teacher's Manual*, p. 223).

2. Separate the students into groups and have them make posters depicting the contrast between Adam and Christ, using one of the comparisons from the chart on the board, i.e., the disobedience of Adam and the obedience of Christ.

3. Have the students continue memorizing Questions 38 and 39.

4. Students may complete their Rosary booklets.

Conclude

1. Read the We Pray section together.

2. Encourage the children to make an Act of Contrition for their sins (see two versions on the facing page). By being sorry for their sins and thanking Jesus for his sacrifice, they can join in Mary's sorrow at the foot of the Cross.

3. Sing "O Cross of Christ, immortal tree," *Adoremus Hymnal*, #361.

18   Jesus Dies for Us

"Greater love has no man than this,
that a man lay down his life for his friends."
John 15:13

The Last Supper happened on a Thursday. That night, after the Supper was over, Jesus went out to a garden to pray. He knew that soon He would be killed, but He wanted to give His life to save us. When soldiers came and took Jesus away the Apostles were afraid, but Jesus was brave. The next day, on Friday, they beat Him with whips. They pressed a crown of thorns onto His head and made fun of Him.

Because Jesus was God He could have stopped them from hurting Him, but He did not. That is because He wanted to suffer for us, because He loves us. His suffering and dying would bring us the gift of grace, God's life, and the ability to go to Heaven.

Later that day, bad men decided to kill Jesus. Jesus had to carry a heavy Cross through the city of Jerusalem and sometimes it made Him fall.

73

Mary met her Son on the way and she suffered very much when she saw the way people were hurting Jesus. Then a man named Simon helped Jesus to carry the Cross until they came to the top of a hill. That is when soldiers crucified Jesus (this means they nailed Him to a wooden cross to die). Mary and Saint John the Apostle stood by Jesus the whole time because they loved Him so much.

After three hours, Jesus died. His friends took Him down from the Cross and buried Him.

Jesus died to make up for Adam's sin and for our sins too. Jesus died to win back the gift of grace for us. Jesus died so that we could live in Heaven forever and ever. We call the day He died **Good Friday** because it is good that Jesus died and opened up the gates of Heaven.

74

Words to Know:

Good Friday

> **Q. 38** *How did Jesus suffer?*
> Jesus was scourged, crowned with thorns, He carried His Cross, He was crucified, and He died (CCC 572, 596, 619).
>
> **Q. 39** *Why did Jesus suffer?*
> Jesus suffered to atone for Adam's sin and our sins, and to open again the gates of Heaven (CCC 615).

We Pray:

Thank you, Jesus, for loving me so much.
I am sorry my sins made You suffer.
Thank You for giving Your life for me. *Amen.*

75

A SIMPLE ACT OF CONTRITION

Dear God, please forgive my sins and help me to be good so I can go to Heaven and be with Jesus and His Mother Mary forever.
Amen.

AN ACT OF CONTRITION

O my God, I am heartily sorry for having offended Thee. I detest all my sins because of Thy just punishments, but most of all because they offend Thee, my God, Who art all good and deserving of all my love. I firmly resolve, with the help of Thy grace, to confess my sins, to do penance, and to amend my life.
Amen.

Preview

In our next lesson, we will review what we have learned this week in class and take a quiz.

Chapter Eighteen: Jesus Dies for Us
Review and Assessment

Aims

To review and assess the children's knowledge of the materials taught in this chapter.

Materials

- Quiz 18 (Appendix, p. A-22)
- "O Cross of Christ, immortal tree," *Adoremus Hymnal*, #361

Review and Enrichment

1. Review the Passion narrative with the children: Christ's foreknowledge of His death, how the soldiers took Him away, how they whipped Him, crowned Him with thorns, and nailed Him to a Cross to die.

2. Have students contrast Adam and Christ. Give them examples of what Adam did, then ask them what Christ did.

3. Ask about the role of Mary in the Passion and how they can follow her example.

4. Review with them the Sacrifice of the Mass.

Name:

Jesus Dies for Us   Quiz 18

Number the event. *Put a 1 beside the first event, a 2 beside the second event, and so on.*

_7_   Jesus died on the Cross.

_1_   Jesus and the Apostles ate the Last Supper.

_2_   Jesus was beaten.

_3_   Jesus was crowned with thorns.

_5_   Jesus was nailed to the Cross.

_4_   Jesus carried the heavy Cross.

_6_   Mary and Saint John stayed by Jesus on the Cross.

Assess

Distribute Quiz 18. Read through it with the children and answer any questions they may have. Administer the quiz. Individually quiz the children orally on the Questions and the Words to Know. When the quiz is completed, review the correct answers with the children.

Conclude

1. Say the We Pray prayer together, found on p. 75 of the textbook (see *Teacher's Manual*, p. 221).

2. Close by singing "O Cross of Christ, immortal tree," *Adoremus Hymnal*, #361.

CHAPTER EIGHTEEN: JESUS DIES FOR US
ACTIVITY BOOK ANSWER KEYS

Name:_____

Write a letter to Jesus. Thank him for dying on the Cross for you.

Dear Jesus,

Answers will vary

_____

_____

_____

_____

_____

Love,

Student's name

Name:_____

The Passion of Christ

Answer the following questions.

1. What day was the Last Supper?

Thursday

2. Where did Jesus go after the supper?

He went out to a garden.

3. What did He do there?

prayed

4. Jesus knew that He would be killed. Why did Jesus want to give His life?

He wanted to suffer for us because He loved us.

5. What did Jesus carry through Jerusalem?

A heavy Cross

6. Who was with Jesus during this time?

Mary, Simon, John the Apostle

7. What day did Jesus die?

Good Friday

Name:_____

Jesus Dies for Us

Draw a picture of yourself under the Cross of Jesus with His faithful followers. Then, color the picture.

Name:_____

Word Search

Can you find these words in the puzzle?
Look carefully! The words go across and down.

CROSS	NAILS
FALL	SIMON
GARDEN	SOLDIER
GOOD FRIDAY	SUFFER
HOLY THURSDAY	THORNS
LAST SUPPER	WHIPS

```
H O L Y T H U R S D A Y
S O L D I E R M N H G G
C X M N R D P D T P O A
R L O V E L L R H N O R
O R W X T F B K O A D D
S Y H X F Y N T R I F E
S R I R S I M O N L R N
B K P F N V L M S S I R
H R S U F F E R J K D T
L A S T S U P P E R A B
B R Z F A L L G V M Y P
C T V L M M J N Z G Z M
```

TEACHER'S NOTES

CHAPTER NINETEEN
JESUS WAS RAISED TO NEW LIFE

Catechism of the Catholic Church References

Apparitions of the Risen One: 641–44
Christ's Resurrection and Ours: 655–58, 992–1004, 1015–17
Easter as the Central Christian Feast: 638, 1169
The Empty Tomb: 640, 657
The Mystery of God's Apparent Powerlessness: 272–74
The Resurrection: Historical and Transcendental Event:
639, 647, 656

The Resurrection as a Work of the Trinity: 648–50
The Resurrection's Meaning and Consequences: 651–55, 658
The State of Christ's Risen Humanity: 645–46
How Do the Dead Rise?: 997–1001

Scripture References

The Resurrection: Mt 28:1–10; Mk 16:1–13; Lk 24:1–43;
Jn 20:1–29

Background Reading: *The Fundamentals of Catholicism* by Fr. Kenneth Baker, S.J.

Volume 1:
"The Resurrection of Jesus," pp. 70–72
"The Glorified Body of Jesus," pp. 72–74
"The Cosmic Effects of Jesus' Resurrection," pp. 75–77
"The Resurrection of the Dead," pp. 113–15

Volume 2:
"Jesus' Glorious Resurrection," pp. 304–7

Volume 3:
"The Resurrection of the Body," pp. 379–82

Summary of Lesson Content

Lesson 1

Christ rose from the dead on Easter Sunday.

Jesus took up His body in the Resurrection.

Christ is truly risen, body and soul.

The first Glorious Mystery is the Resurrection.

Lesson 3

By rising from the dead Jesus won back the gift of grace,
so man can live forever with Him in Heaven.

Jesus gives His life and gift of grace to Catholics through
the Sacraments, and in a special way in Holy Communion.

Lesson 2

The Apostles were filled with joy at the Resurrection of
Jesus.

Catholics celebrate the Resurrection at every Mass, and in
a special way on Easter Sunday.

Lesson 4

Jesus has a resurrected body.

Mary was taken to Heaven, body and soul, which is called
the Assumption.

Catholics believe in the resurrection of the body.

Chapter Nineteen: Jesus Was Raised to New Life
Lesson One: Jesus Is Risen

Aims

Students will learn about the Resurrection of Christ.

They will know that Jesus rose on Easter.

They will begin to understand the risen Christ, truly risen with His body.

Materials

- Children's Bible

- *Activity Book*, p. 73

- Appendix, p. B-28, The Resurrection

Optional:
- "Christ the Lord is risen today," *Adoremus Hymnal*, #415

Begin

Review the story of the Passion and Crucifixion of Jesus with the children. Tell them that if this were the end of the story, it would be very sad. But, this was not the end of the story because Jesus rose from the dead, He came back to life.

Develop

1. Read paragraph 1 of the text with the students.

2. Now read the full story of Easter from a children's Bible, (Mt 28:1–10; Mk 16:1–13; Lk 24:1–43; or Jn 20:1–29), or you may simply choose to show a video of the Resurrection.

3. Discuss with the children what it means that Jesus rose from the dead three days after the Crucifixion:
   - He has life again.
   - He took up His body.
   - He saw His Mother and the Apostles.
   - He is God.

4. Emphasize with the children how great a celebration this is. Jesus had died, but He is now risen! How great is the Lord!

5. Many families celebrate Easter in a special way. Ask the students if they have special family customs for Easter. These may include Easter bread (bread is a symbol of the Eucharist), coloring and hiding eggs for an Easter egg hunt with their family and friends (the egg is a symbol of new life), visits from the Easter Bunny (the bunny is the symbol of rising up from the ground and springing to new life; note, at this age the children may believe in the Easter Bunny, so be sensitive to this). Families may also buy Easter clothes, and some women buy Easter bonnets. An Easter basket full of good things to eat is also often a family custom.

6. Tell the students that the Church has a special Mass the night before Easter called the Easter Vigil Mass. During this Mass, adults who have been studying to become Catholic enter the Church; they are baptized, confirmed, and make their First Holy Communion. These adults have found a new spiritual life in Christ and it is a beautiful time for them to enter the Church.

Reinforce

1. Assign p. 73 of the *Activity Book* (see *Teacher's Manual*, p. 235).

2. Children may be invited to do a family show-and-tell in order to share their family celebrations with the other students. Props, food, and samples for all children would be welcome. You may want to do this project over several days, or wait until Lent is over.

3. This would be a good time to pass out copies of Appendix, p. B-28, The Resurrection, for the children to color.

Note: Appendix, p. B-28 is the first of the Glorious Mysteries coloring pages. These pages may be photocopied and passed out for the children to color as each Mystery is learned and discussed. Once all five have been completed, the pages may be stapled together to form a Rosary booklet, following the Joyful and Sorrowful Mysteries.

Conclude

1. Teach an appropriate song, such as "Christ the Lord is risen today," *Adoremus Hymnal*, #415.

2. Pray the first Glorious Mystery of the Rosary.

19   Jesus Was Raised to New Life

"He is not here; for he has risen, as he said.
Come, see the place where he lay."
Matthew 28:6

On the third day after Jesus died, something wonderful happened. Jesus rose from the dead, which means that He came back to life! That day was the very first **Easter Sunday**. We call this great miracle the **Resurrection**.

Mary and the Apostles were so happy to see Jesus alive again. And we are glad that our Savior is alive too. Because Jesus rose from the dead, we too can share in His life and live forever!

At Mass on Easter Sunday we sing joyful songs that praise and thank God:

"The Lord is Risen!"
"**Alleluia!** Alleluia! Alleluia!"

77

Jesus won the gift of grace for us so now we, too, can come back to life after we die. We will go to Heaven to be with Jesus. One day, our bodies will also rise from the dead and be with us in Heaven too. Because Jesus rose from the dead with His body, we know we will be able to live with Jesus in Heaven—body and soul.

Words to Know:

Easter   Alleluia   Resurrection

78

EASTER CUSTOMS – CASCARONES

In some parts of Mexico and the United States, families celebrate Easter with eggs that are not hardboiled. For weeks these families save the shells (cáscaras) of the eggs that they cook by cracking a hole in the top just large enough to release the contents. After washing and drying the egg shells, the children color and decorate them. Once the dyed shells have dried, their parents fill them with confetti, often homemade, and using a paste made of flour and water they cover the opening with a small piece of tissue or napkin. After Easter morning Mass, the families hide the cascarones in the yard and the children find them, then chase each other and crack the eggs in their hands and rub the confetti in each other's hair.

THE RESURRECTION

Matthew 28:1–10	Mark 16:1–13
Luke 24:1–43	John 20:1–29

Preview

In our next lesson, we will learn that we celebrate the Resurrection at every Mass.

CHAPTER NINETEEN: JESUS WAS RAISED TO NEW LIFE
LESSON TWO: WE CELEBRATE THE MASS

Aims

Students will be able to relate to the Apostles' joy in the Resurrection.

They will understand that Catholics celebrate the Resurrection at every Mass and in particular during Easter Sunday Mass.

Materials

• *Activity Book*, p. 74

Optional:
• Children's Bible

• "Christ the Lord is risen today," *Adoremus Hymnal*, #415

Begin

Ask the children why people celebrate Easter with a party or special foods (to celebrate Christ's rising from the dead). What day did Jesus rise from the dead? (Easter Sunday) What day do Catholics celebrate Christ's rising from the dead? (Easter Sunday, but also every Sunday at Mass) Tell them that today they will learn how they can celebrate Christ's rising from the dead. This will help them attend Mass joyfully.

Develop

1. Read paragraph 2 in the text together with the students.

2. Ask the children to retell scenes of the Resurrection story as you have read it to them from the text and the children's Bible (see Mt 28:1–10; Mk 16:1–13; Lk 24:1–43; or Jn 20:1–29). It may be broken into the following parts:
   • Jesus speaking to Mary Magdalene
   • Mary Magdalene telling Peter and John that she has seen the Lord
   • Jesus meeting the Apostles on Easter Sunday night
   • Jesus walking with the Apostles to Emmaus

Discuss with the students how each person might have felt in each scene listed above.

3. Make the connection for them that at each Sunday Mass (not just Easter) Catholics celebrate the Risen Lord. Just as the Sacrifice of the Cross is made present, so also is Christ's rising; Catholics can receive His life in Holy Communion.

This is a great gift. Discuss with them how they should feel and what they should do when they come to Mass (enter quietly, be joyful, be reverent, pray silently, etc.).

4. Go through the parts of the Mass with the children (see the facing page): the Introductory Rites, the Liturgy of the Word, the Liturgy of the Eucharist, the Communion Rite, and the Concluding Rite. Emphasize the glory given to God during Mass, and the fact that it is not only a memorial of the Sacrifice of the Cross, but also a celebration of the Resurrection.

5. Reinforce the idea that anyone can visit the Risen Lord in the tabernacle. Encourage the students to make a visit with their families in the near future.

6. Attend Mass together as a class if possible, or tell the students to pay special attention to the parts of the Mass next time they attend with their families.

Reinforce

1. Have the children complete p. 74 of the *Activity Book* (see *Teacher's Manual*, p. 235), matching the words of the Mass to the parts of the Mass. You may want to assist them with this.

2. Read Questions 40 and 41 from the text (see *Teacher's Manual*, p. 231).

3. Say a simple prayer of thanksgiving to Jesus for His Resurrection and the gift of life as well as the gift of the Mass. Tell the children they can say a similar prayer to Jesus the next time they are near the tabernacle.

Conclude

1. Sing "Christ the Lord is risen today," *Adoremus Hymnal*, #415.

2. Pray the first Glorious Mystery of the Rosary.

19   Jesus Was Raised to New Life

"He is not here; for he has risen, as he said.
Come, see the place where he lay."

Matthew 28:6

On the third day after Jesus died, something wonderful happened. Jesus rose from the dead, which means that He came back to life! That day was the very first **Easter Sunday**. We call this great miracle the **Resurrection**.

Mary and the Apostles were so happy to see Jesus alive again. And we are glad that our Savior is alive too. Because Jesus rose from the dead, we too can share in His life and live forever!

At Mass on Easter Sunday we sing joyful songs that praise and thank God:

"The Lord is Risen!"
"**Alleluia!** Alleluia! Alleluia!"

77

Jesus won the gift of grace for us so now we, too, can come back to life after we die. We will go to Heaven to be with Jesus. One day, our bodies will also rise from the dead and be with us in Heaven too. Because Jesus rose from the dead with His body, we know we will be able to live with Jesus in Heaven—body and soul.

Words to Know:

Easter   Alleluia   Resurrection

78

PARTS OF THE MASS

Introductory Rites: Entrance Song, Greeting (the Sign of the Cross), Penitential Rite (the Confiteor), Kyrie, Gloria, and Opening Prayer

Liturgy of the Word: First Reading, the Responsorial Psalm, the Second Reading, the Alleluia, the Gospel, the Homily, Credo (Profession of Faith), and the General Intercessions

Liturgy of the Eucharist: Offertory (Preparation of the Altar and the Gifts), Offertory Hymn, Prayer over the Gifts, Preface, Sanctus, the Eucharistic Prayer, and the Consecration

Communion Rite: Lord's Prayer, Sign of Peace, the Agnus Dei, Communion, the Communion Hymn, and the Prayer after Communion

Concluding Rite: the Blessing and Dismissal

THE TABERNACLE

Consecrated Hosts are reserved in a tabernacle that is not see-through and is kept locked. The interior walls must be lined with either fine material or special fabric. A cloth may be hung in front of it. A lamp or wax candle, usually in red glass, must always burn nearby as a sign that Jesus is really there. See also p. 356 of this manual.

Preview

In our next lesson, we will learn more about the Mass, we will hear a message from Jesus, and we will respond to Him.

Chapter Nineteen: Jesus Was Raised to New Life
Lesson Three: We Can Live Forever

Aims

Students will understand that when Jesus rose from the dead He won back the gift of grace.

They will learn that Jesus opened the gates of Heaven so man may go to Heaven.

They will realize that Catholics receive Jesus' life and grace through the Sacraments, especially in Holy Communion.

Materials

• *Activity Book*, p. 75

Optional:
• Construction paper and crayons

• "Christ the Lord is risen today," *Adoremus Hymnal*, #415

Begin

Have the following message written on the chalkboard before the children arrive:

My dear child, I love you and want to share My life with you in Heaven forever. I offer you the gift of My life. Will you receive My gift of grace? Love, Jesus

When the students arrive, ask them if they like to receive presents. Have them look at the board and listen as you read a message from Jesus.

Develop

1. Tell the students that they can choose whether or not they will accept this gift, but that they should know that this gift requires great care. Use the example of an animal, e.g., a pet dog. What care must be taken of this dog? They need to feed it, exercise it, clean up after it, and teach it to behave.

2. Review with the children the sin of Adam. Remind them that because of this sin, people could not go to Heaven; they had lost the gift of grace. Jesus' death and Resurrection won back this grace and opened the gates of Heaven.

3. Remind the children that this gift of Jesus (grace) is His life in the soul and that it requires great care; it is a gift for which the individual must be responsible. A Catholic must feed his soul with prayer and the Eucharist. He must exercise his soul with good deeds and prayer. He must keep it clean by not sinning, and tell God he is sorry if he does sin, and then go to Confession. He cannot leave his soul alone (without grace) for too long

either. He must pray and go to Mass. He must teach it, by reading the Bible, and by listening at Mass and during religion class.

4. Explain to the children that they, too, can be gifts for Jesus. Remind them how to offer up their daily works, joys, and sufferings in a Morning Offering (see two versions in Chapter 11, Lesson 4, p. 133 of this manual). Tell them that loving their neighbor, doing good works, praying, and avoiding sin are all ways to make their lives pleasing to God, and that these things are gifts to God if they are done for Him.

6. Ask the children to think of ways they can offer themselves up to God. They may use a talent to serve Him. They may serve others in charity. They may strive to grow in holiness in some way. Encourage the children to think of many ways so their entire lives can be gifts to God. Let them know that all things can be a gift to God except sin, but that sorrow for sin and making up for our sins can also be a gift to God.

Reinforce

1. Assign p. 75 of the *Activity Book* (see *Teacher's Manual*, p. 235).

2. The children may make cards to respond to Jesus' message. Do they want to accept this gift? Will they be responsible with it? They can offer themselves as gifts to God in their cards.

Conclude

1. Have each child promise to offer up something this week to God as a gift of thanksgiving. It might be TV, a favorite food, or doing a good deed. They can report back next week.

2. Sing "Christ the Lord is risen today," *Adoremus Hymnal*, #415.

3. Pray the first Glorious Mystery of the Rosary.

19   Jesus Was Raised to New Life

"He is not here; for he has risen, as he said.
Come, see the place where he lay."

Matthew 28:6

On the third day after Jesus died, something wonderful happened. Jesus rose from the dead, which means that He came back to life! That day was the very first **Easter Sunday**. We call this great miracle the **Resurrection**.

Mary and the Apostles were so happy to see Jesus alive again. And we are glad that our Savior is alive too. Because Jesus rose from the dead, we too can share in His life and live forever!

At Mass on Easter Sunday we sing joyful songs that praise and thank God:

"The Lord is Risen!"
"**Alleluia!** Alleluia! Alleluia!"

77

Jesus won the gift of grace for us so now we, too, can come back to life after we die. We will go to Heaven to be with Jesus. One day, our bodies will also rise from the dead and be with us in Heaven too. Because Jesus rose from the dead with His body, we know we will be able to live with Jesus in Heaven— body and soul.

Words to Know:

Easter   Alleluia   Resurrection

78

> **Q. 40** *After His death, what did Jesus do?*
> After His death, Jesus rose again from the dead, taking up His body that had been buried (CCC 646).
>
> **Q. 41** *How long did the body of Jesus remain buried?*
> The body of Jesus remained buried from Friday evening to the day that we now call Easter Sunday (CCC 639).

79

SAINT JOHN BOSCO

Saint John Bosco was born of poor parents in a small town near Piedmont, Italy, on August 16, 1815. At age nine he had a dream about his future vocation with boys. He was ordained a priest in 1841 and settled in Turin. He began his ministry by using his gift of juggling to catch the attention of the young boys in town, after which he would teach them, take them to Mass, and hear their Confessions. This apostolate soon developed into the Salesian Order (the order of Saint Francis de Sales). One of his students was Saint Dominic Savio (see p. 155 of this manual). Later he founded an order of women—Daughters of Mary Auxiliatrix— for similar work among girls. He died in 1888 at the age of seventy-two. He was canonized in 1934. His feastday is January 31.

Preview

In our next lesson, we will learn about the doctrine of the resurrection of the body.

CHAPTER NINETEEN: JESUS WAS RAISED TO NEW LIFE
LESSON FOUR: THE RESURRECTION OF THE BODY

Aims

Students will gain a better understanding of Jesus' resurrected body.

They will learn that Mary was taken to Heaven, body and soul.

They will learn that one day, their body will join their soul in Heaven.

Materials

• *Activity Book*, p. 76

Optional:
• Picture of the Assumption

• "Christ the Lord is Risen today," *Adoremus Hymnal*, #415

Begin

Discuss the painting of the Resurrection found on p. 76 in the textbook (see *Teacher's Manual*, p. 227). Ask the students questions to reinforce the fact that Jesus has a body (He is not a ghost). He has His wounds from the Crucifixion. He is radiant and happy. He is outside the tomb and the door is shut.

Develop

1. Read paragraphs 3 and 4 with the class. Explain to the children that because Jesus rose from the dead and took up His body again, He has given everyone a share in this great gift. He wants His children to live with Him forever, body and soul.

2. At a person's death, his body dies, but his soul lives forever. The Church teaches, however, that at the end of time, the bodies of the just will be raised up to join their souls. Catholics profess this at the end of the Apostles' Creed: "I believe in…the resurrection of the body."

3. Jesus gave us a perfect example of this in His Mother, Mary. At the end of her life on earth, she went straight to Heaven body and soul. This is called the Assumption (show a picture of this event if you have one or see Appendix p. B-31). Be sure to emphasize that God raised Mary into Heaven; she did not go of her own power. (This will be discussed in further detail in Chapter 26.)

4. Explain that Catholics trust that their bodies will join their souls in Heaven, too, at the end of time. These resurrected bodies will no longer be subject to pain, disease, or death. They will be spiritual bodies.

5. Tell the children that it is important to take good care of their bodies while here on earth. They need to eat properly, exercise, take care of themselves when they are sick, and take care not to injure others accidentally or with intent. It is important to respect their bodies and the bodies of others because one day these bodies may be raised up to live forever with God in Heaven. Have them suggest ways to care for their bodies and list them on the board:
• Eat healthy foods, i.e., broccoli and spinach.
• Take medicine when ill, even if it tastes bad.
• Get enough sleep at night, i.e., go to bed when told.

Reinforce

1. Assign p. 76 of the *Activity Book* (see *Teacher's Manual*, p. 235), which corresponds with the first two paragraphs of the text of this chapter.

2. Have the children begin to memorize Questions 40 and 41 in the text (see *Teacher's Manual*, p. 231).

Conclude

1. Ask each child to do something good for their body tonight, i.e., eat a vegetable with dinner, exercise, bathe or shower, etc. Tell them you will do something good for your body too. Everyone can share their healthy deed during the next lesson.

2. Sing "Christ the Lord is risen today," *Adoremus Hymnal*, #415.

3. Pray the First Glorious Mystery of the Rosary.

19   Jesus Was Raised to New Life

"He is not here; for he has risen, as he said.
Come, see the place where he lay."
Matthew 28:6

On the third day after Jesus died, something wonderful happened. Jesus rose from the dead, which means that He came back to life! That day was the very first **Easter Sunday**. We call this great miracle the **Resurrection**.

Mary and the Apostles were so happy to see Jesus alive again. And we are glad that our Savior is alive too. Because Jesus rose from the dead, we too can share in His life and live forever!

At Mass on Easter Sunday we sing joyful songs that praise and thank God:

"The Lord is Risen!"
"Alleluia! Alleluia! Alleluia!"

77

Jesus won the gift of grace for us so now we, too, can come back to life after we die. We will go to Heaven to be with Jesus. One day, our bodies will also rise from the dead and be with us in Heaven too. Because Jesus rose from the dead with His body, we know we will be able to live with Jesus in Heaven—body and soul.

Words to Know:

Easter   Alleluia   Resurrection

78

Q. 40   *After His death, what did Jesus do?*
After His death, Jesus rose again from the dead, taking up His body that had been buried (CCC 646).

Q. 41   *How long did the body of Jesus remain buried?*
The body of Jesus remained buried from Friday evening to the day that we now call Easter Sunday (CCC 639).

79

THE ASSUMPTION

The dogma of the Assumption of the Blessed Virgin Mary was declared *ex cathedra* (see p. 241) by Pope Pius XII on November 1, 1950. This dogma declared only that our Lady was assumed into Heaven body and soul; it did not speak of her death. Belief in Mary's assumption has been held by pious Christians since about the fourth century. It is called the feast of the Dormition by Eastern rite Catholics, for they believe that as a perfect human without Original Sin, she did not have to die, therefore she merely fell into a deep sleep (see p. 315 of this manual). The feast of the Assumption of the Blessed Virgin Mary is a Holy Day of Obligation in the United States, and it is celebrated on August 15.

THE STATE OF RESURRECTED BODIES

Impassibility: The body will no longer suffer pain or death; it will not corrupt.
Brightness: The body will be beautiful and brilliant.
Agility: The body will be able to pass through matter and go to all parts of the universe with great speed.
Subtlety: The body will participate more perfectly in the spiritual life.

Preview

We will review what we have learned and take a quiz.

233

CHAPTER NINETEEN: JESUS WAS RAISED TO NEW LIFE
REVIEW AND ASSESSMENT

Aims

To review and assess the children's knowledge of the materials taught in this chapter.

Materials

- Appendix, p. B-1
- Quiz 19 (Appendix, p. A-23)
- "Christ the Lord is risen today," *Adoremus Hymnal*, #415

Review and Enrichment

Play a review game, such as Bible Baseball (see Appendix, p. B-1 for instructions). Be sure to cover the content of all four lessons, including:

- Jesus rose from the dead on the first Easter Sunday. This is called the Resurrection.
- He rose body and soul.
- By rising from the dead, Jesus won back grace for man and opened the gates of Heaven.
- Catholics celebrate the Resurrection on Easter and at every Sunday Mass, and have a foretaste of Heaven by being united with Jesus in Holy Communion.
- Because Jesus rose from the dead, Catholics know they will be in Heaven one day with their bodies, just as Mary was after the Assumption.

Assess

Distribute Quiz 19. Read through it with the children and answer any questions that they may have. Individually quiz the children on the Questions from the textbook. After they have completed the quiz, take time to review the correct answers to reinforce them.

Conclude

Close with a prayer or sing "Christ the Lord is risen today," *Adoremus Hymnal*, #415.

Name:_____

The Easter Season brings new life!

Color the pictures.

We thank Jesus for His grace and we welcome Him into our hearts.

We welcome God's creations into the world.

We welcome our new brothers and sisters into the Church.

Name:_____

The Order of the Mass

Draw a line from the part of the Mass to the words that are said during each part. Then, number the four parts in the correct order.

<u>3</u>   Liturgy of the Eucharist — "Go forth, the Mass is ended."

<u>4</u>   Concluding Rite — "A reading from the holy Gospel according to John."

<u>2</u>   Liturgy of the Word — "This is my Body, which will be given up for you."

<u>1</u>   Introductory Rite — "I confess to almighty God..."

Name:_____

The Gift of Grace

Fill in the blanks using the words below.

thank	Adam and Eve
new life	Confession
prayer	sin
Eucharist	won

1. <u>Adam and Eve</u> lost the gift of grace for us in the Garden of Eden.

2. Jesus <u>won</u> back the gift of grace for us by dying for our sins and rising to <u>new life</u>.

3. We should <u>thank</u> Jesus for the gift of grace.

4. We must "feed" the gift of grace with <u>prayer</u> and the <u>Eucharist</u>.

5. We will lose the gift of grace if we <u>sin</u>.

6. We can receive the gift of grace again if we are sorry for our sins and go to <u>Confession</u>.

Name:_____

Can you fill in the blanks? Use Chapter 19 in your textbook for help.

On the <u>third</u> day after Jesus died, something <u>wonderful</u> happened. <u>Jesus</u> rose from the <u>dead</u>, which means He came back to <u>life</u>! That day was the very first <u>Easter Sunday</u>. We call this great miracle the <u>Resurrection</u>.

<u>Mary</u> and the <u>Apostles</u> were so happy to see <u>Jesus</u> alive again. We are glad that our Savior is alive too. Because Jesus <u>rose</u> from the <u>dead</u>, we too, can <u>share</u> in His <u>life</u> and live <u>forever</u>.

TEACHER'S NOTES

CHAPTER TWENTY
JESUS BEGINS THE CHURCH

Catechism of the Catholic Church References

Apostolic Succession: 75–79, 96, 861–62, 880–87, 935–39
Christ as the Head of the Church: 669
The Church Is Apostolic: 857–65, 869
The Church Is Catholic: 830–35, 838, 868
The Church Is Holy: 823–29, 867
The Church Is One: 813–22, 866
The Church's Origin, Foundation, and Mission: 758–69, 778
The Church as People of God: 781–86

The Episcopal College: 880–87
The Governing Office of the Church: 894–96
The Hierarchical Constitution of the Church: 871–96, 934–39
The Infallibility of the Pope: 882, 891–92, 937
"Outside the Church There Is No Salvation": 846–48
The Pope and Bishops: 816, 2034
The Sanctifying Office of the Church: 893
The Teaching Office of the Church: 888–92

Scripture References

Christ Gives the Keys of the Kingdom to Peter: Mt 16:13–19

Christ Promises to Remain with His Church: Mt 28:19–20

Background Reading: *The Fundamentals of Catholicism* by Fr. Kenneth Baker, S.J.

Volume 3:
"Why Did Christ Establish His Church?", pp. 95–98
"A Hierarchal Church," pp. 101–4
"The Primacy of St. Peter," pp. 107–10
"The Primacy of the Pope," pp. 110–13
"The Pope Is Judged by No One," pp. 113–16

"When Is the Pope Infallible?", pp. 116–19
"Christ Is the Head of the Church," pp. 125–28
The Catholic Church, pp. 128–40
"The Four Marks of the Church," pp. 140–42
"Who Are Members of the Church?", pp. 143–45
"Outside of the Church There Is No Salvation," pp. 146–48

Summary of Lesson Content

Lesson 1

Jesus' mission on earth was to teach the Good News, win back God's grace, and give it to others.

Jesus wanted His work to continue on earth after He returned to the Father.

He founded the Catholic Church to continue His work after He returned to Heaven.

Lesson 2

The Church teaches about Jesus and dispenses His grace.

Jesus works in and through the Church.

Catholics enter the Church when they are baptized.

Lesson 3

Jesus is the founder of the Church.

The four marks of the Church are: one, holy, catholic, and apostolic.

Christ established a hierarchy in the Church.

We will review Apostolic Succession, which began with Peter succeeding Christ as the visible head of the Church.

Lesson 4

We will learn about the present leadership in the Church, including the current Pope and local bishops and priests.

The successor of Peter lives in the Vatican.

CHAPTER TWENTY: JESUS BEGINS THE CHURCH
LESSON ONE: CHRIST'S WORK CONTINUES

Aims

Students will understand that Jesus became man in order to teach the Good News, win back God's grace, and pass it on to others.

They will learn Jesus wanted His work to continue on earth after He returned to Heaven.

They will realize that Jesus founded the Catholic Church in order to continue His work on earth.

Materials

• Children's Bible

• *Activity Book*, p. 77

Optional:
• "The Church's one foundation," *Adoremus Hymnal*, #560

Begin

Instruct the students to open their textbooks to the picture of Jesus giving the keys of the Kingdom to Saint Peter (p. 80). Explain to them that Jesus gave Peter His own work of protecting and guarding the Church. Tell them that today they will learn more about what this meant for Peter and for the Church.

Develop

1. Ask the class what would happen if the teacher gave a student the keys to the classroom. Explain that the student could go in and out freely and could open all the cabinets, drawers, and closets because he would have all the keys. He could let in whomever he chose, but he would also have to take care of the room and be responsible for the space. By giving the keys to Peter, Jesus gave him the authority to guard and protect the Church.

2. Read paragraph 1 from the text aloud with the class. Then read the foundation of the Church from the children's Bible (Mt 16:13–19).

3. Explain to the children that Jesus gave Peter the keys of the Kingdom. This made Peter the first Pope. Although Peter had the keys, he was Jesus' servant. He was not the head of the Church, but instead he was like a butler. A butler takes care of a home, and keeps it safe and clean. He lets the guests in and helps them to follow household rules by inviting them to behave in a pleasing manner (e.g., please take off your coat and wait in the study). The Pope protects the Church (God's house) from incorrect teaching and keeps her free from error. He brings people into the Church and teaches them about Jesus and His laws, so they may please God. The Pope guides Catholics to Jesus in the best way: through the Church. Just as a butler is not head of the household, so the Pope is not head of the Church, but Jesus' servant.

4. Ask the children why Jesus founded the Church (to continue His work, to teach the Good News, to dispense His grace, to guard the truth, and to protect His followers). Explain that Jesus continues to love all people through the Church and that the Church helps people to love Jesus in return. She does this by teaching about Him and how to serve Him and love Him, and by guiding Catholics in ways that are pleasing to Him.

Reinforce

1. Have the children color the Papal symbol on p. 77 of the *Activity Book* (see *Teacher's Manual*, p. 247).

2. Teach an appropriate song, such as "The Church's one foundation," *Adoremus Hymnal*, #560.

Conclude

1. Say a class prayer thanking God for the gift of His Church.

2. Pray one Our Father, one Hail Mary, and one Glory Be for the Pope (see *Teacher's Manual*, p. 367).

20   Jesus Begins the Church

"And I tell you, you are Peter, and on this rock
I will build my Church, and the gates of Hades
shall not prevail against it."
Matthew 16:18

Jesus was alive and with His Apostles again. But He was going to go up to Heaven. Jesus wanted all people to know the Good News of God's love. He wanted people to know Him and He wanted His work to continue on earth. To continue His work, He started His **Church**.

People who belong to the Church can learn about Jesus and receive the gift of grace. He continues to work in and through the Church, so we can come to know His love for us.

Jesus made His Apostles the leaders of His Church and they were the first **bishops**. Then He named **Peter** the head of the Apostles and the very first **Pope**. Do you know who your Pope and bishop are?

81

PAPAL INFALLIBILITY

Papal infallibility is implied in Scripture, though it was not defined until 1870 at the First Vatican Council. This is not to say that the Church did not hold this doctrine to be true, for any doctrine that the Church proclaims is not new, but merely becomes official. In this case, Christ granted a charism (a specific gift or grace of the Holy Spirit which may directly or indirectly benefit the Church) to the successors of Peter so that in declaring doctrine regarding faith and morals, the Holy Spirit protects them from error. This does not apply to everything the Pope says, such as his daily teaching as the Bishop of Rome. Infallibility applies only to the doctrines he officially proclaims for the Universal Church.

VATICAN CITY

Not only is the Pope the visible head of the entire Catholic Church, he is the personal Bishop of Rome and the Head of State of Vatican City with full legislative, executive, and judicial power. The smallest independent state in the world, Vatican City is entirely contained within the city of Rome. The Vatican is immune from Italian taxation, has its own currency, and issues its own postage stamps. The Papal summer residence at Castel Gandolfo also enjoys extraterritorial rights.

PETER

The name Peter comes from the Greek word *petros*, which means "stone, rock." *Petros* is the translation of the Syriac word *kefa*, meaning "stone." Jesus gave Simon the name Cephas or Peter.

Preview

In our next lesson, we will come to understand the work of the Church.

CHAPTER TWENTY: JESUS BEGINS THE CHURCH
LESSON TWO: THE WORK OF THE CHURCH

Aims

Students will recognize that the Church has the authority to teach about Jesus and dispense His grace.

They will learn that Jesus works in and through the Church, even today.

They will understand that Catholics enter the Church when they are baptized.

Materials

• *Activity Book*, p. 78

Optional:
• "The Church's one foundation," *Adoremus Hymnal*, #560

Begin

List the seven Sacraments on the board and briefly discuss how each affects the soul:
  Baptism: Gives God's life (grace)
  Eucharist: Feeds the soul
  Penance: Heals the soul of sin

Confirmation: Strengthens faith in the soul
Holy Orders/Matrimony: Helps one to live faithfully to Christ
Anointing of the Sick: Strengthens the soul and may heal the body

Develop

1. Read paragraph 2 of the text with the students.

2. Discuss the main role of the Church: to continue the work of Jesus. Review with the students the work of Jesus: to teach the Good News, to guard the truth, to teach the Faith, to dispense grace, and to protect His followers and care for their needs.

3. Explain that the Church continues the work of Jesus through the Church leaders. Jesus gave His teaching authority to Peter and to the Apostles in union with Him. This authority has been passed on to the Pope (the successor of Peter) and the bishops (the successors of the Apostles). These men care for the Church and all the people in the Church. They continue to teach the truth about Jesus and His teachings, including the Good News. With the priests, they dispense grace through the Sacraments. The Church cares for all her members just as

Christ cares for His followers (see also Chapter 17, Lesson 2; pp. 204–05).

4. Jesus works through the Church to ensure that all that is taught on matters of faith and morals is the truth. Whenever the Pope declares certain things to be the truth, the Holy Spirit ensures that he makes no mistakes. This wonderful security we have in the Church is because Jesus promised to be with the Church until the end of time (Mt 28: 19–20).

5. Jesus also gives grace to the Church and works through the priests, bishops, and the Pope. They are His ministers. When they celebrate the Sacraments—Baptism, Penance, Eucharist, Confirmation, Matrimony, Anointing of the Sick, and Holy Orders—it is Jesus who works in and through them as they use His words, gestures, and the things He used to celebrate the Sacraments (like bread and wine for the Eucharist).

Reinforce

1. Assign the word search on p. 78 of the *Activity Book* (see *Teacher's Manual*, p. 247).

2. Have the children think of ways that they can receive the Good News, the teachings of Jesus, and His grace. They can raise their hands and share their ideas with the class. Examples: pray, listen to the readings at Mass, tell the Good News to others.

3. Ask the children to memorize Question 42 (see *Teacher's Manual*, p. 245).

Conclude

1. Close with a prayer or the song "The Church's one foundation," *Adoremus Hymnal*, #560.

2. Pray for the Pope.

20   Jesus Begins the Church

> "And I tell you, you are Peter, and on this rock
> I will build my Church, and the gates of Hades
> shall not prevail against it."
>
> Matthew 16:18

Jesus was alive and with His Apostles again. But He was going to go up to Heaven. Jesus wanted all people to know the Good News of God's love. He wanted people to know Him and He wanted His work to continue on earth. To continue His work, He started His **Church**.

People who belong to the Church can learn about Jesus and receive the gift of grace. He continues to work in and through the Church, so we can come to know His love for us.

Jesus made His Apostles the leaders of His Church and they were the first **bishops**. Then He named **Peter** the head of the Apostles and the very first **Pope**. Do you know who your Pope and bishop are?

81

Words to Know:

Church   Pope   bishop   Peter

82

"OUTSIDE THE CHURCH THERE IS NO SALVATION"

"Basing itself on Scripture and Tradition, the Council teaches that the Church . . . is necessary for salvation: the one Christ is the mediator and the way for salvation; he is present to us in his body which is the Church. He himself explicitly asserted the necessity of faith and Baptism, and thereby affirmed the necessity of the Church which men enter through Baptism as through a door. Hence they could not be saved who, knowing that the Catholic Church was founded as necessary by God through Christ, would refuse either to enter it or remain in it."

—*Catechism of the Catholic Church*, 846
Lumen Gentium 14 (cf Mark 16:16; John 3:5)

"EX CATHEDRA"

When the Holy Father speaks on faith and morals, Catholics are obliged to assent to his teaching. The highest authority from which he can speak is *ex cathedra* (from the chair), that is, from the chair of Peter. (Tradition holds that a chair in the back of Saint Peter's Basilica belonged to Peter.) On only two occasions has a Pope spoken solemnly in this way, both times in reference to our Lady: to declare her the Immaculate Conception in 1854, and to declare the doctrine of her Assumption in 1950 (see pp. 233 and 315 of this manual).

THE CHURCH AND SALVATION

The Church offers the fullness of the means of salvation to all people. Catholics enter the Church through Baptism when Original Sin and personal sin is washed away and God fills the soul with grace.

Preview

In our next lesson, we will learn more about the Church leaders and we will review Apostolic Succession.

CHAPTER TWENTY: JESUS BEGINS THE CHURCH
LESSON THREE: THE CHURCH LEADERS

Aims

Students will remember that Jesus is the founder of the Church.

They will learn that the marks of the Church are one, holy, catholic, and apostolic.

They will review Apostolic Succession.

They will also review the hierarchal structure of the Church.

Materials

- An heirloom or personal "treasure"

- *Activity Book*, p. 79

Optional:
- "The Church's one foundation," *Adoremus Hymnal*, #560

Begin

Explain to the children the concept of passing on something from one generation to the next, using the example of a family heirloom or an inheritance. You may want to bring to class a small heirloom, i.e., a piece of art, a brooch, etc. to use as a concrete example. Explain that the authenticity of such an object is known because of family tradition, but also because of documentation, a certificate of authenticity, or a dated letter.

Develop

1. Read paragraph 3 together with the class.

2. Emphasize that when Jesus founded the Church He wanted to be sure His treasures would be passed on to His followers. These treasures are the truths of the Faith and grace.

3. Review with the students what it meant for Jesus to give the keys to Peter: it gave him authority over and responsibility for the Church; the other Apostles, as the first bishops of the Church, helped Peter; Peter was the first Pope. These men were the leaders of the Church and safeguarded the treasures of the Faith and grace.

4. The Apostles passed on their leadership, like a family treasure or inheritance, to other bishops, so that what was passed on did not change, only the leader changed. This concept is very important for the students to understand.

5. To prove the authenticity of its treasured inheritance, the Church has a tradition, but there are also four proofs or marks of the true Church founded by Christ:

One: Jesus founded one Church to witness to Him and unite people to Him through her work.

Holy: The Church is holy because Jesus founded it, and gives her His grace.

Catholic: The Church is for everyone all over the world, throughout time.

Apostolic: The Apostles who learned directly from Jesus were the first bishops, and they passed on their authority, teaching, and leadership from one generation of bishops to the next.

6. You may want to chart the authority of the Church beginning with Jesus, the Apostles with Peter as their leader, and the bishops with the Pope as the successor of Peter, etc. Refer to p. 205 of this manual for examples.

Reinforce

1. Assign p. 79 of the *Activity Book* (see *Teacher's Manual*, p. 247), which asks the students to write sentences about the chapter using certain words. You may want to assist them with this activity.

2. Have the children begin to memorize Questions 43 and 44 from the textbook (see *Teacher's Manual*, p. 245).

Conclude

1. Conclude with the hymn "The Church's one foundation," *Adoremus Hymnal*, #560.

2. Pray for the Pope.

20   Jesus Begins the Church

"And I tell you, you are Peter, and on this rock
I will build my Church, and the gates of Hades
shall not prevail against it."
                                        Matthew 16:18

Jesus was alive and with His Apostles again. But He was going to go up to Heaven. Jesus wanted all people to know the Good News of God's love. He wanted people to know Him and He wanted His work to continue on earth. To continue His work, He started His **Church**.

People who belong to the Church can learn about Jesus and receive the gift of grace. He continues to work in and through the Church, so we can come to know His love for us.

Jesus made His Apostles the leaders of His Church and they were the first **bishops**. Then He named **Peter** the head of the Apostles and the very first **Pope**. Do you know who your Pope and bishop are?

81

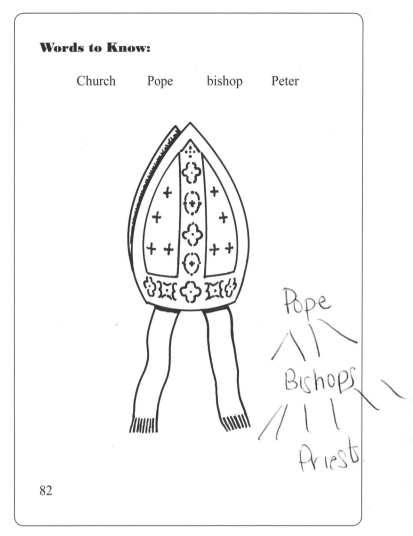

Pope
Bishops
Priest

82

ECUMENICAL COUNCILS

An ecumenical council is a gathering of the college of bishops, at which the Pope presides either in person or through his delegates. A council is considered ecumenical and its conciliar decrees are binding only if the Pope confirms and promulgates them, or at least accepts them. It is the prerogative of the Roman Pontiff to convene, preside over, and confirm the teaching of ecumenical councils. If the Pope dies during a council, it is suspended until a new Pope is elected. A council is not superior to a Pope; collectively he and the bishops represent the entire Church, not in a democratic way, but as successors of the Apostles. Every bishop is invited to attend and vote. The Church, in her supreme authority, can invite and determine the participation of others.

SCRIPTURE AND TRADITION

The Catholic Church differs from the Protestants because it gives equal reverence and acceptance to Scripture and Tradition, the two pillars of the Church. Tradition refers to those things which are unwritten and which have been passed on from Christ to His Apostles. Catholics further believe that Christ instituted the Church with the authority to interpret Scripture and to defend and transmit revealed truth.

VATICAN COUNCIL II

The most recent Ecumenical Council of the Church, Vatican II was called by John XXIII in 1959 and convened in 1962. After his death, Paul VI reconvened the Council in 1963 and its last session ended in 1965. Sixteen documents were formulated and promulagated at this Council: two dogmatic and two pastoral constitutions, nine decrees, and three declarations.

The first five Popes were saints Peter, Linus, Anacletus, Clement I, and Evaristus.

Preview

In our next lesson, we will learn about the present leadership of the Church, and who our current Pope, bishops, and priests are.

243

CHAPTER TWENTY: JESUS BEGINS THE CHURCH
LESSON FOUR: THE CHURCH TODAY

Aims

Students will learn about the present leadership of the Church.

They will be able to identify the current Pope, their local bishop, and parish priests.

They will learn that the Pope lives in the Vatican.

Materials

• Images of the current Pope, local bishop and parish priests

• Picture of the Vatican

• *Activity Book*, p. 80

Optional:
• Construction paper and crayons

• "The Church's one foundation," *Adoremus Hymnal*, #560

Begin

Review the idea of Apostolic Succession with the children. You may want to draw a chart on the chalkboard that outlines this, beginning with Christ, the Apostles with Peter as their head, then the bishops and the Pope as their successors respectively. See p. 205 of this manual for examples.

Develop

1. Read aloud the last sentence of paragraph 3 in the text: "Do you know who your Pope and bishop are?" Ask the children if they can name them for you.

2. Explain that after Peter died, another man was chosen to take his place. As each man died, another was chosen to replace him so that his authority passed from one man to the next. These men are called Popes. Write the word "Pope" on the board. Tell them that today our Pope is _____, and hold up a picture of the current Holy Father. Explain that this man represents Jesus for Catholics here on earth. The Pope is the visible head of the Catholic Church, though Jesus is the invisible and true leader of His Church. Explain also that there is only one Pope for the Church. Show the students a picture of the Vatican and explain that this is where the Pope lives (see "Vatican City" on p. 239).

3. Now hold up a picture of the local bishop. Explain that the Apostles also had men take their places once they died. These men are called bishops. Write the word "bishop" on the board. Explain that there are many bishops in the world today and that they all care for a geographical region. Tell the students the name of their diocese and the name of their bishop. Explain that bishops must obey the Pope, and Catholics must obey them.

4. Explain that the bishop has many people to care for, so he has some priests to help him. Many of these priests have a church and lots of people under their care. Write the word "Priest" on the board. Hold up pictures of the pastor or parish priest(s) and ask the students if they know his name. If they do not recognize any of the priests, tell them their names and encourage them to greet the priests the next time they see them at Mass. Explain that the priest is obedient to the bishop, and he serves the people in place of the bishop as his helper.

Reinforce

1. Have the children answer the questions based on this lesson on p. 80 of the *Activity Book* (see *Teacher's Manual*, p. 247).

2. Play a memory game with the students to reinforce this lesson. Put the pictures of the Pope, bishop, and priest(s) face down on the table. Call on the children to choose a picture and identify each clergyman.

3. Make a list of the ordination anniversaries of the local bishop and parish priests (this can be found in the Catholic Directory or by calling your local diocesan offices). Have the children make cards for the parish priest or bishop on this day.

Conclude

1. Close with "The Church's one foundation," *Adoremus Hymnal*, #560.

2. Pray for the Pope.

20 Jesus Begins the Church

"And I tell you, you are Peter, and on this rock
I will build my Church, and the gates of Hades
shall not prevail against it."
Matthew 16:18

Jesus was alive and with His Apostles again. But He was going to go up to Heaven. Jesus wanted all people to know the Good News of God's love. He wanted people to know Him and He wanted His work to continue on earth. To continue His work, He started His **Church**.

People who belong to the Church can learn about Jesus and receive the gift of grace. He continues to work in and through the Church, so we can come to know His love for us.

Jesus made His Apostles the leaders of His Church and they were the first **bishops**. Then He named **Peter** the head of the Apostles and the very first **Pope**. Do you know who your Pope and bishop are?

81

Words to Know:

Church   Pope   bishop   Peter

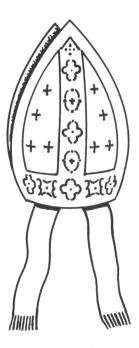

82

Q. 42   *What is the Church?*
The Church is the group of baptized persons who profess the Catholic Faith and come together to worship God. (CCC 751–52).

Q. 43   *By whom was the Church founded?*
The Church was founded by Jesus Christ (CCC 763–66).

Q. 44   *Who is the Pope?*
The Pope is the successor of Saint Peter. He is the visible head of the Catholic Church (CCC 882).

83

THE HIERARCHY OF THE CHURCH

The Pope: He is the direct successor of Peter and the Bishop of Rome. He is the visible head of the Church, the Vicar of Christ on earth.

Bishops: These are the successors of the twelve Apostles; they oversee the priests in a diocese and they ordain new priests.

Priests: They administer the Sacraments; they are often, but not always, associated with a parish.

Deacons: These men receive Holy Orders and may perform marriages, assist at Mass, and preach the homily.

Laity: Those who have not received Holy Orders or vows.

Preview

In our next lesson, there will be a quiz and unit test.

CHAPTER TWENTY: JESUS BEGINS THE CHURCH
REVIEW AND ASSESSMENT

Aims

To review and assess the children's knowledge of the materials taught in this chapter.

Materials

- Quiz 20 (Appendix, p. A-24)
- "The Church's one foundation," *Adoremus Hymnal*, #560

Name: _____

Jesus Begins the Church   **Quiz 20**

Yes or No. *Circle the correct answer.*

1. Did Jesus spend time with His Apostles after He rose?   (Yes)   No

2. Did Jesus start the Church to give us grace?   (Yes)   No

Fill in the blanks. *Trace the gray letters and fill in the rest.*

| Pope   Apostles   bishops |

Word Bank

1. The A p o s t l e s were the first leaders of the Church.

2. The Apostles were the first b i s h o p s .

3. Peter was the first P o p e .

Review and Enrichment

1. Review the passing of the keys from Christ to Peter (Mt 16:13–19).

2. Ask the children questions to review the content of the chapter:
- Why did Jesus found the Church?
- What work does the Church do?
- Who were the first leaders of the Church?
- Who are the present leaders of the Church?
- Who are the bishops? (What do they do?)
- Who is the Pope?

3. Review the hierarchical structure of the Church and her Apostolic Succession, including the current leaders (by name).

Assess

1. Distribute the quiz and read through it with the children. Answer any questions they may have.

2. Orally quiz each child on Questions 42, 43, and 44 as he hands in his quiz (see *Teacher's Manual*, p. 245).

3. Once the children have completed the quiz, review the correct answers with the class.

Conclude

Close by singing "The Church's one foundation," *Adoremus Hymnal*, #560.

Name:_____

Jesus Begins His Church

"And I tell you, you are Peter, and on this rock
I will build my Church, and the gates of Hades
shall not prevail against it."

Matthew 16:18

Color the picture of the Papal symbol.

Faith and Life Series • Grade 1 • Chapter 20 • Lesson 1   77

Name:_____

Word Search

**Can you find these words in the puzzle?
Look carefully! The words go across and down.**

APOSTLES	FOUNDED	LEADERS
BISHOPS	GRACE	PASTORS
CATHOLIC	JESUS	PETER
CHURCH	KEYS	POPE

```
V  C  H  L  P  P  O  P  E  N
D  H  N  L  E  J  E  S  U  S
H  U  C  A  T  H  O  L  I  C
B  R  T  W  E  Y  C  Y  N  R
I  C  G  D  R  G  F  N  L  M
S  H  R  P  A  S  T  O  R  S
H  K  A  P  O  S  T  L  E  S
O  E  C  L  E  A  D  E  R  S
P  Y  E  J  R  F  P  R  J  B
S  S  L  F  O  U  N  D  E  D
```

78   *Faith and Life Series • Grade 1 • Chapter 20 • Lesson 2*

Name:_____

**Write sentences about the lesson using the
following words.**

Apostles: Answers will vary _____
_____

Catholic Church:_____
_____

Peter:_____
_____

Pope:_____
_____

Bishops:_____
_____

Keys:_____
_____

Faith and Life Series • Grade 1 • Chapter 20 • Lesson 3   79

Name:_____

Answer the following questions.

1. What is the Church?

The Church is the group of baptized
persons who profess the Catholic
Faith and come together to worship
God.

2. By whom was the Church founded?

The Church was founded by Jesus
Christ.

3. Who are the leaders of the Church today?

The Pope and bishops

4. What is a Pope?

The successor of Saint Peter and
the visible head of the Church

5. Who is our Pope now?

Students should name the current
Pope.

80   *Faith and Life Series • Grade 1 • Chapter 20 • Lesson 4*

TEACHER'S NOTES

UNIT FIVE TEST
CHAPTERS 17–20

> **CHAPTER SEVENTEEN: THE BEST GIFT OF ALL**
>
> **CHAPTER EIGHTEEN: JESUS DIES FOR US**
>
> **CHAPTER NINETEEN: JESUS WAS RAISED TO NEW LIFE**
>
> **CHAPTER TWENTY: JESUS BEGINS THE CHURCH**

Aims

The students' understanding of the material covered in this unit will be reviewed and assessed.

Materials

• Unit 5 Test, Appendix, p. A-25

Assess

1. Distribute the unit tests and read through them with the students to be sure they understand the questions.

2. Administer the test.

3. After all the tests have been handed in, you may wish to review the correct answers with the class.

Name: _____

Unit 5 Test   **Chapters 17–20**

Fill in the blanks. *Trace the gray letters and fill in the rest.*

Word Bank

rose	Last	Good	best
Church	loves	Pope	

1. Jesus ate the Last Supper with His Apostles.

2. Jesus died on Good Friday.

3. Jesus died for us because He loves us.

4. Jesus rose from the dead.

5. Jesus began the Church.

6. Peter was the first Pope.

7. Holy Communion is the best gift of all.

TEACHER'S NOTES

TEACHER'S NOTES

CHAPTER TWENTY-ONE
JESUS GOES BACK TO HEAVEN

Catechism of the Catholic Church References

The Ascension: 659–64, 665–67
Christ and the Holy Spirit: 727–30, 746
Christ Is Present in the Church: 669

The Final Age: 670
Jesus Will Return in Glory: 668–77, 680
The Mission of the Apostles: 858–60, 869

Scripture References

The Ascension: Acts 1:3–11
The Great Commission: Mt 28:19–20
Jesus Appears in the Upper Room: Jn 20:19–30

Jesus Reveals Himself on the Sea of Tiberias: Jn 21:1–17
Coming of the Savior: Mt 1:18–25; Lk 2:1–20

Background Reading: *The Fundamentals of Catholicism* by Fr. Kenneth Baker, S.J.

Volume 1:
"The Glorified Body of Jesus," pp. 72–74
"Jesus Ascended into Heaven," pp. 77–79
"The Second Coming," pp. 80–82
"The Glory of the Lord," pp. 82–84
"Jesus Will Judge the Living and the Dead," pp. 85–87
"Jesus' Eternal Kingdom," pp. 87–89

Volume 2:
"His Kingdom Will Have No End," pp. 225–28
"The Ascension of Jesus," pp. 308–11

Volume 3:
Eschatology, the Doctrine of the Last Things, pp. 361–88

Summary of Lesson Content

Lesson 1

Jesus spent forty days with the Apostles after His Resurrection.

During this time, Jesus told the Apostles many things which they would need to know to continue His work.

Jesus was going to return to the Father.

Peter was selected as the head of the Church.

Lesson 2

Jesus gave the Great Commission to his Apostles to go forth and baptize.

They were to baptize all nations in the Name of the Father and of the Son and of the Holy Spirit.

The Church baptizes new Catholics just as the Apostles did; through Baptism Catholics enter the Church and receive grace.

Lesson 3

Jesus promised the Apostles that He would be with them always, even if they could not see Him.

Jesus promised that He would send the Holy Spirit after He returned to the Father.

Jesus rose into Heaven body and soul; we call this the Ascension. It is the second Glorious Mystery.

Lesson 4

Two angels appeared to the Apostles after the Ascension.

The angels announced that Jesus would return.

Jesus will come in glory at the end of time.

CHAPTER TWENTY-ONE: JESUS GOES BACK TO HEAVEN
LESSON ONE: JESUS PREPARES TO RETURN TO THE FATHER

Aims

Students will learn that Jesus stayed with the Apostles for forty days after the Resurrection.

They will come to understand that Jesus used this time to teach the Apostles.

They will learn that Jesus was to return to the Father.

Materials

- Children's Bible

- *Activity Book*, p. 81

Optional:
- "Hail the day that sees him rise," *Adoremus Hymnal*, #430

Begin

Review with the children the Resurrection of Jesus. Remind them that He rose and took up His body (He was not a ghost), and that He wanted His work to continue on earth. Ask the children what Jesus' work was: to teach the Good News, to give grace, etc. Ask the children how Jesus wanted to continue His work: through the Apostles, led by the Pope, in the Church, by the priests and faithful. Jesus needed to prepare the Apostles who were to be the first Church leaders. This is what the students will learn about today.

Develop

1. Read paragraph 1 from the text with the children.

2. Explain to the students that leaders need to be prepared to lead. You may use yourself as an example. You are a teacher, you lead the children in instruction of the Faith. You first had to learn your Faith, then be taught how to teach and be guided by lesson plans. You had to accept the responsibility for this class. So too, the Apostles had to be taught and prepared for their roles as leaders in the Church. They had to understand the Scriptures and all that Jesus wanted them to know. They had to understand Jesus' work and how He wanted it to be accomplished.

3. Tell the students that Jesus spent forty days with His Apostles after His Resurrection in order to prepare them to be leaders of His Church after He returned to the Father. The Bible tells us that Jesus spent time with the Apostles as they gathered in an upper room in Jerusalem. He walked with them and talked to them. One day when they had breakfast on the beach, Jesus asked Peter if he loved Him. Jesus asked only Peter, three times, if he loved Him. This is significant, for Peter was the first Pope. When Peter said he did love Him, Jesus gave Peter charge of His flock. He asked him to take care of His sheep, meaning He wanted Peter to take care of the Church.

4. Now read from the children's Bible:
- Jn 20:19–30 (upper room)
- Jn 21:1–17 (Jesus with Peter on the beach)

5. Stress that Jesus spent this time with the Apostles to prepare them for His work. He taught them, let them know that they were important to His work, and helped them to understand all they had seen and heard.

Reinforce

1. Assign *Activity Book* p. 81 (see *Teacher's Manual*, p. 261), the word tsearch. You may want to do this activity together.

2. Have the children memorize Question 45 in the text.

Conclude

1. Ask the children to bring in a picture of their Baptism for the next class. Remind them to write their names on the back of it before handing it in to you.

2. Close by singing an appropriate hymn, such as "Hail the day that sees him rise," *Adoremus Hymnal*, #430.

3. Pray for the Church.

21   Jesus Goes Back to Heaven

"...as they were looking on, he was lifted up, and a cloud took him out of their sight."

Acts 1:9

Jesus spent forty days with His Apostles after He rose from the dead. He told them many things that they should know. Then it was time for Him to go back to God, His Father.

So He took the Apostles to the top of a mountain. "Go," He said. "Teach everyone and baptize them in the Name of the Father and of the Son and of the Holy Spirit." Jesus promised to be with them always even if they could not see Him. He promised to send the **Holy Spirit** to help them, too. Then Jesus rose up to Heaven. We call this the **Ascension**.

The Apostles watched and watched until they could not see Jesus anymore. Then two angels came. They said, "Someday Jesus will come again." Jesus will come again at the end of the world.

85

Words to Know:

Ascension   Holy Spirit

Q. 45 *What did Jesus do after His Resurrection?* After His Resurrection, Jesus remained on earth for forty days, then He ascended to Heaven (CCC 659).

86

THE GOOD SHEPHERD

The image of Christ as the Good Shepherd has always been popular in Catholic and Christian art, even from the time of the catacombs. It is derived from Christ's own words in Chapter 10 of John's Gospel: "I am the good shepherd." Jesus loves his sheep, and He says He will lay down His life for His sheep, which He does at the Crucifixion. This image also applies directly to the Church leaders, for the bishops and priests are shepherds who tend to their flock, the faithful. The Latin word for shepherd is *pastor*. This Scripture passage teaches Christians to follow the voice of their leaders, especially those who speak for Christ, and to trust in them as completely as sheep trust the shepherd.

GOOD SHEPHERD SUNDAY

The Fourth Sunday of Easter is celebrated as Good Shepherd Sunday. Although the readings vary per Church cycle, the Gospel reading is taken from John 10:1–30, where Christ calls Himself the Good Shepherd.

Preview

In our next lesson, we will learn about Jesus' Great Commission: to baptize all nations.

CHAPTER TWENTY-ONE: JESUS GOES BACK TO HEAVEN
LESSON TWO: GO FORTH AND BAPTIZE

Aims

Students will understand that the Church's purpose is to teach and bring God's grace to the world.

They will learn that Jesus Himself commanded that everyone should be baptized in the Name of the Father, and of the Son, and of the Holy Spirit.

They will learn that Catholics enter the Church and receive grace through Baptism.

Materials

• Children's Bible

• *Activity Book*, p. 82

• Bulletin board, tacks, and the words: "In Baptism I entered the Church and received grace"

Optional:
• "Hail the day that sees him rise," *Adoremus Hymnal*, #430

Begin

Remind the children that the role and work of the Church is to continue Jesus' work. The Church teaches the Good News and gives Jesus' grace. Explain that when people enter the Church through Baptism, they receive God's life in their souls. It is in Baptism that Catholics become God's children and enter His family, the Church.

Develop

1. Read aloud paragraph 2 of the text.

2. Now read from the children's Bible about Christ's Great Commission (Mt 28:19–20). Be sure that the students understand that Jesus told His Apostles to do His work, to teach, and to baptize all people.

3. Ask the children if they were baptized (some may not have been baptized yet). Ask if they remember their Baptisms, or if they have ever seen a Baptism.

4. Ask the children in what name (not names) they were baptized? "In the Name of the Father, and of the Son, and of the Holy Spirit." Jesus taught the Apostles to do this. This is Baptism in the name of God who is three Divine Persons but only One God.

5. Discuss the matter (objects or actions), form (words), and minister of Baptism (see the facing page):

Matter: Water (poured or immersed into three times while saying the form)
Form: "I baptize you in the Name of the Father, and of the Son, and of the Holy Spirit"
Minister: Usually a priest but anyone may baptize in an emergency.

Explain to the students that when the matter and form are performed by the minister and there is intent to baptize a person into the true Faith of Jesus, then a person is baptized and becomes a member of the Church. This person also becomes a child of God (He claims him as His own), and receives grace (God's life) in his soul. These new Catholics, especially if they are baptized as infants, are to be taught the fullness of the Faith as Jesus taught the Apostles (this is why the children come to religion class).

Reinforce

1. Have the students complete p. 82 of the *Activity Book* (see *Teacher's Manual*, p. 261), the coloring page for Baptism.

2. Have the children bring up their pictures and ask about their Baptism: when they were baptized, where they were baptized, who was the priest, who are their godparents, etc. Have the children tack their pictures to the bulletin board, and make a display.

Conclude

1. Pray the Our Father as a class (see *Teacher's Manual*, p. 367), and sing "Hail the day that sees Him rise," *Adoremus Hymnal*, #430.

2. Pray for the Church.

21   Jesus Goes Back to Heaven

"...as they were looking on, he was lifted up,
and a cloud took him out of their sight."
Acts 1:9

Jesus spent forty days with His Apostles after He rose from the dead. He told them many things that they should know. Then it was time for Him to go back to God, His Father.

So He took the Apostles to the top of a mountain. "Go," He said. "Teach everyone and baptize them in the Name of the Father and of the Son and of the Holy Spirit." Jesus promised to be with them always even if they could not see Him. He promised to send the **Holy Spirit** to help them, too. Then Jesus rose up to Heaven. We call this the **Ascension**.

The Apostles watched and watched until they could not see Jesus anymore. Then two angels came. They said, "Someday Jesus will come again." Jesus will come again at the end of the world.

85

SACRAMENT	MATTER	FORM	MINISTER
Baptism	Water	I baptize you in the Name of the Father and of the Son and of the Holy Spirit.	Usually a priest, but anyone if needed
Penance	Repentence, Confession, Penance	I absolve you from your sins in the Name of the Father and of the Son and of the Holy Spirit.	The priest
Eucharist	Bread and Wine	This is my Body. This is the chalice of my Blood.	The priest
Anointing of the Sick	Holy Oils	Through this holy anointing may the Lord in His love and mercy help you with the grace of the Holy Spirit. May the Lord who frees you from sin save you and raise you up.	The priest

BAPTISM

The word *baptism* comes from the Greek word, *baptizein* which means "to wash" or "to immerse."

Preview

In our next lesson, we will learn about the Ascension of Jesus.

CHAPTER TWENTY-ONE: JESUS GOES BACK TO HEAVEN
LESSON THREE: THE ASCENSION

Aims

Students will learn Jesus' promise to remain with the Church and to send the Holy Spirit.

They will hear about the events of the Ascension.

They will pray the second Glorious Mystery.

Materials

- Children's Bible

- *Activity Book*, p. 83

Optional:
- Appendix, p. B-29, The Ascension

- "Hail the day that sees him rise," *Adoremus Hymnal*, #430

Begin

Remind the children that after the Resurrection, Jesus prepared to return to the Father. Remind them also that the Father is God; He is everywhere, but He is also in Heaven.

After Jesus rose, it was time for Him to return body and soul to Heaven. Tell the students that today they will learn about this great and miraculous event.

Develop

1. Reread paragraph 2 from the text, then read paragraph 3.

2. You may now want to read the account of the Ascension from the children's Bible (Acts 1:3–11).

3. To help the students visualize the Ascension, discuss the picture on p. 84 of the textbook, asking questions such as:
   - Where are Mary and the Apostles? (They are on top of a mountain.)
   - Where is Jesus? (He is in the sky.)
   - Why is He in the sky? (He is ascending to the Father.)
   - What does 'ascend' mean? (It means to rise.)
   - Is Jesus like a ghost? (No, He has a body; He is ascending body and soul.)
   - Did Jesus leave His Church alone? (No, He left the Apostles as leaders of His Church.)
   - Did Jesus go back to Heaven forever? (No, He promised to return one day, just as He left.)

- What else did Jesus promise the Apostles? (He promised that He would send the Holy Spirit.)

4. Discuss the promises of Jesus with the children:
   A. Jesus promised the Apostles that He would remain with them always. How is this possible? (He does this through His Church, in the Eucharist, through the teachings of the Church, in prayer and the Liturgy, through the Sacraments, by His grace, and through the Holy Spirit.)
   B. Jesus promised to send the Holy Spirit. Who is the Holy Spirit? (The Holy Spirit is God. We know the Holy Spirit is God, because Jesus said so. Jesus said that we are to be baptized in the Name of God the Father, Son, and Holy Spirit, One God in three Persons.)

5. Tell the children that they will learn more about the mystery of the Blessed Trinity in a later chapter (23).

Reinforce

1. Have the children color the picture of the Ascension on p. 83 of the *Activity Book* (see *Teacher's Manual*, p. 261).

2. If they have been working on their Rosary booklets, you may want to pass out copies of Appendix, p. B-29, the Ascension, for the children to color at this time.

Conclude

1. You may lead the children in praying the second Glorious Mystery, The Ascension, as a way of thanking Jesus for His promises.

2. Close by singing "Hail the day that sees Him rise," *Adoremus Hymnal*, #430.

3. Pray for the Church.

21   Jesus Goes Back to Heaven

*"...as they were looking on, he was lifted up,
and a cloud took him out of their sight."*

Acts 1:9

Jesus spent forty days with His Apostles after He rose from the dead. He told them many things that they should know. Then it was time for Him to go back to God, His Father.

So He took the Apostles to the top of a mountain. "Go," He said. "Teach everyone and baptize them in the Name of the Father and of the Son and of the Holy Spirit." Jesus promised to be with them always even if they could not see Him. He promised to send the **Holy Spirit** to help them, too. Then Jesus rose up to Heaven. We call this the **Ascension**.

The Apostles watched and watched until they could not see Jesus anymore. Then two angels came. They said, "Someday Jesus will come again." Jesus will come again at the end of the world.

85

Words to Know:

Ascension   Holy Spirit

Q. 45 *What did Jesus do after His Resurrection?*
After His Resurrection, Jesus remained on earth for forty days, then He ascended to Heaven (CCC 659).

86

ELIJAH OF THE OLD TESTAMENT

Elijah, a Thesbite, was a great prophet of the Old Testament whose life is recounted almost entirely in the First Book of Kings. Elijah wore a garment of animal skins and dwelt in caves or clefts in the mountains. One of the better known incidents in his life is the contest between the priests of Baal and their god, and the True God, Yahweh, on Mount Carmel. All of their pleading could not elicit a response from Baal, while Yahweh answered immediately (I Kings 18:17–40). God took Elijah from this earth alive. One day, while speaking to one of his followers, a chariot of fire with fiery horses appeared from the sky and carried him away in a whirlwind to Heaven (2 Kings 2:11). Tradition holds that Elijah will return as a prophet at the end of the world.

On Holy Thursday evening (see p. 203) many Catholic families hold a Seder dinner ceremony in memory of the Jewish Passover, with roast lamb, bitter herbs, matzah, and wine. An empty place is left for the prophet Elijah.

THE ASCENSION
Acts 1:3–11

Preview

In our next lesson, we will learn that Jesus will come again in glory.

257

Chapter Twenty-One: Jesus Goes Back to Heaven
Lesson Four: Jesus Will Come Again

Aims

Students will learn that now Jesus is in Heaven, but that He will come again.

They will understand that Christians wait in joyful hope for the coming of Jesus Christ.

Materials

- *Activity Book*, p. 84

Optional:
- Children's Bible

- "Hail the day that sees Him rise," *Adoremus Hymnal*, #430

Begin

Remind the students that the time before Christmas is called Advent. It is a time for all Christians to prepare for the coming of the infant Jesus. Remind the children how difficult it was for the people of the Old Testament to wait while they prepared for the coming of the Savior. They had to work hard to be faithful to God and they had to wait in hope for the coming of Jesus. Catholics today are also preparing for Jesus' coming, for His Second Coming, which the students will learn more about today.

Develop

1. Review with the students the excitement of the coming of the Savior at Christmas. (You may want to read Mt 1:18–25 or Lk 2:1–20 from a children's Bible—the story of the Nativity.) Ask them about the response of the shepherds and the wise men. Ask them to imagine how the shepherds and wise men must have felt when they discovered Christ. Ask them to remember and describe how they felt last Christmas morning.

2. Tell the children that on the day of the Ascension the angels said that Jesus will come again. Everyone today still awaits His coming and prepares for His return, just as the people of the Old Testament waited for His first coming.

3. Take some time to reread paragraph 3 from the text.

4. Ask the children how they would prepare for an important guest. What if the president/queen/king or another important person (e.g., the Pope) came to visit? What would they do?

They would put on their best clothes, clean the house, prepare their best meal, be on their best behavior, etc.

5. Tell the students that no one knows when Jesus is coming, so everyone must always be ready. Ask the children how they should prepare for the coming of Jesus, Who is God. Answers may include:
- not sin
- pray
- go to Mass
- receive the Sacraments of Eucharist and Confession (when they can)
- love God
- serve others

6. Talk about how Saints Charles Borromeo and Robert Bellarmine prepared themselves and others for Christ's coming (see the facing page).

Reinforce

1. Assign *Activity Book* p. 84 (see *Teacher's Manual*, p. 261), which is based on Develop #4, the visit of a great guest.

2. Ask the children to decide on one thing that they will do this week as a special way to prepare for the coming of Jesus. You may give them ideas to help them (e.g., pray before bed, help at home, read a Bible story, pay extra attention to the readings at Mass, etc.).

Conclude

1. Pray the second Glorious Mystery of the Rosary.

2. Close by singing "Hail the day that sees him rise," *Adoremus Hymnal*, #430.

3. Pray for the Church.

21   Jesus Goes Back to Heaven

"...as they were looking on, he was lifted up,
and a cloud took him out of their sight."

Acts 1:9

Jesus spent forty days with His Apostles after He rose from the dead. He told them many things that they should know. Then it was time for Him to go back to God, His Father.

So He took the Apostles to the top of a mountain. "Go," He said. "Teach everyone and baptize them in the Name of the Father and of the Son and of the Holy Spirit." Jesus promised to be with them always even if they could not see Him. He promised to send the **Holy Spirit** to help them, too. Then Jesus rose up to Heaven. We call this the **Ascension**.

The Apostles watched and watched until they could not see Jesus anymore. Then two angels came. They said, "Someday Jesus will come again." Jesus will come again at the end of the world.

85

Ascension   Holy Spirit

Q. 45 *What did Jesus do after His Resurrection?*
After His Resurrection, Jesus remained on earth for forty days, then He ascended to Heaven (CCC 659).

86

SAINT CHARLES BORROMEO

Saint Charles, the son of Count Gilbert Borromeo and Margaret Medici, was born at the family castle in Italy in 1538. In 1559 his uncle was elected Pope Pius IV, and at age 22, Charles was named a cardinal and the Pope's Secretary of State. Charles was influential in the Council of Trent and oversaw the resulting catechism, missal, and breviary. He was ordained a priest and consecrated bishop of Milan in 1563. He was a towering figure of the Reformation and brought many lapsed Catholics to the Church, all in great humility. He died in 1584 and was canonized in 1610. His feastday is November 4. He is the patron of learning and the arts.

SAINT ROBERT BELLARMINE

The third of ten children, Saint Robert was born in Italy in 1542. His mother was the niece of Pope Marcellus II and he was dedicated to almsgiving, prayer, and fasting. He entered the newly formed Society of Jesus in 1560. In 1576 he was appointed chair of theology at the Roman College, and named a cardinal in 1598. He was the spiritual father of Saint Aloysius Gonzaga, helped Saint Francis de Sales obtain formal approval of the Visitation Order, and in his prudence, opposed the severe treatment of Galileo. He died in 1621 and was canonized in 1930. His feastday is September 17. He is the patron of catechists and a Doctor of the Church.

If we wish to make any progress in the service of God we must begin every day of our life with new eagerness. We must keep ourselves in the presence of God as much as possible and have no other end in all our actions but the divine honor.

—Saint Charles Borromeo

Preview

In our next lesson, we will review and be quizzed on the materials we learned in this chapter.

Chapter Twenty-One: Jesus Goes Back to Heaven

Review and Assessment

Aims

To review and assess the children's knowledge of the materials taught in this chapter.

Materials

- Quiz 21 (Appendix, p. A-26)
- "Hail the day that sees him rise," *Adoremus Hymnal*, #430

Name: _____

Jesus Goes Back to Heaven   Quiz 21

Fill in the blanks. *Trace the gray letters and fill in the rest.*

Word Bank

will	rose	up
name	Holy	teach

1. Jesus spent forty days with His Apostles after He r o s e from the dead.

2. Jesus told the Apostles to t e a c h everyone about Him.

3. "Baptize them in the n a m e of the Father and of the Son and of the Holy Spirit."

4. Jesus promised to send the H o l y Spirit.

5. Jesus went u p to Heaven.

6. Jesus w i l l come again.

Review and Enrichment

1. Ask the children if they remember what Jesus did after the Resurrection. (He stayed on earth for forty days to teach the Apostles.)

2. Remind the students that Jesus gave the Great Commission that all people should be baptized in the Name of the Father and of the Son and of the Holy Spirit.

3. Jesus promised to stay with the Apostles always and to send the Holy Spirit. He then ascended into Heaven. He will come again in glory so everyone on earth must wait and prepare for His coming.

Assess

1. Distribute Quiz 21 and read through it with the children. Answer any questions that they may have. Administer the quiz.

2. Once the quiz is completed, review the correct answers with the children.

Conclude

Close by singing as a class "Hail the day that sees Him rise," *Adoremus Hymnal*, #430.

Name:_____

Word Search

Can you find these words in the puzzle?
Look carefully! The words go across and down.

ALIVE	CROSS	JESUS
ALLELUIA	DIED	MIRACLE
ASCENSION	EASTER	NAILS
BAPTIZE	GOOD FRIDAY	TEACH
BURIED	HOLY SPIRIT	THORNS

```
B K V J A S C E N S I O N
E A S T E R J E S U S H N
H Q K H A L I V E Y D T A
K E M U K R X C Y I O H I
G D H O L Y S P I R I T L
K I T T E A C H J F B B S
V E G M I R A C L E U A C
J D Y Y L R X G E Y R P R
G O O D F R I D A Y I T O
B G R K T V D K S V E I S
A L L E L U I A T D D Z S
T H O R N S E K E M L E S
```

Faith and Life Series • Grade 1 • Chapter 21 • Lesson 1   81

Name:_____

Baptism

"Go therefore and make disciples of all nations, baptizing them in the name of the Father and of the Son and of the Holy Spirit, teaching them to observe all that I have commanded you..."

Matthew 28:19–20

Color the picture.

82   *Faith and Life Series • Grade 1 • Chapter 21 • Lesson 2*

Name:_____

The Ascension of Our Lord

Jesus went to Heaven to be with God the Father.

Color the picture.

Faith and Life Series • Grade 1 • Chapter 21 • Lesson 3   83

Name:_____

Someday Jesus will come again!
What should I do to prepare?

First, match the words that show how you would prepare if a king were to come to your home.
Then match the words that show how you should prepare for Jesus, the King of Kings, to come again.

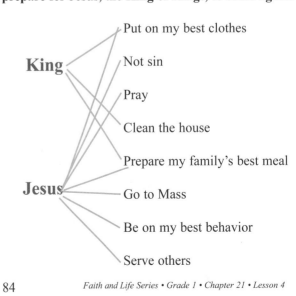

King

Put on my best clothes

Not sin

Pray

Clean the house

Prepare my family's best meal

Jesus

Go to Mass

Be on my best behavior

Serve others

84   *Faith and Life Series • Grade 1 • Chapter 21 • Lesson 4*

TEACHER'S NOTES

CHAPTER TWENTY-TWO
THE HOLY SPIRIT COMES

Catechism of the Catholic Church References

Belief in the Holy Spirit: 683–88
Christian Holiness: 2012–16, 2028–29
The Church Manifested by the Holy Spirit: 767–68
The Church is the Temple of the Holy Spirit: 797–98
The Gifts of the Holy Spirit: 768, 798–801, 1830–31

The Holy Spirit and Justification: 1987–89
Life in the Holy Spirit: 2017
The Name, Titles, and Symbols of the Holy Spirit: 691–701
Pentecost: 731–41, 746–47, 767–68
The Spirit of Christ in the Fullness of Time: 717–30, 745–46

Scripture References

The Descent of the Holy Spirit on Pentecost: Acts 2:1–4
The Spirit and the Old Testament: Is 11:2

Peter Preaching after the Descent of the Holy Spirit:
Acts 2:14–42

Background Reading: *The Fundamentals of Catholicism* by Fr. Kenneth Baker, S.J.

Volume 1:
"The Holy Spirit: Lord and Giver of Life," pp. 90–92
"The Origin of the Holy Spirit," pp. 92–94
"Worship of the Holy Spirit," pp. 95–97
"The Holy Spirit and Prophecy," pp. 97–99

Volume 2:
"The Son and the Holy Spirit," pp. 86–89
"The Origin of the Son and the Holy Spirit," pp. 89–92
"The Origin of the Holy Spirit," pp. 96–99

Summary of Lesson Content

Lesson 1

The Apostles and Mary prayed for nine days before the descent of the Holy Spirit.

On the tenth day, the Holy Spirit came. We call this day Pentecost.

Pentecost was the beginning of the Catholic tradition of nine days of petitionary prayer. This kind of prayer is called a novena.

Lesson 2

The Holy Spirit descended on the Apostles and Mary on Pentecost.

The Holy Spirit filled the souls of the Apostles with grace.

The Holy Spirit helped the Apostles to remember and understand all Jesus taught them.

The Holy Spirit gave strength and courage to the Apostles to do the Church's work.

Lesson 3

The Apostles received strength and courage to do Jesus' work when the Holy Spirit descended on them.

Peter preached after the descent of the Holy Spirit and many were converted. Three thousand were baptized that very day.

Lesson 4

The Holy Spirit is alive in the Church.

The Holy Spirit helps the Pope and the bishops to teach the truth and govern the Church.

The Holy Spirit helps everyone to love one another and become holy.

The seven gifts of the Holy Spirit are: Wisdom, Understanding, Counsel, Knowledge, Fortitude, Piety, and Fear of the Lord.

CHAPTER TWENTY-TWO: THE HOLY SPIRIT COMES
LESSON ONE: THE FIRST NOVENA

Aims

Students will be able to recount the events of the descent of the Holy Spirit.

They will understand that the Holy Spirit came to Mary and the Apostles on Pentecost.

The prayers of Mary and the Apostles are the model for Catholic novenas, nine-day prayers asking for God's assistance.

Materials

- Children's Bible

- *Activity Book*, p. 85

Optional:
- "Come, Holy Ghost, Creator blest," *Adoremus Hymnal*, #443

Begin

Ask the students if their parents have ever had to ask them to do something more than once, such as tidy their room or put away toys. Or ask if they were ever promised something, but for a later time, e.g., on their birthday. Explain to them that with God, people may need to wait for Him to answer a prayer, or they may ask Him many times to let Him know how much they want His help with something. A nine-day prayer is called a novena. Tell the children that the first novena happened after Jesus went back to Heaven and Mary and the Apostles prayed for God to send the Holy Spirit.

Develop

1. Read paragraph 1 aloud from the textbook.

2. Now read the Pentecost narrative from a children's Bible (Acts 2:1–4).

3. Discuss some things for which Mary and the Apostles may have been praying:
- for the Holy Spirit to come
- for the courage to preach
- for greater faith
- for the knowledge to lead the Church
- to help others believe

4. Repeat to the children that the Holy Spirit came on Pentecost. Explain that the Holy Spirit appeared as tongues of fire over each of their heads. Use the picture on p. 88 of the text to demonstrate this. Remind the children that a person receives the same Holy Spirit at his Baptism. No one can see the Holy Spirit, but He comes and lives in our souls anyway. The Holy Spirit brings God's life to the soul, so the faithful baptized person can go to Heaven one day.

5. Discuss with the children how the Church celebrates Pentecost: the liturgical color is red; it is the birthday of the Church; we sing songs about the Holy Spirit and give thanks for His coming.

6. Ask the children to think about what they would have prayed for in the upper room. Have them tell you some things they would now like to pray for from the Holy Spirit.

Reinforce

1. Have the children answer the questions on p. 85 of the *Activity Book* (see *Teacher's Manual*, p. 273).

2. Teach the children the words of "Come, Holy Ghost, Creator blest," *Adoremus Hymnal*, #443. You may need to explain some of the words, especially that Holy Ghost and Holy Spirit refer to the same Person. Tell the children that by praying "Come Holy Ghost" they are saying the same prayer the Apostles said in the upper room.

Conclude

1. Lead the students in prayer, asking the Holy Spirit to bring joy and truth to the children's lives so that they may grow in faith.

2. The children may add their own petitions, e.g., "Come Holy Spirit, and make me strong in my faith"; "Come Holy Spirit, and help me to love my brother/sister/mother/father."

22　The Holy Spirit Comes

"And they were all filled with the Holy Spirit..."
Acts 2:4

For nine days, the Apostles waited for the Holy Spirit to come to them. They stayed in a house with Mary and prayed and prayed. On the tenth day something wonderful happened. The Apostles heard the sound of a great wind. And then the Holy Spirit came! This day is called **Pentecost**.

The Holy Spirit filled their souls with grace and He filled their hearts with love for God. He helped them to remember and to understand all the things Jesus had taught them. He made them very brave and strong so they could continue Jesus' work here on earth.

Now the Apostles could go out and tell all the world about Jesus, just as He asked them to do. So the Apostles went out. Peter began to teach the Good News. "Believe in Jesus, be **baptized**, and you will be saved," Peter said.

87

Many people believed Peter's words, and about three thousand were baptized that very day. Already the Church was beginning to grow.

The Holy Spirit is alive in the Church today. He helps the Pope and the bishops to teach the truth about God. He helps us to love one another and become holy.

Words to Know:

baptized　　　Pentecost

> **Q. 46** *What happened on Pentecost?*
> On Pentecost, the Holy Spirit came to Mary and the Apostles (CCC 731; Acts 2:1–4).
>
> **Q. 47** *What did the Holy Spirit do for the Apostles?*
> The Holy Spirit gave grace to the Apostles, and the courage to continue Jesus' work (CCC 737, 739).

89

PENTECOST = WHITSUNDAY

This feast commemorates the descent of the Holy Spirit. The name *Pentecost* (called the "feast of weeks" by the Jews) comes from the Greek word for fiftieth. This refers to the fact that Pentecost falls fifty days after Easter. (It is ten days after the Ascension which is forty days after Easter.) *Whit* signifies the white garments worn by those who were baptized during the Vigil.

TITLES OF THE HOLY SPIRIT

Paraclete:　He who is called to one's side; a supporter

Advocate:　From the Latin *advocatus* meaning "to call toward oneself; one who pleads a case for someone else"

Consoler:　One Who consoles

Quickener:　He who quickens one's heart with love

Also **Spirit of Truth**, **Spirit of the Lord**, and **Spirit of Glory**

Preview

In our next lesson, we will learn more about what happened when the Holy Spirit came.

Chapter Twenty-Two: The Holy Spirit Comes

Lesson Two: The Holy Spirit Came

Aims

Students will learn about the power of the Holy Spirit in the lives of the Apostles.

They will understand that the Holy Spirit brings grace and safeguards the truth.

They will know that the Holy Spirit helped the Apostles to remember and understand what Jesus taught them.

They will learn the names, titles, and symbols for the Holy Spirit.

Materials

- *Activity Book*, p. 86

Optional:
- Appendix, p. B-30, The Descent of the Holy Spirit

- "Come, Holy Ghost, Creator blest," *Adoremus Hymnal*, #443

Begin

Using the song, "Come, Holy Ghost, Creator blest" (*Adoremus Hymnal*, #443) as a reference, make a list on the chalk board of the different titles given to the Holy Spirit and explain their meaning (see the facing page for other symbols):

Holy Ghost/Spirit, Comforter, Fount of Life, Fire of Love, and Sweet Anointing.
(If you taught the titles of the Holy Spirit yesterday, add these to the list as well.)

review novena, pentecost, filled w/ grace love (questions on pg 8?

Develop

1. Have the children open their texts to p. 88, *Pentecost*, by Titian. Begin discussion using the following questions as examples:

- How many people are in the picture? Who are they? (fourteen people; the Apostles, Mary, and Mary Magdalene)
- What do the flames above their heads signify? (the Holy Spirit)
- What does the dove represent? (the Holy Spirit)
- What does the light represent? (the Holy Spirit)
- What are the people doing in this picture? (praying)
- Where are these people? (in an upper room in Jerusalem)
- How many days after the Ascension did this happen? (ten)

2. Repeat that the dove, light, and flames in this picture all represent the Holy Spirit. The Holy Spirit is God who came at Pentecost. Jesus and God the Father sent the Holy Spirit to

help the Church. In art, there are many symbols for the Holy Spirit (see the facing page).

3. Now read paragraph 2 in the textbook.

4. Talk about what it was like for the Apostles before the descent of the Holy Spirit. They may have been scared to teach and do Jesus' work. They could have been confused by all the events they had seen. The Apostles had Original Sin still, and did not yet have grace. Their faith was probably weakening.

5. Next explain the effects of the Holy Spirit in the lives of the Apostles. Their souls were filled with grace (God's life). Their hearts were filled with love for God. They remembered and understood what Jesus taught them. They became brave and strong and they desired to do Jesus' work.

Reinforce

1. Students may color *Activity Book*, p. 86 (see *Teacher's Manual*, p. 273), the symbols of the Holy Spirit.

2. If they have been working on their Rosary booklets, you may want to pass out copies of Appendix, p. B-30, The Descent of the Holy Spirit, for the children to color at this time.

Conclude

1. You may lead the children in praying the third Glorious Mystery of the Rosary, The Descent of the Holy Spirit.

2. Or you may pray this prayer with the class:

Holy Spirit come to me,
And live here in my soul.
Fill the heart you made for me,
With grace and make me whole.

3. Sing "Come, Holy Ghost, Creator blest," *Adoremus Hymnal*, #443.

22   The Holy Spirit Comes

"And they were all filled with the Holy Spirit..."
Acts 2:4

For nine days, the Apostles waited for the Holy Spirit to come to them. They stayed in a house with Mary and prayed and prayed. On the tenth day something wonderful happened. The Apostles heard the sound of a great wind. And then the Holy Spirit came! This day is called **Pentecost**.

The Holy Spirit filled their souls with grace and He filled their hearts with love for God. He helped them to remember and to understand all the things Jesus had taught them. He made them very brave and strong so they could continue Jesus' work here on earth.

Now the Apostles could go out and tell all the world about Jesus, just as He asked them to do. So the Apostles went out. Peter began to teach the Good News. "Believe in Jesus, be **baptized**, and you will be saved," Peter said.

87

Many people believed Peter's words, and about three thousand were baptized that very day. Already the Church was beginning to grow.

The Holy Spirit is alive in the Church today. He helps the Pope and the bishops to teach the truth about God. He helps us to love one another and become holy.

Words to Know:

baptized   Pentecost

> **Q. 46** *What happened on Pentecost?*
> On Pentecost, the Holy Spirit came to Mary and the Apostles (CCC 731; Acts 2:1–4).
>
> **Q. 47** *What did the Holy Spirit do for the Apostles?*
> The Holy Spirit gave grace to the Apostles, and the courage to continue Jesus' work (CCC 737, 739).

89

TITLES AND SYMBOLS OF THE HOLY SPIRIT

Water: The Holy Spirit works through Baptism; He gives life and cleanses us

Anointing: Sets apart; Christ was anointed by God's Spirit

Fire: The transforming energy of the Holy Spirit

Cloud, Light: Obscures and illuminates God

Seal: The indelibleness of the Holy Spirit's anointing

Hand, Finger: The laying on of hands, written law

Dove: Symbolizes His descent to earth

THE DESCENT OF THE HOLY SPIRIT
Acts 2:1–4

Preview

In our next lesson, we will learn about the Apostles' work.

Chapter Twenty-Two: The Holy Spirit Comes
Lesson Three: The Apostles Go Forth

Aims

Students will review the descent of the Holy Spirit.

They will come to understand the transformation of the Apostles on Pentecost.

They will learn that Peter preached that day and three thousand were converted and baptized.

Materials

• Children's Bible

• *Activity Book*, p. 87

• Index cards

Optional:
• "Come Holy Ghost, Creator blest," *Adoremus Hymnal*, #443

Begin

Open with a discussion of what the Apostles were like before the descent of the Holy Spirit, and how they changed after receiving Him. Remind the children that the Holy Spirit comes to Catholics today at Baptism and in the other Sacraments. This discussion is a review and will prepare them for the following lesson.

Develop

1. Read paragraphs 3 and 4 from the text.

2. Read Acts 2:14–42 from the children's Bible. This passage contains an account of Peter's speech after Pentecost and the Baptism of the three thousand.

3. Discuss this passage with the children:
   • Why did Peter tell the crowd that they were not drunk? How do you think they were acting? (joyous, excited)
   • What did the prophet Joel say about the coming of the Holy Spirit? (sons and daughters would prophesy, they would see visions and have dreams, there would be wonders in the heavens)
   • Peter spoke the truth about Jesus because the Holy Spirit reminded him. What did Peter teach? (Jesus is Christ, Who came to save everyone from sin)
   • Peter said, "Repent, and be baptized…and you shall receive the gift of the Holy Spirit." What does repent mean? (to be sorry for one's sins)

4. Ask the children if they remember what happens during a Baptism. (The priest pours water three times over the person's head and says, "I baptize you in the Name of the Father and of the Son and of the Holy Spirit.") Ask the children how many of them have received the Holy Spirit. Many of them were probably baptized as infants.

5. Explain to the children that like the Apostles, they have received the Holy Spirit because of their Baptism. They, too, will be strong and courageous to do Jesus' work. What works can they already do?
   • pray
   • help friends and parents
   • obey parents/teachers/priests
   • learn their Faith and share it with friends
   Ask the children to add to these examples.

Reinforce

1. Assign the word search found on p. 87 of the *Activity Book* (see *Teacher's Manual*, p. 273).

2. Have the students begin to memorize Questions 46 and 47 in the textbook.

3. Pass out index cards and have the children write down ways that they can be as strong and courageous as the Apostles were because they have received Baptism (see the facing page).

Conclude

1. Say the prayer from the last lesson and have the students repeat it after you. (You may want to make flashcards for them).

2. Sing "Come Holy Ghost, Creator blest," *Adoremus Hymnal*, #443.

3. Pray the third Glorious Mystery of the Rosary.

22 The Holy Spirit Comes

"And they were all filled with the Holy Spirit..."
Acts 2:4

For nine days, the Apostles waited for the Holy Spirit to come to them. They stayed in a house with Mary and prayed and prayed. On the tenth day something wonderful happened. The Apostles heard the sound of a great wind. And then the Holy Spirit came! This day is called **Pentecost**.

The Holy Spirit filled their souls with grace and He filled their hearts with love for God. He helped them to remember and to understand all the things Jesus had taught them. He made them very brave and strong so they could continue Jesus' work here on earth.

Now the Apostles could go out and tell all the world about Jesus, just as He asked them to do. So the Apostles went out. Peter began to teach the Good News. "Believe in Jesus, be **baptized**, and you will be saved," Peter said.

87

Many people believed Peter's words, and about three thousand were baptized that very day. Already the Church was beginning to grow.

The Holy Spirit is alive in the Church today. He helps the Pope and the bishops to teach the truth about God. He helps us to love one another and become holy.

Words to Know:

baptized   Pentecost

> **Q. 46** *What happened on Pentecost?*
> On Pentecost, the Holy Spirit came to Mary and the Apostles (CCC 731; Acts 2:1–4).
>
> **Q. 47** *What did the Holy Spirit do for the Apostles?*
> The Holy Spirit gave grace to the Apostles, and the courage to continue Jesus' work (CCC 737, 739).

89

PENTECOST VESTMENTS

On Pentecost Sunday the priest wears red vestments that signify the fire of God's love as well as the tongues of fire that descended upon the Apostles in the Upper Room.

SAMPLE BULLETIN BOARD

I RECEIVED THE HOLY SPIRIT AT BAPTISM.

LIKE THE APOSTLES I CAN BE STRONG AND COURAGEOUS TO DO JESUS'
WORK BY...

Preview

In our next lesson, we will learn more about the Holy Spirit and the Church.

Chapter Twenty-Two: The Holy Spirit Comes
Lesson Four: The Holy Spirit and the Church

Aims

Students will learn that the Holy Spirit brings life to the Church.

They will realize that the Holy Spirit helps the Pope and bishops to teach the truth and govern.

They will understand that the Holy Spirit helps everyone to love one another.

They will learn the seven gifts of the Holy Spirit.

Materials

• *Activity Book*, p. 88

Optional:
• Appendix, p. B-33, patterns for the Holy Spirit Mobile

• Hangers

• Yarn

• "Come Holy Ghost, Creator blest," *Adoremus Hymnal*, #443

Begin

Review with the children the hierarchy of the Church and the role of the Church (to continue Jesus' work here on earth). Explain that the Holy Spirit makes it possible for the Church to do her job by providing the grace to be dispensed through the Church. Tell them that *to dispense* means "to give out" or "to pass on."

Develop

1. Read paragraph 5 from the textbook.

2. Discuss with the children how the Holy Spirit acts in the Church.
   • The Holy Spirit helps the leaders to understand and promulgate Jesus' teachings.
   • The Holy Spirit works through the Sacraments to dispense grace.
   • The Holy Spirit enters a person's heart at Baptism so he may love others.
   • The Holy Spirit inspires us in our hearts to pray and to serve each other in charity.

3. Teach the children about the seven gifts of the Holy Spirit. The Holy Spirit gives these gifts to help the Church to be faithful in order to do Jesus' work.
   Wisdom: to see things as God does
   Understanding: to recognize the truth in the Catholic Faith

Counsel: to make good decisions
Fortitude: to serve God, even when it is difficult
Knowledge: to know God and how to serve Him
Piety: to love God in our words, deeds, and worship
Fear of the Lord: to be always aware of God's presence

4. Tell the children that they received these gifts at their Baptism. As you explain each gift, ask them how they have used it, or lived an example of it. For instance, fortitude: I have said my prayers every day, even if I did not feel like saying them.

5. Ask the children to think of times they have felt the Holy Spirit present in their lives. This could be at prayer, at Mass, when they felt inspired to help someone, etc.

6. Read Isaiah 11:2 with the students. Explain that this is a prophecy about Christ.

Reinforce

1. Have the children open their *Activity Books* to p. 88 (see *Teacher's Manual*, p. 273), and read the first paragraph with them. This is a review of the seven gifts of the Holy Spirit. You may want to assist them with this.

2. Have the class review Questions 46 and 47.

3. Supervise the children as they make Holy Spirit mobiles (see patterns for dove and flames in Appendix, p. B-33; also see the facing page).

Conclude

1. Pray the Holy Spirit prayer from p. 266.

2. Close by singing "Come Holy Ghost, Creator blest," *Adoremus Hymnal*, #443.

3. Pray the third Glorious Mystery of the Rosary.

22   The Holy Spirit Comes

"And they were all filled with the Holy Spirit..."
Acts 2:4

For nine days, the Apostles waited for the Holy Spirit to come to them. They stayed in a house with Mary and prayed and prayed. On the tenth day something wonderful happened. The Apostles heard the sound of a great wind. And then the Holy Spirit came! This day is called **Pentecost**.

The Holy Spirit filled their souls with grace and He filled their hearts with love for God. He helped them to remember and to understand all the things Jesus had taught them. He made them very brave and strong so they could continue Jesus' work here on earth.

Now the Apostles could go out and tell all the world about Jesus, just as He asked them to do. So the Apostles went out. Peter began to teach the Good News. "Believe in Jesus, be **baptized**, and you will be saved," Peter said.

87

Many people believed Peter's words, and about three thousand were baptized that very day. Already the Church was beginning to grow.

The Holy Spirit is alive in the Church today. He helps the Pope and the bishops to teach the truth about God. He helps us to love one another and become holy.

Words to Know:

baptized   Pentecost

> **Q. 46** *What happened on Pentecost?*
> On Pentecost, the Holy Spirit came to Mary and the Apostles (CCC 731; Acts 2:1–4).
>
> **Q. 47** *What did the Holy Spirit do for the Apostles?*
> The Holy Spirit gave grace to the Apostles, and the courage to continue Jesus' work (CCC 737, 739).

89

HOLY SPIRIT MOBILE

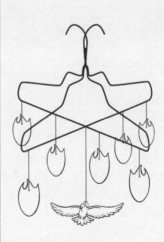

1. Photocopy the patterns from Appendix, p. B-33.

2. Write the names of the seven gifts of the Holy Spirit on the flames.

3. After they are colored, punch out the holes in the patterns and attach to hangers with yarn.

Preview

We will review what we have learned and take a quiz.

CHAPTER TWENTY-TWO: THE HOLY SPIRIT COMES
REVIEW AND ASSESSMENT

Aims

To review and assess the student's knowledge of the materials taught in this chapter.

Materials

- Quiz 22 (Appendix, p. A-27)
- "Come Holy Ghost, Creator blest," *Adoremus Hymnal*, #443

Review and Enrichment

1. Review with the children the events surrounding Pentecost:
   - The Apostles and Mary prayed for nine days.
   - On the tenth day, the Holy Spirit descended.
   - The Holy Spirit gave courage and strength to the Apostles to do Jesus' work.
   - He filled them with grace and love for God.

2. Remind them that the Apostles began preaching and the Holy Spirit helped them to remember and understand and teach the truth. The Holy Spirit inspired the hearts of many and three thousand were baptized that day.

3. Review that in Baptism, the Holy Spirit dispenses God's grace, lives in the soul, and gives his seven gifts: Wisdom, Understanding, Counsel, Fortitude, Knowledge, Piety, and, Fear of the Lord. Students should be able to explain or define these seven gifts. If you give them scenarios, they should be able to name which gift is being used, e.g., when others say going to church is silly, but you go nonetheless: Fortitude.

Name: _____

The Holy Spirit Comes   **Quiz 22**

Yes or No. *Circle the correct answer.*

1. Did Mary and the Apostles pray for the Holy Spirit to come?   (Yes)   No

2. Did the Holy Spirit come at Pentecost?   (Yes)   No

3. Were the Apostles brave without the Holy Spirit?   Yes   (No)

4. Does the Holy Spirit help the Church?   (Yes)   No

5. Does the Holy Spirit help you to love?   (Yes)   No

Assess

Distribute the quiz and answer any questions that the children may have. Orally quiz the children on the questions from the textbook as they hand in their tests. When the quiz is completed, review the correct answer with the children.

Conclude

Conclude by singing "Come, Holy Ghost, Creator blest," *Adoremus Hymnal*, #443.

Name:_____

The Holy Spirit Comes

Answer the following questions.

1. What did Mary and the Apostles do for nine days in the room?

<u>They waited for the Holy Spirit to</u>
<u>come.</u>

2. What happened on the tenth day?

<u>The Holy Spirit came.</u>

3. What sound did Mary and the Apostles hear when the Holy Spirit came?

<u>They heard the sound of great</u>
<u>wind.</u>

4. What do we call the day that the Holy Spirit came?

<u>Pentecost</u>

5. With what did the Holy Spirit fill their souls and hearts?

<u>Grace and love</u>

6. What do we call prayers that last nine days?

<u>Novenas</u>

Faith and Life Series • Grade 1 • Chapter 22 • Lesson 1   85

Name:_____

Symbols of the Holy Spirit

The
Holy Spirit
is God!

86   *Faith and Life Series • Grade 1 • Chapter 22 • Lesson 2*

Name:_____

Word Search

Can you find these words in the puzzle?
Look carefully! The words go across and down.

APOSTLES	GOOD NEWS	POPE
BAPTIZE	GRACE	PRAY
BISHOPS	HEART	SOUL
BRAVE	HOLY SPIRIT	TEACH
CHURCH	LOVE	WIND
	NINE	

```
W Z W G O O D N E W S
Q J F A P O S T L E S
J M L G R A C E B L S
H O L Y S P I R I T O
B H V N L L X B S R U
R G F I L C H A H R L
A N Y N O T P P O P E
V T W E V E R T P J G
E Z V D E A I S K B
W I N D Z C Y Z R N M
C H U R C H H E A R T
```

Faith and Life Series • Grade 1 • Chapter 22 • Lesson 3   87

Name:_____

The Holy Spirit is alive in the Church today. He helps the Pope and the bishops to teach the truth about God. He helps us to love one another and become holy.

Fill in the missing letters to the gifts of the Holy Spirit using the letters below. Then, color the picture.

Wisdo**m**   For**t**itu**d**e   Fea**r** of the
Un**d**er**s**tanding   **K**now**l**edge   **L**ord
Pi**e**t**y**   **C**oun**s**el

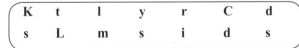

K	t	l	y	r	C	d
s	L	m	s	i	d	s

88   *Faith and Life Series • Grade 1 • Chapter 22 • Lesson 4*

273

TEACHER'S NOTES

CHAPTER TWENTY-THREE
THE BLESSED TRINITY

Catechism of the Catholic Church References

Belief in One God: 199–202, 228
Christians Begin the Day with the Sign of the Cross: 2157
The Divine Works and the Trinitarian Missions: 257–60, 267
The Family as an Image of the Trinity: 2205
Grace: 1996–2005, 2021–24
The Holy Trinity in the Teaching of the Faith: 249–56, 266
The Implications of Faith in One God: 222–27, 229

"In the Name of the Father and of the Son and of the Holy Spirit": 232–37, 265
The Mystery of Faith: 230, 234, 237, 1066
The Persons of the Trinity: 242, 252–57, 685, 689
The Revelation of God as Trinity: 238–48, 261–64
The Trinity in Us: 260

Scripture References

The Great Commission: Mt 28:16–20
Promise of the Counselor: Jn 14:25–26
The Baptism of Jesus: Mt 3:1–17

The Annunciation: Lk 1:31–38
Speaking: Is 49:14–15; 66:13; Ps 131:2–3; Hos 11:1–4; Jer 3:4–19

Background Reading: *The Fundamentals of Catholicism* by Fr. Kenneth Baker, S.J.

Volume 2:
"The Most Holy Trinity," pp. 77–79
"God is Both One and Three," pp. 80–83

Summary of Lesson Content

Lesson 1

In Baptism, persons are baptized, "In the Name of the Father and of the Son and of the Holy Spirit."

There is only one God.

There are three Divine Persons in one God.

The Father is God, the Son is God, and the Holy Spirit is God. They are one God.

Lesson 2

The mystery of the Blessed Trinity is one God in three Persons.

The First Person is the Father, the Second Person is the Son (who became man as Jesus the Christ) and the Third Person is the Holy Spirit.

The Persons are distinct: The Father is not the Son, nor the Holy Spirit. The Son is not the Father nor the Holy Spirit. The Holy Spirit is not the Father nor the Son.

The three Persons had no beginning and have no end. They are equal. No one Person is greater than another.

Lesson 3

Jesus told us about the Blessed Trinity: one God in three Persons.

The Blessed Trinity is a mystery of the Faith.

The family is an image of the Blessed Trinity: father, mother, and child.

Lesson 4

Prayer is said to the Father, through the Son, in the Holy Spirit, therefore calling upon the name of the Blessed Trinity.

The Sign of the Cross reminds Catholics of the mystery of the Blessed Trinity and of the sacrifice of the Son, Who became man as Jesus, and saved mankind by dying on the Cross.

When grace resides in a soul, the Blessed Trinity dwells in it.

Chapter Twenty-Three: The Blessed Trinity
Lesson One: We Believe in One God

Aims

Students will learn that persons are baptized, "In the Name of the Father and of the Son and of the Holy Spirit."

They will learn that Catholics believe in one God.

They will learn that God is three Persons: God the Father, God the Son, and God the Holy Spirit.

Materials

- Green construction paper, scissors, glue

- *Activity Book*, p. 89

Optional:
- "Patrick: Brave Shepherd of the Emerald Isle," video, CCC of America, available through Ignatius Press

- "All hail, adored Trinity," *Adoremus Hymnal*, #462

Begin

Review with the children Jesus' Great Commission to go forth and baptize all nations "In the Name of the Father and of the Son and of the Holy Spirit." Does He say, "in the Names"? (No.) Why? (There is only one God.) But this one God is three Divine Persons: The Father is God, the Son is God, and the Holy Spirit is God.

Develop

1. Read paragraph 1 with the students.

2. In order to demonstrate that God the Blessed Trinity is love, cut out three hearts by folding (green) construction paper in three, then cutting out a heart (each will then be the same size). On the first heart write "God the Father," on the second heart, write "God the Son," and on the third heart, write "God the Holy Spirit."

2. Next, tell the children that these three Persons (Father, Son, and Holy Spirit) are all God. Ask if the children have ever seen a three-leaf clover (shamrock). It is one plant with three leaves (like one God in three Persons). Assemble the three hearts to make a clover leaf. Make a stem that says "is God." This will make a clover leaf that says: The Father is

God, the Son is God, and the Holy Spirit is God. Reinforce that God the Father, God the Son, and God the Holy Spirit love the children very much.

3. Have the children look at the diagram of the Blessed Trinity on p. 89 of their *Activity Book*. This diagram shows that the Father is God, the Son is God, the Holy Spirit is God (but that the three Persons are distinct). It is a diagram of the Blessed Trinity: one God in three Persons (see also pp. 19 and 177 of this manual).

4. You may want to briefly describe the life of the great Saint Patrick (see the facing page) and how he used the three-leaf clover to teach the doctrine of the Blessed Trinity to the Irish. Or you may choose to show a video on his life.

Reinforce

1. Have the children color the diagram of the Blessed Trinity on p. 89 in the *Activity Book* (see *Teacher's Manual*, p. 285).

2. The students may make their own shamrocks after the model you made for them in class. They will need green construction paper, children's scissors, and glue or paste.

3. If time permits and you have not already done so, show the video "Patrick: Brave Shepherd of the Emerald Isle" from CCC of America (available through Ignatius Press; 30 minutes).

Conclude

1. Lead the children in prayer, having the students thank God that they were baptized in His name and claimed for the Blessed Trinity.

2. Sing with the children "All Hail, adored Trinity," *Adoremus Hymnal*, #462.

23   The Blessed Trinity

"Go therefore and make disciples of all nations,
baptizing them in the name of the Father
and of the Son and of the Holy Spirit."

Matthew 28:19

There is only one God. There are three Divine Persons in one God: God the Father, God the Son, and God the Holy Spirit. The Father is God. The Son is God. The Holy Spirit is God. But together They are one God.

We call the three Persons in one God the **Blessed Trinity**. **God the Father** is the First Person of the Blessed Trinity. **God the Son** is the Second Person of the Blessed Trinity. He became the man Whom we call Jesus and Who died to save us from sin. **God the Holy Spirit** is the Third Person of the Blessed Trinity. He helps us to pray and to love one another.

The three Persons of the Blessed Trinity had no beginning. They always were and always will be.

91

The three Persons are equal. The Father is not greater than the Son. The Son is not greater than the Holy Spirit.

We know there are three Persons in one God because Jesus told us about it. But we cannot really understand how God can be both three and one. That is called a **mystery** and we will have to wait until Heaven to understand it better. But it can help if you think about a family. In a family there are the mother, father, and children, all different persons, but they are one family. In the Blessed Trinity there are three Persons, but one God.

We often begin our prayers by calling on the Blessed Trinity. We say, "In the Name of the Father and of the Son and of the Holy Spirit." When we say these words, we make the Sign of the Cross on our bodies. And it reminds us that Jesus saved us by dying on a Cross.

When my soul is filled with grace, the Blessed Trinity lives in me!

Words to Know:

Blessed Trinity   God the Father   God the Son

God the Holy Spirit   mystery

92

SAINT PATRICK OF IRELAND

Saint Patrick was born in Scotland around the year 385 to Roman parents in charge of the colonies in Britain. Around the age of fourteen he was captured and taken to Ireland as a slave and shepherd, at a time when Ireland was a land of Druids and pagans. He learned their language and customs, and at age twenty, escaped to the coast where sailors returned him to Gaul. He became a priest and then a bishop, and returned to Ireland in 433. Patrick preached the Gospel, converted thousands, and built churches all over Ireland. He used the shamrock to teach the Blessed Trinity. He is the patron saint of Ireland. His feast day is March 17.

Preview

In our next lesson, we will learn more about the three Persons of the Blessed Trinity.

Chapter Twenty-Three: The Blessed Trinity
Lesson Two: One God, Three Persons

Aims

Students will review that the one God in three Persons is a mystery called the Blessed Trinity.

They will review that the Persons are distinct, equal, and they always were and always will be.

They will know that the Father is the First Person, the Son is the Second Person, and the Holy Spirit is the Third Person of the Blessed Trinity.

They will learn that Jesus is the Second Person of the Blessed Trinity and, therefore, Jesus is God.

Materials

• *Activity Book*, p. 90

Optional:
• "All hail, adored Trinity," *Adoremus Hymnal*, #462

Begin

Using the example of a clover, ask the children to explain the Blessed Trinity (one God in three Persons). Ask them to name the three Persons: Father, Son, and Holy Spirit. Tell the children that this is a great mystery of faith, called the Blessed Trinity. It is not a problem or a puzzle to be solved, but something that no one can fully understand. We know it is true because Jesus told us.

Develop

1. Read paragraphs 2, 3, and 4 from the text.

2. Now separate the construction paper clover leaves from the last lesson: Father, Son, and Holy Spirit. They are all equal in size. This is like God, for all three Persons are equal; they are all God. No one Person is greater. The Father is not greater than the Son, nor the Holy Spirit. The Son is not greater than the Father, nor the Holy Spirit. The Holy Spirit is not greater than the Father, nor the Son.

3. In the clover, each leaf is the clover: no one leaf is different. Therefore, the clover is like God: the Father is God, the Son is God, and the Holy Spirit is God.

4. Re-emphasize that all three Persons are God. God has no beginning and no end. The Father has no beginning and no end. The Son has no beginning and no end. The Holy Spirit has no beginning and no end.

5. The three Persons have a relation to one another. Just like your dad is your father, and you know him in this relation, and he knows you as his child, so God the Father and God the Son are known by this relationship of love. And, the love between the Father and the Son is the Holy Spirit. This relationship may be modeled by the love of a father, mother, and child.

6. Each Person of the Blessed Trinity is known for His work. The Father is the Creator and is the Father of all creatures. The Son is the Redeemer; He became man in the Person of Jesus and died for the sins of man. God the Holy Spirit is the Sanctifier; He helps to make men holy. The Holy Spirit was sent by the Father and the Son to give life to the Church and help people pray and love one another.

7. The Father, Son, and Holy Spirit are God, and everyone must know, love, and serve this one God in three Persons.

Reinforce

1. Ask the children to fill in the blanks on *Activity Book*, p. 90 (see *Teacher's Manual*, p. 285). They may use Chapter 23 as an aid.

2. Separate the children into pairs and ask them to begin learning Questions 48–51 in the textbook (see *Teacher's Manual*, p. 281).

Conclude

1. End with a prayer, praising each Person of the Blessed Trinity for His works and love for the children.

2. Sing with the children "All Hail, adored Trinity," *Adoremus Hymnal*, #462.

23   The Blessed Trinity

"Go therefore and make disciples of all nations,
baptizing them in the name of the Father
and of the Son and of the Holy Spirit."

Matthew 28:19

There is only one God. There are three Divine Persons in one God: God the Father, God the Son, and God the Holy Spirit. The Father is God. The Son is God. The Holy Spirit is God. But together They are one God.

We call the three Persons in one God the **Blessed Trinity**. **God the Father** is the First Person of the Blessed Trinity. **God the Son** is the Second Person of the Blessed Trinity. He became the man Whom we call Jesus and Who died to save us from sin. **God the Holy Spirit** is the Third Person of the Blessed Trinity. He helps us to pray and to love one another.

The three Persons of the Blessed Trinity had no beginning. They always were and always will be.

91

The three Persons are equal. The Father is not greater than the Son. The Son is not greater than the Holy Spirit.

We know there are three Persons in one God because Jesus told us about it. But we cannot really understand how God can be both three and one. That is called a **mystery** and we will have to wait until Heaven to understand it better. But it can help if you think about a family. In a family there are the mother, father, and children, all different persons, but they are one family. In the Blessed Trinity there are three Persons, but one God.

We often begin our prayers by calling on the Blessed Trinity. We say, "In the Name of the Father and of the Son and of the Holy Spirit." When we say these words, we make the Sign of the Cross on our bodies. And it reminds us that Jesus saved us by dying on a Cross.

When my soul is filled with grace, the Blessed Trinity lives in me!

Words to Know:

Blessed Trinity   God the Father   God the Son
God the Holy Spirit   mystery

92

THE RELATIONSHIP OF PERSONS IN THE BLESSED TRINITY

In Catholic Tradition, certain theological terminology is used to refer to each Person's relation to the other in the Blessed Trinity, which is stated in the Nicene Creed (see p. 283 of this manual). The Church uses the term "substance" (at times "essence" or "nature") to signify the divine being in its unity; the term "person" or "hypostasis" to designate the Father, Son, and Holy Spirit in the real distinction among them; and also the term "relation" to indicate the fact that their distinction lies in the relationship of each to the others. The Father "begets" the Son eternally, and the Father and Son's mutual love results in the "spiration" of the Holy Spirit. See also CCC 249–56.

THE BLESSED TRINITY IN SCRIPTURE

There are many instances of the Blessed Trinity in Scripture, such as:

- Creation: Gen 1:1–2
- The Annunciation: Lk 1:26–38
- The Baptism of Jesus: Mt 3:1–17
- Christ's Priestly Prayer: Jn 14—17
- The Crucifixion: Mt 27:45–50; Mk 15:33–39; Lk 23:44–46.

TRINITY SUNDAY

Pope John XXII (1316–34) promulgated this feast for the Universal Church on the first Sunday after Pentecost. Because it was after the first Pentecost that the Trinitarian doctrine was proclaimed to the world, the feast was chosen to follow Pentecost.

Preview

In our next lesson, we will learn more about the family as an image of the Blessed Trinity.

CHAPTER TWENTY-THREE: THE BLESSED TRINITY
LESSON THREE: THE FAMILY IN THE IMAGE OF THE TRINITY

Aims

Students will learn that Jesus taught that God is three Persons. Even so, this is a great mystery.

They will learn that Jesus spoke to the Father and that He sent the Holy Spirit.

They will learn that the family is an image of the Blessed Trinity.

Materials

- Children's Bible
- *Activity Book*, p. 91

- "All hail, adored Trinity," *Adoremus Hymnal*, #462

Optional:

Begin

Have the children think of their parents in relation to themselves. Each child has a mother and a father. Write "Father, Mother, and You = One Family" on the chalkboard. Remind the students that this family is three persons: a model of the Blessed Trinity. The father is not the mother nor the child, the mother is not the father nor the child, and the child is not the father nor the mother. All three are persons; they are all one family. They know themselves by their relationship. They are three distinct persons, different in their roles, all one family, in love.

Develop

1. Read paragraph 5 in the textbook.

2. Emphasize with the children that the Blessed Trinity is a mystery. A mystery is not a puzzle nor is it a problem to be solved. A mystery is something that a person can know about, and can learn about, but cannot fully understand, even if he spends his entire life thinking about it. The Blessed Trinity is a mystery people know is true because Jesus taught it. The Blessed Trinity is present in other parts of the Bible too. Reading about it in Scripture can help a person to understand the mystery better. Praying to learn more about this mystery can also help a person's faith.

3. Explain that Jesus really did reveal the Blessed Trinity to the Church. He told the Apostles to baptize all nations, "In the name of the Father and of the Son and of the Holy Spirit" (Mt 28:19). The Blessed Trinity is present at the Baptism of Jesus, with God the Father's voice from Heaven and the Holy Spirit descending upon Jesus (Mt 3:1–17). Jesus speaks about His Father and the Holy Spirit; read John 14:25–26 from your children's Bible.

4. Discuss this passage in John. Explain that the term Counselor means someone who guides Christians in truth. A Counselor defends Christians from error or false judgment. The Counselor is a name for the Holy Spirit.

6. Ask the children if they can think of another example of the three Persons of the Blessed Trinity being present in a Bible passage. Perhaps they will remember learning about the Annunciation (Lk 1:31–38) in Chapter 9. The angel Gabriel appears to announce that Mary is to be the Mother of Jesus (God the Son) according to the plan of God, the Most High (God the Father), and she shall conceive by the power of the Holy Spirit. Clearly the Blessed Trinity is there.

Reinforce

1. Assign the word search found on p. 91 of the *Activity Book* (see *Teacher's Manual*, p. 285). The children may write sentences with the words they find in the puzzle.

2. Have the children review and finalize memorization of Questions 48–51.

Conclude

Close by singing "All Hail, adored Trinity," *Adoremus Hymnal*, #462, or saying a prayer to the Blessed Trinity, beginning and ending with the Sign of the Cross (see *Teacher's Manual*, p. 367).

The three Persons are equal. The Father is not greater than the Son. The Son is not greater than the Holy Spirit.

We know there are three Persons in one God because Jesus told us about it. But we cannot really understand how God can be both three and one. That is called a **mystery** and we will have to wait until Heaven to understand it better. But it can help if you think about a family. In a family there are the mother, father, and children, all different persons, but they are one family. In the Blessed Trinity there are three Persons, but one God.

We often begin our prayers by calling on the Blessed Trinity. We say, "In the Name of the Father and of the Son and of the Holy Spirit." When we say these words, we make the Sign of the Cross on our bodies. And it reminds us that Jesus saved us by dying on a Cross.

When my soul is filled with grace, the Blessed Trinity lives in me!

Words to Know:

Blessed Trinity   God the Father   God the Son

God the Holy Spirit   mystery

Q. 48 *Who is the First Person of the Blessed Trinity?*
The First Person of the Blessed Trinity is God the Father (CCC 254).

Q. 49 *Who is the Second Person of the Blessed Trinity?*
The Second Person of the Blessed Trinity is God the Son (CCC 254).

Q. 50 *Who is the Third Person of the Blessed Trinity?*
The Third Person of the Blessed Trinity is God the Holy Spirit (CCC 254).

Q. 51 *Has God always existed?*
God has always been and always will be (CCC 202).

We Pray:

GLORY BE

Glory be to the Father, and to the Son, and to the Holy Spirit, as it was in the beginning is now, and ever shall be, world without end. *Amen.*

SPEAKING OF GOD IN THE MASCULINE

Although God is pure spirit, has no body and is therefore neither male nor female, the Church has always called God "Father". This tradition follows Christ's example in Scripture of calling God not only "Father," but also "Abba," which is "Daddy"

"In no way is God in man's image. He is neither man nor woman. God is pure spirit in which there is no place for the difference between the sexes. But the respective 'perfections' of man and woman reflect something of the infinite perfection of God: those of a mother and those of a father and husband." (Cf. Is 49:14–15; 66:13; Ps 131:2–3; Hos 11:1–4; Jer 3:4–19 as quoted in the *Catechism of the Catholic Church*, 370).

CHALK TALK: THE FAMILY AS A TRINITARIAN IMAGE

FATHER
(FATHER)

MOTHER
(SON)

CHILD
(HOLY SPIRIT)

As the Father has loved me, so have I loved you; abide in my love…just as I have kept my Father's commandments and abide in his love.

—John 15:9–10

Preview

In our next lesson, we will learn about praying to the Blessed Trinity.

CHAPTER TWENTY-THREE: THE BLESSED TRINITY
LESSON FOUR: PRAYING TO THE TRINITY

Aims

Students will learn that Catholics pray to the Father, through the Son, in the Holy Spirit.

They will learn that the Sign of the Cross reminds Catholics of the mystery of the Blessed Trinity because the Second Person, the Son, became man and died on the Cross to save the world from sin.

They will be reminded that grace is God's life, so that when a person has grace in his soul, the Blessed Trinity lives in him.

Materials

- Children's Bible

- *Activity Book*, p. 92

Optional:
- "All hail, adored Trinity," *Adoremus Hymnal*, #462

Begin

Write the word "Grace" on the board. Ask the children if they remember what grace is (God's life). Review with them the fact that Adam and Eve had grace, but they lost it by their Original Sin. Jesus won back grace by dying on the Cross so that people receive grace in Baptism. It remains in a soul when there is no serious sin. Explain to the children that grace is important because when a person has grace, God (the Blessed Trinity) lives in him.

Develop

1. Read paragraphs 6 and 7 in the text.

2. Explain to the children that wherever God's life is, He is there. If a person has grace in his soul, God is in that soul. It does not make a person God, but God does truly live in him.

3. To review the last lesson, read the story of the Annunciation from a children's Bible (Lk 1:31–38).
   - Who was full of grace? (Mary)
   - Where are the three Persons of the Blessed Trinity? (The Father wanted Mary to be the Mother of Jesus; the Son became baby Jesus; the Holy Spirit brought the Son to Mary.)

4. Explain to the students that Mary had the Blessed Trinity living in her in a very special way—as a baby. Any person can have God living in him when he is full of grace (which he receives when he is baptized and every time he receives the Eucharist).

5. Ask the following questions:
   - How does a person receive grace? (through the Sacraments)
   - How can a person lose grace? (sin; use concrete examples covering the Ten Commandments, i.e., stealing or lying)
   - How can a person receive grace again if he loses it? (ask God's forgiveness and go to Confession)
   - How can a person strengthen grace in his soul? (through the Sacraments, prayer, works of charity, penance)

6. Review the Sign of the Cross with the children. Catholics sign over our hearts because we love God, He loves us, and He lives in our hearts when we have grace. Saying, "In the Name of the Father, and of the Son, and of the Holy Spirit" reminds Catholics of the mystery of the Blessed Trinity: one God in three Persons. We make a Cross because the Second Person became man as Jesus and died for man's sins on the Cross, so people can have grace in their souls. The three Persons are united, so if we pray to one Person, we pray to all three.

Reinforce

1. Have the students answer the questions on p. 92 of the *Activity Book* (see *Teacher's Manual*, p. 285).

2. Have the students review Questions 48–51 from the text.

Conclude

1. Pray the Glory Be together as a class (see *Teacher's Manual*, p. 367).

2. Lead the children in a prayer thanking God for grace and for living in our hearts. Begin and end the prayer with the Sign of the Cross (see *Teacher's Manual*, p. 367).

3. Sing "All Hail, adored Trinity," *Adoremus Hymnal*, #462

The three Persons are equal. The Father is not greater than the Son. The Son is not greater than the Holy Spirit.

We know there are three Persons in one God because Jesus told us about it. But we cannot really understand how God can be both three and one. That is called a **mystery** and we will have to wait until Heaven to understand it better. But it can help if you think about a family. In a family there are the mother, father, and children, all different persons, but they are one family. In the Blessed Trinity there are three Persons, but one God.

We often begin our prayers by calling on the Blessed Trinity. We say, "In the Name of the Father and of the Son and of the Holy Spirit." When we say these words, we make the Sign of the Cross on our bodies. And it reminds us that Jesus saved us by dying on a Cross.

When my soul is filled with grace, the Blessed Trinity lives in me!

Words to Know:

Blessed Trinity   God the Father   God the Son

God the Holy Spirit   mystery

92

Q. 48 *Who is the First Person of the Blessed Trinity?*
The First Person of the Blessed Trinity is God the Father (CCC 254).

Q. 49 *Who is the Second Person of the Blessed Trinity?*
The Second Person of the Blessed Trinity is God the Son (CCC 254).

Q. 50 *Who is the Third Person of the Blessed Trinity?*
The Third Person of the Blessed Trinity is God the Holy Spirit (CCC 254).

Q. 51 *Has God always existed?*
God has always been and always will be (CCC 202).

We Pray:

GLORY BE

Glory be to the Father, and to the Son, and to the Holy Spirit, as it was in the beginning is now, and ever shall be, world without end. *Amen.*

93

The Nicene Creed

I believe in one God, the Father almighty, maker of heaven and earth, of all things visible and invisible.

I believe in one Lord Jesus Christ, the Only Begotten Son of God, born of the Father before all ages. God from God, Light from Light, true God from true God, begotten, not made, consubstantial with the Father; through him all things were made. For us men and for our salvation he came down from heaven,

and by the Holy Spirit was incarnate of the Virgin Mary, and became man.

For our sake he was crucified under Pontius Pilate, he suffered death and was buried, and rose again on the third day in accordance with the Scriptures.

He ascended into heaven and is seated at the right hand of the Father. He will come again in glory to judge the living and the dead and his kingdom will have no end.

I believe in the Holy Spirit, the Lord, the giver of life, who proceeds from the Father and the Son, who with the Father and the Son is adored and glorified, who has spoken through the prophets.

I believe in one, holy, catholic, and apostolic Church. I confess one Baptism for the forgiveness of sins and I look forward to the resurrection of the dead and the life of the world to come. Amen.

MARY: SPOUSE OF THE HOLY SPIRIT

After accepting the Father's invitation to become the Mother of God, the Holy Spirit overshadowed Mary and the Son was conceived in her womb. By the power of the Holy Spirit and because of her faith, Mary's virginity became uniquely fruitful. She is often called the spouse of the Holy Spirit.

Preview

We will review what we have learned by playing a game, then take a quiz.

CHAPTER TWENTY-THREE: THE BLESSED TRINITY
REVIEW AND ASSESSMENT

Aims

To review and assess the students' knowledge of the materials taught in this chapter.

Materials

- Appendix, p. B-1
- Quiz 23 (Appendix, p. A-28)
- "All hail, adored Trinity," *Adoremus Hymnal*, #462

Name: _____

The Blessed Trinity   Quiz 23

Multiple choice. *Circle the correct answer.*

1. There is _____ God.

   (a) one)   b) two   c) three

2. There are _____ Divine Persons in God.

   a) one   b) two   (c) three)

3. The Father is _____ , the Son is _____ ,
   and the Holy Spirit is _____ .
   (Circle one word for all three blanks.)

   a) human   (b) God)   c) less

4. Did the Blessed Trinity have a beginning?

   a) yes   (b) no)

A-28   *Faith and Life Series • Grade 1 • Appendix A*

Review and Enrichment

Play a review game, such as Bible Baseball (see Appendix, p. B-1 for instructions). Be sure to cover the content of all four lessons, including the examples of the Blessed Trinity as found in Scripture. Items to review:
- The Blessed Trinity is one God in three Divine Persons.
- All three Persons are distinct.
- All three Persons are equal.
- God has no beginning and no end.
- Jesus taught us about the Blessed Trinity.
- The family is a model of the Blessed Trinity.
- The Sign of the Cross is a prayer that reminds Catholics of the mystery of the Blessed Trinity, and that the Second Person, the Son, became man and died on the Cross to save the world from sin.

Assess

1. Distribute the quiz. Read through it with the children and answer any questions that they may have. Individually quiz the children on Questions 48–51 from the textbook (see *Teacher's Manual*, p. 283).

2. After they have completed them, review the correct answers for reinforcement.

Conclude

End with singing "All hail, adored Trinity," *Adoremus Hymnal*, #462, or pass out prayer cards as little rewards for learning.

Chapter Twenty-Three: The Blessed Trinity
Activity Book Answer Keys

Name:_____

The Blessed Trinity
One God in three Persons

Color the circle with "The Father" red, "The Son" blue, and "The Holy Spirit" yellow. Then color the sections with the word "is" orange, and the sections with "is not" black.

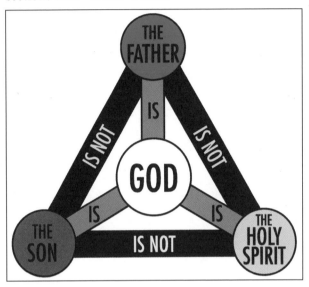

Faith and Life Series • Grade 1 • Chapter 23 • Lesson 1   89

Name:_____

Can you fill in the blanks? Use Chapter 23 in your textbook for help.

There is only **one** God. There are **three** Divine Persons in one God.

We call the three Persons in one God the **Blessed Trinity**. God the **Father** is the First Person of the Blessed Trinity. God the **Son** is the Second Person of the Blessed Trinity. He became the man Whom we call **Jesus** and Who died to save us from **sin**. God the **Holy Spirit** is the Third Person of the Blessed Trinity.

The three Persons of the Blessed Trinity had no **beginning**. They always were and always will be.

The three Persons are equal. The **Father** is not greater than the Son. The Son is not greater than the Holy Spirit.

We know there are three Persons in one God because Jesus told us. That is called a **mystery** and we will have to wait until Heaven to understand.

90   *Faith and Life Series • Grade 1 • Chapter 23 • Lesson 2*

Name:_____

Word Search

Can you find these words in the puzzle? Look carefully! The words go across and down.

BLESSED   JESUS   SON
FATHER   MYSTERY   THREE
GOD   ONE   TRINITY
HOLY SPIRIT   PERSONS

```
V T V X F A T H E R
O N E Y T R R Z K R
H O L Y S P I R I T
T M Y S T E R Y R R
R H M Q N R J Y X D
I B L E S S E D F G
N L M L W O S X J O
I V L V J N S U J D
T H R E E S U S D R
Y R P H H D R T T P
```

Faith and Life Series • Grade 1 • Chapter 23 • Lesson 3   91

Name:_____

We pray to the Blessed Trinity

Fill in the blanks using the words below.

loves	Son
Cross	Second
Holy Spirit	Father

We make the Sign of the Cross before and after each prayer to remind us of the mystery of the Blessed Trinity. We say, "In the Name of the **Father** and of the **Son** and of the **Holy Spirit**. *Amen.*"

The Blessed Trinity lives in our hearts when we have the gift of grace. We make the Sign of the Cross over our hearts to remind us that God **loves** us and we love Him.

We make the shape of a cross to remind us that the **Second** Person of the Blessed Trinity, Jesus, died on the **Cross** so that we could have grace in our souls.

92   *Faith and Life Series • Grade 1 • Chapter 23 • Lesson 4*

285

TEACHER'S NOTES

CHAPTER TWENTY-FOUR
GOD GIVES YOU HIS LIFE

Catechism of the Catholic Church References

Baptism: 1213–16, 1253
Baptism and Sin: 405, 977–78, 985, 1263, 2520
Baptism in the Church: 1226–28
Consequences of Original Sin: 399–409, 416–19
The Definition of a Sacrament: 774, 1131
Fidelity to Baptismal Promises: 2340

Grace and Effects of Baptism: 265, 683, 1262–74, 1279–80
The Importance of Baptism: 628, 1226
Minister of Baptism: 1256, 1284
Necessity of Baptism: 846, 1250, 1257–61, 1277
Original Sin: 388–90, 396–401, 415
The Rite and Signs of Baptism: 1234–45, 1278

Scripture References

The Great Commission: Mt 28:16–20
The Fall of Adam and Eve: Gen 1—3

The Passion of Jesus: Jn 18—19
Book of Names: Rev 3:5; 13:8

Background Reading: *The Fundamentals of Catholicism* by Fr. Kenneth Baker, S.J.

Volume 2:
Original Sin, pp. 159–68
"Never Make Light of Sin," pp. 168–71
Infants Dying Without Baptism, pp. 171–74

Volume 3:
"Man without Grace," pp. 34–37
What is a Sacrament?, pp. 163–71

Sacramental Grace and Character, pp. 172–81
Christ, the Sacraments, and Salvation, pp. 181–94
"Baptism into the Body of Christ," pp. 194–97
"Water and Words," pp. 197–200
"Baptism Has Consequences," pp. 200–2
"The Necessity of Baptism," pp. 202–5
Infants Who Die Without Baptism, pp. 205–8
Ministers and Recipients of Baptism, pp. 208–13 .

Summary of Lesson Content

Lesson 1

All people except Jesus and Mary are born with Original Sin.

The consequences of Original Sin include:
• loss of grace, absence of justification
• spiritual disharmony
• concupiscence, weakened nature
• death and illness
• error in education, politics, social actions, and morals

Jesus died for the forgiveness of sins (including Original Sin).

Lesson 2

Jesus instituted the Sacrament of Baptism.

The symbols for Baptism include:
• Water
• White garment
• Candle
• Oil (Holy Chrism)

Lesson 3

The effects of Baptism on a person's soul include:
• Forgiveness of sins (including Original Sin and personal sin)
• An infusion of grace
• Full membership into the Church
• An indelible mark
• Becoming a new person in Christ
• The seven gifts of the Holy Spirit
• The three theological virtues

Lesson 4

There is a minister, form, and matter for every Sacrament.

The minister of Baptism is a priest or deacon.

The matter for Baptism is water; the form is, "I baptize you in the Name of the Father, and of the Son, and of the Holy Spirit."

Baptism is necessary for salvation.

Chapter Twenty-Four: God Gives You His Life
Lesson One: Jesus Restores the Life of Grace

Aims

Students will review the concept of Original Sin and the need for grace.

They will recall that Jesus won back grace through His death and Resurrection.

They will remember that Catholics receive grace in Baptism, and that grace allows people to go to Heaven.

Materials

- A small toy or treat

- *Activity Book*, p. 93

Optional:
- Children's Bible

- "Sing praise to our Creator," *Adoremus Hymnal*, #500

Begin

Using the pictures from a children's Bible, ask the students to retell the stories of the Fall of Adam and Eve (Gen 1—3), and the Passion and death of Jesus (Jn 18—19). Ask the children if they see how these stories are related: Adam and Eve lost grace through sin, and Jesus won it back through His death and Resurrection.

Develop

1. Read paragraph 1 and the first line of paragraph 2 aloud from the textbook.

2. Now hold up a small toy or treat, something that the children would want. Ask them if they want it, and what they would give you for it (then make the trade). Next, explain that you want it back. What price must you pay? It may be a greater value than that for which you traded it, or the price may be more than what you have. What if you did not have enough to get it back? Then someone else would have to get it back for you. This trade, or bargain, is what Jesus did for Adam and Eve after they sinned and lost grace.

3. Expound on this parallel with grace: Adam and Eve lost the grace in their souls by accepting the forbidden fruit. They were unable to get grace back on their own. They could not buy it back or give up something for it. Jesus, however, being God, perfect, and a man, paid the price for sin and won back grace, which is dispensed in the Sacrament of Baptism.

4. Review with the students how a person receives grace; one way is through Baptism. This Sacrament washes away Original Sin, as well as any personal sin on the soul (if someone is baptized as an adult). God also fills the newly baptized soul with His grace.

5. Explain that anyone who is baptized must care greatly about this gift of grace and should try his best not to lose it again (through sin). Review with the children what sin is: saying no to God. People sin by breaking the Ten Commandments, not loving God or neighbor, or choosing to do a bad thing. Remind the children that if they or anyone loses grace, it can be recovered through the Sacrament of Penance.

Reinforce

1. Ask the children to answer the questions on p. 93 of the *Activity Book* (see *Teacher's Manual*, p. 297). As these are rather involved, you may want to assist them in completing this page.

2. Play a game to review this lesson by asking questions about grace. Outline a scenario, then ask the children if they would lose or receive grace. For example:
- Disobey your parents: lose grace
- Receive Holy Communion: receive grace
- Go to Confession: receive grace
- Steal from someone: lose grace

Conclude

1. Teach the children the hymn "Sing praise to our Creator, *Adoremus Hymnal*, #500.

2. Say a prayer as a class thanking God for Jesus, Who died for our sins and gives us grace in Baptism.

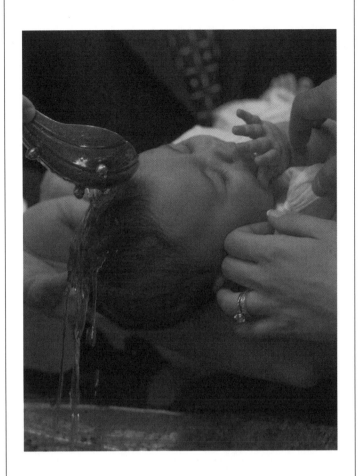

24   God Gives You His Life

"We were buried therefore with him by baptism into death,
so that as Christ was raised from the dead by the glory
of the Father, we too might walk in newness of life."

Romans 6:4

When Adam and Eve sinned, it meant that all the people born after him would have Adam's sin. It is called Original Sin because it was the first sin. You were born with Original Sin on your soul. This means that when you were born, there was none of God's life of grace in your soul. You were made for Baptism.

The Sacrament of Baptism washes away the guilt of Original Sin. When you are baptized, your soul is filled with the grace that Jesus won for you. It gives you God's life. That way you can reach Heaven.

Baptism makes you a child of God. And Baptism makes you a member of God's family, which is the Church.

Jesus wants all of us to share in His life and become children of God. Jesus said to His Apostles,

95

ORIGINAL SIN = THE SIN OF OUR ORIGIN

This is the sin by which the first human pair, in particular the man, Adam, chose to disobey a commandment of God in order to follow their own will. As a result they lost the grace of original holiness and justice with which they were created, became subject to sickness and death, and introduced the world to sin. Because all people now on earth are their descendants, Adam and Eve's sin, the sin of the origin of human life, is passed on to everyone. Every soul has an inclination toward evil; this inclination is called "concupiscence." Although Baptism washes away Original Sin from a person's soul, the inclination to sin remains throughout his life. Partaking of the other Sacraments is a good way to avoid sin.

COMPARISON OF ADAM AND CHRIST

ADAM	NEW ADAM
• Disobedient	• Obedient
• Selfish sin	• Self-sacrifice
• Loss of grace	• Won back grace
• Loss of Heaven	• Opened Heaven
• Death	• Eternal Life

From his fulness have we all received, grace upon grace . . . grace and truth came through Jesus Christ.

—John 1:16–17

Preview

In our next lesson, we will learn some of the signs and symbols of Baptism.

289

Chapter Twenty-Four: God Gives You His Life
Lesson Two: Signs and Symbols of Baptism

Aims

Students will learn some of the symbols of Baptism:
- Water
- Candle
- White garment
- Oil

Materials

- *Activity Book*, p. 94

Optional:
- Appendix, p. B-34

- Index cards including explanations of symbols

- "Sing praise to our Creator," *Adoremus Hymnal*, #500

Begin

Make a large table or chart on the chalkboard:

Symbol:	What it Means:
Water	Cleansing, rebirth
Candle	Light
Oil	Strength, anointing
White Garment	Purity

As you discuss these symbols in the course of the lesson, you may want to have the children follow along on p. 94 of the *Activity Book* (see *Teacher's Manual*, p. 297).

Develop

Explain what each of the following symbols mean in Baptism.

Water: Water is present in the Bible, for example with Noah, when the flood washed away all sin from the earth. Later, Moses split the waters of the Red Sea so that the Israelites could escape the Egyptians who pursued them.

Ask how the children think of water. Water can be fun, for swimming. Water maintains life; it is refreshing and cleansing. It can also be dangerous and take away life, by drowning.

In Baptism, water does these things, but to the soul. All sin is washed away. Baptism refreshes the soul with grace. The newly baptized person dies and rises to new life in Christ by going under and coming up from the water (or having water poured over his head). Baptism is a joyous event.

Candle: Light helps man to see. Fire is hot and is used to cook, to see, and to keep warm.

Jesus is the Light of the World (see pp. 118 and 119 of this manual). Catholics receive Him in Baptism and in grace He

lives in the baptized. Just as fire spreads, so faith spreads from one to another. Wax can be molded into different shapes, just as a newly baptized person takes on the image of Christ.

White Garment: People wear clothes to look nice and for modesty. White is a sign of cleanness and purity.

In Baptism, a person puts on a new self in Christ. He is made beautiful as he is filled with grace. He becomes pure and white without sin.

Oil: Oil is used to make hair and skin beautiful and to heal muscles. In the Bible, oil was used to anoint prophets, priests, and kings.

In Baptism, a person is anointed and shares in the prophetic, priestly, and kingly ministry of Christ; he learns to speak the truth, to worship, and inherit the Kingdom. God gives grace, heals the baptized person of sin, and strengthens him to avoid sin and temptation in the future.

Reinforce

1. Have the children complete p. 94 of the *Activity Book* (see *Teacher's Manual*, p. 297), the symbols of Baptism.

2. Students may draw and cut out shapes to make a baptismal candle, a white garment, oil, and water, or you may pass out copies of Appendix, p. B-34 for them to color.

3. They may begin memorizing Questions 52 and 53 on page 97 of the text (see *Teacher's Manual*, p. 295).

4. Make a bulletin board display with the symbols of Baptism. Have written on individual index cards the meaning of each symbol, i.e., water: washes away sin. Pass out the cards and have the children place them beside the appropriate symbol on the board. See example on the facing page.

Conclude

1. Pray a Glory Be together with the class (see *Teacher's Manual*, p. 367).

2. Sing "Sing praise to our Creator," *Adoremus Hymnal*, #500.

24   God Gives You His Life

"We were buried therefore with him by baptism into death,
so that as Christ was raised from the dead by the glory
of the Father, we too might walk in newness of life."
Romans 6:4

When Adam and Eve sinned, it meant that all the people born after him would have Adam's sin. It is called Original Sin because it was the first sin. You were born with Original Sin on your soul. This means that when you were born, there was none of God's life of grace in your soul. You were made for Baptism.

The Sacrament of Baptism washes away the guilt of Original Sin. When you are baptized, your soul is filled with the grace that Jesus won for you. It gives you God's life. That way you can reach Heaven.

Baptism makes you a child of God. And Baptism makes you a member of God's family, which is the Church.

Jesus wants all of us to share in His life and become children of God. Jesus said to His Apostles,

95

"Go and baptize all people." Like the Apostles, the priest is Jesus' helper. That is why the priest baptizes people.

When the priest baptizes a baby, he pours water on the baby's head and says, "I baptize you in the Name of the Father and of the Son and of the Holy Spirit." Now the baby is a child of God. Now the baby's soul is holy and pleasing to God.

Not everyone is baptized as a baby, but most people are. Ask your parents about your own Baptism. They can tell you all about when you were baptized. Maybe they even took a picture of your Baptism.

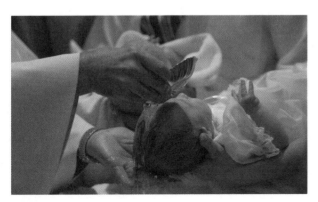

96

BAPTISMAL SYMBOLS

WATER

GARMENT

CANDLE

OIL

Preview

In our next lesson, we will learn about the effects of Baptism.

Chapter Twenty-Four: God Gives You His Life
Lesson Three: Effects of Baptism

Aims

Students will learn the effects of Baptism:
- The forgiveness of sin
- The ability to go to Heaven
- Initiation into the Church
- Receiving an indelible mark on the soul
- Becoming a new person in Christ
- The seven gifts of the Holy Spirit
- The three theological virtues

Materials

- Children's Bible
- *Activity Book*, p. 95

Optional:
- "Sing praise to our Creator," *Adoremus Hymnal*, #500

Begin

Begin the class by reading from the children's Bible the Great Commission, Jesus' instruction to go forth and baptize all nations (Mt 28:16–20). Remind the students that Jesus Himself instituted this Sacrament and said that all people need to be baptized. Tell them that today they will learn about the effects of Baptism.

Develop

1. Read paragraphs 2, 3, and 4 with the students.

2. Explain the effects of Baptism:
- Baptism washes away all sin, Original and personal.

- Baptism confers God's grace (His life), and therefore, the ability to go to Heaven.

- Baptized persons become God's children and members of His Church. They have godparents to help them learn the Faith, live it well, and guide them toward God.

- The baptized receives a permanent mark on the soul which can never be taken away. This mark sets him apart as a son of God; it shows that he is a Christian.

- The baptized becomes a new person in Christ; he takes a baptismal name, which is usually the name of a saint. (Note: students may want to research their saints and draw pictures of them.)

- The newly baptized receive the seven gifts of the Holy Spirit:
  Wisdom: to see things as God does
  Understanding: to recognize the truth in the Catholic Faith
  Counsel: to make good decisions
  Fortitude: to serve God, even when it is difficult
  Knowledge: to know God and how to serve Him
  Piety: to love and worship God and see Him as our Father
  Fear of the Lord: to be always aware of God's presence and His might, having reverence and awe for God

- The newly baptized also receive virtues. (Note: teach only the three theological virtues.) Virtues are habits of doing good. These are gifts from God that help man to serve Him better:
  Faith: to believe in God
  Hope: to trust in all the promises that God has made
  Charity: to love God, and to serve Him in our neighbor

Reinforce

1. Have the children take home p. 95 of the *Activity Book* (see *Teacher's Manual*, p. 297) and ask their parents for help in filling in the blanks about their Baptism.

2. Have the children research their patron saints (or ask their parents at home tonight) and then draw pictures of their saints.

3. Discuss with the children some ways of using the gifts of the Holy Spirit and living the virtues. You may want to use some or all of the questions on the facing page. Answers may vary.

Conclude

1. Ask the children to bring in pictures of their own Baptisms, to write their names on the back, and to be ready to talk about them in class.

2. Lead the students in thanking God for the gifts of the Holy Spirit and the virtues (itemizing them for review).

3. Sing "Sing praise to our Creator," *Adoremus Hymnal*, #500.

24 God Gives You His Life

"We were buried therefore with him by baptism into death,
so that as Christ was raised from the dead by the glory
of the Father, we too might walk in newness of life."

Romans 6:4

When Adam and Eve sinned, it meant that all the people born after him would have Adam's sin. It is called Original Sin because it was the first sin. You were born with Original Sin on your soul. This means that when you were born, there was none of God's life of grace in your soul. You were made for Baptism.

The Sacrament of Baptism washes away the guilt of Original Sin. When you are baptized, your soul is filled with the grace that Jesus won for you. It gives you God's life. That way you can reach Heaven.

Baptism makes you a child of God. And Baptism makes you a member of God's family, which is the Church.

Jesus wants all of us to share in His life and become children of God. Jesus said to His Apostles,

95

"Go and baptize all people." Like the Apostles, the priest is Jesus' helper. That is why the priest baptizes people.

When the priest baptizes a baby, he pours water on the baby's head and says, "I baptize you in the Name of the Father and of the Son and of the Holy Spirit." Now the baby is a child of God. Now the baby's soul is holy and pleasing to God.

Not everyone is baptized as a baby, but most people are. Ask your parents about your own Baptism. They can tell you all about when you were baptized. Maybe they even took a picture of your Baptism.

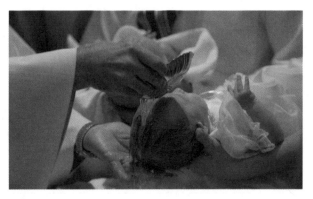

96

WHAT GIFT OR VIRTUE WOULD YOU USE?

1. You pray instead of watching T.V. (Fortitude)

2. You see God's love for you in your daily blessings. (Fear of the Lord, Wisdom)

3. You pray without distraction at Mass. (Piety)

4. You know God hears your prayers. (Faith)

5. You study your religion text. (Knowledge)

6. You want to avoid sin. (Fortitude, Counsel)

7. You look forward to Heaven. (Hope)

8. You bring food to an ill friend. (Charity)

9. You see the Church as doing God's work. (Wisdom, Faith)

10. You take time to say grace before meals. (Piety, Fear of the Lord)

11. You know Jesus is God because it is written in the Bible. (Faith)

12. You tell others to be good and to love God. (Counsel)

13. You accept your daily troubles. (Wisdom)

BAPTISM REGISTRY

In this book are officially recorded the names of the newly baptized who have become part of God's family. Some churches also include Confirmation dates, First Communion, marriages, and religious vows. See the book of names referred to in Revelation 3:5; 13:8.

Preview

In our next lesson, we will learn about the Rite of Baptism.

CHAPTER TWENTY-FOUR: GOD GIVES YOU HIS LIFE
LESSON FOUR: THE RITE OF BAPTISM

Aims

Students will learn about the Rite of Baptism.

They will be able to explain the symbolism and effects of this Sacrament.

They will better understand the Sacrament of Baptism.

Materials

- The Rite of Baptism

- A doll, water (baptismal font or pail of water with a dish from which to pour), a white garment, a candle, oil

- Pictures of the students' Baptisms

- *Activity Book*, p. 96

Optional:
- Have a priest come in to explain and demonstrate this Sacrament

- "Sing praise to our Creator," *Adoremus Hymnal*, #500

Begin

Ask the children if they have ever seen a Baptism. Tell the children that today they are going to learn about the Rite of Baptism and see a demonstration of it.

Take the children to the baptismal font of the church. If this is not possible, set up the classroom to demonstrate a Baptism.

Develop

1. Read paragraphs 5 and 6 with the students.

2. Demonstrate the Rite of Baptism (or have a priest do this). You can find the ceremony in The Rites of the Catholic Church, Volume One, a book most likely available in your parish or diocesan office. Be sure to ask questions frequently. For example: take the children to the baptismal font and ask them what is contained in it (water). Why does it contain water? (Here review the symbolism of water as learned in an earlier lesson.) Continue the Rite, doing the same for the white garment, the candle, and the oil.

3. Be sure to stress the minister, matter, and form of this Sacrament (see p. 255 of this manual).

Minister: Usually a priest, but in case of an emergency, anyone can baptize as long as the person being baptized has never previously been baptized, and the layman has the intent of the Church in mind.

Matter: Holy Water, although in case of an emergency any water will bring about the effect.

Form: While water is poured three times, or the person is immersed under the water three times, the minister says: "N., I baptize you in the Name of the Father, and of the Son, and of the Holy Spirit. *Amen.*"

4. Show the children Holy Water and tell them that Holy Water should remind Christians of their Baptism. Teach them to bless themselves with Holy Water, reverently making the Sign of the Cross. Tell them that making the Sign of the Cross should remind them of the mystery of the Blessed Trinity and of Jesus dying for the sins of man so that people could receive grace in Baptism.

5. Have the students do a "show and tell" of their Baptisms, and put the pictures they have brought in on a bulletin board for display.

Reinforce

1. Have the students draw a picture of the effects of Baptism on *Activity Book*, p. 96 (see *Teacher's Manual*, p. 297).

2. Separate the children into groups to review Questions 52 and 53, and have them begin memorizing Question 54.

Conclude

1. Have the children bless themselves with Holy Water, making the Sign of the Cross reverently (see *Teacher's Manual*, p. 367).

2. Sing "Sing praise to our Creator," *Adoremus Hymnal*, #500.

"Go and baptize all people." Like the Apostles, the priest is Jesus' helper. That is why the priest baptizes people.

When the priest baptizes a baby, he pours water on the baby's head and says, "I baptize you in the Name of the Father and of the Son and of the Holy Spirit." Now the baby is a child of God. Now the baby's soul is holy and pleasing to God.

Not everyone is baptized as a baby, but most people are. Ask your parents about your own Baptism. They can tell you all about when you were baptized. Maybe they even took a picture of your Baptism.

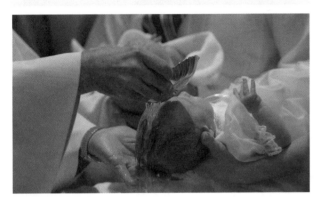

96

Q. 52 *How is Original Sin taken away?*
Original Sin is taken away by the Sacrament of Baptism (CCC 1263).

Q. 53 *What is Baptism?*
Baptism is the Sacrament that makes us followers of Christ, sons of God, and members of His Church (CCC 1213).

Q. 54 *What is a Sacrament?*
A Sacrament is an outward sign made by Christ to give grace (CCC 774, 1131).

"For just as the body is one and has many members, and all the members of the body, though many, are one body, so it is with Christ. For by one Spirit we were all baptized into one body..."
1 Corinthians 12:12–13

97

BAPTISMAL FONTS

In the Early Church, most baptisms, like Christ's, took place in a natural body of water. Indoor Baptism, performed for the sake of privacy and solemnity, soon became the norm. Reverence for the water, which came to receive a special blessing by the priest, led to the construction of basins or fonts for the baptismal ceremony, and eventually, for the preservation of the water. Many fonts were built in an octagonal shape, the eight sides representing the eighth day, i.e., the Resurrection. The fonts were placed at the entrances of churches to symbolize the catechumens' entrance into the Church. Typically made of stone, metal is also an acceptable material. Upright fonts soon became more popular than full immersion basins.

THREE TYPES OF BAPTISM

Water: Through the Rite of Baptism

Desire: Being willing but physically unable to reach a priest for Baptism

Blood: Being martyred for Christ before Baptism by water is possible

VALUABLE RESOURCE

The Rites of the Catholic Church as revised by the Second Vatican Ecumenical Council, Volume One; The Liturgical Press, Collegeville, Minnesota, 1990.

Preview

In our next lesson, we will be quizzed in order to review the materials we have covered this week in class. There will be a unit test, also.

CHAPTER TWENTY-FOUR: GOD GIVES YOU HIS LIFE
REVIEW AND ASSESSMENT

Aims

To review and assess the students' knowledge of the materials taught in this chapter.

Materials

- Appendix, p. B-1
- Quiz 24 (Appendix, p. A-29)
- "Sing praise to our Creator," *Adoremus Hymnal*, #500

Review and Enrichment

Play a review game with the children (see Appendix, p. B-1). Be sure to cover:
- Christ's institution of the Sacrament of Baptism
- The symbolism of the water, the white garment, the oil, and the candle
- The effects of Baptism
- The matter, form, and minister of Baptism

Name: _____

God Gives You His Life   Quiz 24

Fill in the blanks. *Trace the gray letters and fill in the rest.*

Word Bank

all	sin	grace	God	water

1. Jesus said to baptize *all* people.

2. We are baptized with *water* .

3. Baptism washes away *sin* .

4. Baptism gives us *grace* .

5. Baptism makes me a child of *God* .

Faith and Life Series • Grade 1 • Appendix A   *A-29*

Assess

1. Hand out the quiz, and read through it with the children. Answer any questions that they have. Orally quiz each child on the memorization questions as they hand in their quiz (see *Teacher's Manual*, p. 295).

2. Once the children have completed the quiz, review the correct answers with the class.

Conclude

End by praying a Glory Be and singing "Sing praise to our Creator," *Adoremus Hymnal*, #500.

CHAPTER TWENTY-FOUR: GOD GIVES YOU HIS LIFE
ACTIVITY BOOK ANSWER KEYS

Name:_____

Can you answer the following questions?

1. When you were born, did you have Original Sin?
   Yes

2. Where did you get the Original Sin?
   From Adam and Eve

3. When you were born, did you have grace in your soul?
   No

4. What washes away the guilt of Original Sin?
   The Sacrament of Baptism

5. What happened when you were baptized?
   My soul was filled with the grace that Jesus won for me.

6. Who won the grace for you that was put in your soul?
   Jesus

7. How was the grace won for you?
   Jesus died and rose again.

8. After you were baptized, could you go to Heaven?
   Yes

9. Are you happy that you were baptized?
   Yes

Faith and Life Series • Grade 1 • Chapter 24 • Lesson 1   93

Name:_____

**Baptism takes away Original Sin and gives us God's life!
Baptism fills us with grace and makes us children of God.**

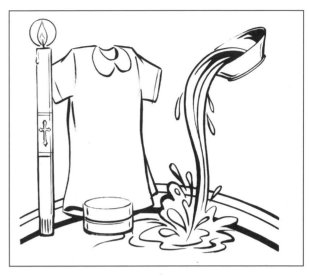

"I baptize you in the Name of the Father and of the Son and of the Holy Spirit. *Amen.*"

94   *Faith and Life Series • Grade 1 • Chapter 24 • Lesson 2*

Name:_____

My Baptism

My name is:

_____

I was baptized on (date?):

_____

I was baptized by (whom?):

_____

I was baptized at (church?):

_____

My godparents were:

_____

I wore:

_____

The priest poured/put me under:

_____

I was anointed with:

_____

I received:

_____

This is how my family celebrated:

_____

_____

Faith and Life Series • Grade 1 • Chapter 24 • Lesson 3   95

Name:_____

Draw a picture that shows that Baptism freed you from sin and opened the doors of Heaven to you!

96   *Faith and Life Series • Grade 1 • Chapter 24 • Lesson 4*

TEACHER'S NOTES

TEACHER'S NOTES

UNIT SIX TEST
CHAPTERS 21–24

> **CHAPTER TWENTY-ONE: JESUS GOES BACK TO HEAVEN**
>
> **CHAPTER TWENTY-TWO: THE HOLY SPIRIT COMES**
>
> **CHAPTER TWENTY-THREE: THE BLESSED TRINITY**
>
> **CHAPTER TWENTY-FOUR: GOD GIVES YOU HIS LIFE**

Aims

The students' understanding of the material covered in this unit will be reviewed and assessed.

Materials

• Unit 6 Test, Appendix, p. A-30

Assess

1. Distribute the unit tests and read through them with the students to be sure they understand the questions.

2. Administer the test.

3. After all the tests have been handed in, you may wish to review the correct answers with the class.

Name: _____

Unit 6 Test   **Chapter 21–24**

Number the event. *Put a 1 beside the first event, a 2 beside the second event, and so on.*

 2   Jesus rises from the dead.

 1   Jesus dies on the Cross.

 4   The Holy Spirit comes.

 3   Jesus goes up to Heaven.

Fill in the blanks with the same word.

1. At my Baptism, I became a child of _God_ .

2. There is only one _God_ .

TEACHER'S NOTES

TEACHER'S NOTES

CHAPTER TWENTY-FIVE
MANY GIFTS FROM GOD

Catechism of the Catholic Church References

Christ's Redemptive Death in God's Plan of Salvation: 599–605, 619–20

Christ Offered Himself to the Father for Our Sins: 606–18, 621–23

"Do this in memory of me": 1341–44, 1409

The Mass of all Ages: 1345–47, 1356–57

The Fruits of Holy Communion: 1391–1401, 1416

The Paschal Banquet: 1355, 1382–90

The Institution of the Eucharist: 1337–40

The Last Supper: 610–11, 621

Parts of the Mass: 1105–6, 1352–54, 1362–66

The Presence of Christ in the Eucharist: 1373–81, 1410

Reception of Communion: 1244, 1385–88

Signs of Bread and Wine in the Eucharist: 1333–36, 1412

Scripture References

The Road to Emmaus: Lk 24:13–32

Eucharistic Discourse: Jn 6:53–58

Man Shall Not Live by Bread Alone: Mt 4:4

Background Reading: *The Fundamentals of Catholicism* by Fr. Kenneth Baker, S.J.

Volume 2:

"Jesus' Sacrifice on the Cross," pp. 289–92

"What Do We Mean by 'Redemption'?", pp. 292–95

"Jesus Died Not for Himself but for All Men," pp. 295–98

Volume 3:

The Real Presence in the Blessed Sacrament, pp. 229–46

The Eucharist, pp. 247–56

The Mass as Sacrifice, pp. 256–70

"Each Mass Benefits All," pp. 271–73

Summary of Lesson Content

Lesson 1

God is all good.

God is Creator of all things: the world, and every person.

God sent His Son to be the Savior of the world so that man can share in God's life forever in Heaven.

Man receives grace in Baptism.

Lesson 3

Jesus appeared and spoke to two Apostles on the road to Emmaus.

The Liturgy of the Word and Liturgy of the Eucharist can be be seen in Christ's words on the way to Emmaus.

Lesson 2

Man is called to respond to God's gifts with thanksgiving and prayer.

People can thank God through prayer or good works.

This gratitude includes reverent behavior at Mass.

Lesson 4

Jesus is made present in the Eucharist through the act of Consecration said by a priest at Mass.

The matter of the Eucharist is bread and wine.

The form of the Eucharist is: "This is my Body"and "This is the chalice of my Blood."

Communion is a sacramental union with Jesus as He is consumed in the Eucharist.

Chapter Twenty-Five: Many Gifts from God
Lesson One: God's Gifts

Aims

Students will review that God is the giver of all good things, He Who gives out of love.

They will review and name some of God's gifts.

They will review the concept of grace: God's gift of His life in a soul.

Materials

• A wrapped present (full of small gifts, e.g., box of candy)

• *Activity Book*, p. 97

• Children's Bibles

Optional:
• "Father, we thank thee who hast planted," *Adoremus Hymnal*, #515

• Magazines, scissors, glue, poster board

Begin

Hold up a wrapped gift. Ask the students who gives presents. (all kinds of people) Why do they give presents? (out of love) Do they expect a present in return? (they should not, but a thank you is appropriate) What are the best kinds of presents? (answers will vary) Are presents always material things? (no, sometimes gifts are of time, and self) How should a person receive a present? (with thanks, gladness) Open the present you brought in, and give some to everyone. Explain that it is wonderful to share gifts too.

Develop

1. Read paragraph 1 of the textbook together as a class.

2. Discuss with the students some of God's many gifts to the world, to their families, and to them individually. Be sure to include material things, spiritual things, and personal qualities. Also stress how good all of God's gifts are.

3. Discuss God the Father's gift of His Son to the world: Christ's coming at Christmas and His example for us. Then discuss God the Son's gift of Himself on the Cross for the sins of man, and also His gift of self in the Eucharist at Mass. Finally, discuss the Father and Son's gift of the Holy Spirit for the life of the Church. Remind them of God's gift of His life, called grace, given first in Baptism, then in the other Sacraments.

4. Talk with the children about the response of thankfulness to a gift. Ask the children how they can show they are thankful (make a thank you card), or how they can tell someone how much they like the gift (praise, use the gift properly and take care of it; this is called stewardship). Share the gift with others (charity). You may discuss examples of thankfulness, praise, stewardship, and charity. For example:
   Thankfulness: Suzy thanked me for the candy I gave her.
   Praise: Johnny said he liked my new shoes.
   Stewardship: Billy takes very good care of the holy card I gave him.
   Charity: Sally shares her gift of singing with others.

Talk about how every person can show these responses to God for His gifts.

5. Ask the children what are some gifts they can offer God. A talent, their prayers, works of charity, etc. They should be able to name specific things.

Reinforce

1. Assign p. 97 of the *Activity Book* (see *Teacher's Manual*, p. 311), a class exercise to help students become familiar with using the Bible. You will need to provide Bibles for each student or group of students.

2. Lead the children in a simple litany of thanksgiving. Each student should say one thing he is thankful for, and all the children should respond with: "We thank you, God."

Conclude

1. Teach the children to sing an appropriate song, such as "Father, we thank thee who hast planted," *Adoremus Hymnal*, #515.

2. Review with the children this simple Morning Offering (from p. 133 of this manual):
   Dear Jesus, I give you my day and everything in it. Please keep me close to You, Your Mother Mary, and my guardian angel as I live today for Your glory. *Amen.*
(See also the version in Develop #6, p. 132.)

25   Many Gifts from God

"Man shall not live by bread alone, but by every word
that proceeds from the mouth of God."

Matthew 4:4

God has given you many gifts. He made you. He gave you a wonderful world in which to live. He gave you your family. God also sent His Son to be your Savior. And He gave you the gift of His life, called grace, in the Sacrament of Baptism.

Do you wonder how you can thank God for all He has given you? One of the best things you can do is to sit quietly at Mass and listen to and join in the prayers.

At every Mass we hear God's Word; God is speaking to us. We listen to a special message from God's book, which is called the Holy Bible. And we hear the Good News about Jesus from a part of the Bible called the **Gospel**.

Jesus is with us at Mass. He offers Himself to

99

God the Father at every Mass, just as He did on Good Friday. We can offer ourselves with Jesus, too.

At every Mass we should remember the Last Supper that Jesus had with the Apostles and how He changed the bread and wine into His Body and Blood. God has given priests the power to do what Jesus did. That is why the priest takes bread in his hands and says the words of Jesus:

"This is my Body"

and the bread becomes the Body of Jesus. Then the priest takes the cup of wine and says:

"This is the chalice of my Blood"

and the wine becomes the Blood of Jesus.

We do not see Jesus on the altar, but He is really there. Jesus is God and He can do anything.

Someday, you will be able to receive Jesus in Holy Communion. Then you will be closer to Him than ever before.

100

SAINT VINCENT DE PAUL

Saint Vincent was born around the year 1580 to poor parents in the village of Pouy, France. In 1596 he went to the University of Toulouse to study theology, and four years later he was ordained a priest. In a 1605 sea voyage he was captured by African pirates and carried to Tunis where he was a a slave for two years. After his providential escape from captivity he returned to France where he began to preach missions and to lay the foundations for a congregation which afterward became the Congregation of the Mission, the Lazarists. He was best known for his charity to all people. His feastday is September 27. He is patron of charitable societies.

Preview

In our next lesson, we will learn more about thankfulness and prayer.

Chapter Twenty-Five: Many Gifts from God
Lesson Two: Thank You, God

Aims

Students will learn that they should receive God's gifts lovingly, and respond with thanksgiving.

They will learn to thank God through actions and prayers.

They will become familiar with reverent behavior in church.

Materials

- A wrapped box

- *Activity Book*, p. 98

Optional:
- "Father, we thank thee who hast planted," *Adoremus Hymnal*, #515

- Arrange a visit to the church

Begin

Write the word "Eucharist" on the chalkboard. Ask the children if they know what this word means. Some may say the Blessed Sacrament, and this is true because the Eucharist is the Blessed Sacrament. *Eucharist* is also a Greek word for "thanksgiving," so the Mass is a great celebration of thanksgiving. In fact, it is the perfect prayer to God the Father. Today, the students will learn about how to be reverent in church, especially during Mass.

Develop

1. Have a child present you with a gift (the wrapped box), and give different responses by pretending:
   - it is something you do not like, and are not grateful
   - it is something you love, but are selfish
   - it is something you are bored with
   - it is something you need
   - it is something you love, and you are really grateful

2. Discuss with the students the best response (the last one). Why is it the best?

3. Ask the students what gift God gives at Mass. What is the best way to respond? How can a person respond? (through his words, actions, expressions, etc.)

4. How should people behave at Mass? Read paragraph 2 from the textbook for the answer.

5. Ask the children how they should prepare for Mass. What should they wear? How should they get ready at home? When they get to the church, what should they do? You may give them scenarios, such as the following: If you and your brother had a big fight, what should you do before Mass? (You should make up, not fight on the way to church, offer to pray for one another, etc.) Ask the children how they should handle different situations, such as having to go to the bathroom during Mass. (Go, and come back quickly and quietly.) What should they do if they cannot understand the readings? (They should pray, listen hard, and read them from the missalette.) What if a friend or sibling wants to speak with them during Mass? (They should kindly tell them to be quiet, and to pray.) What if they do not want to go to Mass? What if they are tired? (They should think about the great gifts God wants to offer them in the Mass, His love for them, and that He desires and deserves their love in return.)

Reinforce

1. Have the students answer the questions on p. 98 of the *Activity Book* (see *Teacher's Manual*, p. 311), which will require them to read the textbook for reinforcement. You may want to do this exercise together.

2. Have the children practice genuflecting, making the Sign of the Cross, and sitting in silence for personal prayer.

3. Have the children begin memorizing Questions 55 and 56.

4. Rehearse the responses to the parts of the Mass: i.e., The Lord be with you. And with your spirit.

Conclude

1. Lead the students in a prayer thanking God for the gift of the Mass, and have the children offer themselves to God by praying the Morning Offering (see two versions on p. 133 of this manual).

2. Sing "Father, we thank thee who hast planted, *Adoremus Hymnal*, #515.

25   Many Gifts from God

"Man shall not live by bread alone, but by every word
that proceeds from the mouth of God."

Matthew 4:4

God has given you many gifts. He made you.
He gave you a wonderful world in which to live. He
gave you your family. God also sent His Son to be
your Savior. And He gave you the gift of His life,
called grace, in the Sacrament of Baptism.

Do you wonder how you can thank God for all
He has given you? One of the best things you can do
is to sit quietly at Mass and listen to and join in the
prayers.

At every Mass we hear God's Word; God is
speaking to us. We listen to a special message from
God's book, which is called the Holy Bible. And we
hear the Good News about Jesus from a part of the
Bible called the **Gospel**.

Jesus is with us at Mass. He offers Himself to

God the Father at every Mass, just as He did on Good
Friday. We can offer ourselves with Jesus, too.

At every Mass we should remember the Last
Supper that Jesus had with the Apostles and how He
changed the bread and wine into His Body and Blood.
God has given priests the power to do what Jesus did.
That is why the priest takes bread in his hands and
says the words of Jesus:

"This is my Body"

and the bread becomes the Body of Jesus. Then the
priest takes the cup of wine and says:

"This is the chalice of my Blood"

and the wine becomes the Blood of Jesus.

We do not see Jesus on the altar, but He is really
there. Jesus is God and He can do anything.

Someday, you will be able to receive Jesus in
Holy Communion. Then you will be closer to Him
than ever before.

Word to Know:

Gospel

> **Q. 55** *What happens during Mass?*
> During the Mass, Jesus comes to earth
> in the Eucharist. We remember the Last
> Supper, His sacrifice, and His death on the
> Cross (CCC 1365–67).
>
> **Q. 56** *Why has Christ given Himself to us in the
> Holy Eucharist?*
> Christ has given Himself to us in the Holy
> Eucharist to be the life and food of our
> souls (CCC 1384).

We Pray:

Jesus, please come to me soon. I want so
much to receive You. *Amen.*

*"Truly, truly, I say to you, unless you eat the flesh of
the Son of man and drink his blood, you have no life
in you; he who eats my flesh and drinks my blood has
eternal life, and I will raise him up at the last day...."*
John 6:53–54

MENDICANT ORDERS

Religious in these orders, by their vow of poverty, rely on their work and the charity of others to survive. Their vow is not merely individual but it is also a community vow. Four great mendicant orders from the Middle Ages (the Order of Preachers, the Friars Minor, the Carmelites, and the Hermits of Saint Augustine) were recognized by the Second Council of Lyons in 1274. It is important to realize that often, receiving charity is in itself charitable, for items may be offered that are not desired. It is vital that a person recognize the hand of God, to trust that He will give what is needed, and always to thank Him for His gifts.

Preview

In our next lesson, we will learn about the unity of the Liturgy of the Word and the Liturgy of the Eucharist.

CHAPTER TWENTY-FIVE: MANY GIFTS FROM GOD
LESSON THREE: THE LITURGY

Aims

Students will learn about the Liturgy of the Word, the Liturgy of the Eucharist, and their relationship in the Mass.

They will hear about Jesus' appearance on the road to Emmaus.

Materials

• Children's Bible

• *Activity Book*, p. 99 with textbook

Optional:
• "Father, we thank thee who hast planted," *Adoremus Hymnal*, #515

Begin

Write the words "Liturgy of the Word" and "Liturgy of the Eucharist" on the chalkboard. Explain to the children that a Liturgy is public worship; it is the work of the Church. The Mass is made up of two parts: the Liturgy of the Word, and the Liturgy of the Eucharist. You will want to explain that the Liturgy of the Word is the part of the Mass with the readings from the Bible, "The Word of the Lord." The Liturgy of the Eucharist is the part of the Mass when Jesus becomes present in the Blessed Sacrament, the Word becomes flesh, and people receive Him in Holy Communion. See p. 229 of this manual for more details.

Develop

1. Read paragraphs 3 and 4 from the textbook.

2. Explain to the children that at the Last Supper, when Jesus instituted the Sacrament of the Eucharist, He and the Apostles had read Scripture before they celebrated the Eucharist because it was part of the Passover tradition. Just as Jesus gave us this example at the Last Supper, there is another example in Scripture. Explain to the children that after the Resurrection, Jesus appeared to some of His disciples on the road to Emmaus.

3. Read the story of Jesus and the disciples on the road to Emmaus (Lk 24:13–32). Discuss with the children what happened in this story. Jesus told the disciples how the Scriptures revealed what happened to Him and how He fulfilled the Old Testament. Then, after sharing the Word of God, Jesus broke bread with the disciples: He shared the Eucharist with them. They recognized Jesus in the breaking of the bread. They asked themselves, "Did not our hearts burn within us while he talked to us?" They knew God in the Word of Scripture, and in the Eucharistic sacrifice.

4. Explain to the children that at the Last Supper and on the road to Emmaus, there were two parts of the Mass: the Liturgy of the Word, and the Liturgy of the Eucharist. The readings from the Old Testament point to Jesus. The New Testament readings teach about Jesus and His Church. In the Mass, the work of Jesus is accomplished. His Good News is proclaimed, the Sacrifice of the Cross is made present on the altar, and Catholics share in His self-gift of love in the Eucharist, that is, in Holy Communion.

5. Teach the children that just as they communicate by what they say and what they do (i.e., how they respond to God at Mass), God communicates His love in what is said (Liturgy of the Word) and done (Sacrifice of the Altar) at Mass.

Reinforce

Have the children complete p. 99 in the *Activity Book* (see *Teacher's Manual*, p. 311). This long exercise incorporates the rest of the chapter and reinforces the text materials as they reread it to fill in the blanks. It is a good preparation for the following lesson.

Conclude

1. Lead the students in a prayer, asking God to help them to better understand the Liturgy of the Word and the Liturgy of the Eucharist. The children may add their own intentions.

2. Sing "Father, we thank thee who hast planted," *Adoremus Hymnal*, #515.

25   Many Gifts from God

*"Man shall not live by bread alone, but by every word
that proceeds from the mouth of God."*

Matthew 4:4

God has given you many gifts. He made you.
He gave you a wonderful world in which to live. He
gave you your family. God also sent His Son to be
your Savior. And He gave you the gift of His life,
called grace, in the Sacrament of Baptism.

Do you wonder how you can thank God for all
He has given you? One of the best things you can do
is to sit quietly at Mass and listen to and join in the
prayers.

At every Mass you hear God's Word; God is
speaking to us. We listen to a special message from
God's book, which is called the Holy Bible. And we
hear the Good News about Jesus from a part of the
Bible called the **Gospel**.

Jesus is with us at Mass. He offers Himself to

99

God the Father at every Mass, just as He did on Good
Friday. We can offer ourselves with Jesus, too.

At every Mass we should remember the Last
Supper that Jesus had with the Apostles and how He
changed the bread and wine into His Body and Blood.
God has given priests the power to do what Jesus did.
That is why the priest takes bread in his hands and
says the words of Jesus:

"This is my Body"

and the bread becomes the Body of Jesus. Then the
priest takes the cup of wine and says:

"This is the chalice of my Blood"

and the wine becomes the Blood of Jesus.

We do not see Jesus on the altar, but He is really
there. Jesus is God and He can do anything.

Someday, you will be able to receive Jesus in
Holy Communion. Then you will be closer to Him
than ever before.

100

Word to Know:

Gospel

Q. 55   *What happens during Mass?*
During the Mass, Jesus comes to earth
in the Eucharist. We remember the Last
Supper, His sacrifice, and His death on the
Cross (CCC 1365–67).

Q. 56   *Why has Christ given Himself to us in the
Holy Eucharist?*
Christ has given Himself to us in the Holy
Eucharist to be the life and food of our
souls (CCC 1384).

We Pray:

Jesus, please come to me soon. I want so
much to receive You. *Amen.*

*"Truly, truly, I say to you, unless you eat the flesh of
the Son of man and drink his blood, you have no life
in you; he who eats my flesh and drinks my blood has
eternal life, and I will raise him up at the last day...."*

John 6:53–54

101

LITURGY

This is public worship or a service done in the name
of, or on behalf of, the people. Through the Liturgy,
Christ the high priest continues the work of our
redemption and salvation.

ADDITIONAL RESOURCES

For the students:
Know Him in the Breaking of the Bread by Fr.
Francis Randolph, Ignatius Press. This book
explains the ceremonies of the Mass and their
meaning for lay people, including the young.

For the teacher:
Ceremonies of the Modern Roman Rite by Msgr.
Peter Elliott, Ignatius Press, 1995. This contains
the Rites of the Eucharist and Liturgy of the Hours.

Liturgical Question Box by Msgr. Peter Elliott,
Ignatius Press, 1998. This work examines and
answers some common questions about the celebration of the Mass and the Sacraments.

Preview

In our next lesson, we will learn about the Consecration of
the Eucharist during Mass.

CHAPTER TWENTY-FIVE: MANY GIFTS FROM GOD
LESSON FOUR: JESUS MADE PRESENT

Aims

Students will learn that the priest has power to consecrate the Eucharist.

They will review that for Jesus to be present, the priest must say the words of Jesus over the bread and wine.

They will learn that Jesus is really and truly present and that when a Catholic receives Him in Communion, Jesus lives in that person.

Materials

- Children's Bible
- *Activity Book*, p. 100
- Take the children to Mass or have a priest visit to explain the Consecration

Optional:
- "Father, we thank thee who hast planted," *Adoremus Hymnal*, #515

Begin

Review the parts of the Mass with the children: the Liturgy of the Word and the Liturgy of the Eucharist. Tell them that just as in Baptism, there is a minister (priest), matter (bread and wine), and form (the words of Christ) for the Sacrament of the Eucharist. They will learn more about this today.

Develop

1. Finish the chapter by reading paragraphs 5, 6, and 7 aloud with the class.

2. Discuss with the students the power of the priesthood. Jesus gave this power to His Apostles, who have passed it on to all priests. What is this power? To do Jesus' works, including to change bread and wine into the Body and Blood of Jesus. Ask the children if you could change the bread and wine into Jesus' Body and Blood? (No, you do not have that power, you are not a priest.) Could a priest change fruit and milk into the Body and Blood of Jesus? (No, it must be bread and wine.)

3. Can a priest change bread and wine into the Body and Blood of Jesus if he makes up his own words, such as, "Hocus Pocus, You're now Jesus!" (No, the priest must say the words of Jesus as He said them on Holy Thursday.)

4. Jesus becomes present in the Eucharist when the priest, who has received the power through his ordination, says the words of Jesus, "This is my Body," and "This is the chalice of my Blood" over the bread and wine. The priest at Mass is acting in the person of Christ, saying and doing what Jesus did at the Last Supper. Only then does Jesus become present on the altar under the apprearances of bread and wine.

5. Emphasize that Jesus becomes really and truly present, Body, Blood, Soul, and Divinity. In every Host, in every part of the Host, and in the chalice, in every drop of the Precious Blood, He is entirely present.

6. When a person receives Jesus in Holy Communion, Jesus comes to live in him, and He shares a special love with him. He is closer to Jesus than ever before! Ask the children if they are excited to someday receive their Lord. Help them to understand what a great gift this is.

Reinforce

1. Assign p. 100 of their *Activity Book* (see *Teacher's Manual*, p. 311), a coloring page on the Eucharist.

2. Have the children work in pairs to memorize Questions 55 and 56. Have them also review and memorize the minister, matter, and form of the Sacrament of the Eucharist.

Conclude

1. Pray the prayer on p. 101 of the textbook: "Jesus, please come to me soon. I want so much to receive You. *Amen.*"

2. Attend Mass or arrange a visit from a priest to explain the Consecration of the Eucharist.

3. Sing "Father, we thank thee who hast planted," *Adoremus Hymnal*, #515.

God the Father at every Mass, just as He did on Good Friday. We can offer ourselves with Jesus, too.

At every Mass we should remember the Last Supper that Jesus had with the Apostles and how He changed the bread and wine into His Body and Blood. God has given priests the power to do what Jesus did. That is why the priest takes bread in his hands and says the words of Jesus:

"This is my Body"

and the bread becomes the Body of Jesus. Then the priest takes the cup of wine and says:

"This is the chalice of my Blood"

and the wine becomes the Blood of Jesus.

We do not see Jesus on the altar, but He is really there. Jesus is God and He can do anything.

Someday, you will be able to receive Jesus in Holy Communion. Then you will be closer to Him than ever before.

100

Gospel

Q. 55 *What happens during Mass?*
During the Mass, Jesus comes to earth in the Eucharist. We remember the Last Supper, His sacrifice, and His death on the Cross (CCC 1365–67).

Q. 56 *Why has Christ given Himself to us in the Holy Eucharist?*
Christ has given Himself to us in the Holy Eucharist to be the life and food of our souls (CCC 1384).

We Pray:

Jesus, please come to me soon. I want so much to receive You. *Amen.*

"Truly, truly, I say to you, unless you eat the flesh of the Son of man and drink his blood, you have no life in you; he who eats my flesh and drinks my blood has eternal life, and I will raise him up at the last day...."
John 6:53–54

101

THE EUCHARISTIC DISCOURSE

"Truly, truly, I say to you, unless you eat the flesh of the Son of man and drink his blood, you have no life in you; he who eats my flesh and drinks my blood has eternal life, and I will raise him up at the last day. For my flesh is food indeed, and my blood is drink indeed. He who eats my flesh and drinks my blood abides in me, and I in him. As the living Father sent me, and I live because of the Father, so he who eats me will live because of me. This is the bread which came down from heaven, not such as the fathers ate and died; he who eats this bread will live for ever."
—John 6:53–58

CATHOLIC TEACHING

- The Eucharist is no longer bread and wine.
- Jesus is only under the appearance of bread and wine.
- The Eucharist is the Real Presence.
- Christ's presence remains.
- He is present in every part of the Eucharist, even if the Host is broken.
- The chalice and Host each contain the entire true presence of Christ.

HERESIES ABOUT THE EUCHARIST

Consubstantiation: The bread and wine remain as bread and wine with Jesus inside of them.

Symbolism: The Eucharist is only a symbol and not the Real Presence.

Temporary: The Real Presence eventually leaves and the Eucharist becomes bread and wine again.

Preview

In our next lesson, we will review the materials we have learned this week.

CHAPTER TWENTY-FIVE: MANY GIFTS FROM GOD
REVIEW AND ASSESSMENT

Aims

To review and assess the students on their knowledge of the materials covered this week.

Materials

- Quiz 25 (Appendix, p. A-31)
- "Father we thank thee who hast planted," *Adoremus Hymnal,* #515

Review and Enrichment

1. Discuss with the children God's many gifts:
   - Creation
   - Life
   - Grace
   - Jesus, the Savior
   - The Mass
   - The Bible
   - The Eucharist
   - Priests
   - His love

2. Remind the children of the two main parts of the Mass: The Liturgy of the Word and the Liturgy of the Eucharist.

3. Review with the students how they should prepare for Mass, behave at Mass, and participate in Mass.

4. Ask the children to name for you the minister, the matter, and the form of the Sacrament of the Eucharist.

Name: _____

Many Gifts from God   Quiz 25

Fill in the blanks. *Trace the gray letters and fill in the rest.*

Word Bank

| This | Word | Bible | my | wine |

1. We hear God's W o r d at Mass.

2. The Gospel is the part of the B i b l e that tells the Good News about Jesus.

3. The priest says, " T h i s is my Body."

4. He also says, "This is the chalice of m y Blood."

5. The bread and w i n e become the Body and Blood of Jesus.

Assess

1. Distribute the quiz, and read through it with the children, answering any questions they may have.

2. As the children hand in their quizzes, orally quiz them on Questions 55 and 56 from the textbook (see *Teacher's Manual,* p. 309). If time permits, review the correct answers with the students.

Conclude

Say the prayer to Jesus found on p. 101 of the student text, or close by singing "Father, we thank thee who hast planted," *Adoremus Hymnal,* #515.

Name:_____

The Bible

Find each of the items in the list below using your Bible. Show a friend and have him write his name beside each item to show that you found it.

The Old Testament: _____

The New Testament: _____

The Gospels: _____

The Book of Matthew: _____

The Book of Mark: _____

The Book of Luke: _____

The Book of John: _____

Faith and Life Series • Grade 1 • Chapter 25 • Lesson 1   97

Name:_____

Circle the right answer.

1. When I go to church, I should genuflect when getting in and out of my pew. (YES) NO

2. When I am in Mass, I should talk to my friends and family.   YES (NO)

3. When I go to Mass, I should listen to the readings. (YES) NO

4. When I go to church, I should sit still and be quiet. (YES) NO

5. When I go to church, I should pray. (YES) NO

6. When I go to Mass, I should receive Communion even though I have not made my First Communion. YES (NO)

7. When I go to Mass, I should go up for a blessing until I have made my First Communion. (YES) NO

8. When I go to Mass, I should sing along with the choir. (YES) NO

9. When I go to Mass, I know when the bread and wine become the Body and Blood of Jesus. (YES) NO

98   *Faith and Life Series • Grade 1 • Chapter 25 • Lesson 2*

Name:_____

Fill in the blanks using Chapter 25 of your textbook.

One of the best things you can do is sit <u>quietly</u> at Mass and listen to and join in the <u>prayers</u>.

At every Mass we hear God's <u>Word</u>, God is speaking to us.   We listen to a special <u>message</u> from God's book, which is called the <u>Holy</u> <u>Bible</u>. And we hear the <u>Good</u> <u>News</u> about <u>Jesus</u> from a part of the Bible called the <u>Gospel</u>.

Jesus is with us at <u>Mass</u>. He offers <u>Himself</u> to God the <u>Father</u> at every Mass, just as He did on Good <u>Friday</u> . We can offer ourselves with Jesus too.

At every Mass, we should remember the <u>Last</u> <u>Supper</u> that Jesus had with the <u>Apostles</u> and how He changed the <u>bread</u> and <u>wine</u> into His <u>Body</u> and <u>Blood</u>. God has given <u>priests</u> the power to do what Jesus did.

When the priest takes bread in his hands and says "This is my <u>Body</u>" it becomes the Body of Jesus. And when he takes the cup of wine in his hands and says "This is the chalice of my <u>Blood</u>" it becomes the Blood of Jesus. We do not see <u>Jesus</u> on the <u>altar</u>, but He is really there. Jesus is <u>God</u> and He can do anything.

Faith and Life Series • Grade 1 • Chapter 25 • Lesson 3   99

Name:_____

When we receive the Body of Jesus, He lives in us and gives us grace.

Jesus, please come to me soon.
I want so much to receive You.
Amen.

100   *Faith and Life Series • Grade 1 • Chapter 25 • Lesson 4*

TEACHER'S NOTES

CHAPTER TWENTY-SIX
OUR MOTHER, MARY

Catechism of the Catholic Church References

The Assumption: 966, 974
Devotion to the Blessed Virgin: 971
The Immaculate Conception: 491–92
Mary's Intercession: 969, 975
Mary as an Eschatological Icon of the Church: 972, 975
Mary as Our Mother: 963–70

Mary in God's Plan: 488–93, 508
Mary's Divine Motherhood: 495, 509
Prayer in Union with Mary: 2673–79, 2682
Prayer of Intercession: 2634–36, 2647
Sacrifice: 2099–2100

Scripture References

Interceding Queen Mother: 1 Kings 2:13–20
The Wedding Feast of Cana: Jn 2:1–11

Jesus Gives Mary to Be Our Mother: Jn 19:26–27
The Queen of Heaven: Rev 12:1

Background Reading: *The Fundamentals of Catholicism* by Fr. Kenneth Baker, S.J.

Volume 2:
"Church Teaching about Mary, the Mother of God,"
pp. 315–17
"Mary Is a Gift of God," pp. 318–20
Mary, Immaculate and Full of Grace, pp. 321–36
The Motherhood of God, pp. 337–56

Mary, Our Mother and Mediatrix, pp. 356–68
The Assumption of Mary, pp. 368–75
"Hail, Holy Queen," pp. 375–78
"Mary Is Our Sure Way to Christ," pp. 378–81
"The Immaculate Heart of Mary," pp. 381–84
"Mary, Mother of the Church," pp. 385–87

Summary of Lesson Content

Lesson 1

The Blessed Virgin Mary is the Mother of God.

Jesus gave Mary to all people to be their Mother by the order of grace.

Mary was assumed (body and soul) into Heaven. The Assumption is the fourth Glorious Mystery of the Rosary.

Mary is the Immaculate Conception.

Lesson 2

Mary is a model of faithful discipleship.

Mary is an intercessor between Jesus and man.

Lesson 3

Jesus is the King of Heaven and earth.

In the Old Testament, the mother of the king is the queen. Using this model, Mary is the Queen of Heaven and earth.

The fifth Glorious Mystery of the Rosary is the Coronation of Mary as Queen of Heaven, earth, angels, and men.

Lesson 4

Mary appeared to children at Fatima.

At Fatima she asked the children to make sacrifices.

We will learn about this apparition, approved by the Church.

Chapter Twenty-Six: Our Mother, Mary
Lesson One: Mary, Mother of God

Aims

Students will learn that Mary is the Mother of God, for she is the Mother of Jesus, Who is God.

They will learn that Jesus gave Mary to all people to be their Mother.

They will learn about Mary's Immaculate Conception and her Assumption into Heaven. The Assumption is the fourth Glorious Mystery.

Materials

- Statue of Mary

- Rosaries

- Children's Bible

- *Activity Book*, p. 101

Optional:
- Appendix, p. B-31, The Assumption

- "Immaculate Mary," *Adoremus Hymnal*, #532

Begin

Prepare a marian shrine in your classroom with a statue of Mary, flowers, and rosaries for all the children. Begin the class by praying the Hail Mary. Ask the children to repeat: "Holy Mary, Mother of God." Ask them what it means. Help them to understand that Mary is the Mother of Jesus, and Jesus is God the Son; therefore, Mary is the Mother of God.

Develop

1. Read paragraph 1 aloud. Ask the children if they know when Jesus gave Mary to be the Mother of all people.

2. To answer this question, read John 19:26–27a from the children's Bible. Explain that in this passage John represents all people. Jesus wanted everyone on earth to have Mary as his Mother because He loves everyone so much. Mary, too, loves all people very much.

3. Ask the children if they remember Eve from the Garden of Eden. She is mother of all who were created; her name means "mother of all the living." Mary is called the New Eve, for she is the Mother of all who have life because of Jesus her son.

4. When a person is baptized, he becomes a child of God. Being a child of God means that God is his Father, Jesus is his brother, and Jesus' Mother, Mary, becomes his Mother too.

5. Ask the children to think of John standing under the Cross with Mary. Jesus gave Mary to John to be his Mother. How do they think John responded? Read John 19:27b: "And from that hour the disciple took her to his own home."

6. Remind the children that Mary had a very special role in God's plan (Chapter 9, Lesson 1; see pp. 102 and 103 in this manual). God saved her from Original Sin. This is a unique gift for Mary. Every other person has Original Sin from a time before he is born. Mary never had it. This gift is called the "Immaculate Conception."

7. Mary received another special gift because she was without sin, and so faithful to God: she went to Heaven with her body and soul. This gives Christians hope because someday, at the end of time, everyone's body will join his soul in Heaven, just like Mary.

Reinforce

1. Have the children open to p. 101 of the *Activity Book* (see *Teacher's Manual*, p. 323), read the directions with them, and have them color the picture of Mary. You may want to reward them with a sticker or holy card for each day the child says his prayers, or for a complete week of prayers.

2. Have the students memorize Question 57 (see *Teacher's Manual*, p. 321).

3. If they have been working on their Rosary booklets, you may want to pass out copies of Appendix, p. B-31, The Assumption, for the children to color at this time.

Conclude

1. You may lead the children in praying the fourth Glorious Mystery of the Rosary, The Assumption.

2. Or you may lead the children in praying the Litany to Mary found on p. 105 of the text (see *Teacher's Manual*, p. 321).

3. Close by teaching and singing "Immaculate Mary," *Adoremus Hymnal*, #532.

26   Our Mother, Mary

"Then he said to the disciple,
'Behold, your mother!'"

John 19:27

Before Jesus went back to His heavenly Father, He left us a special gift. He gave us His Mother for our very own! From her place in Heaven she watches over you with so much love.

You can ask your Blessed Mother to pray for you when you need help. She will pray to God for you. She will help you to get to Heaven.

Jesus is the King of Heaven. Mary is the **Queen of Heaven**. Mary is the Queen of all the angels and all the saints.

Mary is the special friend of children. She has asked all boys and girls to pray and make **sacrifices** so that there will be peace in the world. A sacrifice is when a person goes without something, out of love for God.

103

THE ASSUMPTION = THE DORMITION

This dogma was declared ex cathedra (see p. 241 of this manual) in 1950 by Pope Pius XII in his encyclical *Munificentissimus Deus*: "Finally the Immaculate Virgin, preserved from all stain of original sin, when the course of her earthly life was finished, was taken up body and soul into heavenly glory, and exalted by the Lord as Queen over all things, so that she might be the more fully conformed to her Son, the Lord of lords and conqueror of sin and death" as quoted in the *Catechism of the Catholic Church*, #966. Because there is no declaration regarding her death, the Orthodox Church calls this the Dormition, for they believe Mary merely fell asleep before being assumed into Heaven (see also p. 233 of this manual).

THE IMMACULATE CONCEPTION

This dogma was declared ex cathedra in 1854 by Pope Pius IX in his encyclical *Ineffabilis Deus*: "The Most Blessed Virgin Mary was, from the first moment of her conception, by a singular grace and privilege of almighty God and by virtue of the merits of Jesus Christ, Savior of the human race, preserved immune from all stain of original sin" as quoted in the *Catechism of the Catholic Church*, 491. (See also p. 103 of this manual and *CCC* 492.)

THEOTOKOS

Theotokos is a Greek word that means "Mother of God." The Council of Ephesus used it in 431 to explain and defend that Mary is Mother of Christ even in His divine nature.

THE ASSUMPTION
Catechism of the Catholic Church 966, 974

Preview

In our next lesson, we will learn about Mary as our advocate and intercessor.

315

CHAPTER TWENTY-SIX: OUR MOTHER, MARY
LESSON TWO: PRAY FOR US SINNERS

Aims

Students will learn that they can turn to Mary for help and ask for her prayers.

They will understand that Mary is a good example for all people.

Materials

• Pictures of mothers and children

• Children's Bible

• *Activity Book*, p. 102

Optional:
• "Immaculate Mary," *Adoremus Hymnal*, #532

Begin

Display pictures of mothers and children, then ask the students what mothers do for them:
  • They give them what they need to live. (Mary prays to God to give them what they need, most importantly to give them grace.)
  • They love them. (Mary loves and watches over them from Heaven.)

  • They help them to make good decisions. (Mary is a good example for making decisions that please God.)
  • They listen to their stories. (Mary likes to hear their prayers.)
Now ask the children how Mary can be their Mother, and emphasize how she is a real Mother, and that the most important thing she does is pray for them.

Develop

1. Read paragraphs 1 and 2 from the textbook. Emphasize the fact that Mary watches over all people, including the students. She will pray for the children if they ask her to, and she will help them to reach Heaven.

2. Ask the students to name the two special graces Mary received. (They learned about these in the last lesson: the Immaculate Conception and the Assumption.) Explain that Mary was born without Original Sin, and that she never sinned in her entire life. She never said no to God. God rewarded her for her faithfulness by taking her to Heaven body and soul. She is a model for everyone.

3. Explain to the children that now that Mary is in Heaven, she can help people on earth in a special way. Jesus loves Mary so very much that if she asks Him for something for someone that is for that person's good, He will give it to her.

4. Read the passage of the wedding feast at Cana (Jn 2:1–11), and emphasize the role of Mary. She is praying to Jesus on behalf of others, and though it was not Jesus' time, He did the miracle because Mary asked Him.

5. Tell the children that they can ask Mary to pray for them, and ask favors for themselves as well. This is called intercession. Mary is an intercessor. In this way, she is their helper and she prays that they do only those things that are pleasing to God.

6. Stress that at the wedding of Cana, Mary said, "Do whatever he tells you." Mary was obedient and taught obedience to her Son. She is a model of discipleship for those who follow Jesus.

Reinforce

1. Have the children color the picture of the Assumption found on p. 102 of the *Activity Book* (see *Teacher's Manual*, p. 323).

2. Using the pictures in the Rosary booklets to aid in meditation, ask the children to think of Mary's life, especially in the Mysteries that they have learned: the Annunciation, the Visitation, the Nativity, the Presentation, and the Finding of Jesus. Think about how they can learn from her.

3. Pair the children off to work on Question 57 (see *Teacher's Manual*, p. 321).

Conclude

1. Pray the Hail Mary together as a class, either from the *Activity Book*, or p. 104 of the text (see *Teacher's Manual*, p. 323 or p. 321).

2. You may also pray a decade of the Rosary as a class; this is Mary's prayer.

3. Close with a verse of "Immaculate Mary," *Adoremus Hymnal*, #532.

26   Our Mother, Mary

"Then he said to the disciple,
'Behold, your mother!'"

John 19:27

Before Jesus went back to His heavenly Father, He left us a special gift. He gave us His Mother for our very own! From her place in Heaven she watches over you with so much love.

You can ask your Blessed Mother to pray for you when you need help. She will pray to God for you. She will help you to get to Heaven.

Jesus is the King of Heaven. Mary is the **Queen of Heaven**. Mary is the Queen of all the angels and all the saints.

Mary is the special friend of children. She has asked all boys and girls to pray and make **sacrifices** so that there will be peace in the world. A sacrifice is when a person goes without something, out of love for God.

103

THE BROWN SCAPULAR: OUR LADY'S GARMENT

The brown scapular is a miniature model of the Carmelite Order's religious habit. Tradition holds that in the 13th century, our Lady appeared to Saint Simon Stock (see p. 319 of this manual), Superior General of the Order, and gave him the brown scapular. She told him that whoever wore it would be preserved from eternal damnation and that on the first Saturday after his death, she would take that person to Heaven. A person must be enrolled, or "invested," in the scapular in a special ceremony at which a priest presides. Our Lady of Mount Carmel's feast day is July 16.

THE PROMISE OF THE BROWN SCAPULAR

"Whoever dies wearing this scapular shall not suffer eternal fire."

The brown scapular (there are nearly twenty approved types of scapulars) is a sacramental, that is, a sacred sign resembling a Sacrament and by means of which spiritual effects are obtained through the prayers of the Church. The promise attached to the scapular is contingent on living a chaste life.

CARMELITE SAINTS

Some Carmelite saints are Saint Teresa of Avila, Saint John of the Cross, Saint Thérèse of Lisieux, Saint Teresa Benedicta (Edith Stein). Blessed Titus Brandsma and Blessed Elizabeth of the Trinity are two Carmelite blesseds.

Preview

In our next lesson, we will learn about Mary as Queen of Heaven and earth.

Chapter Twenty-Six: Our Mother, Mary
Lesson Three: Hail Holy Queen!

Aims

Students will learn that Mary is the Queen of Heaven and earth.

They will learn the fifth Glorious Mystery of the Rosary, the Coronation.

Materials

- Children's Bible
- *Activity Book*, p. 103

Optional:
- "Immaculate Mary," *Adoremus Hymnal*, #532

Begin

Have the children turn to p. 102 in their text and ask the following questions:
- What is happening? (a coronation ceremony)
- Who is receiving a crown? Why? (Mary, because she is Queen)
- Who is giving her this crown? (the Blessed Trinity)
- What do we call a woman who wears a crown? (queen)
- What does a queen do? (sits on a throne by the king)
- Of what places is Mary the Queen? (Heaven and earth)
- If Mary is Queen, Who is King? (Jesus Christ)
- If Mary is the Queen, and we are her children, what are we? (heirs to the Kingdom of God)

Develop

1. Read aloud 1 Kings 2:13–20 from the children's Bible. This passage from Scripture shows clearly that the king's mother was queen of the country. She had a very important role, even in this passage, for the king had a throne brought in for her to sit upon. He listened to her advice and said he would not deny her. Mary is the Mother of Jesus the King. He will listen to her requests and will not deny her, if what she asks for is good.

2. Read paragraph 3. Explain that the coronation (crowning) of Mary is a mystery meditated upon in the Rosary. Because Jesus is King of Heaven and earth, angels and saints, and Mary is His Mother, she is the Queen of Heaven and earth, of angels and saints, and of course, Queen of everyone on earth.

3. Read Revelations 12:1, which gives a visual image of such a queen: she is a woman clothed with the sun, with the moon at her feet and a crown of twelve stars.

4. Emphasize the fact that if Mary is everyone's Mother and the Queen, and if Jesus is everyone's brother and the King, those on earth are heirs to the Kingdom of God, which is Heaven. Ask the children what this means for them. How should they behave? How should they treat the Queen and King? How should they prepare to inherit the Kingdom?

5. Ask the children if they have ever seen a coronation ceremony, perhaps an old video of the crowning of British royalty. Ask if they have heard about one, maybe in a fairy tale. Explain that there is a lot of preparation: people wear their best clothes to the ceremony, they bring presents, they attend respectfully, and there is a great celebration. The ruler often takes an oath to God to be faithful, and they have great responsibility to help their people. Saints Elizabeth of Hungary and Bridget of Sweden were real royalty who loved God so much that they went to Heaven and became saints after their death.

Reinforce

1. Have the children answer the questions on p. 103 of their *Activity Book* (see *Teacher's Manual*, p. 323), which are based on the picture in the student text and your discussion in the Begin section.

2. If they have been working on their Rosary booklets, you may want to pass out copies of Appendix, p. B-32, The Coronation, for the children to color at this time.

Conclude

1. Lead the children in a crowning ceremony for Mary at the marian shrine in the classroom. The students may offer her flowers or prayers. They may gather flowers from outside, or make flowers or offering cards for the coronation ceremony, during which you may sing, "Immaculate Mary," *Adoremus Hymnal*, #532.

2. Or you may lead the children in praying the fifth Glorious Mystery of the Rosary, The Coronation of the Blessed Virgin Mary as Queen of Heaven, earth, angels, and men.

26   Our Mother, Mary

"Then he said to the disciple,
'Behold, your mother!'"

John 19:27

Before Jesus went back to His heavenly Father, He left us a special gift. He gave us His Mother for our very own! From her place in Heaven she watches over you with so much love.

You can ask your Blessed Mother to pray for you when you need help. She will pray to God for you. She will help you to get to Heaven.

Jesus is the King of Heaven. Mary is the **Queen of Heaven**. Mary is the Queen of all the angels and all the saints.

Mary is the special friend of children. She has asked all boys and girls to pray and make **sacrifices** so that there will be peace in the world. A sacrifice is when a person goes without something, out of love for God.

103

SAINT ELIZABETH OF HUNGARY

Saint Elizabeth, the daughter of Alexander II of Hungary, was born in 1207. In 1221, she married Louis of Thuringia, a good man who shared her love of virtue. Despite her royal position, she led an austere life, practiced penance, and devoted herself to works of charity. After Louis' death in the Crusades, Elizabeth left the court, made arrangements for her three children, and in 1228 she renounced the world to become a tertiary of Saint Francis. She died in 1231. Her feast day is November 17. She is the patroness of bakers, countesses, the death of children, the falsely accused, the homeless, nursing services, tertiaries, widows, and young brides.

SAINT SIMON STOCK

Little is known about Saint Simon Stock's early life, though the name "Stock," i.e., "tree trunk," derives from the fact that from age twelve he lived as a hermit in the hollow of an oak tree. He became a Carmelite and founded many Carmelite communities, specifically in the university towns of Cambridge, Oxford, Paris, and Bologna, and helped change the order from hermits to mendicants (see p. 305 of this manual). In 1254 he was elected Superior General of his Order at London. He became well known after a marian apparition in Cambridge, England, on July 16, 1251. During this time, the Carmelite Order was being oppressed. Our Lady appeared to him holding the brown scapular in one hand (see p. 317 of this manual).

If you say the Rosary faithfully until death, I do assure you that, in spite of the gravity of your sins "you shall receive a never-fading crown of glory."

—Saint Louis de Montfort

Preview

In our next lesson, we will learn about Mary's special love for children.

CHAPTER TWENTY-SIX: OUR MOTHER, MARY
LESSON FOUR: MARY APPEARS!

Aims

Students will learn about the Church-approved marian apparition at Fatima, Portugal, to three children, Lucia, Jacinta, and Francisco. Mary asked them to make sacrifices and to pray the Rosary. Two of the children have been beatified.

Materials

- Various images of Mary (*The Madonnas of Europe*, edited by Janusz Rosikon, Rosikon Press, Warsaw 2000, available through Ignatius Press)

- *Activity Book*, p. 104

Optional:
- "The Day the Sun Danced," video, CCC of America, available through Ignatius Press

- "Immaculate Mary," *Adoremus Hymnal*, #532

Begin

Show the children different images of Mary and tell them her titles portrayed in each one. Explain that Mary is loved all over the world. Mary has also appeared in different places; she has made visits from Heaven to help man better follow her Son. You may explain by giving an example using yourself, i.e., sometimes you are called by your first name, some- times by your last name, sometimes by your job, sometimes by your relationships, sometimes by where people have seen you (e.g., the lady I saw at the grocery store). The children should come to know that all the titles and images of Mary are for the same Mary, the Mother of God and our Mother.

Develop

1. Read paragraph 4 of the text aloud, then briefly outline the events of the Fatima apparitions (see p. 83 of this manual and the facing page) and Mary's call for sacrifice. Be sure to em- phasize that one of the children, Jacinta, was just six years old, their age, when our Lady first appeared to her.

2. Tell the students about the beatification of Francisco and Jacincta in 2000, and the Feast of Our Lady of Fatima (October 13). Beatification is the first step toward becoming a recognized and canonized saint. However, any person who is in Heaven is a saint, whether the Church has recognized him or not. (Lucia died in 2005.)

3. Explain that by doing what Mary asked of them, two of the children are now in Heaven. They were rewarded for their faithfulness to Jesus, as Mary had taught them to do.

4. Ask the students what sacrifices they can make. List them on the board. Help them understand that they can sacrifice big and little things. Teach them to offer up their sacrifices. Remind them about the morning offering.

5. You may want to show a video about Fatima and discuss it, such as "The Day the Sun Danced" by CCC of America.
   - What did Mary look like?
   - To whom did Mary appear?
   - What did Mary say to the children?
   - Did other people see Mary too?
   - Why did the children see Mary?
   - How did the children change after seeing Mary?
   - Which prayers did Mary ask them to say?
   - What does it mean to make sacrifices? What sacrifices did the children make?

6. You may explain that public revelation is the property of the entire Church and, if approved, must be believed in order to be saved (e.g., the doctrine of the Blessed Trinity, the Incarnation, the Eucharist); public revelation ended with the death of the last Apostle, John. Since then every revelation, such as an apparition, is considered private, and though they may be approved by the Church, they are never necessary for salvation, though the Church may encourage their practice or devotion for personal sanctity. Apparitions are never granted Church approval until they cease.

Reinforce

1. Assign p. 104 of the *Activity Book* (see *Teacher's Manual*, p. 323), Mary is my Mother. You may want to assist the students with this page.

2. If the children have not already finished coloring their Rosary booklets, give them some time to do so.

Conclude

1. Pray a decade of the Rosary; one of the Glorious Mys- teries would be most appropriate. Tell the children that the Fatima prayer (see p. 83 of this manual) may be added between the decades of the Rosary (after the Glory Be).

2. If you have not already done so, show the video "The Day the Sun Danced," the story of Our Lady of Fatima (available through Ignatius Press; 30 minutes).

3. Sing "Immaculate Mary," *Adoremus Hymnal*, #532.

26   Our Mother, Mary

*"Then he said to the disciple,
'Behold, your mother!'"*

John 19:27

Before Jesus went back to His heavenly Father, He left us a special gift. He gave us His Mother for our very own! From her place in Heaven she watches over you with so much love.

You can ask your Blessed Mother to pray for you when you need help. She will pray to God for you. She will help you to get to Heaven.

Jesus is the King of Heaven. Mary is the **Queen of Heaven**. Mary is the Queen of all the angels and all the saints.

Mary is the special friend of children. She has asked all boys and girls to pray and make **sacrifices** so that there will be peace in the world. A sacrifice is when a person goes without something, out of love for God.

103

Words to Know:

Queen of Heaven   sacrifice

> **Q. 57** *Who is Mary?*
> Mary is the Mother of Jesus and the Queen of Heaven, earth, angels, and men (CCC 501, 963, 966).

We Pray:

HAIL MARY

Hail Mary, full of Grace! The Lord is with thee.
Blessed art thou among women, and blessed
is the fruit of thy womb, Jesus.
Holy Mary, Mother of God, pray for us sinners,
now and at the hour of our death. *Amen.*

104

Litany to Mary

Let Us Pray:

Holy Mary...
Holy Mother of God...
Mother of divine grace...
Mother of our Savior...
Health of the sick...
Help of Christians...
Queen of angels...
Queen of prophets...
Queen of Apostles...
Queen of all saints...
Queen of peace...

Pray for us.

105

OUR LADY OF FATIMA

Our Lady appeared six times to three shepherd children (see p. 83 of this manual) between May 13 and October 13, 1917, near Fatima, Portugal. She asked the children to pray the Rosary daily, to wear the brown scapular, and to perform acts of sacrifice and reparation. The children were given a terrifying vision of Hell and, through Mary, predicted the fall of Russia from Christianity and the future outbreak of World War II. Our Lady asked that the faithful attend Mass on five consecutive first Fridays in her honor. She performed the Miracle of the Sun on October 13, 1917. May 13 is the feast of Our Lady of Fatima.

See also *Roses, Fountains, and Gold,* by John Martin, pp. 213–33, Ignatius Press, 1998.

Preview

In our next lesson, we will review the materials covered this week in class and take a quiz.

CHAPTER TWENTY-SIX: OUR MOTHER, MARY
REVIEW AND ASSESSMENT

Aims

To review and assess the students on their knowledge of the materials covered this week.

Materials

- Quiz 26 (Appendix, p. A-32)
- The Litany to Mary, p. 105 of the text
- "Immaculate Mary," *Adoremus Hymnal*, #532

Review and Enrichment

1. Review with the children what they have learned about Mary's presence in Scripture (note: they are not limited to this chapter): the wedding feast at Cana, the Annunciation, the Nativity, the Visitation, the Presentation, the Finding of Jesus in the Temple, standing beneath the Cross with John, etc.

2. Ask the children when Mary became our Mother. (Christ gave her to us from the Cross.)

3. Ask the children what it means to say:
- Mary is Queen of Heaven and earth.
- Mary is the Immaculate Conception.
- Mary was assumed into Heaven.
- Mary is an intercessor.

4. Have the children name some different titles for Mary: the Blessed Mother, the Immacualte Conception, Our Lady of Fatima, Our Lady of Lourdes, the New Eve, Mother of God, etc.

Name: _____

Our Mother Mary   Quiz 26

Yes or No. *Circle the correct answer.*

1. Is Mary the Mother of Jesus? (Yes)   No

2. Is Mary our Mother too? (Yes)   No

3. Is an angel the Queen of Heaven?   Yes   (No)

4. Is Mary the Queen of Heaven? (Yes)   No

Assess

1. Distribute the quiz and read through it with the children. Answer any questions they may have.

2. As the children hand in the quiz, you may want to have them individually recite the Hail Mary (see *Teacher's Manual*, p. 367). When all the quizzes have been turned in, review the correct answers with them.

Conclude

1. Say the Litany to Mary as a class (see *Teacher's Manual*, p. 321).

2. The class may also close by singing "Immaculate Mary," *Adoremus Hymnal*, #532.

Name:_____

Did you know that Jesus gave us His Mother to be our Mother too? We should take time with our Mother Mary. She wants to teach us how to pray.

This week, before bed, pray the Hail Mary. Put a check in the box each day you pray to your heavenly Mother.

Monday	Tuesday	Wednesday	Thursday	Friday	Saturday	Sunday

Faith and Life Series • Grade 1 • Chapter 26 • Lesson 1   101

Name:_____

The Assumption
Mary was assumed into Heaven, body and soul.

HAIL MARY

Hail Mary, full of grace! The Lord is with thee. Blessed art thou among women, and blessed is the fruit of thy womb, Jesus.
Holy Mary, Mother of God, pray for us sinners, now and at the hour of our death.
Amen.

102   *Faith and Life Series • Grade 1 • Chapter 26 • Lesson 2*

Name:_____

Answer the following questions using the picture on page 102 of your textbook.

1. Who is receiving a crown?
   Mary
2. Who is giving the crown to her?
   The Blessed Trinity
3. Upon what is she sitting?
   Choir of angels / clouds
4. What are in the clouds?
   Angels
5. What is God the Father wearing?
   Cloak
6. What is God the Son wearing?
   The same garment as the Father
7. What does the Holy Spirit look like?
   A Dove
8. What is happening in this picture?
   The Blessed Trinity is crowning Mary the Queen of Heaven and earth.

Faith and Life Series • Grade 1 • Chapter 26 • Lesson 3   103

Name:_____

Mary is my Mother
Write some ways in which Mary is our example.

Answers will vary. _____
_____
_____
_____

_____
_____
_____
_____

_____
_____
_____
_____

104   *Faith and Life Series • Grade 1 • Chapter 26 • Lesson 4*

TEACHER'S NOTES

corn

roar

more

pork

soar

store

soar

learn

CHAPTER TWENTY-SEVEN
FOLLOWING JESUS

Catechism of the Catholic Church References

Christ Calls Disciples: 542, 787
Christian Holiness: 2012–16, 2028–29
Forgiveness: 2842–45, 2862
Jesus, Model of Holiness: 468–69, 516, 519–21, 561
Jesus Teaches Us How to Pray: 2607–15, 2621
Mysteries of Jesus' Hidden Life: 531–34, 564
Our Participation in Christ's Sacrifice: 618
Pentecost: 731–41, 746–47, 767–68

Prayers of Blessing and Adoration: 2626–28, 2645
Prayers of Intercession: 2634–36, 2647
Prayers of Petition: 2629–33, 2646
Prayers of Praise: 2639–43, 2649
Prayers of Thanksgiving: 2637–38, 2648
The Sign of the Cross: 2157, 2166
Tasks of Disciples: 425, 1816
What is Prayer?: 2559–65, 2590, 2644

Scripture References

The Call To Be a Disciple: Mt 16:24

The Our Father: Mt 6:9–13; Lk 11:2–4

Background Reading: *The Fundamentals of Catholicism* by Fr. Kenneth Baker, S.J.

Volume 3:
"The Gratuity of Grace," pp. 37–40
"Sharing in God's Life," pp. 65–68

"Children of God," pp. 68–71
"Church and World," pp. 158–60

Summary of Lesson Content

Lesson 1

Jesus called His disciples saying: "If any man would come after me, let him deny himself and take up his cross and follow me" (Mt 16:24).

To follow Jesus is to become His disciple.

Every person has a cross to bear in life which is part of God's plan to help him reach Heaven.

Lesson 2

Jesus is a model of perfection.

By examining the life and teachings of Christ, one can learn to imitate them and follow Him.

By following Jesus, a person can go to Heaven.

Every person should think of how Jesus would act in a given situation and then act accordingly.

Lesson 3

Jesus taught the Apostles how to pray and taught them specifically to pray the Our Father.

Prayer is the lifting of one's heart and mind to God.

There are many forms of prayer. Some of these are Blessing, Adoration, Praise, Prayers of Petition, Prayers of Intercession, and Prayers of Thanksgiving.

Lesson 4

Love is sacrificial.

Children can offer sacrifices of love to God, including: knowing, loving, and serving God, as well as offering works, words, daily sacrifices, talents, and their very selves at Mass.

CHAPTER TWENTY-SEVEN: FOLLOWING JESUS
LESSON ONE: FOLLOW THE LEADER

Aims

Students will learn that they are all called to follow Jesus.

They will learn that to follow Jesus is to be a disciple.

They will learn that to be a disciple, one must deny himself, take up his cross, and follow Jesus.

Materials

- *Activity Book*, p. 105

Optional:
- Children's Bible

- A children's Way of the Cross prayer book

- "Lift high the cross," *Adoremus Hymnal*, #606

Begin

Play "Follow the Leader" with the children. If it is a nice day, you may want to take them outside. Walk in different directions, hop on one foot, spin circles, make hand gestures, etc.

Then allow the children to take turns being the leader. Or, you may simply talk to them about this game and how it is played. The children may have to explain the rules to you.

Develop

1. Now read paragraphs 1 and 2 of the text.

2. Referring to the game you played with them, ask the children where the leader took them. What was their favorite part? Were there times when it was hard to follow the leader?

3. Then ask the children how Jesus is their leader. Where does He lead them? Who are His followers? Is it always easy to follow Jesus?

4. Ask the children if they remember the Way of the Cross, also called the Stations of the Cross (from Chapter 18, Lesson 2, p. 216 of this manual, or perhaps from attending the Good Friday service). Tell them that the Way of the Cross is a prayer that helps people meditate upon the journey Jesus took before he was crucified. He suffered greatly during this journey, but from His suffering He was able to give of Himself, even unto death, and thus give life to the world.

5. Read this passage aloud: Then Jesus told his disciples, "If any man would come after me, let him deny himself and take up his cross and follow me" (Mt 16:24), or read it from a children's Bible. Ask the students what this passage means. It means to put Jesus and others first, to do what is right even when it is hard, and be faithful to Jesus' teachings. By following Jesus, and His teachings, a person can go to Heaven.

6. Ask the children to think of ways they can:
   - Deny themselves
   - Take up their cross
   - Follow Jesus

7. If possible, read through a children's Way of the Cross prayer book with the students. Find practical examples to apply to their lives based on the Stations, i.e., Jesus accepted his sentence by Pilate although innocent, thus the children should do their parents' bidding and pick up after a mess is made, even if they did not make it.

Reinforce

1. Have the children complete p. 105 in the *Activity Book* (see *Teacher's Manual*, p. 335).

2. Review with the children the simple way of praying the Stations that you introduced on p. 216. First, read the title of each aloud, then pray together as a response: "We adore You, O Christ, and we bless You, because by Your Holy Cross, You have redeemed the world." You may want to write this prayer on the chalkboard or pass out printed copies they may read at their desks.

Conclude

1. Lead the children in praying the Morning Offering (see p. 133 of this manual).

2. Teach the students an appropriate hymn, such as "Lift high the cross," *Adoremus Hymnal*, #606.

27   Following Jesus

"No greater joy can I have than this,
to hear that my children follow the truth."
3 John 1:4

When we play "Follow the Leader," we walk behind someone else and we do whatever the person in front of us does. The "leader" doesn't take us to any place special because it is only a game.

But Jesus is our leader on the road of life and that is not a game. It is real. By following Him, we can come to the Kingdom of Heaven. By doing whatever Jesus does, we learn how to live as God's children.

These are some of the things Jesus did that we should follow. Jesus always obeyed His Mother and foster-father, Saint Joseph. He told them the truth. He did the work they asked Him to do. He was kind to everyone. He shared with others. He forgave those who hurt Him. You can do these things too.

107

DEVOTION TO THE WAY OF THE CROSS

According to tradition, our Lady visited the scenes of Christ's Passion every day. After Constantine legalized Christianity in the year 312, the path of the Cross, called the Via Dolorosa, was marked with stations. Saint Jerome, living in Bethlehem in the early fifth century, attested to the many international pilgrims who visited those holy places and followed the Way of the Cross. Shortly thereafter, an interest developed in the Church to reproduce these holy places elsewhere so that pilgrims did not have to travel to the Holy Land. Promotion of this devotion began in earnest with the Franciscans, who were given custody of these places in the Holy Land in the 14th century. Today there are fourteen stations which can be found in many churches.

THE STATIONS OF THE CROSS

1st: Jesus is condemned to die
2nd: Jesus takes up His Cross
3rd: Jesus falls the first time
4th: Jesus meets His Mother, Mary
5th: Simon of Cyrene helps Jesus carry His Cross
6th: Veronica wipes the face of Jesus
7th: Jesus falls the second time
8th: Jesus speaks to the women of Jerusalem
9th: Jesus falls the third time
10th: Soldiers remove the clothes of Jesus
11th: Jesus is nailed to the Cross
12th: Jesus dies on the Cross
13th: Jesus is taken down from the Cross
14th: Jesus is laid in the tomb

THE STATIONS AT HOME

A plenary indulgence (see p. 329 of this manual) is granted to those who piously exercise the Way of the Cross, physically moving from station to station while mediating on the Passion and death of our Lord, in any place where they are legitimately erected. Those who are unable to visit a church may gain the same indulgence by piously reading and meditating on the Passion and death of Christ for a half hour.

Preview

In our next lesson, we will learn more about following Jesus.

Chapter Twenty-Seven: Following Jesus
Lesson Two: Following Jesus' Example

Aims

Students will learn how to follow Jesus' example.

They will realize that as a boy, Jesus had some of the same experiences they have. They can follow his own childhood example.

They will learn to think of how Christ would act in any given situation, and base their behavior on that.

Materials

- *Activity Book*, p. 106

Optional:
- "Lift high the cross," *Adoremus Hymnal*, #606

Begin

Play a Catholic version of "Simon Says" with the children, changing the words to "Jesus Says." If the children do not obey, then they must sit down until the next round. Play the game again, but this time play "Jesus Does." Have the children imitate your actions without being told what to do.

Develop

1. Read paragraph 3 from the textbook.

2. Ask the children to help you name things that Jesus did, and write these on the chalkboard. They can add things to the list if they seem appropriate, e.g., Jesus ate healthy food, Jesus read the Bible, Jesus helped clean the workshop.

3. Have the children think of ways they can imitate Jesus. Tell them that when they are in a situation and don't know what to do, they should think of what Jesus would do, and then do that. This principle is called "What Would Jesus Do?" (WWJD).

4. Give the children various situations and ask them what they should do. Then ask them what Jesus would do. For example: You are doing your chores in the front yard when your friends come to ask you to play, they need you or they will lose the game. Your mother said you could play once you finished your chores. What would Jesus do? What should you do?

5. Remind the children that Jesus is the Leader. Ask them where Jesus is leading them—to Heaven. Help them understand that they follow Jesus by imitating His deeds and obeying his teachings.

6. Review with the children some of Jesus' teachings:
- pray
- obey parents
- share
- help others
- be kind
- forgive others

Ask the children how Jesus lived these teachings. Talk about how they can follow these teachings.

Reinforce

Have the children complete p. 106 of their *Activity Book* (see *Teacher's Manual*, p. 335), which is a reiteration of the principle, What Twould Jesus Do. This is a good exercise to do together as a class because it follows the Develop section well.

Conclude

1. Lead the children in a prayer. Have them ask Jesus to help them follow Him and imitate Him with specific examples, e.g., "Jesus help me to imitate your obedience by cleaning my room when I am told to do so"; "Jesus help me to help others like you did, by helping my sister with her chores."

2. Close with the hymn "Lift high the cross," *Adoremus Hymnal*, #606.

27 Following Jesus

"No greater joy can I have than this,
to hear that my children follow the truth."
3 John 1:4

When we play "Follow the Leader," we walk behind someone else and we do whatever the person in front of us does. The "leader" doesn't take us to any place special because it is only a game.

But Jesus is our leader on the road of life and that is not a game. It is real. By following Him, we can come to the Kingdom of Heaven. By doing whatever Jesus does, we learn how to live as God's children.

These are some of the things Jesus did that we should follow. Jesus always obeyed His Mother and foster-father, Saint Joseph. He told them the truth. He did the work they asked Him to do. He was kind to everyone. He shared with others. He forgave those who hurt Him. You can do these things too.

107

Jesus also showed us how to pray. To pray means to talk with God. You can say the prayers you have learned or you can tell God what you are thinking about. God is interested in anything you have to say and anything you think, or even feel.

Every morning when you wake up, you should kneel down and make the Sign of the Cross. You should offer God everything you will do and say and think that day. At night, kneel down beside your bed and thank God for the things He gave you during the day.

You can ask Him to bless all the people you love and all the people everywhere. Try to remember if you did anything wrong that day, and then tell God you are sorry. Ask Him to make you a better boy or girl tomorrow.

Remember, you can pray anytime or anywhere, and about anything. You can ask God to help people who are sick or unhappy. You can ask God to make you a **saint**. A saint is a good person who has died and gone to Heaven to be with God.

108

Jesus taught us to love God with all our hearts. You can show God that you love Him, too. One way is to work hard to learn about Him. You can try to be good even when it is very difficult. And you can go to Mass and learn to say the prayers of the Mass. With Jesus, you can offer yourself to the Father at Mass.

God has given you so many gifts. Your gift to God is to live as His good child, to thank Him and to love Him.

Word to Know:

saint

> **Q. 58** *What is prayer?*
> Prayer is talking to God (CCC 2559).

109

INDULGENCES

An indulgence is the remission before God of temporal punishment due to sin for which guilt has already been forgiven (i.e., in Confession). A properly disposed Catholic, following the prescribed conditions of the Church, can obtain an indulgence. A plenary indulgence removes all temporal punishment; if some of the punishment remains, the indulgence is partial.

Preview

In our next lesson, we will learn more about prayer.

Chapter Twenty-Seven: Following Jesus
Lesson Three: Let Us Pray

Aims

Students will learn that Jesus taught the Apostles to pray the Our Father.

They will learn the forms of prayer: Blessing and Adoration, Petition, Intercession, Thanksgiving, and Praise.

Materials

• Children's Bible

• *Activity Book*, p. 107

• Cards with prayer phrases

Optional:
• "Lift high the cross," *Adoremus Hymnal*, #606

Begin

Write the word "prayer" on the board. Ask the children if they know what prayer is: it is talking to God, or the lifting of one's heart and mind to God. Some prayers are spoken out loud, and some are said silently in the heart. Some prayers are memorized, and sometimes a person simply talks with God about whatever is on his mind. God likes all kinds of prayer. Today, the students will learn more about prayer and the various forms of prayer.

Develop

1. Read paragraphs 4, 5, and 6 with the students. Explain to the children that prayer is very important because it helps a person establish a relationship with God. Imagine what it would be like to live in your parents' house, but never to speak to them or listen to them. It would be terribly sad.

2. Jesus taught His disciples how to pray, and anyone can read about it in the Bible: Mt 6:9–13 or Lk 11:2–4. Jesus taught the Apostles to pray the Our Father (you may read this aloud). This is a very good prayer, which everyone should memorize. There are many good prayers that should be learned by heart.

3. There are different forms of prayer (see p. 9 of this manual for a brief overview of the various types of prayer). Enumerate these on the chalkboard:
   • Blessing and Adoration
   • Petition
   • Intercession
   • Thanksgiving
   • Praise

4. The Mass is the perfect prayer because it has all of these types of prayer in it. Ask the children if they can think of how the different forms of prayer are said/done during Mass:
   Blessing and Adoration: the Gloria, the Eucharistic Prayer
   Petition: the Prayers of the Faithful
   Intercession: the Prayers of the Faithful
   Thanksgiving: the Liturgy of the Eucharist, the Prayer after Communion, the Dismissal
   Praise: the Sursum Corda, Liturgy of the Eucharist

5. Review with the children the prayers they have learned throughout the year. You may have cards with phrases written on them so that the children can number and order them:
   2 Full of grace
   2 The Lord is with thee
   1 Hail Mary
   4 Blessed art thou among women
   5 And blessed is the fruit of thy womb, Jesus

Reinforce

1. Assign p. 107 of the *Activity Book* (see *Teacher's Manual*, p. 335).

2. Have the children memorize Question 58.

3. Give examples of types of prayer, then have the children make up their own prayers for each form. Examples for yourself:

Blessing and Adoration: I adore You, God, for You are good.
Petition: Please God, help me to teach Your Truth.
Intercession: I pray the angels and saints to ask God that I do not stray from teaching the Truth.
Thanksgiving: Thank You, God, for allowing me to teach Your little ones.
Praise: You are a great God deserving of all our love.

Conclude

1. Close by singing "Lift high the cross," *Adoremus Hymnal*, #606.

2. Pray the Stations of the Cross (see *Teacher's Manual*, p. 327).

27   Following Jesus

"No greater joy can I have than this,
to hear that my children follow the truth."

3 John 1:4

When we play "Follow the Leader," we walk behind someone else and we do whatever the person in front of us does. The "leader" doesn't take us to any place special because it is only a game.

But Jesus is our leader on the road of life and that is not a game. It is real. By following Him, we can come to the Kingdom of Heaven. By doing whatever Jesus does, we learn how to live as God's children.

These are some of the things Jesus did that we should follow. Jesus always obeyed His Mother and foster-father, Saint Joseph. He told them the truth. He did the work they asked Him to do. He was kind to everyone. He shared with others. He forgave those who hurt Him. You can do these things too.

107

Jesus also showed us how to pray. To pray means to talk with God. You can say the prayers you have learned or you can tell God what you are thinking about. God is interested in anything you have to say and anything you think, or even feel.

Every morning when you wake up, you should kneel down and make the Sign of the Cross. You should offer God everything you will do and say and think that day. At night, kneel down beside your bed and thank God for the things He gave you during the day.

You can ask Him to bless all the people you love and all the people everywhere. Try to remember if you did anything wrong that day, and then tell God you are sorry. Ask Him to make you a better boy or girl tomorrow.

Remember, you can pray anytime or anywhere, and about anything. You can ask God to help people who are sick or unhappy. You can ask God to make you a **saint**. A saint is a good person who has died and gone to Heaven to be with God.

108

Jesus taught us to love God with all our hearts. You can show God that you love Him, too. One way is to work hard to learn about Him. You can try to be good even when it is very difficult. And you can go to Mass and learn to say the prayers of the Mass. With Jesus, you can offer yourself to the Father at Mass.

God has given you so many gifts. Your gift to God is to live as His good child, to thank Him and to love Him.

Word to Know:

saint

> **Q. 58** *What is prayer?*
> Prayer is talking to God (CCC 2559).

109

SAMPLE PRAYER PHRASES

____ *Amen.*	____ pray for us sinners
____ and to the Son	
____ is now and ever shall be	____ Mother of God
	____ *Amen.*
____ and to the Holy Spirit.	____ and at the hour of our death
____ Glory Be to the Father	____ Holy Mary
	____ now
____ As it was in the beginning	

Preview

In our next lesson, we will learn about sacrificial love.

CHAPTER TWENTY-SEVEN: FOLLOWING JESUS
LESSON FOUR: LOVE IS SELF-GIFT

Aims

Students will learn that love is sacrificial and that Jesus showed the greatest love by giving Himself on the Cross.

They will learn that by making sacrifices they show their love for God as well as grow in love for Him.

Materials

- *Activity Book*, p. 108

Optional:
- "Lift high the cross," *Adoremus Hymnal*, #606

Begin

Write the word "Sacrifice" on the chalkboard. Ask if the students remember (from the last chapter) what this word means. Explain that to sacrifice something is to give up one thing for another. It is a way a person can show God he loves Him the most by giving up something he really likes. Jesus sacrificed Himself on the Cross and continues to do so in the Eucharist. Remind the children that they can also make sacrifices.

Develop

1. Read the rest of the chapter with the children.

2. Ask the students to name some ways that they can love God with all their hearts:
   - learn about God
   - be good, even when it is hard
   - go to Mass
   - say prayers

Emphasize that all of these are offerings to God, little sacrifices that please Him greatly.

3. In paragraph 8, the text states that the children can offer themselves to the Father at Mass, which is something that should be emphasized. How do the children offer themselves? Jesus gave Himself up to the Father on the Cross. A person can unite himself to Jesus in the Sacrifice of the Mass by also giving himself to the Father. Because the children have not yet received Holy Communion, they can only make a spiritual communion (see facing page). But once they are prepared, they can unite themselves with Jesus in the Blessed Sacrament and give their lives to the Father at Mass in a sacramental as well as spiritual way.

4. Tell the children that they can now unite themselves to Jesus by following His example, keeping His Commandments, obeying His teachings, and praying faithfully.

5. Explain to the students that by giving themselves, their works, words, and all their love back to God, they are making sacrifices of love. They are "lifting high their cross" which will bring them to eternal life and unite them with Jesus.

Reinforce

1. Have the children draw two pictures of themselves making sacrifices to Jesus on p. 108 of the *Activity Book* (see *Teacher's Manual*, p. 335).

2. Teach the children a prayer of spiritual communion (see the facing page).

3. Ask the students to review Question 58.

Conclude

1. Pray the Morning Offering (see p. 133).

2. Sing "Lift high the cross," *Adoremus Hymnal*, #606.

3. Pray the Stations of the Cross (see *Teacher's Manual*, p. 327).

Jesus also showed us how to pray. To pray means to talk with God. You can say the prayers you have learned or you can tell God what you are thinking about. God is interested in anything you have to say and anything you think, or even feel.

Every morning when you wake up, you should kneel down and make the Sign of the Cross. You should offer God everything you will do and say and think that day. At night, kneel down beside your bed and thank God for the things He gave you during the day.

You can ask Him to bless all the people you love and all the people everywhere. Try to remember if you did anything wrong that day, and then tell God you are sorry. Ask Him to make you a better boy or girl tomorrow.

Remember, you can pray anytime or anywhere, and about anything. You can ask God to help people who are sick or unhappy. You can ask God to make you a **saint**. A saint is a good person who has died and gone to Heaven to be with God.

Jesus taught us to love God with all our hearts. You can show God that you love Him, too. One way is to work hard to learn about Him. You can try to be good even when it is very difficult. And you can go to Mass and learn to say the prayers of the Mass. With Jesus, you can offer yourself to the Father at Mass.

God has given you so many gifts. Your gift to God is to live as His good child, to thank Him and to love Him.

Word to Know:

saint

> **Q. 58** *What is prayer?*
> Prayer is talking to God (CCC 2559).

THE CHURCH AND SACRIFICE

Sacrifice is important in the Church, for at every Mass Christ offers Himself in sacrifice to the Father. The Son sacrificed Himself on the Cross so that we might have eternal life. The word *sacrifice* is derived from two Latin words, *sacrum* and *facere*, meaning "to make holy." It is the act of offering something precious to God; the gift is thus set apart from profane items and made holy. A true sacrifice must consist of a visible and/or precious item, be offered by a priest or authorized representative, have as its purpose to recognize the supreme sovereignty of God, and it must visibly represent the invisible or inner sacrifical disposition. See also *Fundamentals of Catholicism*, Fr. Kenneth Baker, Volume 3, pp. 265–67; Ignatius Press.

"OFFER IT UP"

Many Catholics are familiar with this phrase. While some children are told to "offer up" a discomfort, what is really being offered up is the comfort. In a non-religious sense, sacrifice is understood as a surrender of some good for the sake of something better, in this case, for personal edification. These sacrifices can also be offered in reparation for sin or for the souls in Purgatory.

SPIRITUAL COMMUNION

My Jesus, as I cannot receive Thee now in the Most Holy and Blessed Sacrament, I ask that Thee come into my heart, and make it like unto Thy heart. *Amen.*

Preview

In our next lesson, we will review the materials that we have learned this week and take a quiz.

CHAPTER TWENTY-SEVEN: FOLLOWING JESUS
REVIEW AND ASSESSMENT

Aims

To review and assess the children's understanding of the materials covered this week in class.

Materials

- Quiz 27 (Appendix, p. A-33)
- "Lift high the cross," *Adoremus Hymnal*, #606

Review and Enrichment

1. Review with the children that Jesus is the Leader. Ask them how they can follow the leader and where He is taking them (Heaven).

2. Ask the children to explain, "If any man would come after me, let him deny himself and take up his cross and follow me." They should know that to be a follower of Jesus they must do things for other people and follow Jesus' teaching and example even when it is difficult.

3. Ask the children to tell you ways that Jesus is our example. How they can follow His example? Review: What Would Jesus Do?

4. Remind the children about the forms of prayer: Blessing and Adoration, Petition, Intercession, Thanksgiving, and Praise. They should know that prayer is lifting their hearts and minds to God.

5. Students should understand that love is sacrificial: it is to give of oneself. To do so, they must know, love, and serve God. They should be able to list ways of making sacrifices for God in order to love Him with all their hearts.

Name: _____

Following Jesus　　　　　　　　　　　　**Quiz 27**

Matching. *Draw a line from the word to its match.*

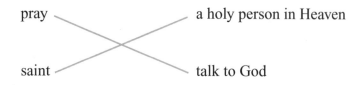

pray　　　　　　　　　　a holy person in Heaven

saint　　　　　　　　　　talk to God

I should follow Jesus. *Circle the things I should do because Jesus did them, too.*

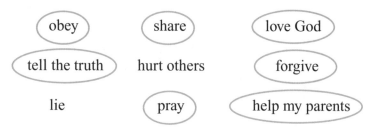

obey　　　　share　　　　love God

tell the truth　　hurt others　　forgive

lie　　　　pray　　　help my parents

Assess

1. Distribute the quiz, and read through it with the children, answering any questions they may have.

2. As the children hand in their quizzes, you may want to test them individually on their prayers.

3. When all the quizzes have been handed in, review the correct answers with the students.

Conclude

1. Make a Spiritual Communion as a class (see *Teacher's Manual*, p. 333).

2. Close by singing "Lift high the cross," *Adoremus Hymnal*, #606.

Name:_____

How can I be a follower of Jesus?

Answer the following questions to find out some ways that you can follow Jesus.

1. Can I teach anyone about Jesus? Whom?

Answers will vary.

2. Can I pray? Which prayers? When?

_____
_____

3. Can I do good deeds?

_____

4. Can I go to Mass? When?

_____

Faith and Life Series • Grade 1 • Chapter 27 • Lesson 1   105

Name:_____

What would Jesus do?

If you ever have to decide what to do and you want to make a good choice, think about what Jesus would do and then do the same thing!

SITUATION	WHAT WOULD JESUS DO	WHAT WILL I DO
I have a test tomorrow.	Answers will vary	
I am going to Mass.		
My friend is eating lunch alone.		
My mom wants help setting the table.		
I got up late for school.		
My friend forgot his lunch.		
A little child is crying.		

106   *Faith and Life Series • Grade 1 • Chapter 27 • Lesson 2*

Name:_____

The Mass is the Perfect Prayer

The Mass contains all types of prayer. Can you match the following types of prayer with the parts of the Mass?

Blessing and Adoration

Thanksgiving

Petition

Intercession

The Prayers of the Faithful—"Lord, hear our prayer."

The Gloria—"Glory to God in the highest…we bless you, we adore you…for your great glory…"

Penitential Act—"I ask blessed Mary ever-Virgin, all the Angels and Saints…to pray for me to the Lord our God."

Eucharistic Prayer—"Let us give thanks to the Lord our God."

Faith and Life Series • Grade 1 • Chapter 27 • Lesson 3   107

Name:_____

My sacrifices make Jesus happy!

Draw two pictures of yourself making sacrifices to please Jesus.

108   *Faith and Life Series • Grade 1 • Chapter 27 • Lesson 4*

335

TEACHER'S NOTES

CHAPTER TWENTY-EIGHT
JESUS WILL COME AGAIN

Catechism of the Catholic Church References

Christ's Resurrection and Ours: 655–58, 992–1004, 1015–17

The Creeds: 185–97

Heaven: 1023–29, 1053

Jesus as Judge of Living and Dead: 678–79, 681–82, 1040

Jesus Will Return in Glory: 668–77, 680

The Last Judgment: 677–82, 1038–41, 1051–52

The Last Supper: 610–11, 621

Man's Vocation to Beatitude: 1718–24, 1726–29

The Mass: 1345–55, 1408

Presence of Christ in the Eucharist: 1373–81, 1410, 1418

Sacramentals: 1667–73, 1677–78

The Second Coming: 673, 1060

Signs of Bread and Wine in the Eucharist: 1333–36, 1412

Sunday: Sabbath and Day of Grace and Rest: 2175–76, 2184–88, 2190, 2193–95

The Sunday Eucharist: 1193, 2177–79

The Sunday Obligation: 2174, 2180–83, 2191–92

Worship/Adoration: 2096–97, 2135–36

Scripture References

Jesus Will Prepare a Place in His Father's House: Jn 14:2–6

Background Reading: *The Fundamentals of Catholicism* by Fr. Kenneth Baker, S.J.

Volume 1:

"The Resurrection of the Dead," pp.113–15

"The Life of the World to Come," pp. 116–18

Volume 3:

"The Law of Death," pp. 361

The Last Things, pp. 364–79

"The Resurrection of the Body," pp. 379–82

The Last Judgment and the End of Time, pp. 382–88

Summary of Lesson Content

Lesson 1

God made man to know, love, and serve Him in this life and share in the beatific vision forever in Heaven.

The Communion of Saints includes the Church Triumphant, the Church Militant, and the Church Suffering.

Saints are in Heaven with God as a reward for their loving faithfulness.

Saints are good examples of discipleship.

Lesson 2

Heaven is eternal.

God's plan for man is to be united with Him forever in Heaven.

In Heaven, the just shall be united with Mary, the angels and saints and those they loved on earth.

Lesson 3

At the end of the world, the bodies of men will rise and be united with their souls for all eternity.

Jesus redeemed the whole man (body and soul) and, therefore, the bodies of the just will rise to share in the glory of the soul.

The qualities of the resurrected body are: impassibility, brightness, agility, and subtlety.

Lesson 4

To go to Heaven, one must die in the state of grace (have God's life in his soul).

Some must go through Purgatory to reach Heaven.

In Heaven, one has the beatific vision: seeing God face to face. The just shall be happy forever.

The heavenly reward is given according to the goodness of the life each person led on earth.

Chapter Twenty-Eight: Jesus Will Come Again
Lesson One: Why Did God Make Me?

Aims

Students will learn that God made them to know, love, and serve Him, and be with Him forever in Heaven.

They will learn that the saints are examples for them. Saints are in Heaven with God.

They will learn about the Mystical Body of Christ.

Materials

- *Activity Book*, p. 109

Optional:
- Saints books for children

- "Lo! he comes, with clouds descending," *Adoremus Hymnal*, #304

Begin

Begin the class by asking the children why God made them. Let the children think for a minute. Remind them that God made them to know, love, and serve Him, and be with Him forever in Heaven. Then ask them what they have learned this year to help them on their way. This is a time for a general year review.

Develop

1. Read paragraph 1 with the students. Then ask them about the saints they have studied this year, saints who exemplified knowing, loving, and serving God. Explain to the children that saints are great examples because they followed Jesus and are now in Heaven.

2. Remind the children that the saints are their friends. They want to help them, as Mary does. The students can ask them for prayers, and they can learn about and imitate their lives.

3. The saints in Heaven are rewarded for following Jesus; their reward is eternal happiness with God. The angels and saints in Heaven are called the Church Triumphant.

4. The Church has three states: the Church Triumphant, the saints happily in Heaven with God; the Church Militant, everyone here on earth who is trying to get to Heaven; and the Church Suffering, those souls who are in Purgatory, waiting and getting ready to go to Heaven.

5. Each person in each of the three states of the Church—Triumphant, Militant, and Suffering—is connected by his love for Christ. All people are united to God through Jesus. Catholics are united when they pray together, when they receive the Eucharist, and when they are charitable to one another. Christians are united through Baptism.

6. Remind the children that the saints loved God faithfully. They kept the Commandments, and made sacrifices. They were prayerful and reverent in their worship. Review with them the types of sacrifices they can make, and how they should behave during Mass and prayers.

7. Tell the children that we can hope to be with the saints in Heaven if we all follow Jesus as our leader.

Reinforce

1. Help the children answer the list of questions on p. 109 of the *Activity Book* (see *Teacher's Manual*, p. 347).

2. The students may draw the pictures of the Church Triumphant, Militant, and Suffering.

3. Using a saints book, read about some of the patron saints of the students. If possible, show them pictures of their patron saints. Ask the children how they can follow their examples.

4. You may teach the children the hymn "Lo! he comes, with clouds descending," *Adoremus Hymnal*, #304.

Conclude

1. Separate the students into pairs and have them begin to memorize Question 59 in the text.

2. Pray the Act of Faith together (see *Teacher's Manual*, p. 367 or p. 79 for the simple version).

[handwritten notes]
Heaven — Triumphant
Purgatory. Suffering.
Earth — Militant
Hell

28   Jesus Will Come Again

"And when I go and prepare a place for you,
I will come again and will take you to myself,
that where I am you may be also."
John 14:3

Do you know why you are here on earth? You are here to learn to know God, to love, and to **serve** God. If you learn how to do these things, you will be ready to live with God forever and ever in Heaven.

We are on earth for only a short time, but Heaven never ends. Heaven is our true home, the place where we will always be happy with Jesus, with Mary, and with those we love.

Someday, the world will end. Then Jesus will come again. He will take all the good people to Heaven with Him. The souls of all the people who have died will be united with their bodies again.

Do you want to start on the road to Heaven? All

111

you have to do is try your best to love God every day. Ready! Set! Go!

Word to Know:

serve

Q. 59 *Why did God make you?*
God made you to know, love, and serve Him in this world, and to be happy with Him forever in Heaven (CCC 260, 358).

CHALK TALK:
THE THREE STATES OF THE CHURCH

Triumphant: These are the angels and saints who are happy with God in Heaven for all eternity.

Militant: These are the faithful on earth who are soldiers for Christ in this world; they struggle to avoid sin, to love God, and to help each other die in the state of grace.

Suffering: These are the holy souls in Purgatory who are suffering for the sins they committed on earth in order to be purified to reach Heaven and eternal happiness.

Preview

In our next lesson, we will learn about Heaven.

CHAPTER TWENTY-EIGHT: JESUS WILL COME AGAIN
LESSON TWO: HEAVEN, OUR ETERNAL HOME

Aims

Students will learn that Heaven is eternal: it lasts forever.

They will learn that God's plan is for them to be with Him forever.

They will realize that in Heaven the just shall be united with Mary, the angels, the saints, and those they loved on earth who have died.

Materials

- *Activity Book*, p. 110

Optional:
- "Lo! he comes, with clouds descending," *Adoremus Hymnal*, #304

Begin

Have the children think of a long period of time, such as the years their grandparents have lived. Now tell them to think of all the years since Jesus lived. Then have them think of all the years since God created Adam and Eve. What if there were no end to it? That is what forever is. Forever is a very long time if you are unhappy (such as when summer holidays come to an end, or when your favorite relatives leave town), but if you are happy and with people you love, it is a great gift to live forever.

Develop

1. Read paragraph 2 aloud with the class.

2. Review with the children how Adam and Eve lost grace through the first sin, and how the gates of Heaven were closed. Jesus opened the gates of Heaven by dying on the Cross and rising from the dead.

3. In Heaven, people are happy forever because their souls, and eventually their bodies, are united with God.

4. People prepare for Heaven by learning to know God, to love God, and to serve God.

5. Ask the children to think of ways they can know God:
- Pay attention in religion class
- Learn about the saints
- Listen to the priest at Mass
- Talk to their parents about God
- Pray

6. Ask the children how they can love God:
- Pray
- Avoid sin
- Obey their parents
- Make sacrifices
- Imitate Jesus or the saints

7. Ask the children how they can serve God:
- Attend Mass reverently
- Be kind to others
- Be good and obey God's Commandments
- Learn their catechism
- Help at the church

Be sure to discuss how doing all of these things will make the students happy here in this life as well as in Heaven.

Reinforce

1. Have the children draw a picture of Heaven on p. 110 of the *Activity Book* (see *Teacher's Manual*, p. 347).

2. You may want to pass out a piece of paper to each student that is folded in three. You should write Know God, Love God, Serve God in each section. Then have the children draw themselves doing something that depicts them knowing, loving, and serving God. *Activity Book*, p. 15 can be used as a review (see *Teacher's Manual*, p. 47).

Conclude

1. The children may "show and tell" about their pictures of Heaven. They may have people they love in the pictures, their guardian angels, etc. Have them talk about their vision of Heaven.

2. End with the Act of Hope (see the facing page).

3. Sing with the children "Lo! he comes, with clouds descending," *Adoremus Hymnal*, #304.

28   Jesus Will Come Again

"And when I go and prepare a place for you,
I will come again and will take you to myself,
that where I am you may be also."

John 14:3

Do you know why you are here on earth? You are here to learn to know God, to love, and to **serve** God. If you learn how to do these things, you will be ready to live with God forever and ever in Heaven.

We are on earth for only a short time, but Heaven never ends. Heaven is our true home, the place where we will always be happy with Jesus, with Mary, and with those we love.

Someday, the world will end. Then Jesus will come again. He will take all the good people to Heaven with Him. The souls of all the people who have died will be united with their bodies again.

Do you want to start on the road to Heaven? All

111

ACT OF FAITH

O My God, I firmly believe that You are one God in three Divine Persons: Father, Son, and Holy Spirit. I believe that Your divine Son became man and died for our sins, and that He will come to judge the living and the dead. I believe these and all the truths that the Holy Catholic Church teaches, because You revealed them, who can neither deceive nor be deceived. *Amen.*

ACT OF HOPE

O my God, relying on Your infinite goodness and promises, I hope to obtain pardon of my sins, the help of Your grace, and life everlasting, through the merits of Jesus Christ, my Lord and Redeemer. *Amen.*

SIMPLE ACT OF HOPE

My Lord and My God, I hope in You, that You will forgive my sins and bring me to Heaven to be with You forever. *Amen.*

SAINT JOSEPH
PATRON OF A HAPPY DEATH

Because he died in the arms of Jesus and Mary, Saint Joseph is the patron of a happy death (see p. 141 of this manual and the Litany on p. 51 of the student text).

Preview

In our next lesson, we will learn about the Second Coming of Jesus.

CHAPTER TWENTY-EIGHT: JESUS WILL COME AGAIN
LESSON THREE: JESUS WILL COME AGAIN

Aims

Students will learn about the Second Coming of Jesus.

They will review the doctrine of the resurrection of the body.

Materials

- *Activity Book*, p. 111

Optional:
- "Lo! he comes, with clouds descending," *Adoremus Hymnal*, #304

Begin

Ask the children to tell you the two parts that make up a person: a body and a soul. Have the children describe their bodies and what their bodies can do. They may talk about their hair color, their eye color, their height, their weight, how they can jump, run, walk, dance, etc. Explain that the souls in Heaven will someday be reunited with their bodies. It will be very different in Heaven. In fact, much will happen before then, which is what they will learn about today.

Develop

1. Ask the children if they remember what happened when Jesus went to Heaven. If they do not, turn to Chapter 21 of their textbook and read the last paragraph to review (see *Teacher's Manual*, p. 257). The angels told the disciples that Jesus would return in the same manner in which He left, in the clouds in glory.

2. Now read paragraphs 3 and 4 of Chapter 28 aloud with the children.

3. Remind the students that Jesus became man, died, and rose from the dead with His body. Jesus saved all men, body and soul, so that everyone now has a chance to go to Heaven when he dies. Jesus prepares a place in His Father's house for us (Jn 14:2–6). Then, at the end of time, the bodies of the just will join their glorious souls in Heaven. Remind them that this is called the Church Triumphant.

4. Review with the children the fact that Jesus went up to Heaven at the Ascension with His body (this is the second Glorious Mystery), and that Mary was also taken to Heaven with her body; this is called the Assumption.

5. The glorified bodies in Heaven will be like Jesus' body after the Resurrection. His Apostles did not immediately recognize Him. The resurrected body will have different qualities:

Impassibility:	The body will no longer suffer pain or death. It will not be corrupted.
Brightness:	It will have a beauty and a brilliance.
Agility:	The body will be able to pass through matter and go to all parts of the universe with great speed.
Subtlety:	The body will be a spiritual body.

When a body is united with its soul, it will share in the glory of the soul. The whole person will be happy with God forever in Heaven.

Reinforce

Assign p. 111 in the *Activity Book* (see *Teacher's Manual*, p. 347), a coloring page of the unification of bodies and souls at the end of time.

Conclude

1. Sing "Lo! he comes, with clouds descending," *Adoremus Hymnal*, #304.

2. End by praying the Acts of Faith, Hope, and Love (see *Teacher's Manual*, pp. 367 and 368).

28   Jesus Will Come Again

"And when I go and prepare a place for you,
I will come again and will take you to myself,
that where I am you may be also."

John 14:3

Do you know why you are here on earth? You are here to learn to know God, to love, and to **serve** God. If you learn how to do these things, you will be ready to live with God forever and ever in Heaven.

We are on earth for only a short time, but Heaven never ends. Heaven is our true home, the place where we will always be happy with Jesus, with Mary, and with those we love.

Someday, the world will end. Then Jesus will come again. He will take all the good people to Heaven with Him. The souls of all the people who have died will be united with their bodies again.

Do you want to start on the road to Heaven? All

111

you have to do is try your best to love God every day. Ready! Set! Go!

Word to Know:

serve

> **Q. 59** *Why did God make you?*
> God made you to know, love, and serve Him in this world, and to be happy with Him forever in Heaven (CCC 260, 358).

112

ACT OF LOVE

O my God, I love You above all things with my whole heart and soul, because You are all good and worthy of all my love. I love my neighbor as myself for love of You. I forgive all who have injured me, and I ask pardon for all whom I have injured. *Amen.*

SIMPLE ACT OF LOVE

My Lord and my God, I love You more than anything in the world because You are so good. I also love everyone, even those who hurt me, and I am sorry if I hurt anyone. *Amen.*

CHALK TALK: THE FOUR LAST THINGS

Death: This is when the soul leaves the body to be judged and then enters either Heaven, Purgatory, or Hell.

Judgment: There are two judgments. The particular judgment takes place at the death of the individual at which time his eternal fate is determined by the Divine Judge; the general judgment occurs at the end of the world in the presence of everyone.

Heaven: The place of perfect and eternal happiness

Hell: The place of eternal damnation

The last words of the Bible are, "Amen. Come, Lord Jesus! The grace of the Lord Jesus be with all the saints. Amen."

Preview

In our next lesson, we will learn that to go to Heaven, we must have grace in our soul.

CHAPTER TWENTY-EIGHT: JESUS WILL COME AGAIN
LESSON FOUR: LIVE FOREVER!

Aims

Students will learn that to go to Heaven, one must die in the state of grace (have God's life in his soul).

They will learn that in Heaven, people see God face to face and that each person is rewarded according to the goodness of his life.

They will realize that the just are happy forever.

Materials

• Thimble, cup, and water

• *Activity Book*, p. 112

Optional:
• "Lo! he comes, with clouds descending," *Adoremus Hymnal*, #304

Begin

Explain to the children that Saint Thérèse of Lisieux taught us something about Heaven. She said that some souls will have greater glory in Heaven, but all souls will be happy. Fill a thimble with water and ask the children if it is full. Yes. Fill the cup with water and ask if it is full. Yes. Even though one holds more water, they are both completely full and could not hold another drop. In Heaven, though some souls will have greater glory, all will be completely happy, and completely filled with God's life—grace.

Develop

1. Tell the children that their reward in Heaven will depend on their goodness here on earth. Ask the children what they must do to obtain the reward of Heaven:
   • Be faithful
   • Do good deeds
   • Pray
   • Listen to God in your heart
   • Obey God's laws

2. Ask the students what things the saints did to obtain their reward in Heaven. They should have already learned about their patron saints. Let them all offer suggestions.

3. Remind the children that they need grace in their soul to go to Heaven. Ask them if they remember when they received grace. They received grace at their Baptism. Do they know how they lose grace? Whenever they sin. Do they know how to get grace back if they lose it? Tell God they are sorry; go to Confession, when they are older. How can God's life of grace grow in their soul? If they do good deeds and acts of charity, and pray and receive the Sacraments, especially the Eucharist once they are old enough.

4. Explain to the children that if they reach Heaven they will see Jesus, their patron saints, their guardian angels, Mary the Mother of God, and possibly their loved ones from here on earth who have passed away. Heaven is a happy and wonderful place, and everyone loves each other and God perfectly.

5. The souls in Heaven see the face of God; they will see God in His majesty. They will see His Kingdom, and they will inherit it because they are children of God.

6. The prayers and penances of the faithful on earth can alleviate the sufferings of the holy souls in Purgatory. Masses may also be offered in their honor. Upon reaching Heaven, it is believed that the just souls thus aided will respond by praying for the faithful on earth who prayed for them.

Reinforce

1. Assign p. 112 of the *Activity Book* (see *Teacher's Manual*, p. 347).

2. You may lead the children in a Litany of Saints, or perhaps the Litany to Saint Joseph, found on p. 51 of the student text, or the Litany to Mary, found on p. 105 of the student text.

Conclude

1. Take some time to review the prayers the children have learned throughout the year.

2. Sing "Lo! he comes, with clouds descending," *Adoremus Hymnal*, #304.

28   Jesus Will Come Again

"And when I go and prepare a place for you,
I will come again and will take you to myself,
that where I am you may be also."

John 14:3

Do you know why you are here on earth? You are here to learn to know God, to love, and to **serve** God. If you learn how to do these things, you will be ready to live with God forever and ever in Heaven.

We are on earth for only a short time, but Heaven never ends. Heaven is our true home, the place where we will always be happy with Jesus, with Mary, and with those we love.

Someday, the world will end. Then Jesus will come again. He will take all the good people to Heaven with Him. The souls of all the people who have died will be united with their bodies again.

Do you want to start on the road to Heaven? All

111

you have to do is try your best to love God every day. Ready! Set! Go!

Word to Know:

serve

> **Q. 59** *Why did God make you?*
> God made you to know, love, and serve Him in this world, and to be happy with Him forever in Heaven (CCC 260, 358).

112

TEACHER'S NOTES

PURGATORY

The doctrine of Purgatory is one teaching of the Catholic Church whose reality is often questioned or even denied by her members. It is important to realize that this is an article of the Catholic Faith that must be believed or one departs from orthodoxy. Purgatory is defined as the place or condition in which the souls of the just are purged before they can enter Heaven. These souls die in the state of sanctifying grace but carry the weight of unrepented venial sin or the temporal punishment due to forgiven mortal sin. Luther, Calvin, and most Protestant Reformers denied the existence of Purgatory because it did not coincide with their altered and erroneous views of justification.

Preview

In our next lesson, we will review the materials we have learned this week and take a quiz and unit test.

Chapter Twenty-Eight: Jesus Will Come Again
Review and Assessment

Aims

To review and assess the children's knowledge of the materials covered this week in class.

Materials

- Quiz 28 (Appendix, p. A-34)

Optional:
- Party supplies
- "Lo! he comes, with clouds descending," *Adoremus Hymnal*, #304

Review and Enrichment

1. Review with the children why God made them: to know, love, and serve Him and be with Him forever in Heaven.

2. Review the definitions of the Church Triumphant, Militant, and Suffering.

3. Review with the children that Heaven is eternal and that in Heaven the souls are united with Mary and the saints and that they will see God face to face.

4. Remind them that at the end of the world, the body will be united with the soul in Heaven. The resurrected body will not have pain or suffering, it will be beautiful and brilliant, it will be able to go to all parts of the universe with great speed, and it will be a spiritual body.

5. Discuss the idea that to go to Heaven, one must die in the state of grace. Every soul will be given its reward according to the goodness of the life each lived on earth. Each soul will be perfectly happy.

Name:

Jesus Will Come Again   Quiz 28

Yes or No. *Circle the correct answer.*

1. Is earth our true home?   Yes   (No)

2. Will Jesus come again?   (Yes)   No

3. Will Jesus take the souls of good people to Heaven?   (Yes)   No

4. Will anyone be sad in Heaven?   Yes   (No)

5. Do we get ready for Heaven by loving God?   (Yes)   No

     Faith and Life Series • Grade 1 • Appendix A

Assess

Distribute the quiz. Read through it and answer any questions the children may have. As the students hand in their quizzes, have them talk about their patron saint. When the students have finished, review the correct answers to the quiz.

Conclude

1. Ask the children to talk about their favorites saints; also ask them to tell you their favorite songs of those they have learned throughout the year, and sing them.

2. Sing "Lo! he comes, with clouds descending," *Adoremus Hymnal*, #304.

3. You might want to have an end-of-the-year party.

Name:_____

Have I done all I can to love God?

1. Do I know and keep the Ten Commandments?
   YES   NO
2. Do I know and say my prayers?   YES   NO
3. Do I take time to learn about God?   YES   NO
4. Do I go to Mass on Sundays?   YES   NO
5. Do I do things to help other people?   YES   NO
6. Do I obey my parents?   YES   NO
7. Do I show my family that I love them?   YES   NO
8. Do I review my old lessons to remember all I learned?
   YES   NO
9. Can I teach my friends about Jesus?   YES   NO
10. Can I sing a song that would please God? YES   NO
11. Do I thank God for all He has given me?   YES   NO
12. Do I tell God that I'm sorry when I do something
    wrong?   YES   NO
13. When I go to church, do I bless myself with Holy
    Water and genuflect?   YES   NO
14. Can I pray with my family?   YES   NO
15. Do I remember often to tell God I love Him?
    YES   NO

Faith and Life Series • Grade 1 • Chapter 28 • Lesson 1   109

Name:_____

This is how I think of Heaven.

Draw a picture of what you imagine Heaven to be like.

110   *Faith and Life Series • Grade 1 • Chapter 28 • Lesson 2*

Name:_____

The Resurrection of the Body

Jesus is God and He returned to Heaven.   Mary was taken to Heaven body and soul.

Your body will join your soul at the end of the world.

Draw a picture of yourself in Heaven at the end of the world.

Faith and Life Series • Grade 1 • Chapter 28 • Lesson 3   111

Name:_____

Read the signs on the road to Heaven.

Draw yourself following Jesus to Heaven.

112   *Faith and Life Series • Grade 1 • Chapter 28 • Lesson 4*

TEACHER'S NOTES

UNIT SEVEN TEST
CHAPTERS 25–28

> **CHAPTER TWENTY-FIVE: MANY GIFTS FROM GOD**
>
> **CHAPTER TWENTY-SIX: OUR MOTHER, MARY**
>
> **CHAPTER TWENTY-SEVEN: FOLLOWING JESUS**
>
> **CHAPTER TWENTY-EIGHT: JESUS WILL COME AGAIN**

Aims

The students' understanding of the material covered in this unit will be reviewed and assessed.

Materials

• Unit 7 Test, Appendix, p. A-35

Assess

1. Distribute the unit tests and read through them with the students to be sure they understand the questions.

2. Administer the test.

3. After all the tests have been handed in, you may wish to review the correct answers with the class.

Name: _____

Unit 7 Test   **Chapters 25–28**

Multiple choice. *Circle the correct answer.*

1. At Mass we

   a) listen and pray   b) give ourselves to God

   c) both a and b

2. Who can change the bread and wine into the Body and Blood of Jesus?

   a) your teacher   b) your parents

   c) your priest

3. Mary is the Mother of

   a) Jesus   b) all of us   c) both a and b

4. Most of all we want

   a) to go to Heaven   b) to make a lot of money

   c) everyone to like us

TEACHER'S NOTES

TEACHER'S NOTES

WE GO TO MASS

In the first grade, students should already be anticipating their first Holy Communion. An integral part of that preparation is beginning to understand the Mass. These pages of the student text provide a concentrated study of the Mass from start to finish. This material can be used at any time during the school year or at the end of the year as a way to set the tone for next year's study.

TEACHER'S NOTES

We Go to Mass

"And beginning with Moses and all the prophets,
he interpreted to them in all the Scriptures the things
concerning himself....When he was at table with them, he
took the bread and blessed and broke it,
and gave it to them. And their eyes were opened
and they recognized him."

Luke 24:27, 30–31

One of God's Laws says, "You must keep the Lord's Day holy." Sunday is the Lord's Day because Jesus rose from the dead on a Sunday. This is why every Sunday we go to Church to **worship** God at Mass.

When we come into Church, we use Holy Water to make the Sign of the Cross. This reminds us of our Baptism and that we are God's children. Before we take our seats, we **genuflect** (kneel down on our right knee) and make the Sign of the Cross to honor Jesus in the tabernacle. Before Mass begins, we kneel down and talk to God for a while.

The priest comes in while we sing a hymn. He begins Mass with the Sign of the Cross: "In the Name of the Father and of the Son and of the Holy Spirit. *Amen.*"

113

Then the priest asks us to think about how we have disobeyed God. And we think, "Dear Jesus, I am sorry for my sins. I want to love You more and more."

And then we usually say: "Glory to God in the highest!" We use the same words the angels sang at Bethlehem to praise God for his goodness.

After that we sit down and hear two readings and a Psalm from the Bible. We should listen carefully and try to understand God's message to us.

Then we stand and listen while the priest reads from the Gospel. The Gospel is the part of the Bible that tells us what Jesus said and did. Through the words of the Gospel, Jesus teaches us about our heavenly Father. Then the priest talks to us to help us understand God's Word.

After that we stand and say the **Creed**. The Creed is what we believe about God and His Church.

Now it is time for the Offertory. That is when we offer gifts of bread and wine, and we offer our money to help take care of our church. We offer ourselves with Jesus to God the Father.

114

At the Last Supper, Jesus changed bread and wine into His own Body and Blood. At Mass, the priest takes the place of Jesus. He takes a special round piece of bread and says the words of Jesus:

"This is my Body."

Then it is not bread anymore. It is the real Body of Jesus.

Next the priest takes the cup filled with wine and says:

"This is the chalice of my Blood."

Now it is the Blood of Jesus. We worship Jesus when the priest holds Him up and we tell Him how happy we are that He is with us.

115

Then we stand and say the prayer Jesus gave us, the Our Father. We may give the Sign of Peace to each other to show that we want to love one another, just as Jesus taught us.

The people go up to receive Jesus in Holy Communion. Someday you will make your First Communion.

After a last prayer, the priest says, "Go forth, the Mass is ended." And we answer, "Thanks be to God."

After the priest leaves, we should kneel down to thank Jesus and say goodbye to Him.

Thank You, Jesus, for the gift of the Mass.
Help me to love God and others this week. *Amen.*

Words to Know:

worship   genuflect   Creed

116

We Go to Mass

Introduction

This section of the *Teacher's Manual* corresponds with the last section in the Student Text, entitled We Go To Mass, which begins on p. 113. Instead of providing a week's worth of lesson plans, the following is a series of informative pages devoted to brief explanations of various aspects of the church building, the Liturgy, and liturgical life. Several of these items were referenced throughout the *Teacher's Manual*, so you may be familiar with them already. What has been written here is for you, the teacher, to read and pass along to students in a manner that is age-appropriate. The two books referenced below are recommended for personal study as they contain more precise explanatory information than is noted in these pages.

Reference Material

Ceremonies of the Modern Roman Rite: The Eucharist and the Liturgy of the Hours
           by Msgr. Peter J. Elliott (San Francisco: Ignatius Press, 1995)

Liturgical Question Box: Answers to Common Questions about the Modern Liturgy
           by Msgr. Peter J. Elliott (San Francisco: Ignatius Press, 1998)

Catechism of the Catholic Church References

The Eucharistic Celebration: 1341–44, 1356
   Elements in the Mass:
   Anaphora: 1352–54
   Collection: 1351
   Communion: 1355, 1382

Epiclesis: 1105, 1353
Fundamental Structures: 1346
Gathering of Christian Faithful: 1348
Liturgy of the Word: 1349
Presentation of the Gifts: 1350

TABLE OF CONTENTS

We Go to Mass
Church Architecture

APSE
The apse is the semi-circular end of the church, characteristic of the early Christian era, which housed the bishop's chair.

BAPTISTERY
As the name indicates, this is the distinct area, which may be located in a small chapel or separate building, where the Sacrament of Baptism is performed. The font itself should be stationary and its appearance befitting of its use. Its name derives from the Latin *baptisterium*, which means "a cold plunging bath."

NAVE
In any church, the area that is designated for the faithful is called the nave. This word comes from the Latin *navis*, meaning "ship," to which the church has been traditionally compared. Among other things, the pews, confessionals, and Stations of the Cross are located in the nave.

SANCTUARY
Derived from *sanctus*, the Latin word meaning "holy" or "sacred," this is the part of the church immediately surrounding the altar where the ceremonial actions of the Mass take place.

SACRISTY
From the Latin *sacrum*, meaning "holy object." In the sacristy are housed the sacred vessels, vestments, linens, books, and other items needed for the Mass. It is also the vesting room for the priest and altar servers; it is not part of the church proper.

SACRARIUM and PISCINA
The sacrarium is a drain leading directly into the earth for the disposal of water that has been used for some liturgical purpose and is no longer needed. The piscina is the sink-like basin to which the sacrarium is connected. The sacrarium and piscina are most often found in the sacristy.

SIDE ALTAR
In many churches can be found side altars or side chapels dedicated to various saints or which act as shrines to our Lord or our Lady.

TRANSEPT
In older churches that were built in the form of a cross, the transepts are the "arms" of the cross.

We Go to Mass
Church Furnishings

Every church is built for the Holy Sacrifice of the Mass, to house an altar, and as a place where God's Word is proclaimed to the faithful. Its structure and furnishings should express the hierarchy of ministry within the Mystical Body; the cathedral is the model for all other churches.

ALTAR
The Holy Sacrifice of the Mass is offered on an altar (from the Latin *altaria*), which is the center and focal point of the church, and upon which Christ is made sacramentally present during the Consecration. In the early days of Christianity, Mass was celebrated on the tombs of martyrs in the catacombs of Rome. Because of this, modern altars have the relics of saints, called the altar stone, upon their surface. Altars are usually made of stone, but may also be made of a solid, well-made wood. They represent two aspects of the Christian mystery: the sacrificial altar where Christ offers Himself for our sins, and the table of our Lord, upon which Christ gives Himself for our food.

ALTAR CLOTH
At least one altar cloth must be used during Mass, the top one of which must be white. To keep it clean outside of Mass, the white of the altar cloth may be covered with a dust cloth.

ANTEPENDIUM
This frontal piece upon the altar, though not obligatory, enhances the altar and usually matches the lectern fall and tabernacle veil. Antependium is from the Latin words *ante*, "before," and *pendere*, "to hang."

TABERNACLE
The tabernacle is a small, box-like receptacle, in which the Blessed Sacrament is reserved in the church; it is usually found on the altar. A tabernacle should be made of solid, nontransparent material and its interior lined with fabric. It is kept locked to prevent desecration of the Eucharist. The word is from the Latin *tabernaculum*, the diminutive of *taberna*, meaning "hut, booth, or tent."

TABERNACLE VEIL
This veil is a sign of the Real Presence of Christ in the tabernacle. It may be white, or the appropriate color for the day, but never black. It represents the holy tent of God; it reveals by concealing.

SANCTUARY LAMP
The sanctuary lamp, which is usually a candle in a red casing, burns day and night whenever the Blessed Sacrament is reserved in the tabernacle to alert the faithful of His presence.

CROSS
A Cross should be located near the altar, either atop it, behind it, or suspended above it. In the Roman Liturgy this designates a crucifix with a figure of Christ upon it.

CANDLES
Mass normally may not be said unless there is the presence of at least two lighted candles on the altar, though more are allowed for High Mass. They should be good quality, clean burning, and white, in most cases. Pure beeswax candles are not obligatory.

CREDENCE
This is the name of the table at the Epistle side of the altar, which holds the cruets (one with wine, another with water), the basin, and the finger towel. Often the credence table holds a ciborium, chalice, paten, and the hosts to be consecrated during Mass, at which time it should be covered with a cloth.

PULPIT, or AMBO
The pulpit, lectern, or ambo is where the readings and Gospel are proclaimed during the Liturgy of the Word. They are built into the church's structure and are immovable. The priest will usually give his homily from behind one of these.

LECTERN FALL
The fall is a cloth hanging in front of the pulpit or ambo that matches the color of the day or season.

PRESIDER'S CHAIR
This is the name of the chair in which the main celebrant sits during the readings and at other times during Mass. It should be located behind or near the altar.

We Go to Mass
Sacred Vessels and Other Accoutrements

The chief sacred vessels in the Latin Rite are the chalice and paten (which must be consecrated by a bishop), the ciborium and pyx (blessed by a priest) and the monstrance. Other vessels used during the Mass are the cruets, thurible, boat, and aspergillum. Once consecrated, these vessels may not be handled by a layman, i.e., a person who has not taken Holy Orders, unless he has been given charge of the sacristy, or in cases of extreme necessity. Those given charge of caring for sacred vessels should use a small linen cloth when handling them, so as not to actually touch them; all sacred vessels must be handled with reverence.

CHALICE

From the latin *calix*, "a cup," the chalice is the most sacred of all the vessels. It is used at Mass to hold the wine, which after the Consecration becomes the Precious Blood of Christ. The chalice is made in the form of a cup with a stem, and may be made of gold, silver, or tin in poorer churches, though the inside should be gilt. The chalice is consecrated with holy chrism by the bishop and is desecrated by profanation. It may be touched only by those clerics and laymen authorized to perform the duties of sacristan.

PATEN

The paten, which comes from the Latin *patena*, "a dish," is a thin circular plate of metal, large enough to rest on top of the chalice and upon which the host of the Mass is laid. A bishop should consecrate each paten, its concave surface, at least, must be gilt, and it is usually made of the same material as the chalice.

PYX

A pyx is a small round metal container (with a hinged lid that is usually made of gold) used to bring the Blessed Sacrament to the sick and to Catholics who cannot attend Mass. Originally a form of tabernacle, either suspended or standing free, its name comes from the Latin *pyxis* or "box."

CIBORIUM

The ciborium resembles the chalice, though it has a lid. Particles of the Blessed Sacrament are kept in the ciborium for distribution of Holy Communion, and to be reserved in the tabernacle. The inside surface, at least, must be gilt, and it is often covered with a veil. Its name is the Latin word for "drinking cup."

MONSTRANCE

From the Latin word, *monstrare*, "to show," the monstrance is a large vessel used for exposition of the Blessed Sacrament and for processions on feasts, such as Corpus Christi. The monstrance consists of a broad base, a stem, and a receptacle in which the Host is exposed; this hinged glass or crystal cover is called a "lunette" from *luna*, the Latin word for the moon. In many churches, the monstrance is made of gold and decorated with jewels.

CRUETS

Cruets are the two small vials made of glass or crystal that contain the water and wine poured into the chalice during Mass. The cruets sit in the lavabo bowl, a small bowl that is used to receive the water in the ceremony of washing the priest's hands.

THURIBLE

Also called a censor, the thurible is a vented vessel in which incense is burned for liturgical purposes, such as Mass and Adoration, to symbolize the zeal of the faithful and their prayers lifted up toward Heaven. It consists of a metal body with a lid to hold the charcoal and incense, three chains attached to the body, and a fourth that lifts the lid. The word thurible comes from the Latin *thuris*, meaning "frankincense."

INCENSE BOAT

A boat-like vessel for holding incense before it is placed in the thurible. It derives its name from its shape. The incense is placed in the thurible with a spoon.

ASPERGILLUM

This is the instrument used to sprinkle Holy Water onto persons or other items in ceremonies either before or during Mass. The word aspergillum derives from the Latin *aspergere*, which means "to scatter upon."

LAVABO	This is the Latin verb "I will wash" said by the priest as he washes and then dries his hands after the Offertory; it is also the name of the washing ceremony, in which the server pours water out of the cruet and onto the priest's fingers.

Other liturgical sacred objects include:

BOOK OF THE GOSPELS	Because this book is the visible sign of Christ the Word, it should be handsomely bound or kept in rich covers that change with the season. The book of the Gospels is the central object of the Mass after the chalice and paten and is carried in procession to the altar.
ROMAN MISSAL	Also called the "Book of the Sacred Mysteries," it contains the prayers and ceremonies of the Mass used by the priest.
LECTIONARY	The lectionary contains the readings and the Gospel for Mass, which are read at the ambo.

We Go to Mass
Vestments

Vestments are the special garments worn by priests and deacons in the exercise of divine worship and during the administering of the Sacraments. The early Church had no special dress requirements; the current vestments in use developed from the everyday clothing of the Roman Empire. When styles changed, the priests continued to wear these clothes so that by the 9th century, Pope Leo IV decided that these garments should be worn during the Holy Sacrifice of the Mass. By the 13th century, vestments became highly decorative, heavy, and recognized as having symbolic religious significance. Today, vestments are lighter and simpler in design, though they should always be beautiful since they are worn during Mass. The sacred vestments include amice, alb, citure, stole, chasuble, and dalmatic.

AMICE

From the Latin *amictus* meaning "garment," an amice is a rectangular piece of white linen cloth with two long strings. This vestment covers the priest's neck and shoulders and is worn under the alb, though it is optional if the alb fully covers the neck. The amice is a symbol of the "helmet of salvation," the "discipline of the tongue," and protection from the devil.

ALB

The name of this vestment is derived from the Latin *tunica alba*, which means "white tunic." An alb is a full-length white linen garment with long flowing sleeves, which may or may not be worn over a cassock. Modern liturgical albs may have hoods and ornamentation; however, decoration should not detract from its character, since the color of the linen is a symbol for purity of heart.

CINTURE

Also called a girdle, the cinture is a long rope made of linen, silk, or cotton with tassled ends. The word cinture comes from the Latin *cintura*. The cinture is worn around the alb as a belt signifying the priest's chastity.

STOLE

This vestment derives its name from the Latin *stola* and the Greek *stole*. It consists of a band of fabric, the color of which varies with the season or occassion, has a Cross stitched on the center back, and which is worn around the neck by bishops and priests and is allowed to hang loose. The stole is a sign of the priest's teaching authority in the Church as a representative of the bishop, who is a successor of the Apostles. Worn over the alb and under the chasuble, the stole is a symbol of justice and immortality. It is also worn in the administration of Sacraments, generally over the alb or surplice. A deacon receives a stole at his ordination; he wears it over his left shoulder, gathered together at the waist on his right side, that is, over the alb and under the dalmatic.

CHASUBLE

This vestment derives its name from two Latin words: *casubla*, or "hooded garment," and *casula*, or "little house." The chasuble is the sacrificial garment proper to the celebrant at Mass. It is made of one piece of cloth with open sides and without sleeves; it is worn over the alb, stole, and amice, hanging from the shoulders in front and behind, down to about the knees. Often, the chasuble, stole, and chalice veil are made as a set of vestments, using the same material, color, and design. Chasubles often have a "Y" cross on them; this is a symbol of charity and represents mercy, so that the stole (justice) and the chasuble (mercy) are worn together by the priest or bishop at Mass.

DALMATIC

Worn first by the 5th century deacons of Rome, the dalmatic is a distinctive diaconal vestment, the fabric and color of which match those of the celebrating priest. It was originally introduced to Rome from Dalmatia (from whence it received its name) as a secular garment. Today, these tunic-like vestments with open sides and wide sleeves are worn without a cinture and over the alb and stole (even when the acting-deacon is a priest), although cardinals or bishops wear them under their chasubles at a Pontifical Mass. The dalmatic has two bands across the front and back that vary in color according to the liturgical season or occassion of the Mass.

TUNICLE

This garment is smaller than a dalmatic and less decorated. It has full sleeves and only one band, which matches the color of the season, across the front and back.

Other priestly vestments and accoutrements used outside of Mass include:

CLERICS   These are the black pants, black shirt, and white Roman collar usually worn by priests on a daily basis. Clerics are the more modern "uniform" of a priest, which help Catholics and others identify him.

CASSOCK   A cassock, the traditional garb of a priest, is an ankle-length black robe that is buttoned down the front and which may be worn with or without a sash. The color is usually black for priests, purple for a bishop, and scarlet for a cardinal. The Pope wears a white cassock.

SURPLICE   From the Latin, *superpellicium,* which means, "over the furs," this shorter form of the alb was used by clergy, beginning in the 11th century, outside of Eucharistic worship and by choristers during the Divine Office. A priest wears a surplice over his cassock when he preaches, joins a procession, acts as a Eucharistic minister, or for Baptisms and funerals.

HUMERAL VEIL   From the Latin word *humerus* or "shoulder," the white humeral veil is a wide oblong cloth used by the priest when carrying the Blessed Sacrament in procession, during Benediction, in carrying the Host to the repository on Holy Thursday, and in returning it on Good Friday. Worn like a shawl with ends that cover the hands, it is fastened across the chest with clasps. In processions of the Blessed Sacrament and at Benediction with a monstrance, only the hands are placed under the humeral veil, otherwise it covers the entire sacred vessel containing the Host. A deacon also wears it around his shoulders whenever he holds a sacred vessel.

COPE   The cope is a long mantle open in front that is held together with a clasp at the breast. It may be worn over an alb or surplice for solemn processions, benedictions, funerals, and weddings, and outdoors in wet weather.

SKULL CAP   Also called a zucchetto, it is worn by some clergy; cardinals wear scarlet, bishops use purple, and the Pope wears a white skull cap.

The following are accessory items for bishops:

PALLIUM   This is a narrow circular band of white wool, ornamented with six dark crosses with two hanging strips, one in front and one behind. It is worn around the neck by archbishops, who receive it from the Pope.

MITRE   From the Latin *mitra*, meaning "headband" or "turban," this item emerged by the 11th century as the distinctive headdress of bishops, though some abbots and others are allowed to wear them. Its origin is from a Roman simple cap. Eastern Orthodox bishops wear a crown-styled mitre. The skull cap is worn under the mitre.

CROSIER   The term crosier, derived from the Middle Latin word *crocia*, is the common name used for the pastoral staff of bishops. It is sometimes spelled crozier.

We Go to Mass
Linens Used During Mass

The linens used during the Holy Sacrifice of the Mass are: the corporal, purificator, pall, and finger towel. These linens, excepting the finger towel, are called the "holy cloths." All are made of white linen. The burse and chalice veil are also used during Mass.

CORPORAL
Taken from the Latin *corpus* or "body," the corporal is a piece of fine linen folded into nine sections with a small Cross stitched in the center of the side nearest the celebrant. It is folded in three from both sides, and may be kept in a burse when not in use. The corporal is the most important of the holy cloths, for the priest spreads it on the altar and places the Host and the chalice on it after the Consecration. A corporal is also placed beneath any vessel containing the Blessed Sacrament; for example, on the "floor" of the tabernacle and beneath the monstrance at Benediction. Because of its close contact with the Blessed Sacrament, the corporal may not be handled by laymen without special permission. The priest first purifies the corporal before others wash it.

PURIFICATOR
From the Latin *purificare*, meaning "to make clean," the purificator is an oblong piece of linen, folded thrice, and placed over the chalice. It is used to to cleanse the chalice before the wine is poured; further, the priest wipes the chalice, his fingers, and his lips with the purificator after receiving the Precious Blood of Christ. Laymen must not handle purificators until a priest has washed them.

PALL
The pall is a stiff, square piece of starched linen, or cardboard covered with linen, which is used to cover the chalice at Mass to protect it from contamination. The upper side may be ornamented; the lower side must be plain. The term pall is from the Latin *pallium*, which means "cover" or "mantle." The use of the pall is optional.

FINGER TOWEL
There is no special significance placed on the finger towel; the priest uses it to dry his fingers after washing them before the Consecration.

BURSE
A burse is a purse or open-ended envelope about 12 inches square, which holds the corporal for Mass. The material of the burse should match the vestments.

CHALICE VEIL
The chalice veil is a square piece of silk used to cover the chalice and paten. It is usually made of the same color and design as the priest's vestments, though it may always be white.

We Go to Mass
Liturgical Colors

During Mass, various colors are used in the altar cloths and vestments. The color of these cloths and vestments varies according to the season of the Church calendar and the event being celebrated. The liturgical colors include: white, red, purple, rose, green, and black.

WHITE

White is the color for vestments worn during the Christmas and Easter seasons. White is also worn on all feasts of our Lord (except His Cross and Passion), for our Lady, the angels, on the feasts of confessors, and for all saints who were not martyrs. White may also be worn during Masses of the dead, when black is not used. White is a color of purity, joy, and holiness. Since the time of Pius V (1566–72) white has also been the ordinary color of papal garments.

RED

Red vestments are worn during the vigil and feast of Pentecost, on the feast of the Precious Blood, during Masses for the Cross, on the feasts of Apostles and martyrs, and during feasts remembering the Passion of our Lord, such as Palm Sunday and Good Friday. Red is the color proper to cardinals and is used by the Pope when he sings a requiem Mass.

PURPLE

During Sundays of Advent and Lent, and also sometimes on the feast of All Souls, purple vestments are worn. Purple is the color for penance, conversion, and expiation.

ROSE

Rose vestments are worn only twice a year: the second Sunday during Advent (Gaudete), and the fourth Sunday during Lent (Laetare). The rose vestment marks the halfway point of each penitential season.

GREEN

The season of Ordinary Time in the Church calls for green vestments. Ordinary Time is any time outside other seasons. Green is a symbol of hope and growth.

BLACK

Black vestments are worn during the Mass of the Presanctified on Good Friday, to celebrate All Souls Day, and at funerals. Black may also be worn during Masses for the dead, though white vestments are often worn instead to express the joy felt for the souls who have gone to be united with God.

GOLD

Vestments made of gold cloth are permitted in place of white, red, and green.

BLUE

This is a liturgical color prescribed in some dioceses of Spain for the feast of the Immaculate Conception.

RESOURCES

The Adoremus Hymnal. San Francisco: Ignatius Press. 1997

Baker S.J., Kenneth. *The Fundamentals of Catholicism*. Volume 1. *Creed, Commandments*. San Francisco: Ignatius Press. 1982 Kenneth Baker, S.J.

Baker S.J., Kenneth. *The Fundamentals of Catholicism*. Volume 2. *God, Trinity, Creation, Christ, Mary*. San Francisco: Ignatius Press. 1983 Kenneth Baker, S.J.

Baker S.J., Kenneth. *The Fundamentals of Catholicism*. Volume 3. *Grace, The Church, The Sacraments, Eschatology*. San Francisco: Ignatius Press. 1983 Kenneth Baker, S.J.

Berger, Barbara Helen. *The Donkey's Dream*. New York: Philomel Books. 1985

de Paola, Tomie. *Poor Man of Assisi*. New York: Holiday House. 1982

Doane, Pelagie. *The Boy Jesus*. Oxford Books for Boys and Girls. New York: Oxford University Press. 1954

Hayward, Linda. *Baby Moses*. New York: Random House. 1989

Hodges, Margaret. *Brother Francis and the Friendly Beasts*. New York: Scriber. 1991

Hooker, Irene H., Susan Andrews, and Miriam Andrews Lademan. *The Caterpillar That Came to Church: A Story of the Eucharist*. Huntington, Indiana: Our Sunday Visitor Publishing Division. 1983

Jones, Mary Alice. *Stories of the Christ Child*. Rand McNally. 1941

Spier, Peter. *Noah's Ark*. Garden City, New York: Doubleday. 1997

Words to Know

The numbers in parentheses correspond to the chapter in which each word can be found.

Abraham (7): A man who lived before Jesus was born. He always did what God wanted, even when it was difficult. He is known as the father of the Jewish people, and our father in faith.

Adam (5): The first man that God made. Eve was the first woman that God made. Adam and Eve are our first parents because everyone came from them.

Alleluia (19): A word that means, "Praise God." We say this at Eastertime to show how happy we are that Jesus rose from the dead.

angels (3): Invisible spirits created by God. Angels are God's helpers.

Apostles (13): Apostles are people sent out by another to help do his work. Jesus had twelve Apostles whom He sent out to tell others about Him after He went back to Heaven. They became the first bishops.

ark (7): A large boat. God told Noah to build an ark to save himself, his family, and the animals from the great flood.

Ascension (21): The return of Jesus to Heaven forty days after Easter.

Baptism (24): Baptism is a Sacrament that takes away Original Sin and gives us grace. It also makes us followers of Christ, sons of God, and members of His Church.

baptized (22): To receive the Sacrament of Baptism.

believe (16): To believe is to accept that what someone says is true, even if you have never heard it before. We believe that Jesus is telling us the truth about Himself and His Father because as God He cannot lie.

Bethlehem (10): The town where Jesus was born.

Bible (14): The holy book that God gave us. It tells us about God's special people and about the beginning of the Church.

bishop (20): A man who has received the power from the Apostles to carry on their work. He takes care of a large group of Catholics.

body (4): The part of you that you can see. The other part of you is your soul.

carpenter (12): Someone who makes chairs, tables, and many other things out of wood. Saint Joseph, the foster-father of Jesus, was a carpenter.

Christmas (10): The day we celebrate Jesus' birth.

Church (20): This is the Catholic Church that Jesus founded. The followers of Jesus are part of the Church. They come together to worship God. The Pope and the bishops are the leaders of the Church.

create (3): To create is to make something out of nothing. God is our Creator. That means He made us and all things out of nothing.

117

118

Creed (We Go to Mass): What we believe about God and His Church.

devils (3): Angels who chose to become bad by turning away from God.

Easter Sunday (19): The Sunday that Jesus rose from the dead.

Eve (5): The first woman that God made. Adam was the first man that God made. Adam and Eve are called our first parents because everyone came from them.

faith (7): Faith is a gift from God that makes us able to believe all that God tells us.

forgive (15): To forgive is to pardon someone who has done something wrong. Only God can forgive sins.

Gabriel (9): The angel that God sent to Mary. He asked her if she would be Jesus' Mother.

genuflect (We Go to Mass): To kneel down on your right knee and then stand up again.

God the Father (23): God the Father is God, the First Person of the Blessed Trinity.

God the Holy Spirit (23): God the Holy Spirit is God, the Third Person of the Blessed Trinity.

God the Son (23): God the Son is God, the Second Person of the Blessed Trinity. God the Son became man and is the Divine Person of Jesus, our Savior.

Good Friday (18): The day that Jesus died on the Cross for our sins and opened the gates of Heaven.

Good News (14): The message that Jesus came to tell us: God loves us all and wants us to be with Him in the Kingdom of Heaven.

Gospel (25): A part of the Bible that tells the Good News of Jesus. In the Gospels, Jesus' friends wrote down many of the things He said and did while He was living here on earth.

grace (5): The life of God in our soul.

guardian angel (4): A special angel given to each person by God who helps to take care of him.

Heaven (2): Heaven is God's home and a place of perfect happiness. God wants us to come to be happy with Him forever in Heaven.

Holy Communion (17): The Body and Blood of Jesus that Catholics receive during Mass.

Holy Spirit (21): The Holy Spirit is God, the Third Person of the Blessed Trinity.

honor (12): To love and obey someone.

Jesus (9): Jesus is God, the Second Person of the Blessed Trinity made man.

Joseph (9): Joseph is the foster-father of Jesus and the husband of Mary.

king (11): Someone who rules over a land. Jesus is King not only of the whole world, but of the Kingdom of Heaven as well.

Last Supper (17): The holy supper that Jesus ate with His Apostles the night before He died. At the Last Supper Jesus gave us His Body and Blood, and He gave the Apostles the power to change bread and wine into His Body and Blood.

manger (10): A wooden box used to hold food for

119

120

animals. Mary had to use a manger for the baby Jesus when He was born.

Mary (9): The Mother of Jesus. Mary is our Mother too.

Mass (17): At Mass, Jesus offers Himself to the Father just as He did on Good Friday. Through the words of the priest, the bread and wine become the Body and Blood of Jesus, as they did at the Last Supper.

miracles (15): Wonderful things done by the power of God and that can only be done by God.

Moses (8): The first prophet. God gave Moses the Ten Commandments.

mystery (23): Something that we know because God has told us, but that we cannot understand completely. The Blessed Trinity is a mystery.

Nazareth (9): The town where Jesus lived with Mary and Joseph.

New Testament (14): The second part of the Bible starting with the life of Jesus Christ.

Noah (7): The good man who obeyed God and built an ark to save his family and the animals from the great flood.

obedient (7): To be obedient is to be someone who obeys; someone who does what he is told to do.

obey (6): To obey is to do what one is told to do. Everyone should obey God's Laws.

Old Testament (14): The first part of the Bible; it tells us about God preparing the people for the coming of Jesus.

121

Original Sin (6): The very first sin committed by Adam and Eve. Adam and Eve are our first parents so we are all born with Original Sin.

Our Father (1): The special prayer that Jesus gave us. We say it to our Father in Heaven.

Pentecost (22): The tenth day after the Ascension when the Holy Spirit came down upon Mary and the Apostles.

Peter (20): The very first Pope. Peter was a fisherman and one of the twelve Apostles chosen by Jesus.

Pope (20): The man who holds the place of Jesus as the visible head of the Catholic Church until He comes again at the end of the world.

prayer (1, 27): Talking with God. You can use prayers you have learned or just tell Him what you are thinking.

priest (17): A man who has received the power from Jesus to forgive sins and offer Mass.

promise (6): To promise is to say you are going to do something and really mean it. God promised to send us a Savior.

prophets (8): Holy men who prepared people for the coming of Jesus, the Savior.

Queen of Heaven (26): The name we give to our Mother Mary to show that she has the highest place in Heaven next to Jesus. She is above all the angels and other saints.

Resurrection (19): The raising of a body from the

122

dead. Jesus rose from the dead on Easter Sunday. Our bodies will be raised from the dead at the end of the world to be reunited with our souls.

Sacrament (24): A Sacrament is an outward sign instituted by God to confer grace. There are seven Sacraments.

sacrifice (26): A sacrifice is a way to show God how much we love Him by giving up something that we like.

saint (27): A holy person who loved God very much on earth and who is now in Heaven. God wants all of us to be saints.

Saint John the Baptist (8): The cousin of Jesus and the last prophet. He told people to be sorry for their sins. He also baptized them to help them prepare for the coming of the Savior.

Savior (6): The one God promised to send to save us from our sins and open the gates of Heaven. Jesus is the Savior.

serve (28): To serve is to follow orders or to help or do work for someone else. We serve God when we do what He wants us to do.

shepherds (10): Men who take care of sheep. When Jesus was born some shepherds were the first to hear the Good News.

Sign of the Cross (2): The shape of the cross that we make by touching our forehead, chest, and shoulders. This shows that we believe that Jesus died on the

123

Cross for us. We also show that we believe in the Blessed Trinity.

sin (6): Sin is saying no to God. It is any bad thing that we choose to do, think, or say. When we sin, we turn away from God.

soul (4): The soul is the part of us that thinks, loves, and chooses what to do. The soul is invisible. The soul never dies.

teacher (13): Someone who shares with others the things that he knows so that they can know them too.

Ten Commandments (8): The moral laws that God gave to Moses on Mount Sinai. These Laws tell us how to live as God wants us to live.

Trinity, Blessed (23): The three Divine Persons in one God. The Blessed Trinity is a mystery.

wise men (11): Men who knew many things about God and the world He made by studying His creation. Three wise men came to Jesus when He was a baby and brought Him presents fit for a king.

worship (10, We Go to Mass): To worship is to give your best love and praise to God.

124

The Alphabet

A is for **Apostles**, the twelve friends of Jesus.

A is also for **angels, Abraham, Adam, Alleluia, ark,** and **Ascension**.

B is for **Baptism**, the first Sacrament. **Baptism** washes away sins and makes us God's children.

B is also for **Bethlehem, Bible, bishop, body,** and **believe**.

C is for **Catholic Church**, God's family.

C is also for **Cross, Christmas, Creator, Creed,** and **carpenter**.

D is for **devil**, an angel who turned away from God and who wants us to sin.

E is for **Easter**, the day Jesus rose from the dead.

F is for **forgive**. Jesus washes away sin.

G is for **God, our Father**, Who made everything and loves us all.

G is also for **Gabriel, Good Friday, Good News, Gospel, grace, genuflect,** and **guardian angel**.

H is for **Heaven**, where we will be happy with God forever.

H is for **Holy Communion** and **Holy Spirit**.

I is for **Israel**, the land where Jesus was born.

J is for **Jesus**, the Son of God. He is our Savior and brother.

125

J is also for **John the Baptist** and **Joseph**.

K is for **king**. Jesus is the King of Heaven and earth.

L is for **Last Supper**, the dinner that Jesus ate with His Apostles the night before He died.

M is for **Mary**, the Mother of God and our Blessed Mother too.

M is also for **Mass, Moses, manger, miracle,** and **mystery**.

N is for **Noah**. He obeyed God and saved his family and the animals from the flood.

N is also for **Nazareth**.

O is for **obey**. We must obey God's Laws. God also wants us to obey our parents.

O is also for **Our Father** and **Original Sin**.

P is for **Pope**, the leader of the whole Church. He has the power to teach all Christians.

P is also for **prayer, Peter, priest, promise,** and **prophet**.

Q is for **quiet**. We are quiet in church so we can pray and hear God's Word.

Q is also for **Queen of Heaven**.

R is for **Resurrection**, the moment when Jesus was raised to new life.

S is for **saint**, someone who loved God on earth and is now in Heaven. There is a saint for almost every name. We all want to be saints too.

126

S is also for **Savior, sin, sacrifice, serve, shepherd, Sign of the Cross,** and **soul**.

T is for Blessed **Trinity,** three Persons in one God: The Father, Son, and Holy Spirit.

T is also for **Ten Commandments** and **teacher**.

U is for **unity**. All Catholics share the same faith in Jesus. We hope that everyone will share our faith someday.

V is for **victory**. Jesus won back the life of grace for us. He conquered sin and death.

W is for **wise men**. Three **wise men** came to adore the Child Jesus and bring Him presents.

W is also for **worship**.

X is **Xmas**, which is another name for Christmas. The X stands for Christ, a name for Jesus.

Y is for **you**, a member of God's family. You can know, love, and serve God. You can be a saint!

Z is for **zeal**, another name for our love of God.

127

TEACHER'S NOTES

WE PRAY

THE SIGN OF THE CROSS

In the Name of the Father, and of the Son,
and of the Holy Spirit. *Amen.*

OUR FATHER

Our Father, Who art in Heaven, hallowed be
Thy Name; Thy Kingdom come; Thy will be
done on earth as it is in Heaven. Give us this day
our daily bread, and forgive us our trespasses, as
we forgive those who trespass against us; and lead us
not into temptation, but deliver us from evil.
Amen.

PRAYER TO MY GUARDIAN ANGEL

Angel of God, my guardian dear,
To whom God's love commits me here,
Ever this day be at my side,
To light and guard, to rule and guide. *Amen.*

MORNING OFFERING

Dear Jesus, I give You my day and everything in it.
Please keep me close to You, Your Mother Mary,
and my guardian angel as I live today for Your glory.
Amen.

HAIL MARY

Hail Mary, full of grace! The Lord is with thee.
Blessed art thou among women, and blessed is the
fruit of thy womb, Jesus.
Holy Mary, Mother of God, pray for us sinners, now
and at the hour of our death. *Amen.*

GLORY BE

Glory Be to the Father, and to the Son, and to the
Holy Spirit, as it was in the beginning, is now, and
ever shall be, world without end. *Amen.*

ADDITIONAL CATHOLIC PRAYERS

SAINT MICHAEL PRAYER

Saint Michael the Archangel, defend us in battle.
Be our protection against the wickedness and
snares of the devil. May God rebuke him, we
humbly pray, and do thou, O prince of the
heavenly hosts, by the power of God, thrust into Hell
Satan and all the evil spirits, who prowl about the
world seeking the ruin of souls. *Amen.*

THE PRAYER OF FATIMA

O my Jesus, forgive us our sins, save us from the
fires of Hell, and lead all souls into Heaven,
especially those in most need of Thy mercy.
Amen.

SPIRITUAL COMMUNION

My Jesus, as I cannot receive Thee now in the
Most Holy Blessed Sacrament, I ask Thee to come
into my heart, and make it like Thy heart. *Amen.*

MORNING OFFERING

O Jesus, through the Immaculate Heart of Mary,
I offer You my prayers, works, joys, and sufferings
of this day, for the intentions of Your Sacred
Heart, in union with the Holy Sacrifice of the
Mass throughout the world, in reparation for my
sins, and for the conversion of all sinners. *Amen.*

ACT OF FAITH

O my God, I firmly believe that You are one
God in three Divine Persons: Father, Son, and
Holy Spirit. I believe that Your divine Son
became man and died for our sins, and that He
will come to judge the living and the dead. I
believe these and all the truths which the Holy
Catholic Church teaches, because You revealed
them, who can neither deceive nor be deceived.
Amen.

ACT OF HOPE

O my God, relying on Your infinite goodness
and promises, I hope to obtain pardon of my
sins, the help of Your grace, and life everlasting,
through the merits of Jesus Christ, my Lord and
Redeemer. *Amen.*

ACT OF LOVE

O my God, I love You above all things with my whole heart and soul, because You are all good and worthy of all my love. I love my neighbor as myself for love of You. I forgive all who have injured me, and I ask pardon for all whom I have injured. *Amen.*

ACT OF CONTRITION

O my God, I am heartily sorry for having offended You. I detest all my sins because of Your just punishments, but most of all because they offend You, my God, Who are all good and deserving of all my love. I firmly resolve, with the help of Your grace, to confess my sins, to do penance, and to amend my life. *Amen.*

PRAYER BEFORE MEALS

Bless us O Lord, and these Thy gifts, which we are about to receive, from Thy bounty, through Christ our Lord. *Amen.*

132

Art Credits

cover   *Genesis: Creation of the Animals*, Raphael, Vatican Palace, Vatican State/ Art Resource, NY
6   *The Creation of the Sun and Moon*, Raphael, Scala/Art Resource, NY
10   *Dance of the Angels and the Just in Paradise* (detail), Fra Angelico, Erich Lessing/Art Resource, NY
14   *Creation of the Animals* (detail), Raphael, Scala/Art Resource, NY
18   *Tobit and Angel*, Rosa, Réunion des Musées Nationaux/Art Resource, NY
22   *Earthly Paradise* (detail), Brueghel, Réunion des Musées Nationaux/ Art Resource, NY
26   *Annunciation* (detail), Fra Angelico, Erich Lessing/Art Resource, NY
30   *Abraham with the Three Angels*, Raphael, Scala/Art Resource, NY
33   *Story of Moses*, Raphael, Scala/Art Resource, NY
36   *Annunciation*, Filippino, © Arte & Immagini srl/Corbis
40   *Nativity*, Barocci, Scala/Art Resource, NY
44   *Adoration of the Magi*, Fra Angelico, Scala/Art Resource, NY
48   *St. Joseph the Carpenter*, Georges de La Tour, Louvre/Art Resource, NY
52   *Calling of Sts. Peter and Andrew* (detail), Ghirlandaio, Scala/Art Resource, NY
56   *Sermon on the Mount and the Healing of the Lepers* (detail), Rosselli, Scala/Art Resource, NY
60   *Jesus Healing the Blind Man of Jericho* (detail), Poussin, Erich Lessing/ Art Resource, NY
64   *Jesus and the Centurion*, Veronese, Erich Lessing/Art Resource, NY
68   *The Last Supper*, Titian, Scala/Art Resource, NY
72   *Descent from the Cross* (detail), Fra Angelico, Erich Lessing/Art Resource, NY
76   *The Seven Joys of Mary* (detail), Memling, Scala/Art Resource, NY
80   *Delivering the Keys of the Kingdom to St. Peter* (detail), Perugino, Scala/ Art Resource, NY
84   *The Seven Joys of Mary* (detail), Memling, Scala/Art Resource, NY
88   *The Pentecost*, Titian, Scala/Art Resource, NY
90   *La Disputa* (detail), Raphael, Erich Lessing/Art Resource, NY
102   *The Coronation of the Virgin*, Velasquez, Erich Lessing/Art Resource, NY
106   *Christ's Entry into Jerusalem*, Fra Angelico, Scala/Art Resource, NY
110   *The Ascension of Christ* (detail), Mantegna, Scala/Art Resource, NY

133

PHOTOGRAPHS:

94   "Baptism of an Infant," Agnusimages.com
96   "Baptism," istockphoto.com/TerryHealy
98   "Mass at the Main Altar of the San Pedro Gonzalez Telmo Church," Ira Block/National Geographic/Getty Images
114   "Pope Celebrates Baptisms at the Sistine Chapel," Pool/Getty Images News/Getty Images
115   WP Wittman Photography
116   "Prayer," istockphoto.com/Jess Wiberg

LINE DRAWINGS, GARY HOFF:

pp. 8, 13, 16, 24, 28, 34, 38, 42, 46, 47, 55, 58, 63, 70, 74, 78, 82, 104

TEACHER'S NOTES

Faith and Life series: Our Heavenly Father
Appendices

APPENDIX A: QUIZZES AND UNIT TESTS

APPENDIX B: STORIES, GAMES, CRAFTS, AND SKITS

Name: _____

God Is Our Father   **Quiz 1**

Fill in the blanks. *Trace the gray letters and fill in the rest.*

Word Bank

God	me	made	Thank	need

1. _G o d_ is my Father.

2. God _m a d e_ me.

3. God gives me what I _n e e d_ .

4. God loves _m e_ .

5. _T h a n k_ You, God.

Heaven Is Our Home   **Quiz 2**

Fill in the blanks. *Trace the gray letters and fill in the rest.*

Word Bank

I	me	home	God

1. _God_ lives in Heaven.

2. God wants _me_ to go to Heaven.

3. In Heaven _I_ will be happy.

4. Heaven is my true _home_.

God Watches Over Everything   **Quiz 3**

Fill in the blanks. *Trace the gray letters and fill in the rest.*

Word Bank

made	all	God	knows	good

1. _God_ is everywhere.

2. God _knows_ everything.

3. God is _all_ powerful.

4. God is all _good_.

5. God _made_ everything.

Name: _____

God's Special Gifts   **Quiz 4**

Fill in the blanks. *Trace the gray letters and fill in the rest.*

Word Bank

helps	me	gifts	angel

1. God gave m e life.

2. God gave me an a n g e l to watch over me.

3. My angel h e l p s me to know, love, and serve God.

4. Thank you, dear Father, for the g i f t s You have given me. Amen.

Name: _____

Unit 1 Test   **Chapters 1–4**

Yes or No. *Circle the correct answer.*

   1. Did God make you?   **(Yes)**   No

   2. Does God love you?   **(Yes)**   No

   3. Can you see God?   Yes   **(No)**

   4. Can you talk to God?   **(Yes)**   No

   5. Do you have your own   **(Yes)**   No
       special angel?

Fill in the blanks.

   To go to Heaven, I must know, love,
   and serve <u>G</u> <u>o</u> <u>d</u> .

Name: _____

Fill in the blanks. *Trace the gray letters and fill in the rest.*

Word Bank

life	grace	God	Eden

1. G__ __ made Adam and Eve.

2. Adam and Eve lived in the Garden of E__ __ __ .

3. God gave them the gift of g r __ __ __ .

4. Grace is God's l__ __ __ in us.

Name: Felicity

A Sad Story   **Quiz 6**

Fill in the blanks. *Trace the gray letters and fill in the rest.*

Word Bank

Adam	lost	send	Sin

1. __Sin__ is saying no to God.

2. __Adam__ and Eve sinned.

3. Adam and Eve __lost__ the gift of grace.

4. God promised to __send__ a Savior.

Yes or No. *Circle the correct answer.*

1. Did God send the Savior
   right away?   Yes   No

2. Did the people need to wait for   Yes   No
   the Savior?

Match the names on the left with the words on the right.

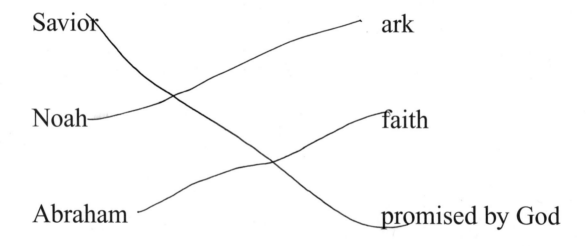

Savior   ark

Noah   faith

Abraham   promised by God

Name: _____

Getting Ready for the Savior **Quiz 8**

Fill in the blanks. *Trace the gray letters and fill in the rest.*

Word Bank

John	prophets	Moses	Ten

1. God sent many p r o p h e t s .

2. God gave M o s e s the Ten Commandments.

3. The T e n Commandments teach us how to live.

4. Saint J o h n the Baptist told people that the Savior was coming very soon.

Fill in the blanks. *Trace the gray letters and fill in the rest.*

Word Bank

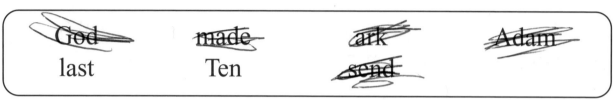

~~God~~   ~~made~~   ~~ark~~   ~~Adam~~

last   Ten   ~~send~~

1. God m a d e Adam and Eve.

2. A d a m and Eve sinned.

3. God promised to s e n d a Savior.

4. Noah built an a r k .

5. Abraham had faith in G o d .

6. God gave Moses the T e n Commandments.

7. Saint John the Baptist was the l a s t prophet.

Mary Hears Some Wonderful News   **Quiz 9**

Fill in the blanks. *Trace the gray letters and fill in the rest.*

Word Bank

| Mary   never   angel   God   yes   Joseph |

1. Mary _n_ _e_ _ _ _ _ _ _ sinned.

2. God sent an _a_ _n_ _ _ _ _ _ _ to Mary.

3. Mary said _Y_ _ _ _ _ to God.

4. _M_ _ _ _ _ _ is the Mother of Jesus.

5. _G_ _ _ _ is the Father of Jesus.

6. Saint _J_ _o_ _s_ _ _ _ _ _ _ is the foster-father of Jesus.

The Savior is Born **Quiz 10**

Fill in the blanks. *Trace the gray letters and fill in the rest.*

Word Bank

Jesus   no   baby   went
sang   Mary   was

1. <u>M a r y</u> and Joseph went to Bethlehem.

2. There was <u>n o</u> room for them at the inn.

3. Jesus <u>w a s</u> born in a stable.

4. Mary laid <u>b a b y</u> Jesus in a manger.

5. Angels <u>s a n g</u> , "Glory to God."

6. The shepherds <u>w e n t</u> to see Jesus.

7. <u>J e s u s</u> is the Savior of the world.

Three Wise Men Arrive **Quiz 11**

Fill in the blanks. *Trace the gray letters and fill in the rest.*

Word Bank

gifts	star	good	save

1. Jesus came to _s_ _a_ _v_ _e_ everybody.

2. A _s_ _t_ _a_ _r_ led the three wise men to Jesus.

3. They gave _g_ _i_ _f_ _t_ _s_ to Jesus.

4. My _g_ _o_ _o_ _d_ deeds are my gifts for Jesus.

Name: _____

Jesus Grows Up   **Quiz 12**

Yes or No. *Circle the correct answer.*

1. Did Joseph make things?   (Yes)   No

2. Did Jesus help Joseph?   (Yes)   No

3. Did Jesus disobey His parents?   Yes   (No)

4. Does Jesus teach us to love
   our parents?   (Yes)   No

5. Is Jesus the Son of God?   (Yes)   No

Fill in the blanks. *Trace the gray letters and fill in the rest.*

Word Bank

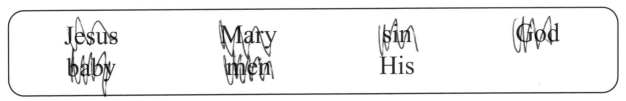

Jesus   Mary   sin   God

baby   men   His

1. M a r y is the Mother of Jesus.

2. Christmas is the birthday of J e s u s .

3. Jesus came to save us from s i n .

4. The angels sang, "Glory to G o d ."

5. The shepherds went to see b a b y Jesus.

6. A star led three wise m e n to Jesus.

7. Jesus obeyed H i s parents.

Fill in the blanks. *Trace the gray letters and fill in the rest.*

Word Bank

God   sent   men   twelve   loves

1. Jesus told people about _G o d_ .

2. Jesus _l o v e s_ little children.

3. Jesus chose _t w e l v e_ men to be His helpers.

4. These _m e n_ were the Apostles.

5. Jesus _s e n t_ the Apostles to teach everyone about Him.

Jesus Tells the Good News   **Quiz 14**

Fill in the blanks. *Trace the gray letters and fill in the rest.*

Word Bank

Bible	~~News~~	Jesus	~~love~~
~~went~~	~~all~~	pray	

1. Jesus and His Apostles w e n t from town to town.

2. They told people the Good N e w s .

3. The Good News is that God loves us a l l .

4. Jesus taught us to l o v e God and one another.

5. Jesus also taught us to p r a y .

6. The B i b l e is the holy book that God gave us.

Matching. *Draw a line from the words to their matches.*

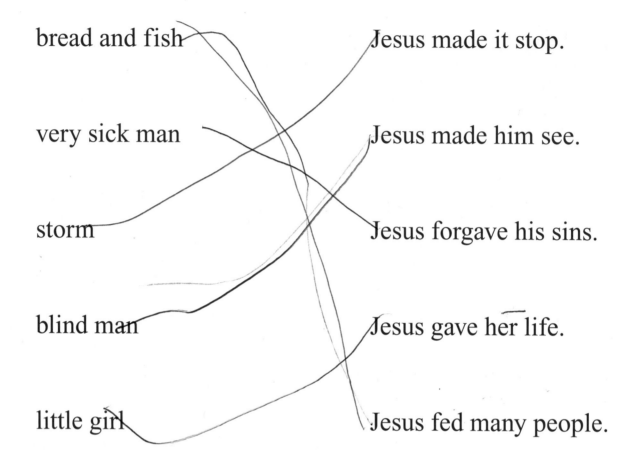

bread and fish   Jesus made it stop.

very sick man   Jesus made him see.

storm   Jesus forgave his sins.

blind man   Jesus gave her life.

little girl   Jesus fed many people.

We Believe in Jesus   **Quiz 16**

Yes or No. *Circle the correct answer.*

1. Did Jesus do miracles?   Yes   No

2. Can a miracle happen without
   God's help?   Yes   No

3. Does everyone believe in Jesus?   Yes   No

4. Does Jesus want everyone
   to believe in Him?   Yes   No

5. Is faith in Jesus pleasing to God?   Yes   No

Fill in the blanks. *Trace the gray letters and fill in the rest.*

Word Bank

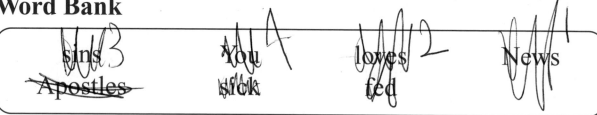

sins   You   loves   News

Apostles   sick   fed

1. Jesus chose Apostles.

2. Jesus and His Apostles spread the Good News.

3. The Good News is that God loves us.

4. Jesus healed the sick.

5. Jesus fed many people.

6. Jesus forgave sins.

7. Jesus, I believe in You.

Fill in the blanks. *Trace the gray letters and fill in the rest.*

Word Bank

Last   Holy   Body   Mass   Blood

1. At the **L a s t** Supper, Jesus was with the Apostles.

2. Jesus changed bread and wine into His **B o d y** and **B l o o d**.

3. At **M a s s**, Jesus gives us His Body and Blood.

4. **H o l y** Communion is the best gift of all.

carry   our   chain   rain

way   play   day   mail

gray   snail

Jesus Dies for Us **Quiz 18**

Number the event. *Put a 1 beside the first event, a 2 beside the second event, and so on.*

6   Jesus died on the Cross.

1   Jesus and the Apostles ate the Last Supper.

2   Jesus was beaten.

3   Jesus was crowned with thorns.   beak

5   Jesus was nailed to the Cross.   speed

4   Jesus carried the heavy Cross.

7   Mary and Saint John stayed by Jesus on the Cross.

Scott

We me feed ceep

becasec wheather

Fill in the blanks. *Trace the gray letters and fill in the rest.*

Word Bank

life   rose   our   body   Jesus

1. Jesus r o s e from the dead on Easter Sunday.

2. After His Resurrection, Jesus was alive b o d y and soul.

3. Because Jesus rose, we can share His l i f e .

4. One day o u r bodies will rise from the dead.

5. Our bodies and souls will be with J e s u s in Heaven.

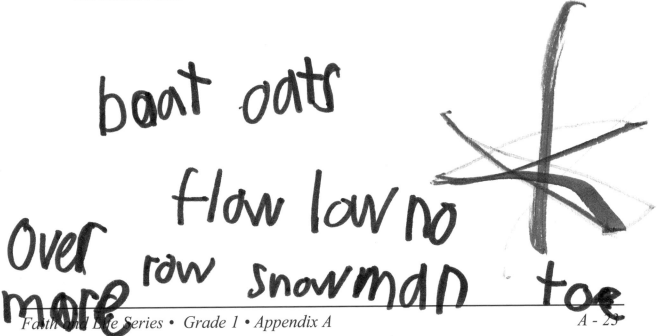

boat oats

flow low no

over

more raw snowman toe

Jesus Begins the Church   **Quiz 20**

Yes or No. *Circle the correct answer.*

1. Did Jesus spend time with His Apostles after He rose?   (Yes)   No

2. Did Jesus start the Church to give us grace?   (Yes)   No

Fill in the blanks. *Trace the gray letters and fill in the rest.*

Pope	Apostles	bishops

Word Bank

1. The A p o s t l e s were the first leaders of the Church.

2. The Apostles were the first b i s h o p s.

3. Peter was the first P o p e.

Fill in the blanks. *Trace the gray letters and fill in the rest.*

Word Bank

| rose | Last | Good | best |
| Church | loves | Pope | |

1. Jesus ate the L a s t Supper with His Apostles.

2. Jesus died on G o o d Friday.

3. Jesus died for us because He l o v e s us.

4. Jesus r o s e from the dead.

5. Jesus began the C h u r c h.

6. Peter was the first P o p e.

7. Holy Communion is the b e s t gift of all.

by Pie cind find
dried cott Brghtdright night
listen

Fill in the blanks. *Trace the gray letters and fill in the rest.*

Word Bank

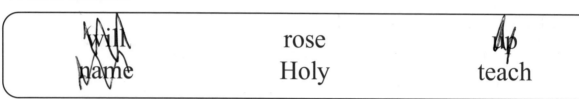

will
rose
up
name
Holy
teach

1. Jesus spent forty days with His Apostles after He
   __r__ __o__ __s__ __e__ from the dead.

2. Jesus told the Apostles to __t__ __e__ __a__ __ch__ everyone
   about Him.

3. "Baptize them in the __n__ __a__ __m__ __e__ of the Father and
   of the Son and of the Holy Spirit."

4. Jesus promised to send the __H__ __o__ __l__ __y__ Spirit.

5. Jesus went __u__ __p__ to Heaven.

6. Jesus __w__ __i__ __l__ __l__ come again.

Yes or No. *Circle the correct answer.*

1. Did Mary and the Apostles pray for the Holy Spirit to come?   **Yes**   No

2. Did the Holy Spirit come at Pentecost?   **Yes**   No

3. Were the Apostles brave without the Holy Spirit?   Yes   **No**

4. Does the Holy Spirit help the Church?   **Yes**   No

5. Does the Holy Spirit help you to love?   **Yes**   No

The Blessed Trinity **Quiz 23**

Multiple choice. *Circle the correct answer.*

1. There is _____ God.

   a) one   b) two   c) three

2. There are _____ Divine Persons in God.

   a) one   b) two   c) three

3. The Father is _____ , the Son is _____ ,
   and the Holy Spirit is _____ .
   (Circle one word for all three blanks.)

   a) human   b) God   c) less

4. Did the Blessed Trinity have a beginning?

   a) yes   b) no

Name: Felicity

God Gives You His Life

Fill in the blanks. *Trace the gray letters and fill in the rest.*

Word Bank

all	sin	grace	God	water

1. Jesus said to baptize __a__ __l__ __l__ people.

2. We are baptized with __w__ __a__ __t__ __e__ __r__ .

3. Baptism washes away __s__ __i__ __n__ .

4. Baptism gives us __g__ __r__ __a__ __c__ __e__ .

5. Baptism makes me a child of __G__ __o__ __d__ .

Name: _____

Number the event. *Put a 1 beside the first event, a 2 beside the second event, and so on.*

   2   Jesus rises from the dead.

   1   Jesus dies on the Cross.

   3   The Holy Spirit comes.

   4   Jesus goes up to Heaven.

Fill in the blanks with the same word.

1. At my Baptism, I became a child of ___God___ .

2. There is only one ___God___ .

Many Gifts from God   **Quiz 25**

Fill in the blanks. *Trace the gray letters and fill in the rest.*

Word Bank

This	Word	Bible	my	wine

1. We hear God's **W o r d** at Mass.

2. The Gospel is the part of the **B i b l e** that tells the Good News about Jesus.

3. The priest says, "**T h i s** is my Body."

4. He also says, "This is the chalice of **m y** Blood."

5. The bread and **w i n e** become the Body and Blood of Jesus.

fern   No   bird   fur

World   Work   Climb   through

her   dirt   burn

Our Mother Mary **Quiz 26**

Yes or No. *Circle the correct answer.*

1. Is Mary the Mother of Jesus?   (Yes)   No

2. Is Mary our Mother too?   (Yes)   No

3. Is an angel the Queen of Heaven?   Yes   (No)

4. Is Mary the Queen of Heaven?   (Yes)   No

Matching. *Draw a line from the word to its match.*

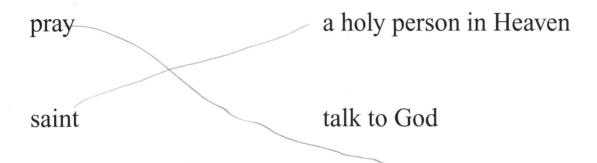

pray   a holy person in Heaven

saint   talk to God

I should follow Jesus. *Circle the things I should do because Jesus did them, too.*

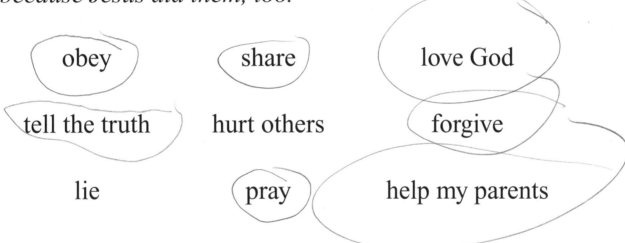

obey   share   love God

tell the truth   hurt others   forgive

lie   pray   help my parents

Name:

Jesus Will Come Again   **Quiz 28**

Yes or No. *Circle the correct answer.*

    1. Is earth our true home?   Yes   ~~No~~

    2. Will Jesus come again?   ~~Yes~~   No

    3. Will Jesus take the souls
       of good people to Heaven?   ~~Yes~~   No

    4. Will anyone be sad in Heaven?   Yes   ~~No~~

    5. Do we get ready for Heaven
       by loving God?   ~~Yes~~   No

Name: _____

Multiple choice. *Circle the correct answer.*

1. At Mass we

    a) listen and pray   b) give ourselves to God

    c) both a and b

2. Who can change the bread and wine into the Body and Blood of Jesus?

    a) your teacher   b) your parents

    c) your priest

3. Mary is the Mother of

    a) Jesus   b) all of us   c) both a and b

4. Most of all we want

    a) to go to Heaven   b) to make a lot of money

    c) everyone to like us

Telephone

Have the children sit in a circle on the floor. The teacher begins the game by whispering a sentence to one of the students. This sentence is taken from the lesson of the day. For example, to reinforce the promise of the Savior, the sentence could be, "God promised Adam and Eve that he would send a Savior." The child, after receiving the message, whispers it to the child next to him. The message continues around the circle in this way until the last person receives it. The last person then stands and repeats it for the entire class. If any child has difficulty understanding the message that is whispered to him, he may say "Operator," which means that he needs to have the message repeated to him again before he can pass it to the next person.

Bible Baseball

1. Set up bases around the room.

2. Choose teams.

3. Ask a question of a student on one of the teams. If he gets the answer, the student goes to first base and the next student is up for a question. If he misses the answer, that student is out. In this case, the next teammate must answer the same question. If three students on the same team cannot answer the question or if three questions are misssed, their team is out and the other team is up.

4. Points are received for "home runs" that is, when a student has passed through all three bases and reached home base.

Tic-Tac-Toe

1. Draw Tic-Tac-Toe grid on the chalkboard.

2. Choose sides. "X" goes first.

3. Ask a student on the first team a question. If he answers it correctly, his team chooses where to put the "X". If he answers incorrectly, the other team has a chance to answer the question. If the "O" team answers, they can choose where to put the "O", and then they get their turn, that is, one student is asked a question. If they answer incorrectly, they merely get their normal turn.

4. The team that has three "X's" or three "O's" in a row wins the round. Losers start the next round.

Did I pray before bed?

Color the picture below.

This week pray the Our Father.
Remember to begin and end with the
Sign of the Cross.

Draw a cross in the box if you prayed that day.

Monday	Tuesday	Wednesday	Thursday	Friday	Saturday	Sunday

Did I pray before bed?

Color the picture below.

This week pray the Our Father. Remember to begin and end with the Sign of the Cross.

Draw a cross in the box if you prayed that day.

Monday	Tuesday	Wednesday	Thursday	Friday	Saturday	Sunday

Creation Mobile

Name:_____

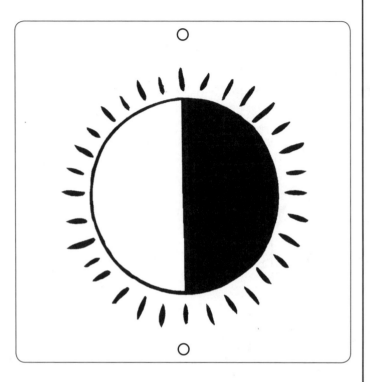

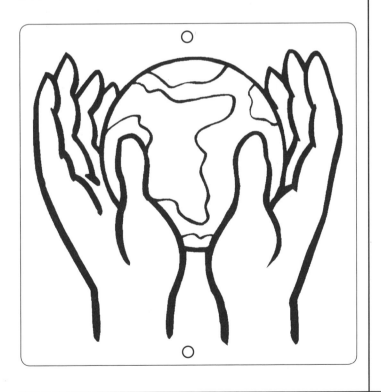

Popsicle Stick Puppets and Shoe Box Theater

The puppets are easily made from popsicle sticks and felt, construction paper, or cut-out pictures. For example:

For the theater, take a large shoe box and cut two slots, one toward the top of the box on one of the long sides, and the other toward the bottom of the box on the opposite long side. (The slot toward the bottom will be where you insert the puppets; the slot toward the top will be for inserting the backdrop or scenery.)

Masks

To identify the different characters in a play without having to make elaborate costumes, it is quite easy to make masks. For example, if you wished to dramatize the temptation and Fall of man, you could make the following masks out of paper and have the students color them; alternatively, the students could make the masks out of construction paper.

To show the change from perfect happiness to the fallen state of Adam and Eve, or the original delight of Satan at man's Fall, then his disappointment at God's promise, make the masks reversible. They may be handheld and flipped.

"TV" Shows

Materials: Cardboard box, long rolls of paper.

1. Cut slots in the bottom of a cardboard box. Cover
   and decorate the box with bottle caps or buttons
   for control knobs.

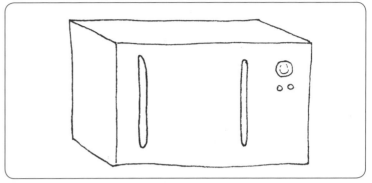

2. Have the students draw the frames on a long roll
   of paper. Leave some space for both a lead and
   an ending frame.

3. Feed the paper through slot A then through slot
   B. Gently pull the frames through the "TV."

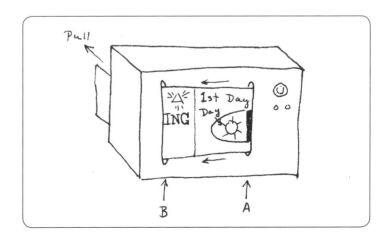

Stained Glass Angel

Adam and Eve before the Fall

EVE

ADAM

GOD

SERPENT

ANGEL

Adam and Eve after the Fall

The Wolf of Gubbio

Saint Francis of Assisi was born in Italy during a time when people lived in castles, knights in armor rode horses to fight for the king, and cities were surrounded by thick walls to keep the townspeople safe from harm.

In a town in Italy called Gubbio, a large, mean, and hungry wolf came to the town one day. He ran around looking for food, scaring the animals and all the people who lived there. They tried to chase the wolf away by shouting and running after him, but he was very mean. Soon no one wanted to go outside anymore. Everyone was afraid of the wolf.

Saint Francis was staying in the town, and since he loved every one of God's creatures— both people and animals—he decided to go out and talk to the wolf. The people said "Please do not go out alone. We are afraid for you. The hungry wolf will attack you!"

But Saint Francis trusted in God Who is Creator of all things, even a mean and hungry wolf. He walked outside to meet the wolf, making the Sign of the Cross and praying that the wolf would listen to him.

"Come here, Brother Wolf," he said, for he believed that all creatures of God were brothers and sisters, even the animals. As all the people of the town watched from a safe distance, the wolf came running toward Saint Francis with his mouth open to show his sharp white teeth. The people were afraid. But Saint Francis made the Sign of the Cross over the wolf and said, "In the name of Christ, please do not harm me or any of these people, Brother Wolf."

The wolf stopped running, closed his mouth and lowered his head. He sat down at the feet of Saint Francis, as if he were a nice dog. He did not bother the people of Gubbio again.

Noah and the Flood

Narrator 1: After the Fall of Adam and Eve, God promised to send a Savior. The Savior would win back God's grace and open the gates of Heaven.

Narrator 2: The Savior did not come right away. The people waited for years and years. Some learned to love and obey God, but others were very wicked. God decided to wash evil from the earth with a flood.

SCENE 1: *Noah goes outside to work, kneels to pray, and hears God's voice.*

God: Noah!

Noah: Here I am.

God: Noah, I will wash the world clean from sin and I want your help. Please build Me an ark. This big boat will keep you and your family safe. I want you to put a male and female of every kind of animal onto the boat. It must be very big. Noah, will you build My ark for Me?

Noah: Yes, God.

SCENE 2: *Noah is building the ark and a crowd is laughing at Noah.*

Crowd member 1: Hey, Noah! Where's the water? There isn't even a lake here!

Crowd member 2: Noah! Your boat is bigger than a house! It will never float. (Crowd laughs and points.)

God: Noah, bring into the ark two of every animal, male and female. Take your family into the ark with the animals.

Narrator 1: It rained and poured for 40 days and 40 nights. God kept Noah and all the animals safe in the ark as it rained and rained. After the rain stopped, they left the ark and gave thanks to God.

(Sing to "Mary Had a Little Lamb": We just want to thank You, God, thank You, God, thank You, God. We just want to thank You, God, for You have saved our lives.)

Narrator 2: God was pleased, and He said to Noah:

God: I will make My covenant with you, that never again shall all creatures be destroyed by a flood. The rainbow will appear in the clouds as a sign of My covenant with you.

Narrator 2: A covenant is a promise that makes us family with God. Noah and his family settled on the earth, planted farms, and their children and their children's children filled the earth.

The Sacrifice of Isaac

SCENE: *Outside in an arid land*

Narrator 1: Many years after the flood and the time of Noah's ark, there was a man named Abraham. Abraham loved and served God. One day, the Lord said to Abraham:

God: Abraham, leave this land and go to a place that I will show you. I will bless you and make you a great nation.

Narrator 2: Abraham trusted God and obeyed Him. He took his wife Sarah and left on a journey for an unknown land. God said:

God: Abraham, look around you. I will give this land to you and your sons forever.

Narrator 1: Abraham built an altar there and worshiped God. Soon he wondered:

Abraham: O God, am I to remain childless?

God: Look up at the sky and count the stars. You shall have just as many descendants as there are stars.

Narrator 2: Very soon, Abraham and Sarah had a son and named him Isaac. Then God tested Abraham's love and faith in Him.

God: Abraham!

Abraham: Here I am.

God: Take your son Isaac, your only son, whom you love, and go to the mountain and sacrifice him to Me.

Narrator 1: So Abraham took Isaac, his only son, and set off for the mountain. Abraham built an altar, tied up Isaac, and prepared to sacrifice him. Suddenly, an angel called to Abraham:

Angel: Abraham! Do not lay a hand on this boy. God knows how faithful you are to Him, since you were willing to give Him your own beloved son.

Narrator 2: Abraham saw a ram caught in a bush by its horns. Abraham offered the ram, instead of his son as a sacrifice to God. God blessed Abraham greatly for his faith.

Narrator 1: As God promised, Abraham's descendants were as many as the stars and became known as God's Chosen People. One of Abraham's descendants was the Savior of the world, Who was promised to Adam and Eve. The Savior's name was Jesus, the Son of God. The End.

The Ten Commandments

Learn this song with your teacher to help you remember the Ten Commandments that God gave us.

Use the tune of "Farmer in the Dell."

Have no gods but Me. (2x)
This is the First Commandment:
Have no gods but Me.

Don't use God's name in vain. (2x)
This is the Second Commandment:
Don't use God's name in vain.

Keep holy the Sabbath day. (2x)
This is the Third Commandment:
Keep holy the Sabbath day.

Honor your mom and dad. (2x)
This is the Fourth Commandment:
Honor your mom and dad.

You shall not kill. (2x)
This is the Fifth Commandment:
You shall not kill.

Do not commit adultery. (2x)
This is the Sixth Commandment:
Do not commit adultery.

You shall not steal. (2x)
This is the Seventh Commandment:
You shall not steal.

You shall not lie. (2x)
This is the Eighth Commandment:
You shall not lie.

Don't covet your neighbor's wife. (2x)
This is the Ninth Commandment:
Don't covet your neighbor's wife.

Don't covet your neighbor's goods. (2x)
This is the Tenth Commandment:
Don't covet your neighbor's goods.

God gave us laws of love. (2x)
They are the Ten Commandments.
God gave us laws of love.

100 Activities Based on the Catechism of the Catholic Church by Ellen Rossini
San Francisco: Ignatius Press 1996; p. 23

Nativity Diorama

Color.
Cut.
Fold tabs.
Glue or tape into a shoe box (or Kleenex box).

SMA, IHM 1987

The Healing of the Blind Man

SCENE: *Outside on a crowded road*

Narrator 1: One day, Jesus and His Apostles were walking on the road to Jericho. Many people were walking with them. A blind man sat begging by the roadside. Hearing the crowd pass, he asked:

Blind man: What is happening?

Person 1 in crowd: Jesus is passing by.

Narrator 2: The blind man heard Jesus walking toward him.

Blind man: Jesus, Son of David, have pity on me!

Narrator 1: The people walking beside Jesus scolded the blind man.

Person 2 in crowd: Be quiet, you! Don't bother Jesus.

Narrator 2: But the blind man cried out all the more.

Blind man: Son of David, have pity on me!

Narrator 1: Jesus stopped and ordered that the man be brought to Him.

Jesus: What do you want Me to do for you?

Blind man: (kneeling) Lord, please let me see.

Jesus: (touching the blind man's eyes) Have sight. Your faith has saved you.

Blind man: Praise God! I can see!

Narrator 2: The man immediately received his sight and followed Jesus, giving glory to God. When the people saw what had happened, they too gave praise to God.

Crowd: Thank You, God!

The Healing of the Centurion's Servant

SCENE: *By the city gates; the servant lies on his bed at one side of the stage.*

Narrator 1: On another day, Jesus and His Apostles were walking toward Capernaum, and a crowd was with them. When Jesus entered the town, a centurion approached Him and said:

Centurion: Lord, my servant is lying at home paralyzed.

Narrator 2: Jesus looked at him and said:

Jesus: I will come and cure him.

Centurion: (kneeling) Lord, I am not good enough to have You enter under my roof. Only say the word, and my servant will be healed.

Narrator 3: The centurion knew that Jesus had the power to cure from far away.

Jesus: Your faith is great. As you have believed, let it be done.

Narrator 4: And at that very hour, the centurion's servant was healed. He rose and thanked God for his cure.

The Annunciation

The Visitation

The Nativity of Our Lord

The Presentation

The Finding of Our Lord in the Temple

The Agony in the Garden

The Scourging at the Pillar

The Crowning with Thorns

The Carrying of the Cross

The Crucifixion of Our Lord

The Resurrection of Our Lord

The Ascension of Our Lord

The Descent of the Holy Spirit upon Mary and the Apostles

The Assumption of Mary into Heaven

The Coronation of Mary as Queen of Heaven and Earth

Holy Spirit Mobile
Pattern for the Dove and Seven Flames

Symbols of Baptism